The Review of
Italian American Studies

The Review of
Italian American Studies

Edited by
Frank M. Sorrentino
and Jerome Krase

LEXINGTON BOOKS
Lanham • Boulder • New York • Oxford

LEXINGTON BOOKS

Published in the United States of America
by Lexington Books
4720 Boston Way, Lanham, Maryland 20706

12 Hid's Copse Road
Cumnor Hill, Oxford OX2 9JJ, England

British Library Cataloguing in Publication Information Available

Library of Congress Cataloging-in-Publication Data

The review of Italian American studies / edited by Frank M. Sorrentino and Jerome
Krase.
    p.   cm.
    Includes index.
    ISBN 0-7391-0159-5 (cloth : alk. paper)
    1. Italian Americans—Study and teaching. I. Sorrentino, Frank M., 1949–
II. Krase, Jerome.

E184.I8 R48 2000
973'.0451—dc21   00-041233

Printed in the United States of America

♾™ The paper used in this publication meets the minimum requirements of American
National Standard for Information Sciences—Permanence of Paper for Printed Library
Materials, ANSI/NISO Z39.48–1992.

Dedicated to

John N. LaCorte

Founder, The Italian Historical
Society of America

Contents

Foreword

Fifty years ago, in 1949, John N. LaCorte was marching down Fifth Avenue in New York City in the St. Patrick's Day Parade. Along the parade route he saw a sign for an organization called the Irish Historical Society. This observation engendered a question: "Why not an *Italian* Historical Society?" Although today that thought does not seem to be particularly radical, at that time it was a rather courageous consideration. Before the civil rights movement, before our raised consciousness about the equality and value of all ethnic heritages, before we came to understand the profoundly destructive effects of all racial and ethnic prejudice, the idea of creating an organization celebrating and encouraging interest in Italian culture was truly revolutionary.

John N. LaCorte was revolutionary: a man of vision and purpose. A man who, in the face of all who maintained "you can't do that" went ahead and did it anyway. Born in New Jersey in 1910, his family returned to their native Sicily while he was still an infant. As the oldest in the family he was expected to remain and tend to family matters, but the siren call of America along with the fact that he was a natural born citizen of this great country never let him rest. His deadline to return was his birthday, 1929, for he had to register for the military draft when he reached his nineteenth year or lose his claim to citizenship. Sicily was an impoverished land and merely eking out a bare existence was a continual and very difficult challenge. Not only did he have to go against the wishes of his family to claim his precious American heritage, he had to overcome daunting financial odds against the possibility of raising enough money to book passage back to the United States. He became the master of odd jobs as carpenter, as electrician, as a laborer, whatever he had to do to achieve his financial goal—and he succeeded.

He arrived but a few months before the beginning of the Great Depression and using the same innate abilities to adapt to his economic environment which he honed as a child, he survived the financial collapse and, eventually, prospered. He was a born salesman, but he was no Willy Loman. Being faced with overwhelming obstacles, he never allowed himself the luxury of self-pity or of giving up. He moved from selling pencils and shoelaces on the corner to selling the latest inventions of the time: refrigerators and vacuum cleaners. He never tried to sell anyone anything he did not believe in. He never tried to sell anything that he did not believe would benefit the buyer. His life was characterized by that kind of integrity. Eventually he was "discovered" by someone in the insurance business and soon he became the family insurance man to many Italian immigrant families. In addition to selling them an insurance policy, which would help minimize financial hardship in the event of death, he would help them with their problems with immigration, translating documents and being a liaison with the appropriate government agency, helping to bring loved ones from their native Italy.

He had achieved the financial success which, as a boy dressed in tattered clothes in his feudal home in Sicily, he could only dream about.. But this hardly satisfied his yearning to do something more—to make a real difference in the world. This desire was fanned by the many stings he endured by being Italian in a world that looked down on them as little more than paupers and criminals. All the great achievements of Italians of the past and present from Galileo to Fermi were completely overshadowed by the antics of the likes of Capone. This provided a moral justification for all who were inclined to vilify and ignore those who were part of that particular ethnic group. Italians became ashamed to be Italians. They changed their names to eliminate the ending vowels. They forbade their children from speaking Italian. The culture was being destroyed from within far more efficiently than any outside forces could accomplish.

"Better to light a candle than curse the darkness." This basic principle of action put forth by the Christophers proved to be the underlying principle of John LaCorte's *modus operandi*. Attacking the attackers would do little, if anything, and probably evoke even greater negativity. However, to be able to proclaim the great contributions of Italians in exploration, the arts and the sciences—now, that could help to dissipate the darkness. The stage was set. The powder primed. Taking the fateful walk down Fifth Avenue, seeing the Irish Historical Society and realizing the acceptance and dignity that once vilified ethnic group had achieved, the question arose: "Why not an Italian Historical Society?"

In 1949, the thirty-nine-year-old John N. LaCorte focused his considerable ability to inspire others to higher action and began to promote his provocative idea. It was recognized by many Italian Americans as the first step in helping to transform their destinies, their relationship to the culture they had adopted as their own. They did have something of which they could be proud after all. They could keep their names, and stand proudly, without shame. At the inaugural ceremony held at the Academy of Music in Brooklyn, New York, some four hundred people joined John N. LaCorte in declaring the beginning of the Italian Historical Society of America, an organization which would thenceforth light a candle and seek to enlighten the world.

"To help perpetuate the names of those of Italian heritage who have contributed to the advancement of mankind and inspired others" became the official motto for the Society.

Among the myriad of those who would fall into this category, there were three that the founder of the Society found most intriguing: Giovanni DaVerrazzano, the first European to sail into Hudson Bay (almost ninety years before Henry Hudson); Charles J. Bonaparte, who in the 1920s under President Teddy Roosevelt, founded what today has become known as the Federal Bureau of Investigation; and Antonio Meucci, the true inventor of the technology that underlies the telephone.

It is the cause of Verrazzano that was indeed the *magnum opus* of John LaCorte and the Society, for it was solely through his taking on the mission that the bridge that came to span the entrance to New York harbor was named after the Western explorer who first laid eyes on it. He achieved great success, as well, in the cause of Bonaparte and with the cooperation of Attorney General Robert Kennedy, a monument was erected in the Department of Justice in Washington, D.C., acknowledging Bonaparte as the founder of the FBI. Finally, the cause of Meucci continues. Primarily because of association in the American consciousness between Alexander Graham Bell (to no small extent perpetuated, ironically, by the Italian actor, Don Ameche, who portrayed Bell in the famous 1940s film), establishing Meucci as the true inventor of the telephone has proven to be a most difficult task. Further, the corporation known as Bell telephone, which existed at the time that John LaCorte was putting forth his greatest efforts on behalf of Meucci, brought its considerable resources to bear to block all acknowledgment of Meucci, including, through legal action, preventing a postage stamp that had already been printed recognizing Meucci as the inventor of the telephone, from ever being distributed.

The work of the Society continues. It seeks to disseminate information that will serve to bring greater awareness of the magnitude of the vast contributions made by those of Italian heritage. No one was more aware than John LaCorte himself of the importance of the printed media in bringing forth such a message. In this vein, in the 1960s he started the *Italian-American Review.* In newspaper format it proclaimed the accomplishments of Verrazzano, Bonaparte, Meucci and others. He intended the *Review* to be a historical document, filled with facts and data that would serve to enlighten present and future generations. It is a continuation of this vision that the Italian Historical Society of America in sponsoring this scholarly journal, *Italian-American Studies.* In its periodical form, this publication will be placed in libraries throughout the United States and beyond, to serve as an ongoing source of information and enlightenment, bringing to all those who take up and read it an understanding and an appreciation of what has been wrought by those who are proud to identify themselves as Italians.

John J. LaCorte, Ph.D.
President, The Italian Historical Society of America
Professor of Philosophy, California State University

Acknowledgments

I   The Essence of Italian American Identity

1)   Richard Gambino, "The Family System" from *Blood of My Blood: The Dilemma of the Italian-Americans*, Guernica Press, 1996. Reprinted by permission of Richard Gambino. Originally published by Doubleday, 1974.

2)   Richard D. Alba, "The Twilight of Ethnicity among Americans of European Ancestry: The Case of Italians," *Journal of Ethnic and Racial Studies*, vol. 8, no. 1, January 1985. Reprinted by permission of *Journal of Ethnic and Racial Studies*.

3)   Rudolph J. Vecoli, "Are Italian Americans Just White Folks?" Proceedings of AIHA Conference 1995. Reprinted by permission of the American Italian Historical Association.

4)   Daniel J. Monti, Jr., "Some Sort of Americans: The Working and Reworking of Italian-American Ethnicity," *Forum Italicum*, Filibrary no. 7, 1994. Reprinted by permission of *Forum Italicum*.

II   Italian American Politics and History

5)   Philip Cannistraro, "Mussolini, Sacco-Vanzetti, and the Anarchists: The Transatlantic Context," *Journal of Modern History*, March 1996. Reprinted by permission of the *Journal of Modern History* and The University of Chicago Press.

6)   Gary R. Mormino and George E. Pozzetta, "Concord and Discord: Italians and Ethnic Interactions in Tampa, Florida, 1886-1930," in Lydio F. Tomasi, ed., *Italian-Americans: New Perspectives in Italian Immigration and Ethnicity*, Center for Migration Studies, 1985. Reprinted by permission of the Center for Migration Studies.

7)   Salvatore J. LaGumina, "From Urban to Suburban: Italian Americans in Transition," Proceedings of AIHA Conference 1988. Reprinted by permission of the American Italian Historical Association.

8) Donna R. Gabaccia, "Italian Immigrant Women in Comparative Perspective," in Lydio Tomasi, ed., *The Columbus People*, Center for Migration Studies, 1994. Reprinted by permission of the Center for Migration Studies.

9) Frank Cavioli, "Columbus, Whitman and The Italian-American Connection," *Forum Italicum*, Filibrary no. 7, 1994. Reprinted by permission of *Forum Italicum*.

III   Italian American Community

10) Judith N. DeSena, "Involved and 'There': The Activities of Italian American Women in Urban Neighborhoods," *Forum Italicum*, Filibrary no. 7, 1994. Reprinted by permission of *Forum Italicum*.

11) Jerome Krase, "Bensonhurst, Brooklyn: Italian American Victims and Victimizers," *Voices in Italian Americana*, vol. 5, no. 2, Fall 1994. Reprinted by permission of *Voices in Italian Americana*.

12) Salvatore Primeggia and Joseph A. Varacalli, "Community and Identity in Italian American Life," in Michael Hughey and Arthur Vidich, eds., *The Ethnic Quest for Community: Searching for Roots in the Lonely Crowd*, JAI Press, Inc., 1993. Reprinted by permission of Elsevier Science.

13) Angela D. Danzi, "Jewish and Italian American Women's Childbirth Choices in the United States, 1920-1940: An Examination of Home Birth," Proceedings of AIHA Conference, 1995. Reprinted by permission of the American Italian Historical Association.

IV   Italian Americans and Literature

14) Robert Viscusi, "*De Vulgari Eloquentia*: An Approach to the Language of Italian American Fiction," *Yale Italian Studies*, Winter 1981. Reprinted by permission of *Yale Italian Studies.*

15) Fred Gardaphe, "The Evolution of Italian American Literary Studies," *The Italian American Review*, Spring 1994. Reprinted by permission of *The Italian American Review.*

16) John Paul Russo, "From Italophilia to Italophobia: Representations of Italian Americans in the Early Gilded Age," *Differentia Review of Italian*

Thought, Spring 1994. Reprinted by permission of *Differentia Review of Italian Thought*.

17)   Mary Jo Bona, "*Mater Dolorosa* No More? Mothers and Writers in Italian American Literary Tradition," *Voices in Italian Americana*, 1996. Reprinted by permission of *Voices in Italian Americana*.

18)   Anthony Julian Tamburri, "In Recognition of the Italian American Writer: Definitions and Categories," *Differentia Review of Italian Thought*, Spring 1991. Reprinted by permission of *Differentia Review of Italian Thought*.

Introduction

The Review of Italian American Studies

Frank M. Sorrentino and Jerome Krase

It has been more than one hundred years since the beginning of the mass migration of Italians to the United States of America. This migration, mostly from southern Italy, was one of the largest in history, ironically coming after the unification of Italy. The six million who came now have descendants numbering close to thirty million. What impact did these individuals have on American society? How did American society and culture affect the immigrants and second, third, and fourth generations of Italian Americans? The Italian American experience is one of the most significant and interesting case studies for those who are interested in American history and culture and/or the Italian American history and culture. This topic traverses the fields of history, political science, sociology, and literature.

This anthology presents many of the most representative scholarly articles that have analyzed the Italian American experience. An outstanding and recognizable scholar in the field writes each article and each article has appeared in a refereed publication. The articles are classified according to four areas: (1) Italian American identity; (2) Italian American politics and history; (3) Italian American community; and (4) Italian Americans and literature. There is a general introduction and there are introductory essays for each section, which attempt to define the context, the relationship and significance of each work.

The first section on Italian American identity presents a series of articles that raise the question of what does it mean to be an Italian

American after more than a century of living, interacting, and intermarrying in America. It also raises the question of the nature and future of ethnicity in general and Italian American ethnicity in particular.

The second section on Italian American politics and history presents the memories and passion of Italian Americans. It will explore events such as the Sacco-Vanzetti episode, Italian American interactions with other ethnic groups in Tampa, Florida, and the suburbanization and transformation of Italian Americans over time. In addition, it presents the problems of investigating Italian immigrant women in comparison to others and last, it will investigate Columbus as an American symbol and icon as perceived through the words and thoughts of Walt Whitman.

The third section on the Italian American community will investigate the question of what do Italian Americans seek and what have they achieved in this ever-changing environment. In addition, it explores what are the characteristics of these communities that are uniquely Italian American in character.

The fourth section on Italian Americans and literature will investigate the diverse and complex area of Italian American expression of their dreams, fears, and experiences in America through the medium of literature. Several authors will present their interpretations of how Italian Americans have reflected on these experiences and how they have impacted and been received in their artistic expression by Italian Americans and by the larger community.

The Review of Italian American Studies will be of interest to those individuals who are interested in the Italian American experience, to those who are interested in the role of ethnicity in American society, to students who are enrolled in Italian American-studies courses and to libraries that are interested in a volume of classic works in this area of study.

This project has received the enthusiastic and widespread support of those scholars who have researched and published on the Italian American experience. This support has been manifested by their desire to lend their names and their work to the success of this project. They all believe that this anthology will prove to be invaluable to scholars and students of the Italian American experience.

Part I

The Essence of Italian American Identity

Introduction

The Essence of Italian American Identity

Frank M. Sorrentino
St. Francis College

According to the United States census, Italian Americans are one of the largest ethnic groups in America. The Census Bureau employs a technique referred to as self-identification—this allows individuals to place themselves into whatever category they select. This raises as many questions as it answers. What does it mean to be an Italian American? To what degree is there consensus among contemporary Americans who identify as Italian Americans? How does our contemporary understanding of Italian American identity compare over time twenty, thirty, forty, or even sixty years ago? Also, how does identity change over the generations fifth, fourth, third, second, and first? What will it mean to be Italian American in the future especially with intermarriages and the loss of any connection to people born in Italy?

This section will explore what is the essence of Italian American identity. It will present Richard Gambino's "The Family System" from his seminal work entitled *Blood of My Blood*; Richard Alba's celebrated work entitled "The Twilight of Ethnicity among Americans of European Ancestry: The Case of Italians"; Rudolph J. Vecoli's, noted historian, provocative work entitled "Are Italian Americans Just White Folks?"; and Daniel J. Monti, Jr.'s synthesizing essay entitled "Some Sort of Americans: The Working and Reworking of Italian American Ethnicity in the United States."

In Richard Gambino's essay entitled "The Family System," he describes that after centuries of invasion, domination and exploitation by many foreigners, Southern Italians had developed a strong system of family to provide for economic, physical, cultural and social, and emotional nurturement. *L'ordine della famiglia* was a system of social attitudes, values and customs that had proven to be impenetrable to the exploitation of any foreigner, no matter how powerful their weapons or clever their devices. Due to its success over many generations in providing them with stability, order and security, *l'ordine della famiglia* was held onto tenaciously by the Italian immigrants.

The second and third generations of Italian Americans faced even more difficult challenges than their immigrant forebears. They could not maintain isolation from American culture. They had to cope with American institutions including the schools, the military, business and other powerful and pervasive cultural forces and entities. This created personality conflicts as well as partial estrangement both from their parents and with the larger American Society. They had not only to adjust to two worlds and their distinct value systems but also to make compromises between their irreconcilable demands.

Gambino argues that the third and fourth generations attempt to integrate American values with a sense of being "Italian," but are not given the necessary cultural values or family guidance upon which this ambition can be defined and pursued. Gambino sees ethnicity as a dynamic concept, one that metamorphizes with each generation but is able to maintain its own essence and identity despite the fact that each group's experience is unique and continuously developing.

Richard Alba's article entitled "The Twilight of Ethnicity among Americans of European Ancestry: The Case of Italians" is one of the most important and controversial scholarly articles because it raises the question as to what degree have Italian Americans been assimilated and acculturated into American culture and society. He concludes that after a century of living in America, Italian American ethnicity has been so transformed that it is virtually indistinguishable from the dominant and larger European American culture.

The immigrants' family structure was developed to deal with social, political and economic realities of their home country, Italy. When these realities were no longer relevant, Italian Americans developed values and attitudes that are similar to other European Americans in the United States. Alba compares education rates among third generation Italian Americans with those of British Americans (WASPs) and determines that the distinctions that were once great have been virtually eliminated for both men and women. In addition, Alba compares attitudes on a variety of cultural issues and concludes that while there are distinctions between WASPs and Italian Americans, they are insignificant. Alba concludes that Italian Americans are in the "Twilight of Ethnicity," where ethnic differences among European Americans remain visible but only faintly so.

Rudolph Vecoli, in his provocative essay entitled "Are Italian Americans Just White Folks?" addresses the question of Italian American identity. Vecoli contends that scholarship that suggests that Italian ethnicity and other European ethnicity is either receding or is merely a racist reaction have misunderstood the concept of ethnicity by treating it as static rather than as a dynamic evolving concept. He observes a revitalization of ethnic pride among third and fourth generation Italian Americans that is manifested by wide variety of cultural, social and academic institutions. He notes that these institutions are different from those created by first and second generation Italian Americans but nevertheless they are vital and significant. Vecoli concludes that the revitalization of Italian American identity reflects this dynamic process. Ethnicity is protean, capable of taking a variety of forms, of being expressed in a range of behaviors and of being revived. Ethnicity is a subjective sense of identity based on common memories and manifested in symbols that evoke those memories.

Daniel J. Monti, Jr. joins the debate on Italian American identity with his essay entitled "Some Sort of Americans: The Working and Reworking of Italian American Ethnicity in the United States." Monti contends that Italian American ethnicity is not declining or being gobbled up by a larger identity but rather it is an important means of organizing a personal identity. He further states that Italian Americans are only now coming to realize their full power and significance as an ethnic group in the United States and that their most vital contributions to the well-being of the people called "Americans" have yet to be made.

Monti traces the history of Italian Americans with the various adjustments they made as a result of an ever-changing environment and interaction with other groups, in addition to significant educational and economic advancement. Monti claims that the idea those minority peoples "lose" their ethnicity as they become more fully integrated into a host culture is inaccurate. Assimilation and pluralism are not mutually exclusive. Ethnicity allows individuals of different education and economic levels to be integrated. In addition, ethnicity allows for different groups to participate in the larger society and to enrich it with their varied ways of looking at the world. Monti concludes that Italian Americans' identity has progressed to the point where they can be full members of American society and culture while retaining their Italian American identity.

Chapter 1

The Family System

Richard Gambino
State University of New York at Stony Brook

During the first sixteen years of my life I lived in Red Hook, Brooklyn. Still largely Italian today, the area then was almost exclusively comprised of Italian American families, many of whose men were longshoremen on Brooklyn's large waterfront. It was typical of the many "Little Italies" in America, and, incidentally, is the area where Arthur Miller chose to set his forceful play about an Italian American longshore family, *A View from the Bridge*. Also typical of many families in the Little Italies, I lived with my parents (my father emigrated from Palermo, Sicily, at age thirteen; my mother was born in Red Hook shortly after her parents came from Palermo) and my maternal grandparents.

One of my early memories is of an event that happened when I was perhaps seven years old. One of my closest friends was an Italian immigrant boy named Tony. One winter day, I forget why, Tony and I fought. We tumbled on the ground and hit each other. Somehow, Tony's nose began to bleed. The sight of the blood on the dirty snow terrified both of us and we each ran home. Because both my parents worked during the day, I went to my grandparents' basement flat rather than to my own, immediately above it. Of course I kept silent about the fight and the blood, preferring to shiver in fear next to the hot coal stove. In a few minutes, the inevitable happened. The doorbell rang, and I watched with a sense of doom as my grandmother walked the long corridor to the outside "gate" of the old brownstone. I thought my fate was sealed a minute later when I heard her call to me in the uniquely sharp, decisive

7

Sicilian dialect, *Veni icca!* (Come here!). My second-generation mother had taught me that fighting was wrong, that hurting someone was wrong, and sometimes reinforced these and other lessons of American morality by spankings. I was thus totally unprepared for the scene I found at the gate. There was my grandmother, a big woman, standing in the doorway facing Tony's mother, totally blocking the latter's view. My grandmother stood squarely on both feet, hands resting on hips, palms turned *outward* from the body—the reverse of the American manner. In the body language of Southern Italy, the stance's meaning was unmistakable—"Don't tread on me or mine!" The two women were engaged in delivering ritual insults to each other, in hissing voices, almost spitting as they spoke. Southern Italians have a name for a game of ritualized oratory—*passatella*. The gist of my grandmother's part of this serious passatella was that Tony was a worthless son of worthless blood and it was a *vergogna* (outrage) to allow him to walk the streets with her *nipotino* (fine little grandson). This was news to me—my grandmother often saw me play with Tony and previously had spoken to his mother with courtesy, hence as a peer. After the confrontation, back inside the house, my grandmother asked me what had happened. Her only comment upon my explanation was that since I shed Tony's blood, he must have committed some *infamia* (infamy)!

I was astonished. My mother, when informed by my teacher of some misbehavior on my part in school, had automatically taken the teacher's side and promised me a beating when I came home—a promise kept. But my grandmother's only punishment to me was a one-sentence lecture on choosing my companions more carefully. She did not even mention the incident to my "American" parents.

My parents were embarked on the *via nuova* (new way), and I suppose my grandmother, in accordance with a Sicilian proverb, considered them too far down the road to recognize what was demanded in such a family confrontation. The proverb is, *Chi lascia la via vecchia per la nuova, sa quel che perde e non sa quel che trova*—"Whoever forsakes the old way for the new knows what he is losing but not what he will find."

At least 85 percent of the total of Italians who immigrated to the United States, and perhaps 90 percent of those who came in the great flood of immigration from 1875 to 1920, were from areas south and east of Rome. Italians call this area the Meridone, Midi, or Mezzogiorno. It is comprised of the six provinces of Abruzzi, Campania, Apulia, Lucania (also known as Basilicata), Calabria, and Sicily. The name Mezzogiorno is rich in connotations. One of the most significant is "the land that time forgot." About 25 percent of the immigrants from the land forgotten by time came from Sicily.

Italian immigrants were overwhelmingly of the *contadino* class—peasant farmers—but also fishermen, artisans, and unskilled urban poor whose ways of life were contadino from such cities as Naples, Palermo, Bari, Messina, Catania, Reggio di Calabria, Foggia, Salerno, Cosenza, Catanzaro, Enna, Ragusa, and Agrigento. In the contadino tradition shared by these people, there was one and only one social reality, the peculiar mores of family life. *La famiglia* and the personality it nurtured were very different from the American nuclear family and the personalities that are its typical products. The famiglia was comprised of all of one's blood relatives, including those relatives Americans would consider very distant cousins, aunts and uncles, an extended clan whose genealogy was traced through paternity. The clan was supplemented through an important custom known as *comparatico* or *comparaggio* (godparenthood), through which carefully selected outsiders became important (but incomplete) extended members of the family.

The only system to which the contadino paid attention was *l'ordine della famiglia,* the unwritten but all-demanding and complex system of rules governing one's relations within, and responsibilities to, his own family and his posture toward those outside the family. All other social institutions were seen within a spectrum of attitudes ranging from indifference to scorn and contempt.

One had absolute responsibilities to family superiors and absolute rights to be demanded from subordinates in the hierarchy. All ambiguous situations were arbitrated by the *capo di famiglia* (head of the family), a position held within each household by the father until it was given to—or, in the case of the father's senility, taken away by—one of the sons, and in the larger clan, by a male "elder" (*anziano*). The contadino showed calculated respect (*rispetto*) to members of other families which were powerful, and *pieta,* a mixture of pity, charity, and haughtiness or indifference toward families less powerful than his own. He despised as a *scomunicato* (pariah) anyone in any family who broke the ordine della famiglia or otherwise violated the *onore* (honor, solidarity, tradition, "face") of the family.

Thus the people of the Mezzogiorno survived a harsh history of invasions, conquests, colonizations, and foreign rule by a procession of tribes and nations (including Phoenicians, Carthaginians, Greeks, Romans, Vandals, Goths, Austrians, Byzantines, Arabs, Normans, French, Spanish, and various Northern Italian powers) and centuries of exploitation by landowners of great estates. Although they rose in violent rebellion many times, these insurrections were always crushed, betrayed, or both. What enabled the contadini to endure and develop their own culture was a system of rules based solely on a phrase I heard uttered many times by my grandparents and their contemporaries in Brooklyn's Little Italy: *sangu du me sangu,* Sicilian dialect for "blood of my blood." (As is typical of Sicilian women, my grandmother's favorite and most earnest term of endearment when addressing her children and grandchildren, and when speaking of them to others, was *sangu miu*— literally "my blood.")

It was a norm simple and demanding, protective and isolating, humanistic and cynical. The unique family pattern of Southern Italy constituted the real sovereignty of that land, regardless of which governments nominally ruled it. Governments and aliens came and went over the centuries. If they brought any customs that might strengthen the family system, these were gradually absorbed. Indeed, in an important sense, all who are derived from this land are descendants of these many cultures, "indigenous" and "alien," of thousands of years. But those customs that were hostile to the family were resisted.

Although much was absorbed from many cultures, the famous Sicilian collector of his island's folklore, Dr. Giuseppe Pitre, was essentially correct when before his death in 1913 he wrote, *"Noi siamo in mezzo a un popolino che non conosce altro galateo di la dal suo, altri usi se non i suoi"*—"We are in the midst of a people who know no other life pattern than their own, no other customs than those of their ancestors."

I was once again reminded of Pitre's words when I visited my sole surviving relatives in Palermo, one great aunt, age seventy-six, and one great aunt by marriage, age eighty-five. They could not understand why my "distant" relatives in America—cousins, great-uncle, etc.—and I do not often see each other. I tried to explain the busy pace of the United States, but they kept returning to the puzzle, at one point asking me if Manhattan (where I live) is very far from Brooklyn and Long Island (where my relatives live). At the end of many attempts at explanation on my part, one of them closed the conversation by saying in a resigned voice, without a trace of irony, "You must all live far from each other."

Among those raised in it, and this to various degrees includes all Italian Americans, it is impossible to be untouched, if not determined, by *la via vecchia*. An understanding of this pattern of family life is critical to any understanding of Italian Americans of any generation, the most "assimilated" third- and fourth-generation young people as well as wizened old immigrants. La via vecchia, cultivated for centuries, does not die quickly and certainly not easily. Even in the life of an urbane man like Luigi Pirandello, it had remarkable stamina. The great writer, whose works probe the philosophical implications of the subtle line between illusion and reality and are among the most sophisticated of our time, lived much of his life away from his homeland. Yet when he decided to marry, he chose to return to his native Agrigento in southwest Sicily to marry a young woman selected for him by his father, *a woman whom the writer had never seen before!*

An example analogous to Pirandello's occurred in my own family about ten years ago. It began with a tragic loss for a cousin of mine, then a woman twenty-four years old. Her Italian-born husband, age twenty-eight, drowned in a boating accident, leaving with her two very young children. Following the morality of la via vecchia, after the proper interval of time for mourning, the dead man's parents took it upon themselves to send word back to their relatives in the homeland to find a suitable new husband for their widowed daughter-in-law and father for their grandchildren. But here the parallel with Pirandello ends. For my cousin is of the third generation of Italian Americans and would not accept a "match." Several other American-born members of my family had to meet with her parents-in-law to explain that she wished to choose her own spouse in her own time. Although they acceded to the *via nuova,* the immigrant parents regarded it with disbelief and alarm. I doubt that they were really resigned to it until sometime later when my cousin married again—to a man of her own choice.

The role played in my cousin's dilemma is typical of the second generation, a generation that forged a great compromise between la via vecchia and la via nuova. Thus, in this example, they interceded between the two ways. Interceding on behalf of the third-generation preference for the via nuova to be sure, but interceding in a manner typical of la via vecchia, *the family interceded.* This pattern of relations between second generation (now mostly middle-aged people) and the third and fourth generations, mostly young adults, teenagers, and children, is common. In my opinion, it will prove to be one of the decisive determinants in the just beginning quest for identity on the part of the younger generations of Italian Americans. The strengths of this pattern will be a boon to them. The weaknesses in the pattern will define some of the chief problems they will have to overcome.

There is an illuminating saying among Southern Italians that the father is the head of the family and the mother the center. The father, as the ultimate retainer of la via vecchia, made all important decisions concerning the family. A living for the family and good marriages for its children were the primary goals toward which decisions were aimed. In this culture, young people had to reestablish in each generation the only social reality of the land, the family, by marriage. Therefore a good marriage was more than just a question of social status. It was tantamount to survival and was treated as a basic bread-and-butter necessity.

In the first aim, a living, the father played an active key role. He labored and maneuvered to gain the most produce and money. In this he acted according to true Machiavellian principles, guarding and guiding the welfare of his family in a dangerous, even treacherous world where *la miseria,* desperate poverty, was a constant plague. He acted as a true monarch for the good of his endangered kingdom, according to the severe rules of *Realpolitik.* Family security, power, status, and necessities of life were goals pursued in this microcosm of the world of sovereign states. And as in the system of nations, they were goals pursued without regard to sentimentality or other moralities that were disastrous in the amoral social world. The father exercised this responsibility without confiding its problems or details to his wife. They were simply *fatti suoi,* his business. He would discuss them only when necessary and then only with close male relatives, most often the clan's elder. To a more guarded degree, he might consult his *padrino* (older godparent) or his *compare* (a close friend, a peer godparent).

In a tradition that continues to puzzle foreigners who have a simplistic stereotyped notion of the Italian man's ideal of manliness, which they mislabel with the Spanish word *machismo,* the father turned over his earnings to his wife for complete management, keeping only a small allowance for his daily needs. Except for reserving the right to intercede in the case of mismanagement or other crisis, the father did not further concern himself with the family budget. Similarly, although he retained the right of veto over any proposed match, often the father was not the one who initiated arrangements for the marriages of his children.

Often he did not enter into the picture until the way for the match had been carefully and quietly arranged by the mothers, aunts, and godmothers of the prospective bride and groom. Usually it was only when a match was virtually assured that the fathers of the respective families would enter into negotiations of which the public was aware. Similarly, the father played a subdued, background role in the raising of young children, stepping in only when he thought it necessary to preserve the overall aim of the process—to turn out children who were *ben educati,* or, in the dialect, *buon educati.* As we shall see, this notion of being well educated had nothing to do with schooling. Rather it meant being brought up to value la via vecchia in thought and feeling, and to honor it in practice.

The family was the major transmitter of its own culture, and other institutions were welcomed only if they aided that goal. Those that were perceived as neither aiding l'ordine della famiglia nor endangering it were tolerated. Hence one source of the Italian's legendary attitude of "live and let live." To be more precise, institutions not affecting la via vecchia were regarded with simple indifference as *cose senza significato,* things of no consequence. But any person or event, idea or institution that was perceived as a threat to la via vecchia or to the members of the family served by the old way was stubbornly, fiercely, and if necessary violently resisted. Not only the father, but every member of the family down to the limit of the *bambini* (roughly the age of seven) was expected to protect the established code of behavior, the onore della famiglia. For example, the sons of the family above the age of puberty were expected to defend any undermining of the welfare of the females of the family, or, worse, any insult to their reputation or status, this being synonymous with an insult to the family's onore.

Individual rights, wishes, and feelings were defined by one's membership in the family. One treated a person according not so much to his individual characteristics as to the status of his family and his particular place in it. In fact, it was difficult to conceive of a "person" in any realistic sense apart from his place and role in a family. The famous book *Christ Stopped at Eboli* offers an excellent proof of this. Its author, Carlo Levi, an artist, physician, and writer from Turin, in Northern Italy, was a vociferous opponent of the Fascist regime of Mussolini. Because of this, he was exiled in 1935 to a small village in the southern province of Lucania (the "anklebone" of the Italian boot).

His book describes the life of the people there. In one passage, Levi tells of a visit to him by his sister, Luisa, and the dramatic difference it created in his status as a person among the contadini. As he tells us, until then he might just as well have been a creature from Mars in the eyes of the people of the Mezzogiorno.

Hitherto they had thought of me as a sort of man from Mars, the only one of my species, and the discovery that I had blood connections here on earth seemed somehow to fill in their picture of me in a manner that pleased them. The sight of me with my sister tapped one of their deepest feelings: that of blood relationship, which was all the more intense since they had so little attachment to either religion or the State. It was not that they venerated family relationship as a social, legal or sentimental tie, but rather that they cherished an occult and sacred sense of communality. A unifying web not only of family ties (a first cousin was often as close as a brother), but of the acquired and symbolic kinship called *comparaggio* [godparenthood], ran throughout the village. . . .

Toward evening, when my sister and I walked arm in arm along the main street, the peasants beamed at us from their houses; "Blessed is the womb that bore you!" they called out to us from the doorways; "Blessed the breasts that suckled you!" Toothless old creatures looked up from their knitting to mumble proverbs: "A wife is one thing but a sister's something more!" "Sister and brother, all to one another." Luisa, with her rational, city [Turin]-bred way of looking at things, never got over their strange enthusiasm for the simple fact that I had a sister.

All obligations, feelings, or rights of radical individuality were repressed by any good father or mother, daughter or son. For example, if a married daughter claimed she or her children were being abused by her husband—which could mean only that be was not conforming to la via vecchia—it was her brothers and, if necessary, other young male relatives who were expected to confront the culprit. Upon confirmation of the charge, the offending husband would be privately warned to mend his ways. In the Mezzogiorno, such a warning of offended onore, like everything else that touched upon the maintenance of la via vecchia, was never taken (or given) lightly.

In their tenacious will to survive inbred over centuries, the contadini paradoxically valued la via vecchia more than their very lives. For survival and the old way had been synonymous for ages.

In the United States today, much of the behavior of Italian Americans becomes more intelligible when its roots in la via vecchia are understood. For example, as recent studies have shown, Italian American families move their homes reluctantly. Further, they do so only when it nurtures the traditional values of their families. The persistence of Little Italy in and near New York's Greenwich Village, side by side with Jewish families in times past, Chinese families until today, and wave after wave of "bohemians," "beatniks," and "hippies" has been cited as an illustrative example. It is only when Italian Americans perceive (correctly or not) some other group behaving in ways that are antithetical to the life of la famiglia that they react with resistance, often merely labeled "intolerance" by the press without further attempts at analysis.

For example, a near race riot in Brooklyn a few years ago was explained by a nun very simply by citing the fact that an Italian American girl had been whistled at and spoken to in rude terms by a Puerto Rican boy. It is a pattern of America's history that it forces the groups at the lowest rung of its socioeconomic ladder to compete and clash with those at the next to lowest rung. In the past, first the Irish, Germans, blacks, and Scandinavians clashed with each other and with those of British background. This was followed by strife between the Irish and Germans, on one hand, and the Poles, Italians, blacks, and Jews, on the other. Now the clash is between poor and working class Irish, Poles, and Italians, those "one rung up," and blacks, Puerto Ricans, and Chicanos on the bottom of the socioeconomic ladder. The simple-minded explanations that Polish Americans, Irish Americans, and Italian Americans are more racist than other Americans is fostered by media coverage which too often "sees all," reports it, and explains little. The fact is that for millions of Italian Americans, the capacity to tolerate anyone is in inverse proportion to the extent that the person's lifestyle is perceived by them as a threat to la via vecchia. No doubt the racism that has played a role in America since its founding as a nation in Lincoln's terms, half slave, half free, has been learned by some Italian Americans. But this only complicates the question of relations between Italian Americans and other groups. Italian Americans fought Irish Americans in America's past, and dozens of other white groups in the history of the

Mezzogiorno who were perceived in various ways as threats to la via vecchia.

As will be seen in the chapter on attitudes toward outsiders, a solution to the problem in the United States today must be based upon an understanding of la via vecchia, which Italian Americans maintain and defend. Mere condemnation of "racism" and moralistic lecturing about it will continue to be ineffective. In Southern Italy one sees complexions ranging from very light to very dark. One need only to walk the streets of a city like Palermo to see evident descendants of Carthaginians and Arabs, who played a part in the history of the Mezzogiorno, and descendants of the blond, blue-eyed Normans, French, and other whites who are part of the history. Although the people of the Mezzogiorno have had many quarrels with many "aliens" and among themselves, there is not now, nor has there ever been, discrimination based on racial characteristics in that part of Italy.

It is instructive to note that there has been no strife between Italian and (nonwhite) Chinese Americans in downtown New York, in spite of many years of living very close to each other, just as there was little friction between Jewish and Italian Americans there in the past. On the other hand there is strife everywhere among Italian and black and Spanish-speaking Americans. This is because the Italian American does not perceive the Chinese and Jewish family-oriented life styles as a threat to la via vecchia and, correctly or not, does perceive the black and Hispanic "street style life" as opposed to it. Thus, the kind of insight often given, e.g., in 1971 by Glazer and Moynihan in their famous book *Beyond the Melting Pot* (M.I.T. Press) is true, but it is really unconstructive:

> Herman Badillo [a Democrat of Puerto Rican background] explaining why he would support Mayor Lindsay [then a Republican] instead of Mario Procaccino [the candidate of the Democratic Party], was quoted in *The New York Times* (July 30, 1969): "When he talks about crime and treating juvenile offenders as adult criminals he's talking about black and Puerto Rican kids. Everyone knows he's not talking about Jewish and Italian kids." Interestingly enough, when you talked about criminals and juvenile delinquents in this city until twenty-five years ago, you *did* mean Jewish and Italian kids.

The father in la via vecchia was the "official" voice of the family in its external relations, and the ultimate authority in its internal affairs. The family of the Mezzogiorno was what anthropologists might call an agnatic group, meaning its organization was defined by relationships to males. This differs from the "bilateral family" definition of Northern European families. Yet the contadino family was no simple patriarchy, if by this word we mean exclusive rule by the father. Except for family emergencies, the father played his role in the everyday internal affairs of the family in a relatively passive way. He did this for two reasons. One was economic necessity. In the Mezzogiorno, the contadino descended from his village to work his fields, often going great distances to do so and not infrequently having to spend several nights a week away from his home. The villages of the Mezzogiorno date from ancient or medieval times and were usually built high up the slopes of the severe, stony mountains of the land for purposes of security against invaders, brigands, and the malaria-filled marshes of the valleys. Virtually all people lived in these villages. There were no equivalents to the system of isolated individual farms typical of rural life in America and elsewhere. Paradoxically, rural life in the Mezzogiorno was town life.

Similarly, because of their vocation the many *pescatori* (fishermen) of the Mezzogiorno were away from their homes much of the time. Although with relatively little land, mainland Italy, Sicily, and Sardinia are a peninsula and two islands and have many miles of coast.

Even the artisans and the poor of the large cities, most of whom were contadino in origin, were influenced by the tradition to stay out of daily household affairs. Like the fathers, the older sons of the family were at work away from the home from the time the father decided they should begin work and turn over their earnings to the family purse, as he did. And the father usually made this decision by following an old formula of the Mezzogiorno that says, "When hair grows between the legs, it is time to work."

Of course, this rule also covered daughters. Females in some areas of the Mezzogiorno, e.g., Sicily, worked in the home and never outside of it, while in other regions, e.g., Calabria, they did light work in the fields as well. (A vestige of these practices is seen in the many gardens of Italian Americans. These are seldom tended by the women.) This was continued in the New World. Many daughters were sent to work by Italian immigrants, and many second-generation women work after their marriages. It is interesting to understand why this last practice changed, for the explanation serves as a model for most of the differences between the life of Italian Americans and the life of their recent ancestors in the old land.

In general, Italian Americans have adopted only those new ways that they perceive as compatible with the family system and its values. Others have been shunned. So, for example, Italian American daughters, and later wives, worked because this contributed to the family welfare. Nevertheless, they were held, and held themselves, close to the home. As in the Mezzogiorno, it was unthinkable for a single woman—or man—to live away from the family. Women left the house in time to get to the job and came home immediately after work. They were found, and later sought, jobs where they could work with other Italian American women. A network of mutual reinforcement of the traditional values was extended. Significantly, they did factory work. No matter how poor, no Italian American woman to this day does work as a domestic. For to work in the house of another family (sometimes an absolute economic necessity in the old land) is seen as a usurpation of family loyalty by her family *and by her.* And if one loses one's place in la via vecchia, there is no self-respect. In American history, there is no Italian counterpart of Irish, German, black, Spanish-speaking, English, Scandinavian, and French maids. In 1950, most of the second generation was into adulthood and together with the Italian-born population in New York City numbered 859,000, according to the United States Census of Population report. The report that year listed only 1 percent of the female Italian immigrant population as employed as private household workers, while the figure for the second-generation female population was 0 percent.

My mother's experience is illustrative. The daughter of immigrants, she was sent to work in a large garment factory as a seamstress, to work together with numbers of other Italian American girls, including a second older sister. The compulsory education law of New York State posed few problems for the younger girls. In common practice, the truant officer was simply bribed to look the other way and to turn in reports that he was "actively pursuing" a child's case until he or she became sixteen and was no longer of legal concern. A working girl was expected to spend all of her remaining time learning the domestic skills. To put it mildly, any activity outside the home was discouraged, and there was no acceptable excuse for not being home on time after work. The immigrants compromised with la via nuova only when it served la via vecchia, and only to the extent that was necessary to serve this end.

The second reason for the father's passive role in daily household affairs, and indeed the only reason it was possible, was the active role played by the mother. Her designation as the "center" of the family might be extended—she was in a crucial way the center of the culture. For it was she who not only maintained the home as the seat of l'ordine della famiglia, but also had responsibility to nurture it in her children with every word, look, and gesture. If the father was monarch in the family kingdom, the mother was the powerful minister of internal affairs.

Italian American homes are kept immaculately clean, so much so that Americans are bemused thereby. Sometimes the bemusement turns to bigoted amusement. Thus the stereotype of the "unliberated" Italian mamma, concerned exclusively with the home, is a source of condescension and outright ridicule. How simple she seems, even shielding the furniture in her working-class living room with covers of transparent plastic. As with most stereotypes, there is here a germ of truth, albeit very distorted.

Traditionally, the home was the site and the source of all that gave meaning to life. A well-kept home was the symbol of a sound family. Furniture that lasted was symbolic of family stability and hence family strength. Plentiful food in the kitchen was a sign of family well-being. But ostentation was shunned. As we shall see, the unique religious attitudes of the Mezzogiorno were an amalgam of Christian doctrines, magic, and pagan beliefs. In this morality, it was considered unwise to display signs of one's wealth. Conspicuous consumption, or anything approaching it, was a sure sign of moral madness. It was a sign of sinful hubris, inviting a punishing nemesis on the part of the forces governing the universe, powers that were believed to be immediate, palpable, and ever present. So to this day, Italian Americans tend to live *below* their financial means. Their homes, clothes, and cars often represent less than they might afford.

In a land where conspicuous consumption, in the style dictated by class-conscious fashion, is the sign of having "made it" in society, the opposed patterns of Italian Americans make them the objects of condescension, ridicule, or at least of misunderstanding. They are tagged as socially gauche, un-chic working-class types stigmatized in the sad American practice of ethnic jokes. Thus, the same joke I heard about Poles in St. Louis and about Italians in Philadelphia: "What is the first thing a flamingo does when it buys a home?" Answer: "It puts a Polack [Italian] out on the lawn." Or to take a case of misunderstanding, in a movie review published in the New York *Post* panning the film *The Godfather,* Emily Genauer noted that the Italian American family in the film was wealthy and she found fault with the film because

> and yet there are no signs of wealth to be seen. The house Don Vito lives in is ugly and commonplace, filled with squalling kids, with women old and young who show none of the appurtenances of wealth.

The reviewer's ignorance of the lifestyle of many Italian Americans is understandable. Yet are we so far into materialism in the United States that we must simply accept Miss Genauer's judgment that the Italian American home is "ugly and commonplace"? Could it be that the current fascination on the part of many Americans with the Italian American home and family reflects a discontent with the hollow, brainless, and heartless ideal of "the beautiful people" incessantly trumpeted by advertising and the media, an ideal that Miss Genauer presumably thinks more appropriate to people who have money? Perhaps we might ponder whether these Americans are attracted to the values of warmth, loyalty, sense of belonging, palpable enjoyment of everyday life, and lack of pretense they perceive in the Italian American home. Further, perhaps we should ponder which set of values is preferable.

The stereotype of the Italian American mother's preoccupation with food also has a kernel of truth in it, although again distorted. To all Mediterranean people, food is the symbol of life, of all that is good and nourishing. We are all familiar with the legends surrounding the importance of food to such peoples as the Italians, the Spanish, the French, the Arabs, and the Greeks. Thus, these people find the attitude of some Americans toward food worse than barbarous. This attitude, characterized in the extreme by the American food stand where one eats bland mass-prepared food on the run, is seen as sacrilegious. To the Italian American, food is symbolic both of life and of life's chief medium for human beings, the family.

I remember the attitude conveyed to me as a child by the adults in my family, immigrants and second generation, that the waste or abuse of food was a sin. They did so not by any attempt to link waste with the Catholic religion, or by inducing guilt through invidious distinctions as in the "think of the starving children of India" approach. On the contrary, I was made to feel that food was the host of life, and not in any remote or abstract sense. It was the product of my father's (or grandfather's, or uncle's, etc.) labor, prepared for us with care by my mother (or grandmother, or aunt, etc.). It was in a very emotional sense a connection with my father and mother, an outreach by them toward me. In a very poignant way, meals were a "communion" of the family, and food was "sacred" because it was the tangible medium of that communion. To this day I cannot bear to see food wasted and tend to save even the smallest quantities of leftovers from a meal. To see edible food thrown in a garbage can has a similar emotional effect on me to seeing a trampled flower in a field, or a dead animal by the side of the highway.

Respect for food as the host of life is upheld even in the most anonymous, poor, and crowded of circumstances. While in Palermo, I spent some time wandering through the area of the city where my father lived as a boy. It is a maze of streets in the old medieval heart of the city around the Via Porta di Castro. The streets and alleys are impossibly narrow, congested with people, and squalid. The buildings are archaic. Except for the presence of electricity, the area is a kind of casbah, unchanged for centuries and as impoverished as perhaps any area in Europe. I watched life there as I had heard it described by my father. Swarms of people walking past groups of others sitting on chairs in the streets, most of which are too narrow to permit automobiles. The earnest chatter of adults animated by swift arabesques of hand gestures and punctuated by the shouts and squalls of children. The women who lower baskets by rope from their windows to accept the objects of the errands their young children run for them. The open stalls that are the counterpart of both our shops and workshops. The artisans and workmen in the latter, laboring in tiny one-room cubicles. The fantastic, elaborate, and odorous outdoor markets where every kind of meat, fish, and produce is prepared and displayed, in exactly the same way as it had been on Court Street, Smith Street, and Union Street when I was a boy in Brooklyn. The cacophony of smells of my boyhood was replayed. Salted fish *(baccala, stoccafisso),* fresh fish, dried peppers, newly baked bread, the sickly smell of bloody cuts of meat, the spicy odor of sausages, the cutting smell of enormous cheeses, the tang of oranges, the allure of garlic and oregano were all blended yet distinguishable.

And here I would eat lunch, in this medieval anachronism just a short walking distance from Palermo's "Fifth Avenue," the Via Macqueda, where one finds long rows of sophisticated shops like Elizabeth Arden's flanking the headquarters of Sicily's Communist Party opposite the famous opera house, the Teatro Massimo at the Piazza Giuseppe Verdi. (The party incessantly blasted forth propaganda from its building via an earsplitting, high-decibel PA system, to the evident disgust of the many passersby who included sleek girls in minis and old women dressed in the traditional black. The only verbal response to the magnified exhortations for "a new Italy" coming from the large building was from a man, about twenty-five years old and dressed in mod clothing à la London's Carnaby Street. He looked up to shout *cafone*—a term meaning a vulgar, undignified person; roughly, a "slob"—at the voice from the loudspeakers and proceeded to harangue it on the subject of *buon costume*, proper behavior! I burst out laughing. It was as if John Lennon were to embark on one of my grandparents' lectures on traditional Sicilian good behavior.)

Lunch at one of the open stall restaurants consisted of typical foods, dishes I used to enjoy in the sawdust-floored longshoremen's restaurants in Brooklyn. I feasted on my favorites—arancine (deep-fried rice balls, each the size of a baseball, stuffed with chopped meat, peas, and spiced tomato sauce) and *panelle* (a type of flat, rectangular pancake made from chickpea flour, deep fried and eaten with or without bread). The prices of the food reflected the poverty of the area. Lunch could be had for 125 lire, about a quarter. Being accustomed to the hot dog stand in America, the first time I ate at one of the "luncheonettes" of Palermo's poor, I began to wolf down the food at the counter while standing in the street. (The people who live in the area buy the food hot and take it home to be eaten at leisure, often at a doorside table.) The lone proprietor and cook immediately invited me to come sit inside (the sole room being the kitchen), and set a makeshift table for me on a food counter. In the midst of the hurlyburly and destitute poverty, the natural manner was one of medieval chivalry, so cherished in Southern Italy. The ceremony of eating was to be honored.

I was reminded of a conversation I had a few years ago with a retired social worker in New York City. In her career, she had visited the homes of the succeeding ethnic waves of New York's poor. She related to me how struck she was when she first went into Italian American homes during the depression of the 1930s. Nothing of any consequence could be discussed until at least some token meat was shared. Entering into the family communion was a prerequisite to partaking in any of its affairs, even for that most distrusted class of people, agents of the state.

On my first, unannounced, visit to my great-aunts in Palermo, I was greeted with great enthusiasm. Yet despite their obvious curiosity, they would not presume to ask me questions until I had shared some of their strong black Italian coffee. My first sip was a cue that we could now talk as *cristiani*. (In an unbroken medieval tradition the term for "human being" used in the Mezzogiorno is cristiano.)

Of course, the social worker told the story to stress how impressed she was with Italian hospitality. This is a common feeling among Americans, who do not realize that the Italian words for hospitality and guest *(ospitalita, ospite)* are not used in the Southern Italian homes. Even among second-generation Italian Americans, "friends" is a preferred word to "guests" and "good manners" is a term used more than "hospitality." This derives from their immigrant parents' use of *buon costume and amici,* the latter a term that means more than "guests" to the contadini but considerably less than "friends" in any intimate sense. For one was truly intimate only with the family.

The paradox of a legendary hospitality without use of the word is cleared up when we understand that l'ordine della famiglia carefully prescribes a hierarchy of categories of people. They are, from top to bottom: One, family members, "blood of my blood." Two, *compari and padrini* and their female equivalents, *commare and madrine* ("godparents," a relationship that was by no means limited to those who were godparents in the Catholic religious rites of baptism and confirmation, and which would be better translated as "intimate friends" and "venerated elders"). Three, *amici or amici di cappello* (friends to whom one tipped one's hat or said "hello"), meaning those whose family status demanded respect. And four, *stranieri* (strangers), a designation for all others, including people one may speak to everyday—for example, shopkeepers or fellow workers on the job. It is an iron rule that one has nothing to do with *stranieri.* One had to go up the hierarchy from the class of "stranger" to "friendly acquaintance" before one could even have human discourse. In a curious psychological twist of the logic, the rule was observed by permitting passage from one class to the next highest through the rite of sharing a meal (or just coffee), a symbolic entering into the ceremony of family communion.

In the tradition, each meal is significant. The noontime meal, *colazione,* was taken whenever possible by the entire family. Workers in Italy still prefer to come home for "lunch" rather than eat at work. Often this was impossible for workingmen because of distances. But even in the field, the contadini ate with family—sons, brothers, cousins, etc. Of course, it was unthinkable that young children ate anywhere but at their mother's table. Despite the well-publicized and economical (state-subsidized) hot lunch program at Public School 142 in Brooklyn, almost all of us walked home for lunch. Although it was frowned upon by Board of Education dietitians who (erroneously) considered Italian food to be of inferior nutritional value, the practice was fine with us. A good home-cooked lunch of the *paese,* for example, fried eggs and potatoes on Italian bread, was indescribably delicious and much preferred to the school's institutional "balanced meals."

One of the first signs of liberation of us second- and third-generation boys was permission to eat lunch at the "candy store" (a local luncheonette serving Italian sandwiches, before they were called "heroes"). It was a hard-won privilege, the granting of which was resisted by parents and grandparents for as long as possible. It was never granted to girls, of course.

Obedience to parental authority was a strictly enforced value, exemplified in the saying that he who disobeys parents *fa la morte di un cane* (will die like a dog). Yet in a paradox Americans have never understood, boys had the boldness to disobey, to assert their developing ability to be *furbo* (foxy), because it was really expected that they should develop this ability to deal with the world outside. The ability had to be honed, so friction against the world on one side was encouraged, and friction against the family from the other side was provided and defiance allowed gradually to succeed. However, because this worldly capacity was not deemed necessary or desirable for females, any such assertive disobedience by girls was always severely punished. It was never permitted to win the day.

Pranzo, dinner, was a gathering of the entire family. The only outsiders to be sometimes invited were godparents and occasionally honored "friends" (in the Mezzogiorno someone demanding "respect," i.e., of an equal or better family). The American custom of children regularly visiting at their friends' homes for dinner was unknown in my neighborhood. Whenever one of us (influenced by the media) would broach the idea with parents, the response was always an unyielding "You come home for dinner!"

The major meal of the week was the one at which time and circumstances permitted the most leisurely and largest gathering of la famiglia. It was the Sunday pranzo, which began in midafternoon—breakfast has never been an important meal for Southern Italians—and lasted until early evening, or even late into the evening. It is a relaxed social gathering of the clan, featuring intimate conversations as much as well-prepared courses. Often it began with an antipasto, featuring all the tasty cheeses, fish, and salamis familiar to Americans, as well as others which few Americans know, such as fatty ham cold cuts known as *capocollo* and *mortadella*. These last were often served with melons when in season. The meal always included a pasta dish, followed by one or more main dishes—meat, fish, or poultry—with side dishes of vegetables. Dessert in the old tradition meant fresh fruits and nuts, peeled and shelled by each person at the table. Desserts of sweets were introduced only as the immigrants and their children learned American ways. Coffee was served black, with a choice of anisette, mint, or nuts.

Although the routine of American life has altered the schedule, especially of daytime weekday meals, Italian Americans still cling to the ceremonies of the evening and Sunday *pranzi*. In addition, the favorite foods of the Mezzogiorno are as current as ever. These include not only those most Americans know from the countless Italian restaurants in the United States, all but a fraction of which serve Southern Italian dishes, but also many that most Americans would find exotic, to say the least. As a carryover from the "waste not" practice of the old land where meat was seldom plentiful, Italian Americans now eat for enjoyment foods that were necessary to sustain life for their ancestors. These include dishes made from the internal organs of livestock. Special favorites are lungs (often sliced and fried and served with grossly grated cheese), kidneys, brains, and tripe. As a boy I savored tripe prepared in soup, or with tomato sauce and cheese, and loved not only the honeycomb variety (stomach), but also the bitter intestines. I understand the latter has since been banned for sale in New York by the Board of Health.

I remember my grandmother eating, along with fish bodies, fish heads, including the eyes, and commenting that it was "the best part." To this day, one can see a particular favorite of the Mezzogiorno in the windows of butcher shops on Union Street, Mulberry Street, and Arthur Avenue, three avenues which are market centers of New York City's three Little Italies, respectively in Brooklyn, Manhattan, and the Bronx. It is the heads of goats, all parts of which are eaten. The same is true of eels, also plentiful in the three markets. Snails, conch *(scungigli)*, squid *(calamari)*, and mussels are all favorites and conjure up childhood memories of gustatory delight for me.

Similarly, the common vegetables of the old land are now loved for their tastes by American-born Italian Americans. These include squashes, eggplants, unbearably hot cherry peppers, and escarole. The last was eaten by contadini from all parts of the Mezzogiorno in the belief that *scarola* was needed at least once a week "to cleanse the intestines." Often repeating this credo, which I doubt he believed, my father insisted on a pattern that almost every Monday evening's meal included escarole, either made with pasta or as a side dish dripping in olive oil and spices. Chickpeas in olive oil spiked with garlic and parsley are still one of my favorites of the old dishes of *la miseria* (poverty). And the two lowliest of all meals are now enjoyed as a special treat. These are hard, even stale, pieces of Italian bread dipped in olive oil, pepper, and oregano; and the dish mildly scorned in the old land as the mark of desperation, *fave foglie,* beans mashed with greens into a paste bonded by olive oil.

Coming from a land where it was folly to eat the meat of an animal not freshly slaughtered, the immigrants shunned canned meats and hamburger meat. When I went shopping for poultry with my grandmother, we would go to a market that had live chickens, select one, and watch as it was decapitated. Succeeding generations of Italian Americans prefer to shop in Italian markets, where even the cold-cut meats are of gourmet quality not to be compared to the plastic-encased, bland specimens of the supermarket. It is quite common for Italian American housewives to travel considerable distances for their food; for example, to drive into the center city "old neighborhood" from homes in the outlying suburbs. They return to neighborhoods like that of my childhood, for there the pushcart vendors had shouted the traditional assurance of the old *paese.* It was only years later that I understood the significance of the vendors' shouting, *Roba dalla mia*—my own goods.

As it was in the Mezzogiorno, Italian Americans still prepare the special dishes appropriate to specific holidays. Christmas Eve has always been the chief among these. Following the tradition, my family would gather, several dozen strong, in the home of my grandparents. Tables would be set end to end, supplemented by makeshift ones arranged from planks set across chairs or wooden horses. The meal was served after midnight, and the conversations would continue sometimes until dawn. Dinner on Christmas Day, although an important family gathering, was an anticlimax for Italian Americans, and many of them met the American tradition halfway by serving ham or turkey then—typically preceded by an Italian pasta dish. The Christmas Eve feasts featured fish dishes. Typically, at my grandparents' house, *purpo* (octopus served hot or cold with lemon juice, olive oil, garlic, and spices) was the main dish, usually flanked by other "holiday" fish, sea urchins being a most treasured one.

In the wee hours of the morning the group might have soft-boiled eggs—
not eaten with a spoon, but "drunk" in the old-fashioned way, that is,
sucked from the shell.

As is the case on all holidays, children were permitted to stay up
until three or four in the morning. A second-generation friend recently
reminisced about how he and the other children in his family would be
picked up and carried off to bed one by one as they dozed off in the sleep
of exhaustion. They would awaken on Christmas Day, lying side by side
in neat rows, a half-dozen or so children on the grandparents' bed.

I remember that during a break in the meal, my grandfather would
roast chestnuts on the coal stove that warmed his combination living
room-dining room. He took orange peels that lay on the printed oilcloth-
covered table and placed them on the stove, creating a sour-sweet room
redolent of Southern Italy. He would also deep-fry in a pot that seemed
to me the largest and heaviest utensil in the world, significantly called
the "laundry pot," a special treat called *zeppole*. These are little balls of
sweet dough, about double the size of a golf ball, dipped in white
powdered sugar. We would watch anxiously to see which of us would
bite into the annual practical joke—a zeppola stuffed with absorbent
cotton. Each holiday had special dishes, e.g., the incredibly delicious,
rich, and dense *pizza di gran* (grain pie) of Easter. It is a dish that
bespeaks the miracle of life's springtime renewal with its grain, ricotta
cheese, and diced fruit prepared to a creamy texture.

Of course, all meals were taken with wine. A traditional saying has
it that a day without wine is like a day without sun: *Un giorno senza vino
i come un giorno senza sole.* The contadino custom of mixing wine with
fruits was followed (fresh peach slices dipped in dark red wine is still my
idea of ambrosia), and was extended in America by mixing wine with the
fruity carbonated soft drinks of the new country. Wine is quite properly
considered a natural food, and to the consternation of American
schoolteachers, social workers, and visiting nurses, immigrants regularly
gave their children small quantities of wine from the age of two on up.
As a young child I never cared for beef, and I remember my grandfather
dipping pieces of the meat in his wine to make it more palatable for me.
Perhaps, predictably, it gave me a love of wine I have to this day, but I
continue to dislike beef.

It is altogether fitting, then, that the mother would be the creator of
all these meals, the daily communions, and the holiday celebrations. For

her role as the family's center was celebrated by her culinary arts, and not limited to it as the stereotype would have it.

To be sure, in the Mezzogiorno a wife would never contradict her husband in public. Often she went so far as to address him in public by the formal "you" or "thou" (*lei*) rather than the informal *tu*. Yet she had her ways of expressing herself within the walls of the home. This sometimes included—as in the case of my grandmother, a volatile woman—stormy argument which my grandfather endured by blowing clouds of dense acrid smoke into the air from the appalling, wrinkled, black Di Nobili cigars that he all but chain-smoked. Finally, after she had had ample say, he would erupt with a *"basta!"* (enough!). This would be followed by about an hour of silence, while both privately meditated what form the compromise action would take. The resolution, whether it involved only them or some business with the outside world, was never spoken, but merely implemented.

In the Mezzogiorno people considered the death of the mother the ultimate in disasters, far worse than a father's dying. For a family could endure the loss of the father, but seldom the mother. A new family head could be found, but not as easily a new center. A new woman coming into the home as mother would mean more children. She would either bring them from a former marriage if a widow, or bear them if marrying for the first time as a young girl—usually a very young girl with many childbirths before her, for most girls married well before the age of twenty and the average Italian immigrant family had six children.

A father's replacement, on the other hand, if need be was accomplished quite simply by endowing the oldest son with responsibilities as family head. If he was still a child, the mother would rule as de facto "regent" until the boy reached the age, as the contadini would say, *quannu vennero i sentimenti* ("when responsibilities come"— puberty). Although she usually continued in reality to make the family decisions, a widowed mother would defer to her son in public as soon as he showed signs of puberty. Needless to say, the death rate of immigrant fathers being high, many a second-generation boy of twelve or so was absolutely bewildered by the contradictory behavior toward him of his mother. In the home she would treat him as a mere child, and in public as a superior. As one man remembers, his mother would simply slap his face if he dared to command her in the home, and rather obsequiously obey him if he did so in public! To complicate matters further, his high school teachers knew nothing of the private relationship and considered the public side of it outrageous. If the phrase had been in vogue then, they would no doubt have cited his case as a perfect example of the "male chauvinism" of the Italian American. Following centuries of precedent by Southern Italian women, his mother had real power but neither displayed it nor sought any public sign or recognition of it. This reality is behind the paradox of the two contrary images the outside world holds of the Southern Italian woman. These are the fiery, sensuous, outspoken, willful "Sophia Loren" image (indeed, the actress is a native of Naples) and the jolly, all-loving, naive, rotund *mamma mia* image.

In an interview, the author Mario Puzo said that he deliberately set out to write a sensational bestseller about violent crime in *The Godfather* after writing an award-winning but commercially unsuccessful novel of an Italian American woman and her family, *The Fortunate Pilgrim*. The widowed Lucia Santa Angeluzzi-Corbo of this beautiful novel combines a great nourishing maternal love with the equally great shrewdness of a vixen and toughness that the contadini call *figatu* ("guts," from *fegato*, meaning liver). She is the quintessential immigrant Italian American mother. Confrontations on the question of male-female relationships between her and her eighteen-year-old daughter, Octavia, are typical. Octavia is a girl lashed both with the cultural conflict of the second generation and the sexual conflicts of a virgin grown to maturity.

As the years pass, Octavia comes to realize that the most formidable human being she knows is this mother of hers with her deceptively simple verbalizations. Regarding the question of how to raise Octavia's younger siblings, the mother said to the disgust of the sophomoric daughter, "If you want a house to give orders in, get married, have children, scream when they come out of your belly. *Then* you can beat them, then you can decide when they will work and how, and who works."

Again, in contrast to the apparent patriarchal image of la famiglia, the mother's family played an important part in her life after her marriage and in the lives of her children, especially in the formative young years. The maternal relatives formed the only insurance she had against the possibility of her husband's death. In the event of her widowhood while her oldest son was still a child, the responsibility for her welfare and that of her children would be assumed by her family, and not by her husband's. Thus, despite the pre-eminence of the husband, the wife's role in the economics of the family was considerable, comprising both management and insurance. And her pre-eminent power to shape her family in its daily affairs was enhanced by the fact that female members of her maiden family usually were daily company to her and her children. Thus the nurturing of children was very strongly in the pattern of the maternal family, the father's dominance notwithstanding. Indeed, the father was formal chief executive of the family, but the actual power was shared with the mother in an intricate pattern of interactions in which the famous female tactic *pigghiami cu bonu* (stooping to conquer) played a major part.

Because so much was at stake, the selection of those outsiders who were to be admitted into the family relationship was done with great care. The institution of comparaggio was thus carefully systematized. These intimates or "godparents" were of two classes. In neither case were they necessarily godparents of the Church, i.e., those who had "stood up for" a child in the baptism or confirmation rites of Catholicism. The first class consisted of compari (male intimates) and commare (female intimates) who were one's peers in age and often were also the Church godparents of one's children. The second class were padrini (males) and madrine (females). These godfathers and godmothers were older people whom one treated with some of the respect accorded to parents. Their word was heeded, and due parental deference paid to them. Often they were also godparents in the Catholic institution. Sometimes these elders were called "uncle" and "aunt" *(zio, zia)*. Thus, one's peer intimate was one's compare and at the same time was padrino or zio to one's children.

Godparents were consulted on important matters, treated with respectful courtesy, and their advice heeded. They were chosen for their prestige, wisdom, and power. Since to be invited to be an intimate was one of the greatest honors, and to refuse the invitation a great insult, the procedure of offering and accepting this role was ritualized. Usually the two people involved gradually became more intimate in their conversations through degrees of codified, circumspect conversation. If one accepted the gambit offered by the other, then one or the other would move to the next degree. If the gambit was refused, the relationship went no deeper and its progress stopped well short of the point of an honor offered and refused. It was typical of all social relations among the contadini, who believed so much in the power of human passions that they evolved a careful system of directing and controlling their fulfillment with a minimum of the destruction attendant to unbridled passions. Often the process of emerging intimacy between two peers or between an elder and a junior took a considerable period of time. In the Mezzogiorno, the process sometimes lasted for years. Thus each party to the relationship was permitted to try it and assess it at graduated levels before making a permanent commitment.

Although the privileges and obligations of being a compare or padrino were considerable, they fell short of those of blood relationships. The confidence and trust one extended to a compare or padrino was never complete as it was with one's brother or father. Conversely, the obligation to look after the welfare, status, and power of one's compare or *figlioccio* (godchild) was circumscribed. The limit was not precise. It could be best understood by saying that relationships of comparaggio could approach the absoluteness of blood connections, but they could never quite reach that point. Of course, in any conflict of interests between the blood and godparents, the blood came first.

Through comparaggio, a network of connections was spread throughout the towns of the Mezzogiorno. The network complemented and extended l'ordine della famiglia, giving it much greater vitality and making it considerably more impervious to disruptive forces, especially those from the outside. This pattern continues today among Italian Americans. The legends of the cohesiveness of Italian American families, friendships, associations, and communities are well founded.

The social value played by comparaggio is considerable. It can be understood by looking at its origin in ancient history. Indeed, comparaggio is traceable to the system of "adoption" widely practiced in ancient Rome. In order to ensure their welfare and their society's, Roman families often adopted promising children or young adults, giving them full legal status within the family, sometimes entrusting the family's destiny to them in preference to natural children. For example, Julius Caesar adopted his sister's grandson, Octavius, and bequeathed to him the larger part of his personal fortune as well as his name, making him his personal and political heir. Upon the murder of Julius, the young Octavius avenged the murder and assumed power, later calling himself Augustus Caesar. The great emperor and Stoic philosopher Marcus Aelius Aurelius Antoninus (originally named Marcus Annius Verus) was the adopted son of his natural aunt's husband, the Emperor Antonius Pius. Unfortunately the great Marcus broke with the practice of adoption and insisted that his natural son, Commodus, succeed him as emperor.

The rule of this stupid, despotic son (A.D. 180–92) was a calamity for the empire.

In retrospect, the evolution of comparaggio over the centuries might be viewed as an attempt to correct the dangers of loving one's own blood unwisely, as with Marcus Aurelius. Family love is a natural passion and hence is considered undeniable. Its fulfillment was protected against its own parochialism by permitting wise intimates to act as checks and balances over family policies. Comparaggio plays an important internal role, as well as a broader social role, in the ordine della famiglia.

The family system, extended by comparaggio, also meant that the old and infirm were cared for. No one went to poorhouses, orphanages, or other institutions of charity in the Mezzogiorno except those few unfortunates without any family intimates. Somewhat cruelly and without mincing words, the contadini called these unfortunates *poveri vergognosi* or "shame-laden poor."

Commenting on the social conditions of the poor in America at the turn of the century, the great social reformer and journalist Jacob Riis noted that the percentage of pauperism among the Italian Americans was lowest of all ethnic groups. "It is curious," he said in *How the Other Half Lives,* "to find preconceived notions quite upset in a review of the nationalities that go to make up this squad of street-beggars." He went on to give figures. "The Irish lead the list with 15 percent, and the native American is only a little behind with 12 percent, while the Italian has less than 2 percent. 8 percent were German. The relative prevalence of the races *[sic]* in our population does not account for this showing."

Phyllis H. Williams, in her *South Italian Folkways in Europe and America* (1938), notes that during the Depression of the 1930s, the percentage of Italian Americans in institutions of charity was remarkably low. She records that in one city where one-third of the population was Italian American, only eighteen of 348 people in the poorhouse were of Italian background.

An interesting set of statistics was published in 1901 by the State Board of Charities of New York regarding the pauperism in New York City. Three tables were included and are reprinted in *The Italian in America* (1905), by E. Lord, J. J. D. Trevor, and S. J. Barrows. The first showed the number and birthplaces of persons admitted to the almshouse in 1900. Italy was lowest on the list and disproportionately low in relation to the numbers of Italians in New York at that time. In fact the number was lower even than groups whose numbers in New York City were very few compared with Italians. The figures are: U.S. 554, Ireland 1,617, England and Wales 198, Scotland 39, France 21, Germany 374, Scandinavian countries 28, Italy 19, others 86; total 2,936. The second table shows the numbers and places of birth of those admitted to the Incurable Hospital in 1900. Again, Italy has the lowest figure, one out of a total of thirty. The last chart is of those admitted to the Blind Asylum in the same year. Italy again had the lowest figure, one out of a total of ninety-seven.

In 1902, the Associated Charities of Boston issued its annual report, which was also reprinted in *The Italian in America.* It noted that although in District Six, the Italian quarter in the North End (still Italian today), where "Italian families largely outnumber the others," the variation in the number of Italians applying for assistance is interesting. "Fifty-four families came to us in 1891, and only sixty-nine in the last year, though the Italian population of this city has in the meantime increased from 4,718 to 13,738. . . . The majority of the Italians are apparently fairly thrifty and those who have trouble are often helped by their countrymen. The little that we have been called upon to do has in some cases set a family at once upon their feet."

A report of the U.S. Bureau of Immigration in 1904 on the nativity of people in America's charitable institutions showed that Italians and "Hebrews" tied for the lowest figure, 8 percent each.

It should also be noted that Italian Americans were at this time at the very bottom of the labor picture. As shall be seen, they were then without exception the "last hired, first fired" and had an appallingly high rate of illiteracy. In short, they had only one advantage over others among the poor—l'ordine della famiglia.

These facts are cited not to make insidious comparisons with other ethnic groups, but to stress the importance of the Italian family and its value of self-care. It is in this context that we should view the discontent with today's welfare system among some Italian Americans, discontent that is again blithely labeled "reactionary" by some in the media. In the tradition Italian Americans learn that to be the object of public *pieta or carita* (charity) is a most humiliating experience. So it is that the credit ratings of even poor Italian Americans is high, as I am told by non-Italian businessmen. Debts are paid on schedule, by oneself or one's relations. For one should never permit himself or any member of the clan to be the object of *pietai.* To do so is to admit the moral inadequacy of one's family, and hence to be truly one of the poveri vergognosi, one of the shameful poor.

The most shameful condition of all, however, was to be without a family. Except for a very low number of illegitimate babies (as we shall see, the rate of illegitimacy in Italy was lowest in the South), this condition only befell one who was a *scomunicato,* one who violated l'ordine della famiglia and was excluded from all respected social intercourse by all families. Indeed, it was difficult even to survive in the Mezzogiorno as a scomunicato. Male outcasts could only become mountain hermit shepherds or, more commonly, the lowest component of the lowest economic class, *glornalieri* (day laborers). As the humblest day laborer, he would be hired only when the work demand was so great that all others before him were already employed. This was a most rare occurrence in Southern Italy. A female outcast could only become a whore or beggar. Because the sanction was so severe, excommunication from the family was applied only in cases of the most treacherous and/or scandalous violations of the onore della famiglia. For to be without family was to be truly a nonbeing, *un saccu vacante* (an empty sack) or as Sicilians say, *un nuddu miscatu cu nenti* (a nobody mixed with nothing).

On the other hand, the devotion shown to loyal kin is difficult for outsiders to imagine. While in Sicily, I visited the Cappuccini Catacombs in Palermo. Unlike the ancient catacombs near Rome, these are recent. The Cappuccini Catacombs were used in the last century. The sight that greets one in them is ghastly (a woman fainted there during my visit). Row upon row of corpses line the walls, most of them tied in standing positions. Because they are relatively recent dead, they are in various states of decomposition. Corrupted flesh, staring eyes, and grinning teeth are visible through ruptures in parchment skin. Each corpse is dressed in Sunday clothing, with a name plate hung around the neck giving the name, age, date of death (most were in the 1860s through the 1880s), and often also some inscription by the family. The most common of the handwritten inscriptions began, *"La sua vita fu tutta dedita alla famiglia"* ("His life was dedicated entirely to his family"). The corpses, perhaps several thousand of them, were arranged in this fashion *so that their surviving relatives could come and visit with them!* Usually on Sundays and holidays.

While in the catacombs, I spoke to a woman from Florence who was obviously upset and kept commenting in a voice not at all quiet that this had been a "barbarous practice . . . what savagery," etc. Although I tried to explain the basis of familial devotion, she seemed psychologically incapable of understanding such feelings. Thus the irony, an Americano of Sicilian ancestry explaining the ways of the not so distant past Mezzogiorno to an uncomprehending native Italian, even if a Northern Italian. Little wonder, then, that to most Americans the Chinese character is probably more scrutable than that of millions of their own countrymen who are Italian Americans.

This background of the ordine della famiglia helps illuminate the confused situation of Italian Americans today. As all of us are confronted with the conflicts of our loyalty to a sovereign state vs. our cosmopolitan aspirations, so the Italian American has found himself in the dilemma of reconciling the psychological sovereignty of his people with the aspirations and demands of being American.

To the immigrant generation of Italians, the task was clear: hold to the sovereignty of the old ways and thereby seal out the threats of the new "strangers," the American society that surrounded them. The complicated customs and institutions of la famiglia had been marvelously effective in neutralizing the influence of a succession of aliens in the Mezzogiorno. In the old land, the people survived and developed their own identity over centuries not so much by their periodic violent rebellions, a futile approach because of the small size, exposed location, and limited resources of Southern Italy. Instead they endured and built their culture by sealing out the influence of strangers.

The sealing medium was not military or even physical. It was at once an antisocial mentality and a supremely social psychology, for it formed the very stuff of contadino society. It constituted the foundation and hidden steel beams of a society that historically had been denied the luxury of more accessible (and vulnerable) foundations or superstructure. This is a reason for the contadino's famous pride. L'ordine della famiglia was a system of social attitudes, values, and customs that had proven to be impenetrable to the *sfruttamento* (exploitation) of any stranieri, no matter how powerful their weapons or clever their devices. But like all defenses, this lifestyle had exacted costs in the old land. These were the vexing social and economic problems that Italians lump together under the terms *Problema del Mezzogiorno or questione merldionale,* meaning "the Southern problem." The problem became catastrophic after the founding of the Italian nation in 1860–1870. And as we shall see in the next chapter, millions of contadini were forced by the specter of starvation to immigrate to other lands.

Because it had worked for so long in the old land in providing them with stability, order, and security, the ordine della famiglia was held to tenaciously by the immigrants in the new country. Thus the immigrants were able to achieve their twofold goals. One, they found bread and work no matter how dismal and exploitive, for it was better than the starvation they fled. Two, they resisted the encroachments of la via nuova into their own lives. In their terms, their audacious adventure has to be judged a success. But the price in the United States was very high. It included isolation from the larger society.

The immigrants' children, the second generation, faced a challenge more difficult to overcome. They could not maintain the same degree of isolation. Indeed, they had to cope with American institutions, first schools, and then a variety of economic, military, and cultural environments. In so doing, what was a successful social strategy for their parents became a crisis of conflict for them. Circumstances split their personalities into conflicting halves. Despite parental attempts to shelter them from American culture, they attended the schools, learned the language, and confronted the culture.

It was a rending confrontation. The parents of the typical second-generation child ridiculed American institutions and sought to nurture in him la via vecchia. The father nurtured in his children (sons especially) a sense of mistrust and cynicism regarding the outside world. And the mother bound her children (not only daughters) to the home by making any aspirations to go beyond it seem somehow disloyal and shameful. Thus outward mobility was impeded.

The great intrinsic difference between American and Southern Italian ways was experienced as an agonized dichotomy by the second generation in their youth. They lived twisted between two worlds, and the strain was extreme. The school, the media, and the employer taught them, implicitly and sometimes perhaps inadvertently, that Italian ways were inferior, while the immigrant community of their parents constantly sought to reinforce them.

Immigrants used "American" as a word of reproach to their children. For example, take another incident from my childhood. Every Wednesday afternoon, I left P.S. 142 early and went to the local parish church for religious instruction under New York State's Released Time Program. Once I asked one of my religious teachers, an Italian-born nun, a politely phrased but skeptical question about the existence of hell. She flew into a rage, slapped my face, and called me a *piccolo Americano,* a "little American." Thus the process of acculturation for second-generation children was an agonizing affair in which they had not only to "adjust" to two worlds, but to compromise between their irreconcilable demands. This was achieved by a sane path of least resistance.

Most of the second generation accepted the old heritage of devotion to family and sought minimal involvement with the institutions of America. This meant going to school but remaining alienated from it. One then left school at a minimum age and got a job that was "secure" but made no troubling demands on one's personality or the family life in which it was imbedded.

Another part of the second generation's compromise was the rejection of Italian ways, which were not felt vital to the family code. They resisted learning higher Italian culture and becoming literate in the language, and were ill-equipped to teach them to the third generation.

Small numbers of the second generation carried the dual rebellion to one extreme or the other. Some became highly "Americanized," giving their time, energy, and loyalty to schools and companies and becoming estranged from the clan. The price they paid for siding with the American culture in the culture-family conflict was an amorphous but strong sense of guilt and a chronic identity crisis not quite compensated for by the places won in middle-class society. At the other extreme, some rejected American culture totally in favor of lifelong immersion in the old ways, many of which through time and circumstance virtually fossilized in their lifetimes, leaving them underdeveloped and forlorn.

The tortured compromise of the second-generation Italian American left him permanently in lower middle-class America. He remains in the minds of Americans a stereotype born of their half understanding of him and constantly reinforced by the media. Oliver Wendell Holmes said a page of history is worth a volume of logic. There are few serious studies of Italian Americans, particularly current ones. It is easy to see why this has left accounts of their past, their present, and their future expressed almost exclusively in the dubious logic of stereotypes.

In the popular image, the second-generation Italian American is seen as a "good employee," i.e., steady, reliable, but having little "initiative" or "dynamism." He is a good "family man," loyal to his wife, and a loving father vaguely yearning for his children to do better in their lifetimes, but not equipped to guide or push them up the social ladder.

Thus, Americans glimpse the compromise solution of this generation's conflict. But the image remains superficial, devoid of depth or nuances.

We come, thus, to the compound dilemma of third- and fourth-generation Italian Americans, who are now mostly young adults and children with parents who are well into their middle age or older. The difference between the problems of the second generation and those of the third is great, more a quantum jump than a continuity.

Perhaps a glimpse at my own life will serve as an illustration. I was raised simultaneously by my immigrant grandparents and by my parents, who were second generation, notwithstanding my father's boyhood in Italy. So I am at one time both second and third generation. I learned Italian and English from birth, but have lost the ability to speak Italian fluently. In this, my third-generation character has won out, although I remain of two generations, and thus perhaps have an advantage of double perspective.

My grandfather had a little garden in the back yard of the building in which we all lived in Brooklyn. In two senses, it was a distinctly Sicilian garden. First, it was the symbolic fulfillment of every contadino's dream to own his own land. Second, what was grown in the garden was a far cry from the typical American garden. In our garden were plum tomatoes, squash, white grapes on an overhead vine, a prolific peach tree, and a fig tree! As a child, I helped my grandfather tend the fig tree. Because of the inhospitable climate of New York, every autumn the tree had to be carefully wrapped in layers of newspaper. These in turn were covered with waterproof linoleum and tarpaulin. The tree was topped with an inverted, galvanized bucket for final protection. But the figs it produced were well worth the trouble. Picked and washed by my own hand, they were as delicious as anything I have eaten since. And perhaps the difference between second- and third-generation Italian Americans is that members of the younger group have not tasted those figs. What they inherit from their Italian background has become so distant as to be not only devalued but quite unintelligible to them. It has been abstracted, removing the possibility of their accepting it or rebelling against it in any satisfying way.

I was struck by this recently when one of my students came to my office to talk with me. Her problems are typical of those I have heard from Italian American college students. Her parents are second-generation Americans. Her father is a fireman and her mother a housewife. Both want her to "get an education" and "do better." Yet both constantly express fears that education will "harm her morals." She is told by her father to be proud of her Italian background, but her consciousness of being Italian is limited to the fact that her last name ends in a vowel. Although she loves her parents and believes they love her, she has no insight into their thoughts, feelings, or values. She is confused by the conflicting signals given to her by them: "Get an education, but don't change"; "go out into the larger world but don't become part of it"; "grow, but remain within the image of the 'house-plant' Sicilian girl." In short, maintain that difficult balance of conflicts which is the second generation's lifestyle.

When the third-generation person achieves maturity, he finds himself in a peculiar situation. A member of one of the largest minority groups in the country, he feels isolated, with no affiliation or affinity for other Italian Americans. This young person often wants and needs to go beyond the minimum security his parents sought in the world. In a word, he is more ambitious. But he has not been given family or cultural guidance upon which this ambition can be defined and pursued. Ironically, this descendant of immigrants despised by the old WASP establishment embodies one of the latter's cherished myths. He rationalizes his identity crisis by attempting to see himself as purely American, a blank slate upon which his individual experiences in American culture will inscribe what are his personality and his destiny.

But it is a myth that is untenable psychologically and sociologically. Although he usually is diligent and highly responsible, the other elements needed for a powerful personality are paralyzed by his pervasive identity crisis. His ability for sustained action with autonomy, initiative, self-confidence and assertiveness is undermined by his yearning for ego integrity. In addition, the third generation's view of itself as a group of atomistic individuals leaves it unorganized, isolated, diffident, and thus powerless in a society of power blocs.

The dilemma of the young Italian American is a lonely, quiet crisis, so it has escaped public attention. But it is a major ethnic group crisis. As it grows, it will be more readily recognized as such, and not merely as the personal problem of individuals. If they are to realize this sooner rather than later, these young people must learn whence they came and why they are as they are. A "page of history" will expose the logic of their problems and thus make them potentially solvable.

The page must begin with an understanding of why their immigrant grandfathers left their homes in the old land. This is not a tangential problem, as it may seem. In the Mezzogiorno, these same people and many generations before them cherished their humble, even destitute homes and would have defended them with their lives (and often did). To this day, the typical contadino in the Mezzogiorno lives and dies where he was born. My elderly great-aunts have lived in the same building all their lives. It is the building where my grandmother was born.

A second-generation Italian American in Buffalo told me of his father's first impression of the United States. As the immigrant stood on the deck of a miserable ship that had just entered New York's harbor, an official boat pulled alongside. An immigration officer shouted up to the would-be American, asking him in Italian how he liked his new country. Looking out at the great mass of skyscrapers, the contadino responded: *"Non so come si puo vivere in questo fuoco!"* ("I don't know how it is possible to live in this fire!"). It is time to look at the reasons why the immigrant Italians left the austere, beautiful land that had mingled into their blood over countless generations. And it is time to look at their experiences and those of their descendants in "the fire."

Chapter 2

The Twilight of Ethnicity among Americans of European Ancestry: The Case of Italians

Richard D. Alba
State University of New York at Albany

The course of ethnicity in advanced industrial societies continues to be debated without satisfactory resolution. Earlier social theorists, inspired by a vision of the erosion of traditional structures under the impact of a tide of modernization, tended to see ethnicity as receding. More recently, sociologists and others have proclaimed the resilience of ethnicity; for some, this is because ethnicity is an affiliation apart, primordial and only superficially modified by currents of modernization, while for others, it is due to ethnicity's moorings in durable structures of inequality.

Proponents of the view that ethnicity is resilient are the dominant voice in contemporary discussions, but their dominance is by no means assured, since the conceptual groundwork for interpreting ethnicity remains unsettled. There is in fact no consensus on the proper vantage point from which to view ethnicity, "assimilation" having been dethroned as the crowning concept of the field over the last two decades (Blauner, 1972; Greeley, 1977).

This paper examines some of the interpretative difficulties surrounding ethnicity through the experiences of one group, Italian Americans. In particular, Italians are taken to constitute a strategic test case for some reigning assumptions in the study of ethnicity of European-ancestry groups in the United States. I will argue that the Italian experience demonstrates the importance of boundary-shifting processes, as opposed to assimilation at the individual level only, and that these shifts require for their explanation the invocation of historical contingencies, rooted in structural changes external to the group.

Assimilation and Ethnic Boundaries

For a long time, assimilation appeared as one of the most successful and important concepts for the study of ethnicity; this status is reflected in its classic treatment at the hands of Milton Gordon (1964). But much recent writing on ethnicity rejects or avoids assimilation as a focus of major concern. At least part of the reason appears to lie in an implicit model of assimilation, which is ahistorical, individualistic and incrementalist—which, in other words, does not connect assimilatory processes to macrostructural dynamics, but instead conceives of them as individual decisions played out against a static background. Such a conception naturally places the emphasis on social psychological constructs, including the acceptability of a group's members to the majority or core and, perhaps more importantly, their motivation to merge with the majority. At the same time, it is implicitly one-directional: assimilating individuals are affiliating with a new group, thereby dropping the cultural and other garb of their original one.

This individualistic conception makes it easier to understand why assimilation has slipped out of the inner circle of concern. Since it assumes that assimilation hinges on the willingness of individuals to surrender to the majority, then the importance of assimilation would appear to decrease as this willingness does. This is precisely what seemed to happen during the 1960s, in what appeared to many as a revival of ethnicity among American groups, both the racial minorities and, somewhat surprisingly, those of European ancestry. The revival meant, to use a characterization that, with minor variations, rings throughout the literature on ethnicity in America, that the ethnics were refusing to assimilate (e.g., Novak, 1972).

One difficulty with this diminishing of the importance of assimilation as a concept is that statistical indicators, such as intermarriage rates (Alba and Chamlin, 1983), suggest the cresting of assimilatory processes in recent decades. The apparent contradiction with the presumed ethnic revival indicates the limitations inherent in the individualistic conception of assimilation and the need to reconceptualize it in a way that allows it to be linked to structural processes of group formation and dissolution. One way to achieve this is to explicitly include the notion of group boundaries within the focus of assimilation. Group boundaries in this context refer to the recognition of ethnic distinctions in interaction, and thus are premised upon "criteria for determining membership and ways of signaling membership and exclusion" (Barth, 1969: 15). Ethnic distinctions are socially maintained by such boundary markers as language, speech mannerisms, food, culture more broadly, and physical appearance, all of which can serve to identify group members to each other and to outsiders.

Reexamining the concept of assimilation with the notion of group boundaries in mind forces the recognition of two ideal types of assimilation. One is the type envisioned by the individualistic conception described above: namely, an individual moves across an ethnic boundary, transferring allegiance to another group, but without any change to the boundary itself. Assimilation of this kind can be viewed as a sort of population trade between different ethnic blocs (e.g., Newman, 1973; Greeley, 1971). Research advancing such an interpretation has emphasized such consequences of intermarriage as the conversion of one spouse to the religion of the other (Newman, 1973: 162–4). The consequences of this kind of assimilation for ethnic change are problematic; it can be plausibly argued that it does not weaken ethnicity.

The second kind is a group form: it is assimilation accomplished through a change in ethnic boundaries, either through a weakening to reduce their salience or through a shift that removes a previously recognized distinction. By definition, such boundary changes mean changes to ethnicity as well. That they may occur is made plausible by the much-noted observation that the coincidence of ethnic and other boundaries, such as those of occupation and residence, tends to enhance ethnic solidarity (Glazer and Moynihan, 1970; Hechter, 1978; Yancey et al., 1976); consequently, a dilution through mobility of ethnic considerations in particular occupational strata or neighborhoods might be expected to weaken ethnic boundaries.

Empirically, of course, there is not necessarily a sharp distinction between the two types. Nonetheless, a separate recognition for the second type is valuable because it forces attention to the structural factors that may enhance or detract from ethnic solidarity, such as those stemming from the cultural division of labor (Hechter, 1978), group size (Blau, 1977), and the institutional completeness of ethnic communities (Breton, 1964).

The type of assimilation at the group level also underlines the cardinal importance of studying interethnic relations, since they provide a means of detecting ethnic boundaries and the changes that occur to them. The same does not hold true for the "content" of boundaries, i.e., the cultural and other signs of group membership, which may change without change to the boundaries themselves (Barth, 1969); for this reason, the study of culture by itself is not decisive for resolving questions of ethnicity. The occurrence, even the frequent occurrence, of interethnic relations also need not contradict the existence of an ethnic boundary, but the maintenance of such a boundary requires that interethnic contacts be asymmetric in some fundamental way, as would be true of relations between members of groups of unequal status (Barth, 1969). Interactions structured by ethnicity help to maintain ethnic distinctions. This is generally not the case for symmetric, nonsegmental relations, such as those of friendship and marriage. A change in the pattern of such relations is a signal of a change in ethnic boundaries.[1]

A Case in Point: The Italian Americans

Italian Americans provide an intriguing example of the significance of boundary shift processes as well as a litmus test for the most frequently advanced interpretations of ethnicity. Thus, those who argue for the persistence or revival of ethnicity generally point to white ethnic groups such as the Italians to support their arguments. In this view, Italians remain entrenched in ethnicity partly because of their recency of arrival and partly because their core values—in particular, the values embodied in the family—have enabled them to maintain solitary ethnic communities, manifest for example in vital urban neighborhoods.

These contemporary arguments find an echo in older ones. Few argued on behalf of the assimilability of the Italians at the time of their arrival, for they entered as one of the most despised of European immigrant groups (Higham, 1970). The bulk of the Italian immigration before the close of mass immigration in the 1920s came from the rural villages of the south, or *Mezzogiorno*, although because of the imprecision of both American and Italian statistics, it is not possible to estimate precisely the proportion from southern provinces (Sori, 1979).[2] The available statistics, however, do clearly support the well-known overall picture of an immigration swollen with a dislocated peasantry. For example, tabulations published by the Immigration Commission of

1911 reveal that in the crucial period 1899–1910, when 2.22 million Italian immigrants arrived on American shores (44 percent of the total from 1820 to 1970), 32 percent of those with European work experience described themselves as farm laborers and an additional 43 percent as laborers (Kessner, 1977: 33–4). The general category of "laborer," or *bracciante* in Italian, included many who had only recently been forced out of agricultural work (Sori, 1979).

The experiences of southern Italians hardly constituted preparation for integration into an urban, industrial society. The *Mezzogiorno* presents a classic picture of an underdeveloped society where the penetration of capitalist markets of land and labor created severe dislocations, uprooting peasants from the land and transforming them into a rural proletariat. By the latter part of the nineteenth century, many rural dwellers were forced to work the land of others, frequently under sharecropping or other tenancy arrangements that gave them little return for their efforts. Patterns of landholding and land use, combined with unfavorable climate and topography, produced an agriculture of scarcity, characterized by chronic shortages of work and food (Covello, 1972; Schneider and Schneider, 1976; Sori, 1979). The nature of the work bore little relation either to farm or industrial work in the United States. The tools were primitive, so that, according to the immigrant writer, Constantine Panunzio, "When they come to America, the work which comes nearest to that which they did in Italy is not farming or even farm labor, but excavation work" (Panunzio, 1928: 78; quoted by Kessner, 1977: 39).

The cultural values engendered by the social and material contours of the *Mezzogiorno* also did not mesh well with the exigencies in the United States. In such a landscape of scarcity, a supreme value was placed on the family. It has been observed many times that the family, not the individual, was the basic social atom of *Mezzogiorno* society; in the well-known words of Robert Foerster,

> Life in the South exalts the family. It has been said of Sicily that the family sentiment is perhaps the only deeply rooted moral sentiment that prevails. (Foerster, 1924: 95)

This was not, however, the "amoral familism" of Banfield (1958), which portrays *Mezzogiorno* life as a Hobbesian war pitting each nuclear family against all others. Southern Italian social structure was constituted in good part from filaments of family-like relations extending beyond the nuclear family, such as extended kinship, fictive kinship created through the institution of godparentship *(compareggio)*, and friendship *(amicizia)* (Chapman, 1971; Schneider and Schneider, 1976).

An aspect of the southern Italian ethos with repercussions for Italians in America lay in the presumption that family interests should take precedence over individual ones. A well-known instance of this occurred in relation to marriage. Since the position of a family was affected by the marriages of its members, families attempted to exert considerable control over the choice of a spouse, to the point that many marriages were arranged. Family control was enhanced by the sexual provisions of the *Mezzogiorno*'s code of honor, which drastically restricted contact between eligible men and women (Chapman, 1971). A second instance lay in the economic value attached to children. In peasant families, children were generally expected to make an economic contribution as soon as they were able to work, beginning usually during adolescence. The early initiation to work brought an abrupt transition to adulthood. It also generally spelled the end of formal schooling. This was in any event in accordance with the family-centered culture, in which education was regarded with suspicion, as a potential danger to family solidarity (Covello, 1972: 257; Gambino, 1974).

This occupational and cultural background powerfully shaped the niche the immigrants were able to establish for themselves. The majority of Italian immigrants sought work in urban labor markets, in part because they frequently intended to repatriate after earning enough money to improve their position and this limited them to places where employment was readily available. But immigrants fresh from the peasantry discovered upon their arrival that only "peek and shuvil" work, as Panunzio described it (quoted by Kessner, 1977: 58), was open to them. In 1905 in New York City, i.e., at the height of immigration in the city with the largest concentration of Italians in the United States, nearly 60 percent of Italian household heads did unskilled or semiskilled manual labor, working on construction gangs or as rag pickers and longshoremen (Kessner, 1977: 52–9). The reasons were not limited to a shortage of skills that could be applied in the industrial sector. Culturally engendered expectations about the nature of work, carried from the *Mezzogiorno*, also constrained occupational possibilities. That many immigrant men took jobs in construction or on the docks was partly a result of a prefer-ence for outdoor work, an attempt to reproduce familiar work cycles and conditions. This preference tended to consign Italians to seasonal work outside the regular channels of blue-collar mobility, which were found in factories (Yans-McLaughlin, 1977: 35–44).

Culture also limited the work horizons of women. One of the *Mezzogiorno*'s strongest prohibitions was directed against contact between women and male strangers, and this powerful norm went far toward defining what was an acceptable work situation for women. Work in the home was strongly preferred. Some took in boarders (generally relatives or *paesani* in order not to compromise the family honor), and others homework such as laundering or the manufacture of artificial flowers. One instance where Italian women did work outside the home occurred in the New York City garment industry, where women could work among other women (Yans-McLaughlin, 1977: 50–4).

Immigrant adjustment was complicated by the intention to repatriate. The number who ultimately returned to the *Mezzogiorno* is uncertain, but clearly it was large; one estimate is that 1.5 million Italians returned from the United States in the years between 1900 and 1914 (Caroli, 1973: 41). The sojourner's orientation toward the homeland, felt undoubtedly also by many who stayed, delayed such important adaptations as the acquisition of citizenship and the learning of English.[3] Lieberson's study of ten cities, for example, shows that in 1930, at a point when new immigration had all but ceased, Italians had the highest percentage of foreign-born who did not speak English in nine of the cities (they ranked second highest in the other); and they had the first or second highest percentages of immigrants who were not citizens in eight (Lieberson, 1963: 206–18). Obviously, this retarded adaptation had a large impact on the group, disadvantaging it relative to other immigrant groups who arrived around the same time (particularly in relation to Jews, who did not wish to return to the European societies from which they fled [Kessner, 1977: 167]).

The prospects for Italians seemed bleak also on the basis of American reactions to them. The Italian group arrived in a period when racial ideologies were widespread in the United States; and its arrival served to stimulate their further development, as Italians became a focus for explicitly racist thinking and stereotypes. The Italians were perceived as prone to crime, both organized and that spurred by passion and vengeance, the latter symbolized for Americans by the stiletto (Higham, 1970: 66–7). The Italian distinctiveness was perceived in physical terms as well: the immigrants were "swarthy" and seemed to bear other signs of physical degradation, such as low foreheads. In the racially conscious climate, at a time when race theoreticians were attempting to draw biological distinctions among European peoples to the disfavor of those from the south and east, the question of color may have been unavoidable. It would go much too far to say that Italians were viewed as nonwhites, but their color position was problematic. This is evident in the common epithet for them, "guinea," which was derived from a term referring originally to slaves from the western coast of Africa (Mencken, 1963: 373; Craigie and Hulbert, 1940: 1192–3).

The Situation in the 1930s

The assimilability of the Italians continued to seem unlikely in the 1930s, after the close of the period of mass immigration. This is not to deny that significant cultural changes had taken place by then; these were especially evident in the transition to the second generation. Important aspects of the family-centered culture of the *Mezzogiorno* were so attuned to southern Italian situations that they could not be reestablished successfully in the United States. For example, strict control over unmarried daughters was only workable in southern Italian villages, where parents were in a position to evaluate the suitability of all potential suitors. Parental superiority broke down in American ghettos, since more acculturated children were better able to make appropriate matches for themselves. The extent of change in family norms is suggested by Ware's study of Greenwich Village in the early 1930s (Ware, 1935: 180–202). In a survey of its Italian residents, she found clear-cut differences between older and younger respondents, a division that no doubt corresponded well with generational status (i.e., foreign versus native born). Older Italians were less likely than younger ones to reject such *Mezzogiorno* family norms as "girls should not associate with men unless engaged" and parental arrangement of marriages.

But in other ways, the same survey indicates second-generation fidelity to the southern Italian cultural heritage. Only half the younger group rejected the proposition that "a child should sacrifice his personal ambition to the welfare of the family group"; and only 15 percent denied that 'children owe absolute obedience to parents' (Ware, 1935: 193).

One area in which the remaining power of the family ethos was undeniably manifest was that of education. The conflict between the school system and the family that had existed in the *Mezzogiorno* was renewed in America. Immigrant families perceived many points of friction in the contact between these culturally alien worlds. These occurred even in seemingly innocuous matters such as school recreation, which immigrant parents saw as creating moral and physical risk for teenagers, who in their eyes were already adults (Covello, 1972: 325–6). Undoubtedly, the most important conflict centered on the economic contribution expected of children, which was jeopardized by compulsory attendance laws, greatly resented by Italian parents.

As a result of the clash between school and family, Italian children had high rates of truancy and frequently left school as early as the law allowed (Covello, 1972). In fact, during the height of mass immigration, it is estimated that as many as 10 percent of the immigrant children in New York City managed to avoid school altogether (Kessner, 1977: 96). But even as late as 1930, only 11 percent of Italian Americans who entered New York City high schools graduated from them, at a time when over 40 percent of all the city's high school students stayed through to receive their diplomas (Covello, 1972: 285). The obvious consequence was low ultimate educational attainment for second-generation Italians and a channeling of them towards jobs where educational credentials were not important, mostly in the blue-collar ranks.

The ultimate assimilation of the Italians was also put in question by attitudes of the Italians themselves. Two studies of Italian American ghettos, in Boston and New Haven, offer relevant testimony. Whyte's (1955) classic study indicates a split among Italians in their attitudes towards assimilation. He portrays the division in terms of "college boys," oriented toward mobility into the larger society, and "corner boys," loyal to their peer groups and held on ghetto corners by that loyalty. Whyte did not provide direct evidence on the relative popularity of these two orientations, but Child's (1943) New Haven study did. Child depicted the attitudes of Italians as defined against a background of virulent prejudice directed at their group, which hedged in the possible choices with the risk of potential losses. Identification with the Italian group meant risking complete exclusion by other Americans and the loss of any prospects for mobility. On the other hand, identification with Americans, and hence a positive valuation of assimilation, risked a double rejection: by non-Italians as a result of prejudice and by other Italians on the grounds of disloyalty to the group. According to Child, the most common response to this double-bind situation was one he labeled "apathetic": a denial of the meaningfulness of nationality distinctions and of the existence of prejudice against Italians. Individuals displaying the apathetic response remained through inertia within the orbit of Italian American social and cultural life, for it required deliberate action to break this social gravity and move into non-Italian spheres. Because of the risks involved, few maintained such intentions.

The 1940s and 50s: The Watershed

By the end of the 1930s, an analysis based solely on the group's experiences and its cultural and occupational background would seem to have doomed Italian Americans to a perpetual position of inferiority and separateness in American society. Such an analysis would have been misleading because other developments were taking place in the larger society that affected the context within which Italian American preferences would be played out. These factors came to a head during and shortly after World War II.

Some had been in the background all along, but the war sharpened their effects. One such was the transformation of the occupational structure and the attendant structural mobility. Between 1930 and 1970, for example, the white-collar proportion of the national labor force expanded rapidly from 29.4 to 44.8 percent (all figures are from U.S. Bureau of the Census, 1975: 139); about half this change, moreover, was concentrated in the upper part of the white-collar spectrum, the category of professional and technical workers, whose share of the labor force increased in this period from 6.8 to 13.7 percent. Although the proportion in the combined blue-collar and service occupations hardly changed, within them a significant realignment was taking shape. In particular, unskilled laborers, a category which included many Italian Americans in the earlier part of the century, declined sharply from 11.0 to 4.4 percent. The structural mobility engendered by such shifts in the occupational distribution holds a special significance for disadvantaged ethnic groups because it does not have a "zero sum" character. Thus, the upward mobility of an individual or group can occur without the complementary downward mobility of another; and as a result, it is not likely to produce a heightened salience of group boundaries among more advantaged groups, intended to keep the disadvantaged in their place.

The effects wrought by structural mobility were most sharply felt in those places where Italian Americans were concentrated: the metropolitan areas of the north. This is made clearest by examining the kinds of jobs that were opening up and closing out in different places in the postwar interval, since it is the changes at the margins that chiefly dictate the occupational options for young people entering the labor force and thus shape intergenerational occupational mobility. Over the period 1940–60, metropolitan areas in general were the places of greatest job growth (Stanback and Knight, 1970). In the older metropolises of the Northeast and Midwest, growth was primarily concentrated in white-collar rather than blue-collar jobs (Berry and Kasarda, 1977: ch. 12).

A corollary of structural occupational shifts during the 1940s and 1950s was another kind of structural mobility: the rapid expansion of higher education and its transformation from a selective system to a mass one. In 1940, only 15 percent of the college-age group actually attended college, but by 1954 the rate of college attendance had climbed to 30 percent; by 1960, it was almost 38 percent (Trow, 1961). This expansion played an important role in reducing status differences because, in addition to propelling occupational mobility, higher education extends a sense of equality among its students through an experience that is viewed as a sharp alteration in status and is sanctified by the selectivity of colleges and universities.

World War II acted as a catalyst for both kinds of mobility. The war helped to drag the United States out of the Depression and open up an era of prosperity and economic growth, signaled by a steady growth in real income beginning in the early 1950s (Miller, 1971); and it specifically fueled the expansion of higher education through the G.I. Bill. But the impact of the war was much wider than the socioeconomic changes it helped to stimulate, for the war had a powerful effect on American perceptions of nationality and national origins.

The crux of the wartime situations during this century is that they have turned ethnic identity into a matter of national loyalty, thereby giving ethnicity a subversive appearance and ultimately hastening a de-emphasis on nationality differences. The diversity of the origins of Americans and the substantial proportion of those of recent origins, particularly from combatant nations, have made Americans sensitive to the potential frailty of national solidarity. During World War I, the presence of millions of recently arrived European immigrants provoked intense anxieties about the immediate loyalties of aliens and the potential for subversion from within, leading to overt xenophobia and demands for the "pressure-cooker assimilation" and "100 percent Americanization" of the immigrants (Higham, 1970). By the 1940s, the flood tide of immigration had receded; the groups with the potential for loyalty to enemy nations were increasingly comprised of the native-born, and the responses of Americans were accordingly different.

This is not to say that the war did not stimulate anxieties over national loyalty. The internment of Japanese Americans demonstrates indisputably that it did. In the case of European ethnics, clouds of suspicion gathered early during the war over Germans and Italians, but then largely gave way to a cultivated national unity that was also a response to the wartime strains. The melding of Americans of different nationalities was almost ritualistically promoted by festivals to celebrate the contributions of immigrant groups to America (Polenberg, 1980: 54). More significant, wartime reporting and films about the war made for domestic consumption that self-consciously highlighted the spirit of unity among American fighting men from different backgrounds, portraying the armed forces as a melting pot in miniature (Blum, 1976: 63).

The war no doubt seemed to drive home the perils of too strong an ethnic identification for many ethnics. One of Child's New Haven respondents sharply formulated a general problem:

> Then a lot of times in the show you see Mussolini on the screen and they all start to razz him. Then I feel, "How the hell do I stand?" (Child, 1943: 88)

A frequent response on the part of the ethnics was a push toward further assimilation. Ethnics had high rates of enlistment in the military, and there was massive adoption of American citizenship by the foreign-born—more than 1,750,000 became citizens in the period 1940–45 (Polenberg, 1980: 57). Movement toward acculturation is evident in the waning of the foreign language press that occurred during the war. The number of radio stations broadcasting in immigrant languages dropped by 40 percent between 1942 and 1948 (Polenberg, 1980: 55).

An ultimate impact of the war was to render the perceptions of the ethnics more fluid and thus open to the possibility of change. One realm in which this influence is visible is in novels about the war, published during it and afterwards. Norman Mailer's *The Naked and the Dead,* James Jones's *From Here to Eternity,* Harry Brown's *A Walk in the Sun,* and John Hersey's *A Bell for Adano,* which were all popular novels made into successful films, presented a very different version of American society from that which prevailed before the war. Like many wartime films, these novels depicted military groups that contained American ethnic diversity, or more precisely the part of European ancestry, in microcosm, and showed ethnics as the moral equals of those of "old stock" origins (Blum, 1976). The novels, which served to interpret the war experience for many Americans, signaled a shift in attitudes towards ethnics.

Thus, World War II stands as a watershed for European ethnics, partly because it lies at a fortuitous conjunction of forces—structural transformation of the labor force, demographic transition from the immigrant to the second generation among the ethnics of recent European origins, and a cultural relaxation of the attitudes towards ethnics—that served to fluidify the boundaries separating ethnics from old stock groups. It remains still to confirm that these massive forces actually had an effect on the life chances of ethnics. Relevant evidence is supplied by Lieberson's recent study (1980), which reveals a prodigious socioeconomic leap for the 1925–35 cohort of second-generation South–Central–Eastern European ethnics, which came to maturity during and shortly after the war (Lieberson, 1980: 200–6, 328–32).

The boundary fluidity associated with the large-scale mobility in the aftermath of the war was further advanced by the enormous residential movements of the 1950s and 1960s. In the single decade from 1950 to 1960, the population in the suburbs increased by nearly 50 percent, from 41 to 60 million (Polenberg, 1980: 128). For ethnics and others, the suburban exodus was often directly connected with occupational chances—and not merely the result of increasing affluence—since the bulk of newly created jobs were to be found in the suburban fringes, not central-city areas (Berry and Kasarda 1977: Ch. 12). But the exodus was full of portent for ethnic groups because it disrupted urban ethnic communities and brought many mobile families into an ethnically heterogeneous milieu, a shift with obvious ramifications for the next generation. The residential changes of Italians are exemplified by the group's distribution in the metropolitan region centered around New York City and Newark, which contained nearly a third of the Italian Americans the census counted in 1970. By then, the second generation had significantly dispersed to the suburbs. According to census figures, 47 percent were living in the area's smaller places, those with fewer than 100,000 residents; and 41 percent were living in places with fewer than 50,000. These figures are only slightly lower than those for whites generally (50 percent and 45 percent, respectively). However, first-generation Italians remained distinctly more concentrated in the region's larger cities. Only 35 percent were in places smaller than 100,000 in population, and 29 percent in places smaller than 50,000.[4]

Obviously, the changes of the postwar period did not mean a complete dissolution of ethnic communities and subcultures. Gans's (1962) study of Boston's West End in the late 1950s establishes that many, particularly in the urban working class, remained firmly in the grip of ethnic worlds. But a process had been initiated, one that spelled a gradual lowering of ethnic boundaries among European ancestry groups and an upward shift in the life chances of their younger members.

The Contemporary Situation of Italian Americans

This process of boundary shift has had a profound impact on Italian Americans, and recent evidence points to a convergence with other European ancestry groups, including those of older stock. As one demonstration, consider the educational trajectory across different cohorts of second- and later-generation Italians, compiled in Table 1 from the November 1979 Current Population Survey.[5] To provide a rigorous yardstick against which to measure change, comparable figures are also provided for third- and later-generation Americans of exclusively British ancestry (defined as those who report ancestry only from England, Scotland, and Wales). Such a comparison group avoids the confusion that might be introduced by including other recent ethnics in the reference group and also compares the Italians to an ethnic category that is indisputably part of the American core, thus underlining the sharpness of the changes. For similar reasons, the focus in the table is exclusively on rates of college attendance and graduation.

What stands out in the table is a pattern of convergence across cohorts. Although the pattern is complicated somewhat by an unsustained peak in college education among British Americans in the 1946–50 cohort (which may be part of a Vietnam era phenomenon revealed by a recent census report) and by some wandering of the numbers from a simple trajectory of linear change, its basic nature is clear: a gradual narrowing of Italian differences from British Americans and the achievement of parity in the youngest cohort (who were in their mid-twenties in 1979). This convergence holds for both men and women, and indeed what the table also reveals is the relatively greater disadvantage of Italian American women in the past, especially in the second generation. For this last group, the rise in college attendance (from 9.1 percent to 50.4 percent) across a twenty-year time span, from the 1930–35 cohort to that of 1951–56, is very strong. The convergence also holds for both generations, and underlining the historical nature of the convergence is the fact that the generations do not seem much different, although the third generation shows some tendency to take the lead in rising rates of college attendance.

Evidence of cultural convergence is provided by survey items that tap attitudes and values connected with the stereotypical family-centered ethos presumed to color Italian American life (e.g., Greeley and McCready, 1975).[6] One widely cited expression of this is greater loyalty to kin groups, purportedly evident for instance in a reluctance to move away from the family (Gambino, 1974; Vecoli, 1978). Another is conservatism on family-related matters, ranging from hostility toward changes in sexual mores and the position of women to a low frequency of divorce (Greeley, 1974; Femminella and Quadagno, 1976).

The thinness of any residual cultural patina among individuals of Italian heritage is evident from Table 2, which reports the analysis of items from the General Social Surveys for the years 1975 through 1980 (the table is a selection from a larger set discussed in Alba, 1985).[7] The comparison is again to those of British ancestry (more precisely: since the General Social Surveys ask for the religion in which a respondent was raised, the comparison group contains those with Protestant ancestry from the British Isles). The table presents the comparison without any controls and also with controls for: current region and size of place as well as those where the respondent was raised; education and occupation of respondent and parents; and sex and age.[8]

On items relating to traditional family roles, Italians are generally quite similar to WASPs. They do not significantly differ from WASPs in terms of acceptance of abortion, for example, although they appear slightly more conservative after controls are applied because of their greater concentration in areas where liberal attitudes prevail.[9] Italians do not differ from WASPs in their acceptance of women outside the home.[10] Similarity between the groups is also found, albeit with an important exception, in attitudes toward the raising of children. Italians have been depicted as emphasizing traditional values, rather than those of self-direction (Rosen, 1959; Schooler, 1976). But in terms of their rating of the desirability of various traits in children, they are not meaningfully different from British Protestants.[11] Worthy of mention for its echo of the

Mezzogiorno is one trait on the list, "that he [the child] obeys his parents well." Just a quarter of the Italian American respondents prize obedience as one of the most desirable traits in children, a figure not statistically different from that for WASPs (28 percent). The exception to this general similarity concerns whether young people should be taught "by their elders to do what is right" or "to think for themselves even though they may do something their elders disapprove of." About half of Italians agree with the position consistent with the family-centered ethos— namely, that young people should be taught by their elders—compared to 38 percent of WASPs. Nonetheless, the Italian percentage is not far from the one for all Americans, 45 percent of whom favor the traditional option.

Despite their conservative image, Italians are more liberal than WASPs in certain respects, apparently because of their location in the metropolitan northeast, where cosmopolitan outlooks are frequent. They are less likely to condemn adultery, premarital sex, and homosexuality as "always wrong." They are also less likely to feel that divorce laws should be tightened to make divorce more difficult to obtain. (The proportion who have ever been divorced or separated is also, incidentally, not statistically different from that found among British Americans.) But in all these cases, the differences disappear after statistical controls are introduced, and an inspection of the regressions indicates that the reduction is chiefly brought about by the controls for place.

Broadly speaking, then, there is little support for the image of a distinctive Italian conservatism on family matters. Where there does appear to be greater evidence for an Italian American ethos is in terms of loyalty to the family group, but at best its remaining strength seems no more than moderate. This loyalty can be examined through two items in Table 2.

One tests the idea that Italians remain rooted in one place because of their reluctance to move away from family. Indeed, an impressive 53 percent reside in the same place where they grew up; however, the percentage of WASPs who do so also is high, 40 percent. Moreover, the Italian percentage could be expected to be higher on the grounds that Italians have more frequently grown up in the cosmopolitan magnets that attract others from their hometowns (New York City is the prototype) and also have lower overall educational and occupational attainment, factors associated with less residential mobility. When controls are applied, the difference between the two groups is only modest, 7 percentage points.[12]

Finally, the Italian pattern of socializing with relatives, emphasized by Gans (1962) in his depiction of the "peer group society," still persists to some degree. Nearly half of Italians socialize with family members weekly or more frequently, compared to only a third of WASPs. This difference is not explained very much by the background variables, as the tendency to socialize within the family is not much affected by socioeconomic variables, and this is counterbalanced for WASPs by the fact that it is somewhat higher among those who live in smaller places. After controls, Italians are still 10 percent more likely to socialize on a weekly basis with relatives.

Thus, what remains of the family-centered ethos is a slightly greater tendency to remain in the same place, greatly diluted from ancestral peasant rootedness, and a moderately greater willingness to keep company with relatives. The evidence of cultural convergence seems substantial,[13] but there is still more imposing evidence of convergence and assimilation: in intermarriage rates. Intermarriage stands as the cardinal indicator of boundary shift for several reasons (cf. Merton, 1941). To begin with the obvious, because marriage is an enduring and intimate relation, intermarriage provides a stringent test of group perceptions, of the social distance between Italians and others. Moreover, an intermarriage is not simply an isolated crossing of ethnic boundaries but carries far wider ramifications, including most importantly those for the next generation, which will be raised in an ethnically heterogeneous milieu. Finally, the occurrence of intermarriage implies the occurrence of other relations that penetrate ethnic boundaries.

The intermarriage rates of Italians, calculated from the 1979 Current Population Survey, are presented in Table 3. In the case of marriage, it makes little sense to combine individuals of part Italian ancestry with those of wholly Italian parentage, because the social contexts in which the two types are raised are so different that their intermarriage rates are likely to be as well; and consequently, they are shown separately in the table. The marriage rates are also decomposed by generations and birth cohort, and presented separately for men and women.

The table indicates a rapid rise in the intermarriage rate, which has reached the point that, of Italians marrying recently, generally two-thirds to three-quarters, depending on the category of the group, have intermarried. Revealing of the changes is the trend by birth cohort for persons with unmixed Italian ancestry, especially in the second generation. Among those born before 1920, i.e., during the era of mass immigration, about 60 percent of this second generation chose spouses of wholly Italian percentage. But this strict endogamy falls off with each new cohort. Among men, a sharp drop occurs with the cohort born during the 1930s; for women, such a drop occurs with the cohort born in the next decade. This rapid change has, among men, closed the gap between the second and third generations. For both, only about 20 percent of men born since 1950 have chosen wives with all Italian parentage, while another 10 to 15 percent have chosen wives with part Italian ancestry. The gap between the generations is not quite closed among women; second-generation women have the highest rate of endogamy in the youngest cohort, although this may be a statistical aberration, since a small number of cases are involved. In any event, the great majority of Italian Americans in this cohort belong to the third or later generations, where high intermarriage rates prevail.

Individuals of wholly Italian ancestry provide a conservative estimate of intermarriage rates. Individuals of mixed background have higher intermarriage rates and, moreover, the overall Italian rates will increasingly resemble theirs, since the group is more and more composed of them (this will be made clear shortly). For example, if the two ancestry groups are combined among men, then nearly three-quarters of third-generation men born since 1950 have chosen wives with no Italian ancestry. The comparable third-generation figure among women is nearly identical to that for the men.

It might be argued that these high intermarriage rates do not establish by themselves a relaxing of boundaries between Italians and other groups because they do not show whom Italians marry when they marry outside. Thus, it remains possible that other boundaries, enclosing clusters of culturally and socially similar groups, constrain their choices. It is true that, like other European ancestry groups, Italians are very unlikely to marry Hispanics and nonwhites (Alba and Golden, 1984). But this important exception aside, two pieces of evidence damage the thesis of selective intermarriage. One is Alba and Kessler's (1979) analysis of marriage patterns among Catholics, demonstrating that very little selectivity is visible among those who marry across nationality lines. The second emerges from data that reveal fairly high rates of marriage across religious lines. For example, Alba (1985) shows from General Social Survey data that about half of Italian Catholics born since World War II have married Protestants. So, in other words, it appears that the elective affinities of intermarrying Italians are not narrowly channeled to a few groups, but range widely across the spectrum of European ancestries.

The rising rate of intermarriage is bringing about a profound transformation of the Italian ancestry group. The character of this transformation is quite evident when the proportion of individuals with mixed Italian ancestry is displayed by birth cohort, as is done in Table 4.[14] The figures reveal a striking relationship of mixed parentage to cohort, with a percentage change between the oldest and youngest cohorts of over 75 percent. These dramatic figures indicate that a tremendous swing in the nature of the Italian ancestry group is destined to take place by the end of this century, as members of older cohorts, for the most part of unmixed ancestry, die and are replaced by younger persons of mixed parentage. Thus, in the Current Population Survey, persons with only Italian ancestry make up two-thirds of the adult ancestry group, a comfortable majority. But counting individuals of all ages, including children, they were a scant majority: 52 percent. Taking into account the expected mortality in the older group, these figures suggest that individuals with one non-Italian parent will comprise a majority of the ancestry group by the end of the next decade.

It is doubtful that even the mild distinctiveness of Italians on matters of family solidarity can withstand such higher intermarriage rates. Intermarriage not only tests the extent of existing cultural differences among groups, but it ultimately alters the cultural boundary. Johnson's (1982) study of kinship contact among Italians in Syracuse, New York, illustrates the general process. She compared in-married and out-married Italians to each other and to Protestants of non-Italian background in terms of the frequency of their contact with parents, siblings, and other relatives. Although contact with the relatives on the Italian side appeared dominant among the intermarried Italians, in the sense that both spouses saw more of them than of the non-Italian relatives, the frequency of contact was diminished; the intermarried group stood intermediate between the in-married Italians, the majority of whom had daily contact with parents and with siblings, and the Protestants, the majority of whom had comparatively infrequent contact with their relatives. Johnson's research implies that high rates of intermarriage are associated with further erosion of what Herbert Gans labeled as the "peer group society" in the 1950s.

Conclusion

Italian Americans are on the verge of the twilight of their ethnicity. "Twilight" appears an accurate metaphor for a stage when ethnic differences will remain visible, but only faintly so. The metaphor acknowledges the claims of many (e.g., Glazer and Moynihan, 1970; Greeley, 1977) that indeed ethnicity has not speedily disappeared and, therefore, the optimism of the melting-pot portrayal of American society seems to have been ill-founded. At the same time, it also captures the reality that ethnicity, at least among whites, seems to be steadily receding.

The approach of this twilight may seem deceiving, for when Italians and some other white ethnic groups are observed in the aggregate, their ethnic features still appear prominent. But in the case of the Italians, this happens because earlier generations and older cohorts are quite different from old stock Americans on such factors as educational and occupational attainment. Hence, it is only when the group is analytically decomposed by generation or birth cohort that the leading edge of change can be discerned.

Properly analyzed, the evidence on behalf of the looming ethnic twilight among Italians appears overwhelming. Despite the widely accepted image of an intense, family-centered Italian American culture, the group's cultural distinctiveness has paled to a feeble version of its former self. Paralleling this change, the social boundary between Italians and other Americans has become easily permeable; intermarriage, an irrevocable indicator of boundary shifts, takes place quite freely between Italians and those of other European ancestries. Acculturation and social assimilation have been fed by a surge in the educational attainment of Italians, which has brought cohorts born since World War II to the brink of parity with British Americans, the quintessential American group. Moreover, this profound transformation of the Italian group has taken place at a time when the fourth generation, the first generation without direct contact with the immigrant experience, is small (Steinberg, 1982; Alba, 1985). This generation will grow substantially in size during the rest of this century and simultaneously, the first and second generations, which presently constitute the majority of the group, will shrink.

In a number of respects, events among the Italians seem to parallel those among other groups descended from European immigrants, although because of differences in their times of arrivals, the specific situations that greeted them, and their occupational and cultural heritages, no two groups are following exactly the same pathways to the twilight stage. Yet among virtually all white ethnic groups, one can observe a progressive, if gradual, dampening of cultural distinctiveness. Core values have been overwhelmed by a common American culture so that even though cultural uniformity has not been the end result, the remaining differences among groups are so mild as to constitute neither a basis for group solidarity nor a barrier to intergroup contact. Additionally, among almost all groups, one can see a spreading pattern of intermarriage, testimony to the minor nature of remaining group differences and guarantee of additional assimilation (e.g., Alba, 1976). The strength of this pattern is confirmed by events among Jewish Americans, who provide the acid test of pervasive intermarriage. Historically, the rate of Jewish-Gentile intermarriage has been quite low, but recent studies have confirmed a sharp rise in this rate, starting in the 1960s (Cohen, 1983).

Such pervasive intermarriage suggests the emergence of a new ethnic group, one defined by ancestry from anywhere on the European continent. This need not mean that ethnic differences within this group will disappear altogether, but rather that their character is being fundamentally altered. This appears to be increasingly the case with ethnic identity. As Herbert Gans (1979) has observed, many mobile ethnics attempt to maintain some psychological connection with their origins, but in such a way that this attachment does not prevent them from mixing freely with others of diverse backgrounds. This contemporary form of ethnicity is private and voluntary, intermittent and undemanding; it focuses on symbols of ethnic cultures, rather than the cultures themselves, and tends to be confined to leisure time activities. There is a wide latitude available for this "symbolic ethnicity"—for Italians, it can range from a liking for pasta to a repudiation of criminal stereotypes—but the crucial point is that it is the individual who decides on the appropriate form. Such an ethnic identity is, in other words, a personal style, and not the manifestation of membership in an ethnic group.

The impending twilight of ethnicity among those of European ancestry is not matched by equal changes among most of America's non–European minorities. Black Americans stand as the extreme case. Though their socioeconomic progress in recent years has been debated, no informed observer claims that they are even close to parity with whites (Farley, 1985). It hardly needs saying, then, that racial boundaries remain salient. Residentially, blacks are still extremely segregated from whites, and the incidence of black-white intermarriage is very small (Heer, 1980).

The position of some other minorities *is* more ambiguous. Some older non-European groups that were voluntary immigrants to the United States evidence developments like those among the white ethnics, though these are not as far along. For example, Japanese Americans, despite the bitter legacy of World War II internment, have been quite successful in socioeconomic terms, with high rates of college attendance and occupational mobility. In tandem with this upward movement have come increases in intermarriage, frequently with whites (Montero, 1981; Woodrum, 1981). Although in the future it may become appropriate to speak of an ethnic twilight among Japanese Americans, the picture for non-European groups *is* complicated by the large-scale immigration from Asia, the Caribbean, and Latin America since immigration laws were revised in 1965. Immigrants from Colombia, Cuba, Haiti, Korea, Mexico, the Philippines, Taiwan, Hong Kong, Vietnam, and still other places are adding new parts to the American ethnic tapestry. Thus, although twilight may be descending on those ethnic groups whose forebears came from Europe, ethnicity itself *is* not subsiding as an issue for American society. In the future, the salient ethnic outlines may stem from non-European origins, *just* as those of European origins have been prominent *in* the recent past.

Notes

A preliminary version of this paper was presented at the 1983 meetings of the American Sociological Association. I am grateful to Robert K. Merton for his comments and to Prentice–Hall for permission to use materials from my book

1. This, of course, coincides with the importance that Gordon (1964) attributes to "structural assimilation," that is, large-scale primary relations across ethnic boundaries.

2. Although American immigration authorities began to keep statistics on "southern" and "northern" Italians in 1899, the racial intent of the distinction distorted the definition of a "southern" Italian to include anyone from the "peninsula proper" (as well as the islands of Sicily and Sardinia). According to the Bureau of Immigration's definition, "even Genoa is South Italian" (U.S. Senate, 1911: 81)! While

American statistics were weakened in this way, Italian statistics depend largely on applications for the *nulla osta,* or exit permit, which required a destination to be stated. But many applicants either did not subsequently leave or went somewhere other than where they stated (Caroli, 1973: 30; Sori, 1979).

Nonetheless, both sources, though imprecise, are broadly consistent.

3. Jerre Mangione's (1981) memoir of Italian American life in Rochester paints a very clear portrait of the sojourner's mentality among his Sicilian relatives.

4. These figures are for the New York, N.Y. Northeastern New Jersey Standard Consolidated Area, which in 1970 contained 1.4 million foreign-stock Italian Americans. The figures are my calculations from Tables 17, 23, and 81 of the *Characteristics of the Population,* Parts 32 and 34 (Bureau of the Census, 1973).

5. This survey included the same ethnic ancestry question that appeared in the long form of the 1980 census. This question, "What is . . .'s ancestry?" is superior to questions asked in previous Current Population Surveys and decennial censuses, because it does not constrain answers by a predefined list of responses and hence does not eliminate the many individuals with mixed ancestry. However, by the same token, it offers a too-inclusive definition of the Italian American group, since it forces the inclusion of individuals with any reported degree of Italian ancestry, regardless of its magnitude and of the extent of their identification with the Italian group (for a more detailed discussion, see Alba, 1985).

A virtue of this survey for the study of socioeconomic change is that its large sample size allows for refined breakdowns.

6. The focus here must be on this ethos, rather than the outward forms of culture since these tend to wither away within the first two generations. This is true, for example of the everyday use of Italian. According to the Current Population Survey, over four million claim Italian as a mother tongue, a language spoken in their childhood home, but only 1.4 million (about 12 percent of the group) claim to speak it in their current home (U.S. Bureau of the Census, 1982: 14). Since the total size of the ancestry group is around twelve million and that of the first generation, whose members are very likely to continue to speak their native tongue at home, is 800 thousand, it is clear that only a small part of the second and third generations continues to use the language on an

everyday basis. For further analysis of external culture, see Crispino (1980).

7. The General Social Surveys offer a narrower definition of the Italian American group than does the November 1979 Current Population Survey. The GSS ask individuals with mixed ethnic ancestry to identify, if they can, the group to which they feel closer. This is then reported as their ethnic category.

8. The adjusted difference between the groups reported in the table is the coefficient for the Italian dummy variable taken from a regression analysis. To achieve stable estimates of the effects of the control variables, the regression analysis includes all whites; the comparison to WASPs is effected by making them the omitted category.

9. The value of the anti-abortion scale is the number of times the respondent would deny a legal abortion in three situations where a presumably healthy pregnancy has resulted from voluntary sexual activity (Davis et al., 1980: 143–4). Such situations are the litmus test for abortion attitudes, as most Americans would allow an abortion for such circumstances as a life-endangering pregnancy, or one resulting from rape.

10. The anti-feminism scale is a summative scale composed of responses to four questions such as "Do you approve or disapprove of a married woman earning money in business or industry if she has a husband capable of supporting her?" For the wordings of the other three, see Davis et al. (1980: 142).

11. These items are derived from the well-known ones developed by Melvin Kohn and his colleagues. But there is no pretense here of replicating Kohn's work, since he has explicitly confined the validity of his scale to parents with children in a certain age range (Kohn, 1976). Such a limitation is not feasible here.

The scale I report is calculated by counting a +1 for each time a respondent rated as desirable a trait associated with self-direction and also each time he or she rated as undesirable a trait associated with conformity, and counting a −1 when the reverses occurred. Positive numbers on the scale thus indicate a valence toward self-direction.

12. Since simultaneous controls for both current and original location amount to controls for mobility itself, one has to be removed from the list of independent variables for this analysis; current location (both region and size of place) has been deleted.

13. This does not imply that Italians and WASPs are similar in all ways. For one, they differ in their political party allegiances, with Italians notably more tied to the Democratic Party. But the crucial point is that they are similar on many traits bearing on the family-centered ethos. (For more details and discussion, see Alba, 1985).

14. The 1980 census yields a somewhat lower estimate of the percent age of Italians with mixed ancestry, 43.5 (versus 48.0), and presumably will show lower rates of mixed ancestry in younger cohorts when tables of ancestry by age become available. Nevertheless, there appears to be good reason to give greater credence to the CPS rather than the decennial census in this case. The markedly lower estimates of mixed ancestry in general in the census suggest that ancestry responses were more cursory to the census's mail survey than to the face-to-face interviewing of the CPS (for further discussion of the differences between the two, see Bureau of the Census, 1983: 4–5).

References

ALBA, RICHARD. 1976. "Social assimilation among American Catholic national origin groups." *American Sociological Review* 41 (December): 1030–46.
———. 1981. "The twilight of ethnicity among American Catholics of European ancestry." *The Annals* 454 (March): 86–97.
———. 1985. *Italian Americans: Into the Twilight of Ethnicity.* Englewood Cliffs: Prentice–Hall.
ALBA, RICHARD, and MITCHELL CHAMLIN. 1983. "A preliminary examination of ethnic identification among whites." *American Sociological Review* 48 (April): 240–7.
ALBA, RICHARD, and REID GOLDEN. 1984. "Patterns of ethnic marriage in the United States." Paper presented at the annual meetings of the American Sociological Association.
ALBA, RICHARD, and RONALD KESSLER. 1979. "Patterns of interethnic marriage among American Catholics." *Social Forces* 57 (June): 1124–40.
BANFIELD, ROBERT. 1958. *The Moral Basis of a Backward Society.* New York: The Free Press.
BARTH, FREDRIK. 1969. "Introduction," pp. 9–38 in Fredrik Barth (ed.), *Ethnic Groups and Boundaries.* Boston: Little, Brown.
BERRY, BRIAN, and JOHN KASARDA. 1977. *Contemporary Urban Ecology.* New York: Macmillan.
BLAU, PETER. 1977. *Inequality and Heterogeneity: A Primitive Theory of Social Structure.* New York: The Free Press.

BLAUNER, ROBERT. 1972. *Racial Oppression in America.* New York: Harper & Row.

BLUM, JOHN MORTON. 1976. V *Was for Victory: Politics and American Culture During World War II.* New York: Harcourt Brace Jovanovich.

BRETON, RAYMOND. 1964. "Institutional completeness of ethnic communities and the personal relations of immigrants." *American Journal of Sociology* 70 (July): 193–205.

BUREAU OF THE CENSUS. 1973. *1970 Census of the Population, Volume I, Characteristics of the Population.* Washington: U.S. Government Printing Office.

————. 1975. *Historical Statistics of the United States, Colonial Times to 1970.* Bicentennial edition, Part 1. Washington: U.S. Government Printing Office.

————. 1982. "Ancestry and language in the United States: November 1979." *Current Population Reports,* Special Studies, Series P—23, No. 116. Washington: U.S. Government Printing Office.

————. 1983. *1980 Census of the Population, Ancestry of the Population by State: 1980, Supplementary Report.* Washington: U.S. Government Printing Office.

CAROLI, BETTY BOYD. 1973. *Italian Repatriation from the United States 1900–1914.* Staten Island: Center for Migration Studies.

CHAPMAN, CHARLOTTE GOWER. 1971. *Milocca: A Sicilian Village.* Cambridge, Mass.: Schenkman.

CHILD, IRVIN. 1943. *Italian or American? Second Generation in Conflict.* New Haven: Yale University Press.

COHEN, STEVEN. 1983. *American Modernity and Jewish Identity.* New York and London: Tavistock.

COVELLO, LEONARD. 1972. *The Social Background of the Italo–American School Child.* Totowa: Rowman & Littlefield.

CRAIGIE, WILLIAM, and JAMES HULBERT. 1940. *A Dictionary of American English on Historical Principles,* Vol. II. Chicago: University of Chicago Press.

CRISPINO, JAMES. 1980. *The Assimilation of Ethnic Groups: The Italian Case.* Staten Island: Center for Migration Studies.

DAVIS, JAMES, TOM SMITH, and C. BRUCE STEPHENSON. 1980. *General Social Surveys, 1972–1980: Cumulative Codebook.* Chicago: NORC.

FARLEY, REYNOLDS. 1985. "Recent changes in the social and economic status of blacks: Three steps forward and two back?" *Ethnic and Racial Studies* (January).

FEMMINELLA, FRANK, and JILL QUADAGNO. 1976. "The Italian American family," in Charles Mindell and Robert Habenstein (eds.), *Ethnic Families in America: Patterns and Variations.* New York: Elsevier.

FOERSTER, ROBERT. 1924. *The Italian Emigration of Our Times.* Cambridge, Mass.: Harvard University Press.
GAMBINO, RICHARD. 1974. *Blood of My Blood.* Garden City, N.Y.: Doubleday.
GANS, HERBERT. 1962. *The Urban Villagers: Group and Class in the Life of Italian Americans.* New York: The Free Press.
———. 1979. "Symbolic ethnicity: The future of ethnic groups and cultures in America." *Ethnic and Racial Studies* 2 (January): 1–20.
GLAZER, NATHAN, and DANIEL MOYNIHAN. 1970. *Beyond the Melting Pot.* Rev. ed. Cambridge, Mass.: MIT Press.
GORDON, MILTON. 1964. *Assimilation in American Life.* New York: Oxford University Press.
GREELEY, ANDREW. 1971. *Why Can't They Be Like Us?* New York: Dutton.
———. 1974. *Ethnicity in the United States: A Preliminary Reconnaissance.* New York: Wiley.
———. 1977. *The American Catholic: A Social Portrait.* New York: Basic Books.
GREELEY, ANDREW, and WILLLIAM McCREADY. 1975. "The transmission of cultural heritages: The case of the Irish and the Italians," pp. 209–35 in Nathan Glazer and Daniel Moynihan (eds.), *Ethnicity: Theory and Experience.* Cambridge, Mass.: Harvard University Press.
HECHTER, MICHAEL. 1978. "Group formation and the cultural division of labor." *American Journal of Sociology* 84 (September): 293–318.
HEER, DAVID. 1980 "Intermarriage," in Stephan Thernstrom, Ann Orlov, and Oscar Handlin (eds.), *Harvard Encyclopedia of American Ethnic Groups.* Cambridge, Mass.: Harvard University Press.
HIGHAM, JOHN. 1970. *Strangers in the Land: Patterns of American Nativism 1860–1925.* New York: Atheneum.
JOHNSON, COLLEEN LEAHY. 1982. "Sibling solidarity: Its origin and functioning in Italian American families." *Journal of Marriage and the Family* (February): 155–67.
KESSNER, THOMAS. 1977. *The Golden Door: Italian and Jewish Immigrant Mobility in New York City, 1880–1915.* New York: Oxford University Press.
KOHN, MELVIN. 1976. "Social class and parental values: Another confirmation of the relationship." *American Sociological Review* 41 (June): 538–45.
LIEBERSON, STANLEY. 1963. *Ethnic Patterns in American Cities.* New York: The Free Press.
LIEBERSON, STANLEY. 1980. *A Piece of the Pie: Blacks and White Immigrants since 1880.* Berkeley: University of California Press.
MANGIONE, JERRE. 1981. *Mount Allegro: A Memoir of Italian American Life.* New York: Columbia University Press.

MENCKEN, H. L. 1963. *The American Language.* Abridged. New York: Knopf.

MERTON, ROBERT. 1941. "Intermarriage and the social structure: Fact and theory." *Psychiatry* 4 (August): 361–74.

MILLER, HERMAN P. 1971. *Rich Man, Poor Man.* New York: Thomas Y. Crowell.

MONTERO, DARREL. 1981. "The Japanese Americans: Changing patterns of assimilation over three generations." *American Sociological Review* 46 (December): 829–39.

NEWMAN, WILLIAM. 1973. *American Pluralism: A Study of Minority Groups and Social Theory.* New York: Harper & Row.

NOVAK, MICHAEL. 1972. *The Risk of the Unmeltable Ethnics.* New York: Macmillan.

PANUNZIO, CONSTANTINE. 1928. *The Soul of an Immigrant.* New York.

POLENBERG, RICHARD. 1980. *One Nation Divisible: Class, Race, and Ethnicity in the United States.* New York: Viking.

ROSEN, BERNARD. 1959. "Race, ethnicity, and the achievement syndrome." *American Sociological Review* 24 (February): 47–60.

SCHNEIDER, JANE, and PETER SCHNEIDER. 1976. *Culture and Political Economy in Western Sicily.* New York: Academic Press.

SCHOOLER, CARMI. 1976. "Serfdom's legacy: An ethnic continuum." *American Journal of Sociology* 81 (May): 1265–86.

SORI, ERCOLE. 1979. *L 'emigrazione italiana dall' Unita alla seconda guerra mondiale.* Bologna: Il Mulino.

STANBACK, THOMAS, and RICHARD KNIGHT. 1970. *The Metropolitan Economy.* New York: Columbia University Press.

STEINBERG, STEPHEN. 1982. *The Ethnic Myth: Race, Ethnicity, and Class in America.* Boston: Beacon Press.

TROW, MARTIN. 1961. "The second transformation of American secondary education." *International Journal of Comparative Sociology* 2: 144–66.

U.S. SENATE. 1911. *Reports of the Immigration Commission: Dictionary of Races or Peoples.* Washington: Government Printing Office.

VECOLI, RUDOLPH J. 1978. "The coming of age of the Italian Americans." *Ethnicity* 5 (June).

WARE, CAROLINE. 1935. *Greenwich Village, 1920–1930.* Boston: Houghton Mifflin.

WHYTE, WILLIAM FOOTE. 1955. *Street Corner Society,* 2nd ed. Chicago: University of Chicago Press.

WOODRUM, ERIC. 1981. "An assessment of Japanese American assimilation, pluralism, and subordination." *American Journal of Sociology* 87 (July): 157–69.

YANCEY, WILLIAM, EUGENE ERICKSEN, and RICHARD JULIANI. 1976. "Emergent ethnicity: A review and a reformulation." *American Sociological Review 41* (June): 391–403.
YANS–MCLAUGHLIN, VIRGINIA. 1977. *Family and Community: Italian Immigrants in Buffalo 1880–1930.* Urbana: University of Illinois.

Table 1. Rates of college education among Italian Americans, by sex, generation, and cohort and compared to those of third-generation British Americans[a]

	Second Generation		Third Generation		Third-Generation British Americans	
Cohort	% attended college	% finished 4 or more yrs.	% attended college	% finished 4 or more yrs.	% attended college	% attended 4 or more yrs.
Men						
1951–	56.6	28.9	54.4	25.8	53.2	27.1
1946–50	42.1	32.8	55.9	29.1	66.4	38.1
1941–45	45.4	26.2	51.8	35.7	55.7	38.5
1936–40	42.9	30.3	42.3	22.1	51.5	35.1
1931–35	33.0	18.7	39.0	18.4	50.3	31.3
1926–30	24.9	11.7	31.5	15.2	42.1	27.8
1921–25	22.1	16.0	20.1	7.7	43.9	23.8
1916–20	17.5	3.9	13.4	11.3	35.7	20.1
–15	16.3	7.9	15.2	6.2	30.1	17.4
Women						
1951–	50.4	20.2	46.6	26.3	46.6	24.0
1946–50	35.0	17.1	40.5	20.0	53.5	31.8
1941–45	27.3	13.1	32.1	13.5	44.7	22.5
1936–40	28.3	13.2	18.2	3.9	39.0	21.7
1931–35	9.1	4.4	17.9	10.5	33.2	16.1
1926–30	14.6	5.7	27.6	9.2	41.8	23.0
1921–25	8.2	4.5	22.6	5.1	29.7	14.5
1916–20	7.0	4.2	30.1	20.2	37.6	17.8
–15	5.1	1.8	2.7	0.0	26.5	12.3

Source: My tabulations from November 1979 Current Population Survey
[a] Table restricted to individuals older than 22. The "third generation" contains all native-born group members with native-born parents and thus encompasses the third and later generations.

Table 2. Cultural comparison between WASPs and Italian Americans

	WASP mean	Italian mean	Difference	Diff. After Adjustment
Anti-abortion scale	1.33	1.42	.09	20%
Anti-feminism scale	1.26	1.25	−01	08
Premarital sex is "always wrong"	34.5%	22.6%	−11.9*	1.3
Adultery is "always wrong"	69.8%	58.6%	−11.2*	−3.5
Homosexual sex is "always wrong"	69.3%	60.4%	−8.9*	−4.7
Ever divorced or legally separated	25.7%	21.9%	−3.8	−4.4
Divorce should be "more difficult"	50.1%	41.3%	−8.8*	−3.1
Scale of value put on self-direction for children	1.24	1.17	−.07	−.12
Young people "should be taught by their elders"	37.9%	53.0%	15.1*	19.8*
Reside in same place where grew up	39.5%	53.2%	13.6*	6.6*
Socialize with relatives weekly	33.8%	46.8%	13.0*	10.4*

*Indicates statistical significance.

Source: Tabulations from the NORC General Social Surveys, 1975–80.

Variables for which adjustment has been made include: current region and size of place and those where respondent grew up, education and occupation of respondent and parents, age and sex.

Table 3. Marriage patterns of Italian Americans, by sex, generation, and cohort

| | Men | | | |
| | Second generation Spouse's ancestry is ... | | Third generation Spouse's ancestry is ... | |
Cohort Ancestry	Wholly Ital. %	Wholly Non-Ital. %	Wholly Ital. %	Wholly Non-Ital. %
1950–				
Wholly Ital.	20.3	64.1	20.0	70.5
Wholly Non-Ital.	—	—	5.4	78.9
1940–49				
Wholly Ital.	30.0	60.0	24.4	69.2
Wholly Non-Ital.	0.0	82.7	10.7	76.8
1930–39				
Wholly Ital.	29.8	62.9	24.1	63.3
Wholly Non-Ital.	17.8	81.5	6.9	80.1
1920–29				
Wholly Ital.	44.6	51.7	38.8	60.9
Wholly Non-Ital.	15.7	83.7	4.8	90.0
Before 1920				
Wholly Ital.	56.7	41.7	42.7	57.3
Wholly Non-Ital.	—	—	15.8	78.6

Table 3. Continued

	Women			
	Second generation Spouse's ancestry is …		Third generation Spouse's ancestry is …	
Cohort Ancestry	Wholly Ital. %	Wholly Non-Ital. %	Wholly Ital. %	Wholly Non-Ital. %
1950–				
Wholly Ital.	38.7	53.2	23.8	72.7
Wholly Non-Ital.	—	—	10.3	79.1
1940–49				
Wholly Ital.	25.7	71.3	31.7	58.4
Wholly Non-Ital.	20.7	72.1	11.7	77.8
1930–39				
Wholly Ital.	38.8	61.0	49.4	46.6
Wholly Non-Ital.	17.0	83.0	17.2	75.6
1920–29				
Wholly Ital.	54.9	44.6	34.6	61.7
Wholly Non-Ital.	10.3	89.7	18.6	69.3
Before 1920				
Wholly Ital.	59.5	37.6	40.8	60.2
Wholly Non-Ital.	—	—	11.5	78.5

Source: My tabulations (weighted) from November 1979 Current Population Survey.
—Percent not reported because it is based on 10 or fewer cases (unweighted).

Richard D. Alba

Table 4. Type of Italian ancestry by age (1979)

	% with mixed Italian Ancestry
All ages	48.0
65 and over	5.9
55 to 64	11.4
45 to 54	18.5
35 to 44	36.1
25 to 34	48.1
18 to 24	60.5
14 to 17	71.3
5 to 13	77.8
Under 5	81.5

Source: November 1979 Current Population Survey, report in U.S. Bureau of the Census (1982): Table 2.

Chapter 3

Are Italian Americans Just White Folks?

Rudolph J. Vecoli
University of Minnesota

Although Chicago is not my home town, the Windy City holds a special significance for me, personally and as a scholar. Chicago was my first big city experience, coming into town on liberty from the Great Lakes Naval Training Station in 1945; but that is another story. Today I want to tell you about my experience when I was researching my dissertation on Italians in Chicago during the fifties.[1]

Over a period of several years, I witnessed the death of Chicago's Little Italies. The old neighborhoods were under siege from urban "renewal," highway construction, and changing population patterns, but when I first arrived they were still here. Halsted Street was still the heart of the West Side colony, lined with *fruttistendi, grosserie, and stori.*[2] Hull House was still a functioning institution, not a museum. As my research stretched over several years, I witnessed the destruction of that neighborhood. Images remain etched in my memory. A vast desolate area (like the bombed-out cities of wartime Europe) where houses and stores had been bulldozed; finally the only building standing was the Italian Church of the Guardian Angel *(la Chiesa dell'Angelo Custode).* One day, as I watched from a distance, a procession emerged from the church and paraded through the empty streets with the statue of the patron saint—a Felliniesque vision.

On the Near North Side was Little Sicily (also called Little Hell) where Father Luigi Giambastiani had presided over the parish of St. Philip Benizi for fifty years. Though the church still stood, the houses of his parishioners had been leveled to make way for public housing. Padre Luigi was a bitter man, his parishioners scattered and his church soon to be destroyed; many Italians I spoke with during those years were bitter. Their lives were literally reduced to heaps of rubble.

I tell you this not to indulge in nostalgia about life in the old neighborhoods, but to remind us that the death of the Little Italies in the 1950s (a subject which deserves a book and a film), not only in Chicago, but across the country, marked the end of the first chapter of the history of the Italians in America. At the time I thought it was the end of the story. The old immigrants were dying; their children were headed for the suburbs hell-bent upon becoming 100 percent American. My own research was driven by the fear that they (including part of me) would disappear without a trace. Oblivion is the worst thing that can happen to a people.

In the fifties, there was no American Italian Historical Association (AIHA), there was no field of Italian American studies. The last substantial work, Robert Foerster's *The Italian Emigration of Our Times,* had been published in 1919. The assumption dominating the public culture, including history and the social sciences, was that the European nationalities (the term "ethnicity" did not come into currency until the 1960s) were rapidly disappearing from the American scene. Israel Zangwill's melting pot, it seemed, had worked its magic.

Of course, today we know that was not the case. For varied and complex reasons, the sixties brought an explosion of repressed identities that erupted through the surface of Anglo-American hegemony and revealed the true pluralism of this society. And lo and behold, the Italian Americans had not disappeared after all; here they were tarantellaing in public, staging protest rallies, and writing books about themselves. By and large these were not the *old paesani,* but second- and third-generation Italian Americans. As part of this phenomenon, the founding of the AIHA in 1966 signified the emergence of a mature scholarship on the Italian American experience, one that was to yield a bountiful harvest of monographs, dissertations, articles, novels, poems, films, and plays. The decades of the sixties and seventies also witnessed a revitalization of Italian American communal life. While the old *societa di mutuo soccorso* became fewer and fewer, new cultural, political, and social organizations sprang up. The voices of Italian Americans could be heard in the public dialogue about the character and future of this "new pluralism," as it was called. Italian America was alive and well, or so it seemed.

Then came the eighties and nineties and suddenly we are told it was all a mirage, that we don't really exist, that we are in the twilight of Italian American ethnicity. What happened? In the parlance of football, we were blindsided; we were hit high and low. From the late seventies neo-nationalists began decrying what they termed the excesses of ethnic "tribalism" which threatened the ungluing, the fragmenting of America, what Arthur M. Schlesinger, Jr., has described in his shrill polemic as *The Disuniting of America* (1991). At the same time, they sneered that the "ethnic revival" was nothing more than a pipedream of would-be ethnic demagogues, and called for a return to the Melting Pot. If the neo-nationalists/assimilationists perceived European American ethnicity in general (and Italian American ethnicity in particular) as annoying distractions that did not need to be tolerated as did ethnicity among "people of color," neo-Marxists dismissed "white ethnicity" as a smokescreen for racism. While the ethnic nationalism of people of color could be accommodated under their model of indigenous resistance to colonial oppressors, Americans of European ancestry who affirmed their ethnicities were simply reactionary fascists.

Much of the intellectual underpinnings for this attack on the "new ethnicity" has come from sociologist Herbert Gans and his followers. Gans's theory of symbolic ethnicity is based on the assumption of straight-line, inevitable assimilation; Gans argued that what had been perceived by some as an "ethnic revival" was really a form of acculturation and assimilations.[3] What was new was that the "symbolic ethnicity" of European Americans consisted of subjective identity which was not based in lived culture or social networks. Gans recognized that Italian Americans still ate spaghetti, attended religious festivals, and might on occasion dance the tarantella, but he dismissed these as leisure-time activities, simply hobbies, like collecting stamps or butterflies. In serious matters, Italian Americans were becoming indistinguishable from their suburban, middle-class European American neighbors.

In recent years, Richard Alba and Mary Waters have buttressed the theory of symbolic ethnicity with their sociological studies. They have particularly sought to resolve the contradiction that they perceive between high levels of ethnic identity with alleged low levels of actual ethnic involvement. It is Alba who condemned Italian Americans to the "twilight of ethnicity." [4] Seconding Gans, he concluded that particularly for the third and fourth generations, ethnicity had become muted, voluntary, and private. What some thought was an ethnic revival was really an expression of receding ethnicity. But Alba has further argued that a new ethnic group is emerging from the Melting Pot, the "European Americans," in part a result of extensive intermarriage, but also as a response to African–American militancy. In her book, *Ethnic Options,* Waters distinguished between the ethnicity of people of color that is due to oppression and thus real and involuntary, and that of whites that is symbolic and voluntary, and, she adds, "contentless."[5] White ethnics, she declared, oppose removing barriers for ethnics of color because they do not understand the difference between the two forms of ethnicity. Waters gratuitously vilified European ethnic groups as sexist, racist, clannish, and narrow-minded. Obviously, I disagree vigorously with Gans et al. for reasons that I hope to make clear.

First, however, a word about multiculturalism.[6] In the seventies, we thought that persons who shared a common identity (a sense of peoplehood) constituted an ethnic group and that pluralism described a society in which there were a number of such ethnic groups. Now we are told the appropriate term is multiculturalism—a word I first encountered when the Canadian government adopted a policy of inclusive multiculturalism in 1971. However, in the American version of multiculturalism, certain "preferred minorities" are to be nurtured by the benign rays (and funds) of multiculturalism while "others" are condemned to the eternal night of non-groupness. Race, Gender, and Class became the trinity worshipped by the cult of multiculturalism; however, social class is assigned a minor role, since biological differences stemming from skin pigmentation and sexual organs are regarded as the prime sources of group identity.

Drawing eclectically upon postmodern, semiotic, and feminist theories, American multiculturalism in its more extreme forms has as its agenda the radical transformation of the polity and curriculum of American universities—and other institutions as well. Given their project of deconstructing patriarchy, racism, and capitalism, which are identified with European–American male domination, multiculturalists privilege (to use one of their favorite terms) the literatures, histories, and cultures of "people of color" and of the Third World. Meanwhile, the ethnicities of European Americans are suspect as an ideological cover for racial and sexual exploitation.

If radical theories of postmodernism and feminism have provided the intellectual firepower behind the multicultural movement, strangely enough the political clout has come from the federal government. While the Civil Rights Act of 1964 mandated equal opportunity "regardless of race, color, religion, sex, or *national origin,*" its subsequent implementation specified particular racial/ethnic populations, as well as women, as the beneficiaries of affirmative action programs. In 1977, the Equal Employment Opportunity Commission's Directive No. Fifteen: *Race and Ethnic Standards for Federal Statistics and Administrative Reporting* established the following categories for compliance purposes: White, not of Hispanic Origin; Black, not of Hispanic Origin; Hispanic, regardless of race; American Indian or Alaskan Native; and Asian or Pacific Islander. These categories, of course, have no basis in biology or ethnology, mixing egregiously racial, cultural, and geographic criteria, and lumping together populations that have wildly divergent histories and cultures—and, be it noted, totally ignoring class as a determinant of disadvantage. Yet this bureaucratic formula has legitimated the five-part division of the American people; university administrators, educators, foundation officers, etc. have embraced these categories as designating distinctive peoples. Private sector as well as governmental programs in ethnic studies, institutes on pluralism, diversity curricula, fellowships, multicultural workshops, and conferences legally restrict their scope to those "protected classes" to the exclusion of persons of European, North African, and Middle Eastern origins who are classified as "white."

How often have you been confronted with forms in which you are asked to indicate your "race and ethnicity" by checking a box with "White" (or the totally dehumanizing "Other") as the only alternative to American Indian or Alaskan Native, Asian or Pacific Islander, Black or Hispanic? Does this upset you? It upsets me, not only because the "white" option automatically excludes me from the multicultural umbrella with all its perks, but even more by the impudence of those who would deny me my history, my culture, my identity and relegate me to the realm of non-being.

The Office of Management and Budget held hearings this past summer on the revision of the race and ethnic standards for federal statistics. The hearings make fascinating reading. Forceful objections were voiced by several witnesses to the "white" category on the grounds that the term did not describe either a race or an ethnicity. A number argued for a European American category, but others demanded specific recognition of their groups as Arab Americans, Hawaiians, or German Americans. I was disappointed that no one appeared to protest the submergence of Italian Americans into the white pool. [7]

Perhaps you can understand my personal chagrin in finding myself (and my people) consigned to the shadowlands of peoplehood just as in the 1950s, the public and academic cultures deny the validity of Italian American claims to a place in the country's ethnic spectrum. Perhaps I was witnessing the last chapter of Italian American history in the fifties, but I think not. I am persuaded that this is not the twilight of Italian American ethnicity for several reasons. First, my conception of ethnicity as a dynamic, evolving form of adaptation is the antithesis of the Gans et al. notion that it is a static quantity, a commodity, which once dissipated, is gone forever. In my conception ethnicity is protean, capable of taking a variety of forms, of being expressed in a range of behaviors, and of being revived. Does one need to speak the mother tongue, live in a particular neighborhood, worship in a specific church, or even eat spicy foods, to be ethnic? I think not; what is essential now as it always has been is a subjective sense of peoplehood based in common memories, and manifested in symbols that evoke those memories (a flag, a ritual, a song, a fig tree).[8]

Second, I believe in my own experience as a participant in and student of Italian American life more than I do in the charts and tables of sociologists.[9] That experience teaches me that while the context and content of Italian American identity have been drastically altered over the past half century, that identity persists in significant ways for many. For how many? The 1990 U.S. census reported that almost fifteen million persons claimed Italian ancestry (making them the fifth largest ancestry group). While the census report does not tell us what that response meant, the fact that they were willing to declare their Italian antecedents means something—as does the fact that only 5 percent of all respondents reported their ancestry as just "American," and less than 1 percent answered "white."[10]

Beyond statistics, I spy abundant evidence of vitality and creativity in Italian American life, which compared to its moribund status in the fifties, tempts me to speak of a *rinascimento.* What is this evidence? Certainly not a revitalization of the Little Italies, except as tourist attractions. But in this age of faxes and e-mail, group affiliation does not depend upon physical proximity. In recent years, old organizations such as the Order Sons of Italy in America (OSIA) and UNICO have taken a new lease on life, while new organizations, devoted to cultural and heritage activities, have proliferated.[11] A new generation of Italian American publications has seen the light of day: community newspapers like Chicago's excellent *Fra Noi,* and scholarly journals such as *VIA and Italian Americana.* Of particular importance, more than ever before, Italian Americans are articulating their experiences through fiction, poetry, films, theater, and exhibits. Meanwhile, in their search for roots, many journey to ancestral *paesi,* scour archives and cemeteries, and reestablish ties with long-lost cousins. If you know genealogists, you would not demean their passionate quest by dismissing it as simply a hobby. [12]

What distinguishes this interest in Italy today from the philofascism of the 1930s is that it is not inspired by politics. Rather it increasingly takes the form of a reaffirmation of specific regional or local origins. Associations based on such ties are burgeoning: *Figli di Calabria, Piemontesi nel Mondo, Trentini nel Mondo, Cuore Napoletano, Lucchesi nel Mondo,* etc. Noting this trend the late Robert Harney commented that this revival of *regionalisms and campanilismo* was the "undoing of the Risorgimento."[13] Indeed, it reflects the growing regionalism in Italy since the devolution of authority and funds to the regions in 1970. Of course, the regions and provinces promote contacts with their far-flung emigrants and descendants for reasons of tourism and commerce. But my experience suggests that genuine interest in distant *paesani* also animates these initiatives. For myself, I derive a greater satisfaction from my Lucchese–American identity based on specific cultural traditions than the more abstract idea of being Italian American. Since I abhor the idea of all melting pots, I applaud this revival of localized dialects and traditions.

If we need more evidence of the vitality of Italian America, I would cite this conference itself. To scan the varied program and to see all these bright minds engaged in exploring the myriad facets of the Italian American experience is itself convincing evidence. Certainly we are not gathered to mourn the obituary of Italian America. That we think the Italian American experience worthy of study signifies that we are involved intellectually and emotionally not with a dead past, but with a living present. Even as we examine our history, we are reflecting and affecting the contemporary realities of being Italian American today. Forty years ago in my wildest dreams, I could not have imagined that I would be addressing an audience of Italian American scholars on this topic in 1994. None of what I have just described to you would have been conceivable forty years ago.

By now you probably have guessed my answer to the question posed by the title of this paper. So, if Italian Americans are not just plain white folks, what are they? I have elsewhere presented my ideas about Italian American ethnicity and rather than recapitulate them here I refer you to those writings.[14] Suffice it to say, that to be an Italian American today obviously means something very different from what it meant fifty or seventy–five years ago. We have learned from our AIHA conferences that meaning varies according to geography, generation, gender, social class, and political disposition. We would be hard pressed to define what it is that we share as Italian Americans today, but of one thing I am certain, we are once again in the process of reinventing our ethnicity.

In the meantime, how do we position ourselves in this increasingly diverse and contentious American society? If we reject being lumped as white European Americans, what are our options? Could we pass as African Americans or Latinos? I don't think our black or Chicano brothers and sisters would have us. Which brings us to the subject of race and Italian Americans. In the years of massive immigration, the racial classification of Italians was in doubt. Many Anglo–Americans questioned that these "swarthy sons of sunny Italy" were really white. Employers and labor leaders referred to them as "black labor," while the color line was invoked to keep them out of certain neighborhoods, schools, and organizations. Nor was this peculiar to the South. I recently discovered the charter of the Washington League of Knights and Ladies of Minneapolis, established in 1902, which specifically excluded Negroes and Italians. I need not remind you of the animus of racial nativists towards southern and eastern Europeans—and Italians in particular. The current controversy swirling about *The Bell Curve* reminds me that in the 1920s, IQ scores were cited to prove the inferiority (and thus undesirability) of Italians.[15] Innocent of the racial code in this "free country," newly arrived immigrants often worked with and lived among African Americans. Such association was itself taken as confirmation of the Italians' ambiguous racial status. Once they became aware of the terrible price to be paid for being "black," they hastened to distance themselves from African Americans and to be accepted as white. The historical relationships of Italian Americans and African Americans are, of course, much more complex than that; they would require a big book, a book that needs to be written.[16]

Let me tell you where I stand. As an unreconstructed pluralist, I believe that true multiculturalism must be inclusive of the full range of ethnic groups that comprise the society, and that ethnicity is a cultural, not a biological, phenomenon. Races, as discreet populations sharing unique hereditary qualities (common gene pools), do not exist; in this conclusion, I am in the company of geneticists and anthropologists. Race, as a cultural construct, and racism, as an ideology, have played a powerful and pernicious role in the history of the past two hundred years. The source of peoplehood is not blood, but shared history and culture. On that basis, we, Italian Americans, have as much a claim to our peoplehood as any other segment of society.

Since ethnicity is not transmitted from generation to generation via germ plasma, it has to be learned from parents, teachers, clergy, community leaders, and the media. How good a job have we been doing of teaching our children about their Italian American heritage? Despite my earlier upbeat remarks, we have reason for concern about the future of Italian America. In part, this is because the mainstream institutions, the schools, films, press, television, either omit Italian Americans or portray them in an ugly, distorted fashion. An irony is that persons of Italian ancestry who fill important positions in such institutions, either because they are de-ethnicized or because of ethnic self-hatred, acquiesce in or even propagate such stereotypes. I applaud the work of the Commission on Social Justice of the OSIA, the National Italian American Foundation, and the Joint Civic Committee of Italian Americans in Chicago. But we need to do more, and we need more muscle to put an end to such group defamation.

Yet we must admit that the transmission of cultural heritage within families and by Italian American institutions is often done poorly, if at all. The result is that we are raising a generation of lost souls. As other groups adopt militant forms of ethnic affirmation, young people without a clear and strong identity are at a disadvantage. We encounter them in our classrooms, kids with Italian names but without an inkling of the history those names carry with them. Some hunger to be Italian American, but don't know how. Some adopt as their role models the *mafiosi* of the gangster films. Or they take on the dress, music, behavior of other ethnics; they become Latinos or Wiggers; and yet others become skinheads.[17] I am not faulting the youth; *it is we who have failed them.*

To quote Lenin: "What is to be done?" I have no panacea, but I think that we who are the self-chosen custodians of Italian American heritage have a special role and responsibility. Ethnicity is a form of memory, and many Italian Americans are suffering from amnesia. Freud observed that forgetting is "the avoidance of the pain of remembering." There was much that was painful in the Italian American experience. I don't believe that we should connive in those silences; our job is to bring to the surface the painful memories of bigotry, repression, and conflict. In addition to writing our books and articles, we need to connect with Italian Americans where they live. Exhibits, oral history projects, films, family histories—these are the means of engaging Italian Americans in the process of recovering often traumatic, but also inspiriting, memories. As we deal with our real history, I think we will engage the imaginations of our young people. Let me with you a letter I recently received from an aspiring fourth-generation student:

> I have a strong attachment to my ethnic roots and am eager to learn more about the "true" story of Italian Americans—not the stereotypical, thin version presented by the media and so widely believed. The Italian experience . . . is complex and varied and I hope to further flesh out, in my small way, the incomplete story of my ancestors.

I realize that I am preaching to the converted, that many of you have been and are engaged in such projects—and I applaud you. The AIHA, which from its inception has been dedicated to the purpose of disseminating understanding of the Italian American experience, has made enormous contributions to a reawakening of Italian American consciousness. What too often has been lacking has been the political and economic support from Italian American organizations and individuals whose resources could have amplified many fold the work of the AIHA. A long-standing tradition of anti-intellectualism among Italian Americans has restricted the essential linkage of wealth and power with intellect and creativity.[18]

But you may ask, why bother? Why invest our time, energy, and money in revitalizing Italian American ethnicity when there are so many other urgent matters to tend to? Why not simply submerge ourselves in the vanilla frosting and enjoy the perks of being "white" in a racist society? Replies will vary, but I have a couple of answers for myself. First let me say I am not into ethnic chauvinism. I am as opposed to Italocentrism as I am to Anglocentrism or Afrocentrism. Beyond the personal significance of the Italian American experience in which I am willy-nilly a participant, as a humanist I argue for the intrinsic significance of that experience. It is an epic story of a diaspora, the story of the tragedies and triumphs of millions, the story of generations struggling to reconcile the old and the new. It is neither grander nor meaner than the story of other migrant peoples, *but it is our story.*

Knowledge of that story can enrich and inspire our lives; it can provide us with a center and a compass in these turbulent times.

The Italian American experience has a larger significance that transcends its meaning for us as individuals. Over the past century we have collectively comprised a considerable segment of the American population; there is no sphere of life in which our presence has not been manifest. To delete that experience is to omit a big slice of American history. Further, we need to ponder what meaning that experience has for understanding the character of this society and the critical issues which confront it today. Sheldon Hackney, the Chairman of the National Endowment for the Humanities, has called for a "National Conversation" about our sources of diversity and of unity. What makes us different? What makes us American? Italian American voices need to be heard in that conversation. Based on our historic experience, I think we have something to contribute to it. Of course, we would not speak with one voice, since there have been a variety of Italian American experiences subject to a variety of interpretations.

I would argue that our experience has taught us firsthand of the evils of racism and nativism. Guido Calabresi was recently sworn in as a judge of the Second U.S. Circuit Court of Appeals (on the 55th anniversary of the arrival of his family from Italy). Speaking of American history, Judge Calabresi observed: "Our tragic moments—for which we are still paying and will long pay—are those times when our laws furthered bigotry and discrimination." We, as Italian Americans, should respond to those words, particularly in these times when the latest arrivals in this Promised Land are the object of nativist attacks. We, the descendants of *contadini*, should not tolerate those who say, "Oh, but our immigrant ancestors were different. They suffered hardships, but because they were hardworking, self-reliant, honest, etc., they made it."[19] Anyone who has studied Italian American history knows that this is a gross oversimplification, if not falsification, as well as a slander on the new immigrants.

Our experience has taught us the fallacy of the very idea of race and the mischief of racial labels. It has taught us that both total assimilation and total separatism are will-o'-the-wisps, not achievable—and undesirable if they were. It has taught us that a healthy ethnicity is compatible with, indeed essential to, a healthy America. For these reasons, we, Italian Americans, have something important to contribute to the national dialogue.

Finally, we must say no to both the neo-nationalists and the multiculturalists who would deny us the right to define our own identities as Italian Americans. We must say no to the xenophobes and bigots whether we or others are their targets. Neither white, not black, nor brown, nor red, nor yellow, we are distinguished by our unique experience in these United States. Let us claim our rightful inheritance as Italian Americans.

Notes

1. "Chicago's Italians Prior to World War 1: A Study of Their Social and Economic Adjustment" (University of Wisconsin, 1963).

2. For a superb study of linguistic adaptation of the Italian immigrants, see Hermann W. Haller, *Una lingua perduta e ritrovata: l'italiano degli italo–americani* (Florence: La Nuova Italia, 1993).

3. Herbert J. Gans, "Symbolic Ethnicity: The Future of Ethnic Groups and Cultures in America," *On the Making of Americans: Essays in Honor of David Riesman,* ed. H. J. Gans (Philadelphia: University of Pennsylvania Press, 1977), 193–220. For a slightly revised version of this formulation, see Herbert J. Gans, "Comment: Ethnic Invention and Acculturation, A Bumpy-Line Approach," *Journal of American Ethnic History* 12 (Fall 1992): 42–52.

4. Richard D. Alba, *Italian Americans: Into the Twilight of Ethnicity* (Englewood Cliffs, NJ: Prentice–Hall, 1985). See also Alba, *Ethnic Identity: The Transformation of White America* (New Haven, CT: Yale University Press, 1990).

5. Mary C. Waters, *Ethnic Options: Choosing Identities in America* (Berkeley: University of California Press, 1990).

6. The literature relating to the controversies swirling about multiculturalism is extensive, but for a critical review of its extreme form, I recommend Richard Bernstein, *Dictatorship of Virtue: Multiculturalism and the Battle for America's Future* (New York: Knopf, 1994).

7. Ramona Douglass, however, did testify before the House Subcommittee on the Census on behalf of establishing a "multiracial/multiethnic category." Douglass, who is president of the Association of Multiethnic Americans, identified herself as Sicilian American on her mother's side, while her father is of Oglala Indian and African–American ancestry. Douglass's testimony was reprinted on the

Internet (H–Ethnic) on November 25, 1994 from *International/ Intercultural Connection,* the newsletter of the Chicago-based Biracial Family Network

8. For an elaboration of this view I refer you to Kathleen Neils Conzen, David A. Gerber, Ewa Morawska, George E. Pozzetta, and Rudolph J. Vecoli, "The Invention of Ethnicity: A Perspective from the U.S.A.," *Journal of American Ethnic History* (Fall 1992): 3–41.

9. For an attempt to articulate the influence of personal experience on the writing of history, see Rudolph J. Vecoli, "Italian Immigrants and Working-Class Movements in the United States: A Personal Reflection on Class and Ethnicity," *Journal of the Canadian Historical Association* 4 (1993): 293–305.

10. U.S. Department of Commerce, *1990 Census of Population Supplementary Reports: Detailed Ancestry for States* (I 190 CP–S– 1 –2) (Washington, DC: Bureau of the Census, 1992).

11. Sando Bologna, author of *The Italians of Waterbury,* writing about the lively Italian American cultural and associational life of that city, concluded: "Prof. Alba would find a long sunset of Italian ethnicity in Waterbury." Letter of July 5, 1995.

12. A lively exchange of information and views takes place on the Italian Genealogy Bulletin Board on the Internet. To subscribe send e-mail to LISTPROC@JSoft.COM, no subject line, and type in the body of the text: subscribe PIE your first name, your last name.

13. "Undoing Elie Risorgimenio: Emigrants from Italy and the Politics of Regionalism," *If One Were to Write a History . . . Selected Writings by Robert E Harney,* ed. Pierre Anctil and Bruno Ramirez (Toronto: Multicultural History Society of Ontario, 1991), 201–26. In a personal communication, Andrew Canepa confirmed my impression of the resurgence of regional and local associations, citing a lengthy list of such organizations in California.

14. "The Search for an Italian American Identity: Continuity and Change," *Italian Americans: New Perspectives in Italian Immigration and Ethnicity,* ed. Lydio Tomasi (New York: Center for Migration Studies, 1985), 88–112; "The Coming of Age of the Italian Americans," *Ethnicity* 5 (1978): 119–47.

15. William McDougall, professor of psychology at Harvard College, presented essentially the same argument regarding the hereditary and racial basis of intelligence in *Is America Safe for Democracy?* (New York: Scribner's, 1921). McDougall reported that

Italians scored 84, while Colored scored 83 as compared with the score of 106 of "All Americans." He noted, however, that "the recent Italian immigrants are not probably a fair sample of the population of Italy" (64).

16. For provocative discussions of the ambiguous racial status of Italian immigrants, see Robert Orsi, "The Religious Boundaries of an In-between People: Street *Feste* and the Problem of the Dark-Skinned Other in Italian Harlem, 1920–1990," *American Quarterly* 44 (Sept. 1992): 313–47; and David R. Roediger, *Towards the Abolition of Whiteness* (London: Verso, 1994), particularly Chapter 11: "Whiteness and Ethnicity in the History of "White Ethnics' in the United States."

17. Donald Tricarico, "Guido, Fashioning an Italian American Youth Style," *The Journal of Ethnic Studies* 19 (Spring 1991): 41–66, is a fascinating account of an Italian American youth culture.

18. For a discussion of the present status and future of Italian American organizational life, see Joseph Maselli, ed., *Year 2000—Where Will Italian American Organizations be in the Year 2000?* (Washington, DC: The National Italian American Foundation, 1990).

19. Anna Quindlen, "Hypocrisy from a Nation of Immigrants," *Star Tribune* (Minneapolis, MN). Quindlen's maternal grandparents were immigrants from Italy. A leading proponent of Proposition 187 in California, Sally Vaughn, who also had Italian grandparents, declared, "I resent them [current immigrants] comparing themselves to my grandparents, who came here legally, worked hard, learned to speak English and tried to be good citizens" (*Star Tribune*, 6 Nov. 1994).

Chapter 4

Some Sort of Americans: The Working and Reworking of Italian American Ethnicity in the United States

Daniel J. Monti, Jr.

Introduction

We are reminded of the continuing importance of ethnicity in our lives by recent events in Europe and the United States. Several European nations today are having great difficulty accommodating people from different countries who have been in residence for varying lengths of time. Elsewhere in Europe, people are reasserting long-standing claims of nationalism against neighbors who have customs, languages, and religions different from their own. While the United States has been spared the worst excesses of xenophobia witnessed across Europe, it has experienced violent outbursts against the lingering remnants of its own racist past. The United States also is serving as host to the emergence of a large and brand new ethnic group comprised of Hispanic people from Mexico, Central and South America, and the Caribbean. The problems and progress of this group will be juxtaposed and sometimes tied to the continuing plight of Americans of African descent.

Against the backdrop of such dramatic events, it might seem little more than an academic exercise to consider the past and future of Italian Americans. These are, after all, people belonging to an ethnic group whose members generally have succeeded in making a good and safe

89

place for themselves in the United States. These also are people whose own ethnicity, because of their successes, has been declared to be in its twilight and more symbolic than substantial in character.[1] Whatever meaning or significance being an Italian American once had, it is thought today to have become less helpful for sorting out one's personal identity and less vital to the well-being of the people called "Americans."

One finds no less sensitive an observer of United States ethnic relations than Herbert J. Gans who argues that the apparent resurgence of ethnicity during the 1970s was peculiar to "poorer ethnics." These were people who, in his estimation, "have been less touched by acculturation and assimilation than middle-class ethnics, and who have, in some cases, used ethnicity and ethnic organizations as a . . . defense against the injustices from which they suffer" in their country. The ethnicity they pursued was "largely a working-class style" that sometimes masked reactionary political ideas.[2]

Alongside these gritty holdovers of enclave ethnicity were third generation, largely middle-class people, more interested in maintaining an ethnic identity than in reviving immigrant customs or invoking immigrant beliefs. Ethnicity for these persons, Gans argued, took an "expressive rather than instrumental" form and became "more of a leisure-time activity" in a way to earn a living or make a family.[3] It was for these reasons that Gans called their ethnicity "symbolic." It did not regulate most aspects of peoples' lives and could be expressed as little or much as one wanted. Feeling "ethnic" took precedence over being an "ethnic," insofar as being an ethnic entailed carrying on a "working-class" way of life.

The success enjoyed by people of Italian American descent, among other Catholic groups of European origins, is thought to have made the dilution or abandonment of ethnicity all but inevitable. In the United States, economic mobility ordinarily is associated with geographic mobility. Individuals measure the pace and distance of their social ascent by how far and quickly they move away from less well-to-do areas. This combination of individual economic and physical movement erodes two important bases for what is commonly thought to be an ethnic way of life: a similar and low economic standing and propinquity.

Ethnicity, according to Richard Alba, "flourishes" among individuals who occupy one niche in the social class hierarchy, have a common ancestral line, and live in the same town.[4] Such individuals also adhere to identical religious beliefs and social customs. What distinguishes an ethnic group, then, is the degree to which its members share certain important traits, and a way of life that persists for generations in a particular location.

Economic and social mobility are thought to undermine the willingness of individuals to stay with their fellow ethnics and to maintain customary ways of acting and thinking. The boundaries of the ethnic world loosen. More mobile individuals leave or introduce new ways of thinking and behaving to their less mobile peers. In either case, they become a bit less ethnic and a bit more like people in the larger society in terms of the customs they follow and the thoughts they hold.

It is under such conditions, Alba reasons, that ethnicity appears to subside or decline. The twilight of ethnicity may last a long time and be marked by occasional flare-ups like the "ethnic resurgence" of different peoples in the United States during the 1970s. Ethnicity could be celebrated, then, "precisely because assimilation had proceeded far enough that ethnicity no longer seemed so threatening and divisive."[5] Nevertheless, the trajectory of ethnicity is unmistakably downward.

Insofar as Italian Americans are representative of a people whose ethnicity is in decline and is being carried on largely through the clever manipulation of symbols that evoke memories of a common past, it may be right and fair to speak of the twilight of their ethnicity in the United States. I, for one, do not think that Italian American ethnicity is in decline or lives on only as the flickering afterglow of a once-bright star that long ago collapsed upon itself or was gobbled up by a larger neighbor. A declaration that one is of Italian descent through either one or both parents remains an important means of organizing a personal identity. Moreover, I believe that Italian Americans are only now coming to realize their full power, and significance as an ethnic group in the United States. Their most vital contributions to the well-being of the people called "Americans" have yet to be made.

Italian Americans Then and Now

Though a definitive social history of Italian Americans has yet to be written, much information does exist and the broad outlines of their story seem clear. I will touch upon only a few themes in that story. In so doing, my intention is to highlight those parts of the Italian American experience that can help us to address important ideas about the meaning of ethnicity in a post-industrial society like the United States.

The ultimate object of this analysis will be to shed some light on the contemporary Italian American population and the extent to which it retains features crucial to the maintenance of an ethnic group. There is no doubt that the twelve million persons of Italian American descent in the United States today are different from the nearly four million Italian immigrants who arrived between 1880 and 1920. It is just as likely that their understanding of what constituted an ethnic group would be different, given the changes in that population and the larger society of which it is a part. Thus, I will endeavor to reconcile our traditional ideas about ethnicity with the possibilities and prospects for ethnicity in the modern world.

Approximately 400,000 Italians came to the United States between 1820 and 1890. Most were from northern Italy, and they tended to be relatively skilled. In the thirty years between 1890 and 1920, the size and composition of Italian immigration changed dramatically. Most immigrants came from southern portions of the country, and they were largely unskilled agricultural workers who labored at menial chores. Many were migratory workers who returned to Italy or traveled to South America for jobs during the winter season in the United States.

It was this latter collection of southern Italians that was responsible for filling many inner-city neighborhoods in the northeastern portion of the United States. They also were the people who built enclaves that became the basis for Italian American community life at the start of the twentieth century. Our understanding of Italian Americans as an ethnic group is rooted in those places and the style of life pursued there.

The attitude of many Americans toward the newcomers at that time was one of unbridled ambivalence. It was a view shared afterward by several generations of theorists. The Italians provided good, cheap labor. Unfortunately, they also were perceived as a threat to the way of life practiced by more established groups. It was expected that the Italians would find a place in this society, but it was not clear how well the society would hold up under the strain. One theologian around the turn of the century put it this way. "Within the next decade," he said, "Italians will be assimilated. They will be Americans of some sort. The battle is begun." His only question was whether "our Protestantism" would "bear the test."[6] The assimilation of Italians into a Protestant America was a foregone conclusion. The period of adjustment might be rocky, but it would not take too long.

Notwithstanding the stigma attached to their different look and customs and to their early poverty, many of the newcomers did make substantial progress. Early on, they congregated with persons from their own province or town, but that pattern broke down as "immigrants mingled with newcomers from other towns and provinces." This had a great impact on everyone involved. They started to think of themselves," Humbert Nelli tells us, "as Italians rather than as members of a particular family. [A] community identity and ethnic consciousness began to evolve."[7] They were becoming Italian Americans. Their ethnicity, Andrew Greeley says, was "not a way of looking back to the old world" but "a way of being American."[8]

The period of their introspection coincided with attempts to reach out to a broader array of persons and places. Almost immediately, the immigrants saved money, bought property, and started businesses that served non-Italians as well as their own people. Nor were they confined to areas populated exclusively by other Italians. There was much mobility in and out of the so-called "Little Italies" that were ethnic enclaves.[9] Some Italians moved into "better" areas, even as others stayed relatively close to "the old neighborhood."

There were other ways in which Italian Americans simultaneously reached out to the broader society and developed their own community. As expanding industrial economy provided many persons with jobs outside of their neighborhood, local politics drew Italian Americans into the public arena where they had to reconcile their needs and desires with those of other groups. The more important changes to occur within Italian American neighborhoods involved the creation of institutions to supplement the work of families and churches. Mutual benefit societies and Italian-language newspapers served both as bridges between Italian Americans and walls between them and the outside world. Their numbers declined over the course of several decades, and the social satisfaction garnered from the work of these organizations became more important than the economic and social protection they initially provided their members and customers.

Reductions in immigration following World War I coupled with the increased economic and social mobility of their people made Italian American enclaves less important. More people of Italian descent were staying in school longer and marrying non-Italians. They became suburbanites along with many others in the years after 1950. Though many enclaves persisted, they were beset by problems common to older city neighborhoods. New immigrants such as Hispanics, along with migrating blacks and poor whites from rural parts of the United States, also occupied some of the areas once considered Italian American neighborhoods. The prosperity and mobility enjoyed by more individuals of Italian American descent were associated with the erosion of an Italian American community and personal identity. Many Italian Americans were becoming better assimilated into the broader society. They were, in some sense, perhaps much more "American" than they were "Italian," just as early twentieth-century reformers and social theorists had predicted.

There is no doubt that Italian Americans are different today from their counterparts earlier in the century. There are very strong signs however that, despite their "assimilation," they have retained many of the social features that distinguished them as a distinct ethnic people. If this is so, and bearing in mind that their character as "Italians" was shaped largely after their emigration to the United States, then it may be too soon to speak of Italian Americans as though they were in the twilight of their ethnicity.

The size of the Italian American population in the United States is larger today than it has ever been. There were approximately 4.5 million Italian Americans in the United States as of 1960 and they constituted about 2.5 percent of the country's population.[10] By 1990, there were between ten and twelve million Italian Americans and they represented approximately 5 percent of the national population.[11] The number and percentage of persons claiming Italian ancestry doubled between 1960 and 1990. Many of these people have only one parent who is of Italian descent. Nonetheless, growth in the Italian American population has been steady.

Italian Americans are more geographically dispersed than they once were, but they remain concentrated in the Northeast and in urban areas. Many Italian Americans were pushed from their city neighborhoods after 1950 as a result of urban renewal projects. Others chose to join the exodus of persons who moved to the suburbs after World War II. However, more than half of all Italian Americans still live in the Northeast. Even more impressive is the fact that no other ethnic group is as concentrated in that region or in the urban areas of that region.[12] Italian Americans may no longer enjoy the warmth and intimacy that was once shared in ethnic enclaves, but they are readily available to each other in numbers sufficient to constitute an impressive social or political bloc.

The Italian American population continues to be replenished by a small, but steady stream of Italian immigrants. The number of Italians entering the United States as immigrants exceeded 20,000 each year between 1966 and 1973, but it has dropped steadily since then. As late as 1980, however, in excess of 830,000 of all Italian Americans had been born in Italy. Just over 30 percent of these persons arrived after 1960. While most Italian immigrants became citizens, nearly 22 percent retained their status as resident aliens. Given their great concentration in the urban centers of the Northeast, these immigrants act as a communal anchor and cultural memory for many Italian Americans.

The social profile of Italian Americans is also interesting. Italian Americans tend to hold politically conservative and socially liberal views when compared to other persons. Their social customs are comparable to those of working-class and middle-class families generally. Some members of the Italian American population have moved beyond the earning power and job status of their parents. However, there also are some distressing signs that Italian Americans are lagging behind other Americans in terms of their occupational and educational accomplishments.

There is unmistakable evidence that many persons of Italian descent are becoming more like other Americans, but not in all ways or especially quickly. For instance, they are less likely to marry other persons with Italian ancestry. Among those Italian Americans born since 1960, only 22 percent are marrying other people from the same background. The national average is 26 percent. In addition, fewer Italian Americans are married today (i.e., 59 percent) than was the case during the 1970s (i.e., 69 percent); but the decline was greater among non-Italian Americans. The proportion of Italian Americans being raised by divorced parents, on the other hand, has increased. Approximately 5 percent were being reared in this way during the 1970s. That figure increased to 12 percent in the early 1990s.

The religious identification of Italian Americans with Catholicism still is strong (i.e., 70 percent), even if their participation in services is rather nominal. They also tend to hold less traditional religious beliefs than was once the case. They are well integrated into other social and organizational networks. On the other hand, today they tend to be less involved with groups catering to ethnic concerns or whose membership consists largely of other Italian Americans.

Since 1972, Italian Americans have witnessed an increase in the prestige of the jobs they hold and in their average level of educational attainment (i.e. 13 years). More are graduating from high school (i.e., 60 percent) and college (i.e., 15–20 percent). Nevertheless, their progress has not been overwhelming. More than 40 percent of women and 54 percent of men who are of Italian descent have less than twelve years of formal education. Their average annual income has hovered around $33,600 since the 1970s, though it still is a little higher than the national average of $29,800. Among all European ethnics, however, they have the lowest rates of educational and occupational achievement. Furthermore, that situation is not improving. The occupational status and mobility of Italian Americans today is leveling off. Young Italian Americans no longer have much better jobs than those held by their parents, and members of other ethnic groups are increasing their occupational mobility at a faster rate.

Italian Americans are integrated into many spheres of life in the United States, but their penetration has been uneven and their rise has been more plodding than meteoric. The passing of ethnicity is said by theorists to be connected in a clear and unmistakable way to the assimilation of a people into a different culture. If Italian Americans are to be included among the groups said to have been "assimilated" into American society, then it must be conceded that their absorption has been of a middling sort. The twilight of their ethnicity is not yet upon them.

Making Sense of Ethnicity in a Modern World

This thesis was advanced during the noisy ethnic revival of the 1970s by persons who have been called "ethnic pluralists," but not in a way that was especially helpful. Ethnic pluralists saw renewed interest in ethnicity as a sign that assimilation had not advanced as quickly or far as many persons thought. The pluralists, argues Stephen Steinberg, "celebrated what they viewed as the triumph of ethnicity over the forces of assimilation."[13] They soon were taken to task by certain individuals whom we shall call "assimilationists" who saw no great accomplishment and much partisan mischief in the ethnic revivalism of white persons with European pedigrees. The rediscovery of tribalism by European ethnics was little more than a temporary distraction. The march toward assimilation had not halted. Indeed, all the rhetorical thumping engaged in by white ethnics merely affirmed just how far the basis for ethnic pluralism in the United States had been undermined. The argument between advocates of pluralism and assimilation was provocative and acquired a great deal of attention in both academic and non-academic circles. It was useful, but not particularly revealing, however, because the partisans on both sides of the issue were operating under an identical assumption. They thought of assimilation and the persistence of ethnicity, or pluralism, as though they were antagonistic. Thus, it was altogether logical for pluralists to speak of ethnicity as a force resistant to assimilation and no less reasonable for their critics to point out that the putative ethnics were not quite so close to their immigrant forefathers as their champions. Representatives on both sides believed that assimilation was a state in which ethnicity was lost or persisted in only diffuse and symbolic ways. Ethnicity was driven down or out in a society where a people with a distinct culture was gradually taken in by a more dominant group whose own ways of thinking and behaving were different from its own. The idea that minority peoples "lose" their ethnicity as they become more fully integrated into a host culture has become a cherished idea in the United States. It is the premise from which most theories about ethnic relations are derived, and it dominates discussions on how best to bring minority citizens into American society more fully and effectively. It also happens to be wrong. Ignored in all the arguing about assimilation and pluralism is the fact that ethnicity is far more complex a phenomenon that is commonly appreciated. A particular ethnic group might display elements of assimilation even as it retains certain aspects of its ethnic character. Assimilation and pluralism need not be mutually exclusive states.[14] Another way of envisioning ethnicity in this way is to understand that some individual members of a particular ethnic group may have experienced more assimilation than other members. Rates of assimilation or acculturation can vary within ethnic groups as well as between ethnic groups. The boundaries of an ethnic group can change as the society around it changes, and some members can find their way more easily into the larger society than can others. What it means to be an ethnic under these circumstances also changes. Another important insight into the nature of ethnicity in the modern world is that the very size and complexity of industrial and post-industrial societies creates numerous opportunities for ethnicity to be reasserted. It is only by organizing "around larger scale cultural identities" such as ethnicity that groups will be able to mobilize successfully. The boundaries around an ethnic group are expanded so that its membership can influence and be incorporated into the bigger institutions of post-industrial societies.[15] These insights were developed in response to the pervasiveness and persistence of ethnicity in the modern world. The same ideas would have been just as applicable for societies before they became industrialized. Indeed, ethnic groups first appeared in the cities of proto-industrial Europe. Ethnic attachments in medieval cities helped in organizing social and economic relations through the use of guilds. Though resistant to innovations in the way goods were manufactured, guilds could not stop the introduction of new ways of organizing work that were introduced after the Middle Ages. More movable forms of capital accumulation, such as those created by merchant entrepreneurs, also began to erode the importance of land holding as a means to amass wealth. The world of work and the arrangement of people into social classes became more freewheeling and complex. There was much antagonism and some violence over the unequal distribution of wealth and power in proto-industrial cities. On the other hand, serious attempts were made to limit or direct the expression of ill feeling over such inequities into less destructive channels. There were public ceremonies and festivals that brought different persons together in common celebration of a larger community to which they all contributed and from which they all took a measure of security. Religion, too, continued to make a union between the higher and lower members of a community. Ethnic attachments, however, made their own independent contribution to this effort. Persons of unequal status and wealth could find that they had much in common that was important. Ties and appeals based on one's lineage and place of origin, shared customs, a peculiar dialect, or time-honored grudges were folded together in the unsteady mix of ideas and practices we call "ethnicity."[16] The rich ceremonial life of medieval guilds revolved around festivals and parades that reinforced and legitimized the work of different groups of persons who often had a common history. In some ways, guilds were the first "ethnic enterprises" in cities.[17] They provided meaningful work and mutual support for people with a shared past. Ethnic groups in proto-industrial cities were not so tightly bound to particular crafts or types of work; but their contribution to the creation of an orderly way of life in urban areas was no less important. They served as bridges between the several social classes represented among their members. In this way, ethnic groups provided a working model for how individuals with unequal wealth or power could be brought together by appealing to their common history and destiny. Ethnic groups also managed to affirm the place of their members in the larger city, even as they defended or celebrated the smaller quarters or neighborhoods in which these persons lived and worked. This was the same problem that city leaders generally were trying to address, but they were working with a larger number and variety of people. Rituals and institutions were created with the explicit intention of drawing together the diverse inhabitants of an ethnic enclave or city. Neither the leaders of cities nor the leaders of ethnic groups were able to erase differences among their co-residents and co-ethnics. Nevertheless, they tried to show how such differences could be muted and their effects softened even as the hard work of inventing a people went forward. The legacy of these efforts was passed on to the inhabitants of industrial cities and to their several ethnic populations. Furthermore, this happened not only in Europe but also in the United States.[18] The lesson in this for students of ethnic relations is that attempts to "assimilate" the city's different residents into one large community did not obscure or render superfluous the work of those who were fashioning themselves into an ethnic group. That both campaigns could be mounted concurrently and succeed to varying degrees does not mean there was no tension between their respective leaders and followers. More elite leaders of cities in the United States certainly made many strong attempts to cajole or push the members of successive immigrant populations to become more like "regular Americans." Nevertheless, the partly successful efforts to build a sense of community in the city as a whole even as would-be ethnics were working to the same end in their enclaves does speak to a convergence in their methods and goals.

An effective campaign to integrate all the inhabitants of a city into a union may need to be balanced by an equally strong effort among its varied residents to define for themselves smaller and more workable communities based on their ethnicity. It may be more feasible to create a congenial social order in cities when we have a "them" that justifies the making of an "us." To transpose this language into the rhetoric of race relations one would say that assimilation and pluralism are not mutually exclusive states. The existence and success of one requires the active presence of the other.

The validity of this assertion becomes clear when examining the past and present state of an ethnic people such as Italian Americans. There are members of this population who have made their way into the economy of the United States and enjoy a degree of material security that rivals and, in some cases, surpasses the success of persons whose ancestors have been there longer. A modest portion of all Italian Americans also have become highly educated or have acquired notoriety in other institutional arenas. A number of these persons are now ensconced in the American middle class, have married non-Italians, and practice the kind of "symbolic ethnicity" described by Gans and others. On the other hand, there are even more people of Italian American descent who have not made that much material and social "progress" or whose mobility has been stalled for some time and, perhaps, for reasons not of their making. It is these individuals who are expected to carry on whatever traditions are associated with being an Italian American. Ethnicity for these individuals is thought to be an important part of their daily lives. The problem with this formulation is that it draws much too sharp a distinction between those Italian Americans who have been more successful in the United States and those who have not yet succeeded and perhaps never will. It is not just the less prosperous Italian Americans who are involved more actively in a way of life that is self-consciously "ethnic" in its tone and content. More well-to-do Italian Americans also belong to ethnic organizations, contribute time and money to ethnic causes, and associate with any persons who are their "co-ethnics." Indeed, some of the very persons who would be expected to be "symbolic ethnics" are among the most active in their respective communities. They may not speak the language of their ancestors or carry on some of the customs of their grandparents, but they have a healthy regard for themselves as Italian Americans and contribute much of themselves to Italian American activities. Many working-class Italian Americans, by contrast, may be deeply involved in groups or personal relations with other Italian Americans, but not have much interest or ability to speak to broader audiences about issues of concern to themselves. The point simply is that both sets of Italian Americans are making a contribution to the maintenance and success of their ethnic group. We in the United States have a limited and ideologically tainted view of ethnicity. We imagine ethnic people to be quaint folk who practice arcane customs and wear brightly colored peasant clothing. It is hard to think of people who are professionals dressed in expensive suits as "ethnics." We do not imagine, as did the inhabitants of proto-industrial cities, that an ethnic people could have its feet in two worlds simultaneously. We also do not accept the possibility that to be effective as a group an ethnic people must have its feet in both its own small community and the larger world occupied by persons different from themselves. The idea of ethnicity advanced here is identical to that advanced nearly eighty years ago by Horace Kallen. Kallen wrote of a "democracy of nationalities" where groups would be free to nurture their ethnic differences even as they participated in the major economic and political institutions of the United States. His notion of pluralism did not hide ethnic peoples behind the shutters of their small communities but had them participating in the larger society and enriching it with their varied ways of looking at the world.[19] The progress of the Italian American people in the United States has brought them to the point that they finally do have their feet planted firmly in both these worlds. It is now possible for them to more clearly articulate a vision for the United States that includes both themselves and the many other people who inhabit it. It is feasible for them to do so only because they have the experience of having lived in both the immigrant and modern world. They are now poised to show what sort of Americans they have become and to show how the United States might someday become the democracy of nationalities that Horace Kallen envisioned.

Notes

1. Richard Alba, "The Twilight of Ethnicity Among American Catholics of European Ancestry," *Majority and Minority,* ed. Norman Yetman (Boston: Allyn and Bacon, 1991), 420–429. Herbert J. Gans, "Symbolic Ethnicity: The Future of Ethnic Groups and Cultures in America," *Majority and Minority,* ed. Norman Yetman (Boston: Allyn and Bacon, 1991), 430–443.

2. Gans, 434.

3. Gans, 435.

4. Alba, 420.

5. Alba, 420.

6. Silvano Tomasi, "The Ethnic Church and the Integration of Italian Immigrants in the United States," *The Italian Experience in the United States,* ed. Silvano Tomasi and Madeline Engel (Staten Island: Center for Migration Studies, 1970), 170.

7. Humbert Nelli, *From Immigrants to Ethnics: The Italian Americans* (Oxford: Oxford University Press, 1983), 59–60.

8. Andrew Greeley, "The Ethnic Miracle," *Majority and Minority,* ed. Norman Yetman (Boston: Allyn and Bacon, 1991), 282.

9. Robert Harney and J. Vincenza Scarpaci, eds., *Little Italies in North America* (Toronto: The Multicultural History Society of Ontario, 1981).

10. Joseph Velikonja, "Italian Immigrants in the United States in the 1960s," *The Italian Experience in the United States,* ed. Silvano Tomasi and Madeline Engel (Staten Island: Center for Migration Studies, 1970), 27.

11. The data cited in the text that deal with the current profile of Italian Americans are drawn from two sources: Tom Smith, *A Profile Of Italian Americans: 1972–1991* (University of Chicago: National Opinion Research Center, 1992); and Graziano Battistella, ed., *Italian Americans in the '80s: A Sociodemographic Profile* (New York: Center for Migration Studies, 1989).

12. Battistella.

13. Stephen Steinberg, *The Ethnic Myth* (Boston: Beacon Press, 1989), 49.

14. Nhlton Gordon, *Assimilation in American Life* (New York: Oxford University Press, 1964).

15. Michael T. Hannan, "The Dynamics of Ethnic Boundaries in Modern States," *National Development and the World System,* eds. John Meyer and Michael Hamm (Chicago: University of Chicago Press, 1979).

16. Ivan Light, *Cities in World Perspective* (New York: Macmillan Publishing Company, 1983); and Paul Hollenberg and Lynn Holen Lees, *The Making of Urban Europe: 100–1950* (Cambridge: Harvard University Press, 1985).

17. Ivan Light, "Immigrant and Ethnic Enterprise in North America," *Majority and Minority,* 307–318.

18. Paul Boyer, *Urban Masses and Moral Order in America, 1820–1920* (Cambridge: Harvard University Press, 1978).

19. Steinberg, 254.

Part II

Italian American Politics and History

Introduction

The Politics and History of
Italian Americans

Frank M. Sorrentino
St. Francis College

This section will explore the history and politics of Italian Americans. History represents a common set of memories both joyful and sorrowful. These memories are the common bonds of ethnicity. Politics represents the divisions and passions of a people. It is impossible to truly understand a group without visiting these two important dimensions.

In Philip Cannistraro's article entitled "Mussolini, Sacco-Vanzetti and the Anarchists: The Transatlantic Context," he explores Mussolini's movement in the Sacco-Vanzetti episode leading to the trial, appeals, and execution. Although Sacco and Vanzetti were anarchists and therefore the enemies of fascism, Mussolini had a grudging admiration for them and was concerned for the implications of how Italian nationals were being treated in America. Mussolini also desired good relations with the United States especially on the issues of debt relief and immigration. In addition, politics in the 1920s within the United States with its Red Scare and xenophobia further complicated matters. Cannistraro demonstrates that Mussolini continued to press for the freedom of Sacco and Vanzetti for national, ideological reasons, as well as for a concern for how the situation would play politically in Italy. This article demonstrates the complex set of political relationships on both sides of the Atlantic which posed great risks for all those involved.

Gary R. Mormino and George E. Pozzetta, in their article entitled "Concord and Discord: Italians and Ethnic Interactions in Tampa,

Florida, 1886-1930," explore the relationship of Italian immigrants with other immigrant groups in Tampa, Florida. The article's focus on inter-minority relationships rather than majority/minority relationships is what makes this piece of scholarship so significant. In general, most minority groups, and Italians in particular, settled in neighborhoods that were inhabited by other minority immigrant groups. These groups have an extremely important impact on each others' socialization and the assimilation process of each other.

Italians went to work in the cigar making factories that were initially dominated by Spanish cigar makers. From their co-workers, Italians learned to form organizations that provided health insurance, while also allowing for ethnic pride and providing social outlets. Furthermore, these organizations provided them with a group identity as Italians, which in turn helped them to become integrated into the larger society. Italians utilized their strong family system, coupled with their great capacity to save, to purchase homes and to start small businesses that served the cigar making industry of Tampa. This entrepreneurial activity facilitated their later success in the more complex economy that ultimately developed in Tampa.

The article gives us an understanding of the complex set of relationships and processes that Italian immigrants have traveled in their American Odyssey.

Salvatore J. LaGumina's article entitled "From Urban to Suburban: Italian Americans in Transition," explores the migration of Italian Americans from the Little Italies of New York to Long Island. The article is an important contribution to our understanding of the choices made by the early immigrants and their descendants on lifestyles and where they would like to live.

Many Italian Americans purchased land on Long Island very inexpensively with many building houses themselves or with the help of their family members. This allowed them to own a piece of land on which they could grow vegetables and raise animals. This represented either a lifestyle that they were accustomed to in Italy or one in which they aspired to achieve.

Moving to different Long Island communities also allowed many of them to have their extended family close by and to live among fellow immigrants from the same region in Italy. Both of these were highly desired values. In addition, this migration permitted them to escape some of the harsh discrimination that many had experienced in the city and to pursue work that was more hospitable to their prior experience and values in Italy. LaGumina also explores the rich community involvement of Italian Americans in this more compatible environment. This article contributes to our understanding of the complex and diverse set of choices made by Italian Americans that reflected the values and experience they brought from Italy and the new set of conditions they confronted in America.

Donna R. Gabaccia's article, entitled "Italian Immigrant Women in Comparative Perspective," is a path-breaking analysis of the problems incurred in historical research. If all knowledge is comparative then an important set of decisions needs to be made with regard to with whom you compare Italian immigrant women and the criteria you employ in the comparison.

Gabaccia analyzes the implications of comparing Italian women to other immigrant women in America, to American women in general, and to Italian women in other nations. Each presents a series of insights and challenges. In addition, she notes that the criteria employed might also reflect cultural and ideological biases.

Gabaccia's interest in Italian immigrant women reflects an important intellectual choice between gender and ethnic culture. The question of to what degree these women are different due to their "Italianess" reflects a major intellectual as well as a methodological challenge. Gabbaccia's article is a major contribution to understanding the challenges facing those investigating Italian immigrant women in America.

Frank Cavioli's article, entitled "Columbus, Whitman and the Italian American Connection," is a penetrating analysis of the symbolism of Columbus in America. Columbus was utilized as a symbol for America—a new world—a breaking away from the chains of feudal Europe. Columbus represented to the citizens of America individualism and democracy coupled with a sense of mission and courage. Cavioli explores how Walt Whitman utilized Columbus in his own works as a great hero whose work was not fully appreciated in his own time. Whitman sensed in Columbus a man of deep faith and a sense of purpose that was undeterred by the physical, political, or social obstacles that he faced.

Cavioli also demonstrates how Whitman used Columbus as a metaphor for himself. Both men defied convention on the way to innovation and were heavily criticized and lambasted in their own times. He then explains that much of this symbolism of Columbus came before the great migration of Italians from Southern Italy. Ironically, Columbus was an American symbol that was adopted by the Italian American community. While Whitman was influenced by Italian culture and by Italian Americans, it was Columbus as an America icon that was most pervasive for him and his work. Finally, Cavioli demonstrates how the changing perceptions of Columbus have had complex implications for Italian Americans in particular and for Americans in general.

Chapter 5

Mussolini, Sacco-Vanzetti, and the Anarchists: The Transatlantic Context

Philip V. Cannistraro
Queens College, City University of New York

In *The Big Money* (1936), John Dos Passos reminds us that for left-wing militants the execution of Nicola Sacco and Bartolomeo Vanzetti on August 23, 1927, defined the political discourse of the age by polarizing society into "two nations"[1]: on one side of the great divide stood the popular, progressive social elements that had fought to save the two anarchists from the electric chair; on the other side were arrayed the reactionary forces that sustained the capitalist order, from American nativism to Italian Fascism. Vanzetti, who anxiously followed the rise of Benito Mussolini's Fascist movement from his prison cell, had arrived at the same conclusion, believing that the judge who condemned him and Sacco wore the American face of the conservative interests propped up by the Italian dictator. The choice, Vanzetti believed, was "either fascismo, or revolution."[2]

Mussolini did not see Sacco and Vanzetti in these stark ideological terms; as the duce of Fascism and as dictator of Italy, reasons of state shaped his policies toward the case. Moreover, even as the leader of a radical right movement engaged in a bloody war against the left, he admired the anarchists, whom he believed were morally and politically superior to socialists and communists. As late as 1934, he continued to speak of Sacco and Vanzetti in a way that suggests personal sympathies for them and for anarchism, attitudes unrecognized by historians who emphasize his unremitting crusade against the left. The two Italian anarchists had been innocent, he protested indignantly to a friend, but the Fascists in America "did not lift a finger . . . to save Sacco and Vanzetti. The socialist ranks among the emigrants, anarchist and maximalist did much more."[3]

Mussolini remained proudly attached to the memory of his own radical past, and his reactions to the Sacco-Vanzetti case can be best understood in that context. Although his intellectual formation was largely the product of Marxism and revolutionary syndicalism, Mussolini was also influenced by anarchist ideas; the anti-Fascist historian Gaetano Salvemini thought he was more an anarchist than a socialist.[4] His father, Alessandro Mussolini, had been a member of Bakunin's anarchist International in Italy in the 1870s and had admired both Carlo Cafiero and Andrea Costa, two of its principal chieftains. During his youthful exile in Switzerland he had known Carlo Tresca and other radicals, and he maintained a lifelong respect for the anarchist leader Errico Malatesta.[5] Mussolini also knew his anarchist literature, including the works of the German individualist anarchist Max Stirner and the Russian anarchist communist Peter Kropotkin. He even translated anarchist works from French into Italian, including two of Kropotkin's major books, *Parotes d'un revolte'* and *La grande revolution, 1789-1793.*[6]

Nor was the Sacco-Vanzetti case the first instance in which Mussolini reacted to political repression in the United States. As a young radical, he had bitterly attacked the capitalists of the United States because of the execution of the anarchist "martyrs" of the Haymarket affair of 1886-87. When reformist socialist Filippo Turati accused Gaetano Bresci, the anarchist who left Paterson, New Jersey, in 1900 to assassinate King Umberto I, of being insane, Mussolini defended Bresci as a hero—and blandly described tyrannicide as "the occupational hazard of being a king."[7] Later, as a socialist editor in the Romagna, he again railed against the "violent and brutal" bourgeoisie that dominated the United States, where two Italian Industrial Workers of the World (IWW) leaders, Joseph Ettor and Arturo Giovannitti, faced murder charges resulting from the Lawrence textile strike of 1912. Mussolini had then tried to rally Italian workers as part of an international protest in support of the two labor activists, much as anarchists would do later for Sacco and Vanzetti.[8]

Sacco and Vanzetti's defenders dismissed the notion that Mussolini tried to save the two anarchists, and some have even argued that he secretly encouraged American officials to prosecute them. In 1927 the anarchist Raffaele Schiavina charged that, in spite of his public statements, Mussolini told U.S. authorities privately that execution would be fully justified. In the 1950s, Howard Fast, in his novel *The Passion of Sacco and Vanzetti,* perpetuated this picture of a cynical Mussolini playing a double game. Sacco's grandson Spencer believes that Mussolini told President Coolidge that he did not want Sacco and Vanzetti returned to Italy.[9] Recalled one Italian American, "If there had been another government in Italy at the time, Sacco and Vanzetti would not have died, but Mussolini washed his hands like Pilate."[10]

Scholarly opinion holds that Mussolini was "complacent and uninterested" in Sacco and Vanzetti's fate and "made no representation" on their behalf.[11] But without access to recently released Italian records, scholars could not have been aware of the full scope of Mussolini's activities or of his real attitudes toward the case. The impression persists that the dictator made only one perfunctory effort to help Sacco and Vanzetti,[12] in the form of a private communication to American ambassador Henry P. Fletcher written shortly before the execution. In what Mussolini described as a letter "of an absolutely confidential nature," he urged Fletcher to prevail upon Governor Alvan T. Fuller of Massachusetts to commute the death sentence, arguing that clemency would reveal the difference between Bolshevik and American methods and would avoid creating two leftist martyrs.[13]

Neither the partisan nor the scholarly view is correct. Italian involvement in the Sacco-Vanzetti case began in 1920, but it consisted largely of reluctant gestures by a Liberal government that had long shown deep-rooted hostility toward anarchism.[14] In the two years before Mussolini took office in October 1922, none of the Liberal prime ministers issued a formal protest against the treatment accorded Sacco and Vanzetti, nor did they appeal privately to American authorities. Yet although Mussolini's repression of the anarchists at home after he came to power represented continuity with Liberal policy, he actually did more than his predecessors to assist Sacco and Vanzetti.[15] During the struggle for power between 1919 and 1922, while his Blackshirts battered the socialists in the streets, Mussolini simultaneously extolled anarchist revolutionary fervor and publicly favored the cause of Sacco and Vanzetti. As prime minister, he reluctantly tempered his support for the

defendants so as not to antagonize American sensibilities. But behind
Mussolini the diplomat lurked a onetime revolutionary who harbored an
instinctive solidarity with two anarchists trapped in the judicial
machinery of a "plutocratic" state he had once violently excoriated and
continued to detest.[16]

On both sides of the Atlantic in 1919-20, a climate of right-wing
reaction prevailed, a climate marked by political violence and
widespread social unrest in which Italian anarchists were the targets of
much of the repression. In the United States, the Italian community
included Carlo Tresca and Luigi Galleani—as well as followers of
Galleani such as Sacco and Vanzetti—among the ranks of foreign-born
anarchists.[17] But Italian American anarchism was already caught in the
last stages of a cycle of government suppression that had begun with the
American entry into World War I in April 1917, when federal agents
cracked down on radical groups in a mounting wave of repression. The
Red Scare in America reached its height in the Palmer Raids of 1919 and
the deportation of alien subversives. In Italy, the period 1919-20—
known as the "red biennium"—also witnessed a rising tide of left-wing
radicalism that climaxed in the "Occupation of the Factories." The
Liberal government stood by while Mussolini's newly formed Blackshirt
squads launched a bloody war against "subversives" and then replied
with a police crackdown against the anarchists.[18]

Galleani and his chief disciple, Schiavina, were deported from the
United States along with seven others, arriving back in Italy in July 1919,
four months after Mussolini had founded the Fascist movement.[19] They
maintained close contact with their American comrades and in January
1920, using money collected in the United States, they revived in Turin
Cronaca Sovversiva, the anarchist paper that had been suppressed in
New England.[20] That September, in the heat of his tirades against the
socialists, Mussolini invoked Galleani as a radical of high principle who
could testify to his charge that maximalist socialist Giacinto M. Serrati
had, while serving as editor of the New York-based *Il Proletario* in
1902-3, betrayed the subversive code by informing police authorities of
Galleani's whereabouts. By reopening the old polemic, Mussolini hoped
to further divide the left and gain anarchist support in his struggle against
the socialists.[21]

In December 1919 Erricio Malatesta returned to Italy from his exile
in London. Mussolini immediately saw Malatesta as introducing a new,
vital element into the revolutionary possibilities of the moment: "From

1892 to 1918, Italian anarchism was an almost insignificant element in politics. Today, no longer. Today Malatesta is the star that obscures all the leaders of the Socialist Party. His influence on the Italian working masses is extremely powerful."[22]

Malatesta soon launched a major anarchist daily in Milan, *Umanita' Nova,* and Galleani's followers in New England, including Sacco and Vanzetti, raised funds to buy a linotype machine for the paper. Mussolini began to contrast his respect for the anarchists, based on their willingness to act while others only talked and on their personal courage, with what he described as the do-nothing rhetoric of the socialists. "We are always ready," proclaimed Mussolini, "to admire men who are willing to die for a faith they believe in selflessly."[23]

Mussolini's admiration for the anarchists was sometimes reciprocated, especially by young anarchists who saw him as a vigorous leader in sharp contrast to the socialist politicians they too ridiculed.[24] For a time in 1920 Mussolini courted the anarchists so assiduously that some speculated that he was about to join the movement. Uncertain of his own ideological direction, he could even exclaim, "For we who are the dying vestiges of individualism there is nothing left . . . but the religion—by now absurd but always comforting—of Anarchy!"[25] When the government tried to cut off the supply of printing paper to Malatesta's *Umanita' Nova* Mussolini offered him stock from his own *Popolo d'italia* but the offer was refused.[26]

As Malatesta pushed for a united revolutionary front with socialists and republicans, Mussolini became convinced of the growing political importance of anarchism. In order to prevent this leftist alliance, Mussolini tried to drive the wedge between the socialists and anarchists deeper.[27] He grew more concerned over news of a possible alliance of anarchists and socialists with the poet-soldier Gabriele D'Annunzio, whose legionnaires had occupied the city of Fiume in September 1919. Alarmed that this unlikely combination might seize power, Mussolini exposed the secret discussions in his own newspaper.[28]

The long ordeal of Sacco and Vanzetti began amidst continued anarchist violence and government repression on both sides of the Atlantic. The two men were arrested on May 5, 1920, on suspicion of having participated in the murders that accompanied a robbery at a shoe factory in South Braintree, Massachusetts. In June, while Vanzetti was being tried on charges of having taken part in a separate holdup in Bridgewater, an anarchist-inspired insurrection broke out among military units in Ancona, where the disorder threatened to spread until the movement was crushed.[29] News of Vanzetti's conviction on the Bridgewater charge first appeared in Italy in the pages of *Cronaca Sovversiva*.[30]

Sacco and Vanzetti were both indicted for the South Braintree murders on September 11. In retaliation, Mario Buda, one of their Galleanisti comrades—he described the two as "the best friends I had in America"—struck back at the American authorities. Buda was responsible for the explosion that blasted Wall Street on September 16, and after escaping the police dragnet he left the United States and made his way back to Italy.[31] Within weeks of his return, a violent engagement took place between police and anarchists in Bologna, followed by a bomb explosion in Milan. These incidents led the Liberal government to arrest some eighty anarchists, including Malatesta, and later Galleani and Schiavina. *Cronaca Sovversiva* was shut down, never to reappear. Schiavina fled to Paris and eventually went back clandestinely to the United States, where he edited the Galleanista paper *L'Adunata dei Refrattari* (New York).[32] With the mass arrests and the subsequent collapse of the Occupation of the Factories in early October, Mussolini was moved to speculate that even the anarchists had begun to lose their hold on the workers. And while he claimed to take no pleasure in seeing the aged Malatesta in jail, he expressed satisfaction that "the arrest of the *duce* of Italian anarchism has not greatly moved the proletariat."[33]

The Italian public first learned of the Sacco-Vanzetti case while the two anarchists awaited trial in Massachusetts and Malatesta languished in a Milanese jail without formal charges. After contacting prominent Italian radicals, Fred Moore, Sacco and Vanzetti's attorney, sent the young left-wing journalist Eugene Lyons to Italy to stir up public opinion.[34] From their prison cells in Massachusetts Sacco and Vanzetti kept abreast of events in Italy, Vanzetti expressing his belief that "my comrades in Italy will not deny me their support."[35]

Lyons arrived in November with letters of introduction for socialist leaders, including Leone Mucci, a deputy from Sacco's hometown in Puglia, and Francesco Saverio Merlino, an attorney who had once been a leading figure in the anarchist movement before becoming an independent socialist. Merlino, then preparing to defend Malatesta in court, agreed to serve as the Sacco-Vanzetti defense attorney in Italy.[36] Lyons also met with Sacco's brother Sabino, a reformist socialist whom Lyons described as "a mighty fine fellow and devoted with all his heart to Nicola."[37] Lyons placed articles about the case in leftist newspapers and helped to set up an Italian organization to coordinate efforts with the Sacco-Vanzetti Defense Committee just formed in Boston by anarchist Aldino Felicani—who, incidentally, had met Mussolini in jail in 1911 when both were serving time for protesting against the Italo-Libyan war. "I have little doubt," Lyons reported, "but that a nationwide agitation for the two boys is in the making."[38] To Sacco and Vanzetti he sent word that "their friends in Italy, particularly those, who were in America, are interested and speak of them in high terms." In December, Mucci and Michele Maitilasso, another deputy from Puglia, raised the issue on the floor of parliament, charging that Italians in the United States were being persecuted for their political beliefs.[39]

The Sacco-Vanzetti Defense Committee intensified its publicity campaign in 1921, sending letters and a leaflet to Italy detailing the "frame-up" and stressing that the two men were being condemned because they were anarchists. The committee solicited contributions and asked friendly Italian newspapers to publish the leaflet.[40] In the Romagna, Mario Buda organized rallies and Malatesta's *Umanita' Nova* published articles about the trial.[41]

In the midst of these activities, Mussolini continued to demonstrate his ambivalent attitudes toward the anarchists. On March 22, an anarchist named Biagio Masi was delegated by comrades in Piombino to kill Mussolini, whose Blackshirt squads were responsible for a mounting wave of bloody reaction. Instead of carrying out the deed, however, Masi confessed his mission to Mussolini, who placed the young man under his protection.[42] The very next day, Mussolini denounced the government for having kept Malatesta in prison without a trial for more than five months. With the anarchist movement in disarray following the arrests, Mussolini felt secure enough to call for Malatesta's provisional release, arguing that "a Malatesta danger does not exist."[43]

But as Mussolini penned these lines, anarchists became the center of a storm of controversy when Milan was rocked by a powerful explosion at the Teatro Diana. The blast killed twenty-one people and injured 172. Three young anarchists had planted the bomb in protest against the government's treatment of Malatesta and his comrades, who had begun a hunger strike in prison.[44] Feeling the pressure of the tremendous outcry that arose against the anarchists, both among the middle classes and among the hard-liners within his own Fascist movement, Mussolini reversed his previously indulgent stance and sprang to the defense of the established order. Fascist squads destroyed the editorial offices of *Umanita' Nova* as well as of the Socialist Party's *Avanti!* and they attacked the syndicalist headquarters of the Unione Sindacale Milanese. Denouncing the "barbaric" act, Mussolini blustered that innocent blood demanded "vengeance."[45]

In the reaction that followed the Diana bombing, Italian authorities expelled Eugene Lyons with the tacit approval of the American embassy. Lyons left Italy on May 25, just as the Sacco-Vanzetti trial opened in Boston.[46]

Italian consul Agostino Ferrante, concerned that Sacco and Vanzetti's anarchist beliefs would hurt their case, insisted on portraying them simply as criminal defendants, and when he visited them in prison before the trial began he urged them to avoid appearing "subversive" in court. Ferrante also seems to have gone to Judge Thayer's home in Worcester to explain the Italian government's position, which he later described to a reporter this way: "The Italian authorities are deeply interested in the case of Sacco and Vanzetti, and this trial will be closely followed by them. They have complete confidence that the trial will be conducted solely as a criminal proceeding, without reference to the political or social beliefs of anyone involved."[47] Ambassador Vittorio Rolandi Ricci assured Italians in Boston privately that his government would do everything it could to help the accused.[48]

On July 15—the same day that Malatesta was found innocent and released from prison—Ferrante reported the guilty verdict to his embassy, along with his own opinion that Thayer had been prejudiced.[49] The defense committee immediately sent telegrams to Rome, and within weeks communist and socialist deputies raised the issue again in parliament. Taking a different approach, socialist Alberto Malatesta asked the government what it proposed to do for "the protection of emigrants." The General Confederation of Labor telegraphed to President Warren G. Harding protesting the proceedings. In response, the government of Prime Minister Ivanoe Bonomi ordered Rolandi Ricci to "take every possible step toward the [American] government to secure a pardon for our nationals Sacco and Vanzetti," but it then decided to wait until the appeals process was concluded before making a formal request for a pardon. From Villafalletto in northern Italy, Vanzetti's father sent a personal appeal to Bonomi but received no response.[50]

Errico Malatesta, now editing *Umanita' Nova* in Rome, called on Italian workers "to make their voices heard loudly in every way possible."[51] At first he had argued that Sacco and Vanzetti had been found guilty because they were anarchists, but then he recognized that a more effective tactic would be to project them as Italian emigrants who were mistreated by foreign governments. "As anarchists they are devoted but modest militants. . . . But in addition to being anarchists, they are also Italians: they belong to a rejected and despised people who can be murdered without concern. Will the patriots of Italy allow that?"[52]

Unlike Sacco, who seemed resigned to his fate, Vanzetti was optimistic about the impact of the Italian protests. "The Italian workers," he wrote to his sister, "have our lives and our liberty in their hands because they have the power to make tyrants across the ocean tremble. . . . Even the government of Italy will be forced by the pressure of public opinion to intervene seriously."[53] In Italy, anarchists joined with socialists, communists, syndicalists, and republicans in protest meetings, the first of which took place in Rome and Bergamo in late September, and in Milan and Bologna on October 2.[54] Over the next three weeks, rallies were coordinated in more than sixty cities. The Liberal government, worried over the strength of public sentiment, refused to issue permits for the use of public facilities, confiscated leaflets, prevented organizers from marching, and ordered prefects to protect American consulates and citizens against possible anarchist violence.[55]

A second, smaller wave of demonstrations took place in January 1922, while protests were also held in a dozen countries in Europe and Latin America and bombs were planted in Paris, Lisbon, Rio de Janeiro, and Marseilles.[56] Telegrams demanding justice for Sacco and Vanzetti from local worker organizations flooded the American embassy, some containing threats of violence. In Rome, the *Arditi del Popolo-an* armed leftist group dedicated to fighting the Fascists declared that it would kill all American diplomats in Italy should Sacco and Vanzetti be executed.[57]

But although most of the Italian demonstrations were peaceful, they had the effect of inflaming the already raw tensions between Fascists and radicals. For two years, the level of Fascist violence had risen steadily. By the spring of 1921 Lyons had found that the "guerilla war" waged by the Fascists was making agitation in favor of Sacco and Vanzetti difficult, and Malatesta had begun to write with concern about the "civil war" that was ripping apart Italian society.[58] Mussolini found it increasingly difficult to control his Blackshirt squads in the provinces, where they were beating and killing socialists, anarchists, and other radicals without distinction. In many instances, therefore, the Sacco-

Vanzetti rallies became occasions for confrontation between left-wing activists and local Blackshirts: while anarchists and socialists combined attacks against Fascism with speeches on behalf of Sacco and Vanzetti, Fascist squads counter-demonstrated, organized marches, and threatened violence. In Massa-Carrara, an anarchist stronghold, organizers at first agreed to let the secretary of the local Fascio speak but then refused him entry, and in Pavia both sides took part in a public debate. More often than not, police had to keep the two factions apart in order to prevent bloodshed.[59]

The tensions between Sacco and Vanzetti's radical supporters and Mussolini's Blackshirts was complicated by the fact that the Fascist movement had been undergoing an ideological transformation from its original left-wing program to the more rightist orientation of the provincial *squadristi*. Indeed, the Blackshirts had already forced Mussolini to abandon the truce with the socialists he had signed in August 1921. Despite the attitudes of his more intransigent followers, however, the Sacco-Vanzetti case reminded Mussolini of the Ettor-Giovannitti affair that had so stirred his radical imagination a decade earlier. Nor could his instinct for propaganda fail to recognize that in the plight of "the good shoemaker and the poor fish peddler" facing the electric chair, the left—and especially the anarchists—had found an energizing symbol around which to rally their forces and influence public opinion. Personal inclinations therefore combined with political instincts to persuade Mussolini to take a public stand in favor of Sacco and Vanzetti.

It was Malatesta who, having appropriated Sacco and Vanzetti's Italian nationality in the campaign to save them, showed Mussolini the way out of his dilemma. At a meeting in Milan on October 31, Mussolini presented the following motion: "The Central Committee of the *Fasci Italiani di Combattimento* . . . while in no way intending to associate itself with the demonstrations staged by those extremist elements, enemies of Fascism, who exploit the situation to increase their demagogic propaganda, formally invites the minister of foreign affairs to be vigilant and to take action to prevent these suspects and innocent men from being condemned—as has happened before—merely because they belong to the Italian race and the Italian nation."[60] The program of the newly created Fascist National Party, adopted the following month, contained a provision calling for "protection of Italians living abroad."[61]

While Mussolini now supported Sacco and Vanzetti, the Liberal government continued to try to quiet the protests in Italy, ostensibly to prevent anti-American sentiments from hurting the chances of a favorable appeal.[62] Behind the scenes the foreign ministry cooperated with Moore in securing a postponement of a deportation order for Frank Lopez, a defense witness who worked for the defense committee. From Rome came the order that "at the opportune moment nothing must be overlooked in obtaining clemency."[63] But when a socialist deputy protested the expulsion of Lyons and the government's failure to help Sacco and Vanzetti, Rome responded that the radicalization of the case had worked against the defendants, and that Lyons had been "invited" to leave Italy because of his subversive activities. Ambassador Rolandi Ricci underscored the government's position, reporting a growing sense of American irritation over the foreign protests. When Judge Thayer eventually denied the first defense motion, Ferrante blamed the "deplorable agitation."[64]

Toward the end of 1921, the defense committee issued a public criticism of the Italian government for the first time, and Vanzetti became convinced that Rome was working against their interests. Some members of the defense committee advised Moore to cut off all contact with Italian authorities, and when Felicani insisted that a formal diplomatic protest be lodged in Washington and Rome, Ferrante told him that was impossible.[65] In March, after Mucci raised further questions in parliament, Ferrante asked Moore to try to stop his criticisms of the American legal system. Nevertheless, as Sacco and Vanzetti awaited the outcome of appeals and motions, Ferrante acted on his own initiative to aid the defense by soothing public opinion in Boston.[66]

To counter Sacco and Vanzetti's radical profile, Rolandi Ricci began to employ the same nationalist strategy adopted by Mussolini, declaring in a speech in Philadelphia that he was responsible for acting as "guardian of the Italian colonies in the United States," implying thereby that such protection was needed. But while the statement drew sharp criticism from the American press and an apology from Rome, the ambassador assured his superiors that he would continue to assist Sacco and Vanzetti "for the dignity of the good Italian name." *La Notizia,* the Boston newspaper for which Aldino Felicani worked, quoted him as saying that the conviction of Sacco and Vanzetti had as much to do with their being Italian as with their being anarchists.[67]

Mussolini was concerned that Rolandi Ricci's Philadelphia remarks had damaged relations with Washington, and when he became prime minister on October 29, 1922, he appointed a new ambassador, Prince Gelasio Caetani. Mussolini had actually made clear his desire for friendship with Washington even before he assumed power.[68] The day he arrived in Rome to form his government, he told foreign journalists that war debts and immigration policy were the two main issues in Italian American relations, and he wrote to Secretary of State Charles Evans Hughes of his desire for close economic cooperation between the two countries. Over the next several years the new premier sought to lift restrictions on Italian immigration imposed by the Immigration Act of 1921 and to secure American loans.[69]

In the first years of his government, Mussolini's treatment of the anarchist movement was distinguished from that of the previous government only by the violence of the Blackshirts. On October 29, 1922, while small bands of anarchists fought to keep the *squadristi* from occupying Rome, in Piazza Cavour Fascists mounted a picture of Malatesta on bayonets and burned it. The following night, Blackshirts broke into the offices of *Umanita' Nova* and partially wrecked the presses, a task completed later in a second assault. Malatesta managed to put out two additional issues of the paper, both of which contained blistering attacks on Mussolini, before it was closed down permanently.[70] Malatesta himself was not personally harmed but with his paper gone he had now, at the age of sixty-nine, to make a living once again by working as an electrical mechanic; for the rest of his life he remained under constant police surveillance.[71]

Hardly was Mussolini in office when the Sacco-Vanzetti case forced itself on his attention. On December 4, Vanzetti's sister, Luigia, addressed a petition to him. "It is true," she wrote, "that as the accused are subversives they cannot have your sympathy, but we believe that justice must be practiced above all ideas and all parties." At the same time, one of the three McAnarney brothers assisting Fred Moore went to Rome to ask Mussolini's government for help. Ambassador Caetani was ordered to approach both federal and Massachusetts officials "in favor of our fellow countrymen." But in view of recent proposals to restrict immigration further, Caetani advised Mussolini not to make a major point of contention out of Sacco and Vanzetti, who were hardly the kind of Italians that American officials wanted in their country.[72]

Mussolini's coming to power divided the Italian immigrant community in the United States. Italian American Fascists were as politically reactionary as their counterparts in Italy. Agostino De Biasi, who founded the first *Fascio* in the United States as early as 1921, used his journal, *Il Carroccio* (New York), to attack immigrant "subversives" as brutally as did the American authorities and carried only brief factual notices about the case. Domenico Trombetta, himself a former anarchist, followed suit in his *Grido della Stirpe* (New York).[73]

But while the leftist papers pounded away at the Fascists, only the anarchist *L'Adunata dei Refrattari and Il Martello* stood unflinchingly by Sacco and Vanzetti. The mainstream Italian-language press took the more cautious position of New York's *Il Progresso Italo-Americano*, the largest-circulation Italian paper, which condemned Sacco and Vanzetti's political ideas but expressed solidarity for fellow Italians falsely accused. The rise of nationalist sentiment among Italian Americans in the 1920s, fueled by Fascist propaganda, encouraged many immigrants to rally behind Sacco and Vanzetti while simultaneously exalting Mussolini.[74]

One exception occurred on March 4, 1923, at a Sacco-Vanzetti rally in Lawrence, Massachusetts, where someone in the audience shouted "Down with Italy, down with Fascism!" A fight then erupted between Fascists and anti-Fascists, during which the head of the local Italian veterans' organization was wounded.[75] As in Italy, violent clashes between Fascists and Sacco-Vanzetti activists in the United States worried Mussolini, for they raised American fears of Fascism and threatened to disrupt the good rapport he hoped to establish with Washington. When Caetani urged Mussolini to bring the American *Fasci* under centralized control from Rome, Mussolini went further by assuring the United States that he would close down all the *Fasci* in North America rather than damage relations between the two countries.[76]

Helping to make the Sacco-Vanzetti case an Italian rather than an ideological issue for Mussolini was Italian journalist Luigi Barzini. In December 1922, Barzini, who had not yet declared himself a Fascist, had founded an Italian daily in New York, *Il Corriere d'America*. In March 1923, Barzini threw the paper behind the defense, noting that "whatever ideas Sacco and Vanzetti have are unimportant." He urged the creation of an Italian American "united front" and persuaded state senator Salvatore Cotillo and Congressman Fiorello La Guardia to help the defense.[77] Barzini then accused the defense committee of being interested only in subversive propaganda, and he formed a committee of his own—the

Comitato Pro Sacco-Vanzetti—run by a group of conservative Italian American *prominenti.* Giovanni Di Silvestro, one of the Comitato's vice presidents and a former socialist turned Fascist, brought the membership of the Sons of Italy behind the defense. These efforts by conservative Italian Americans even prompted support from Carlo Barsotti, publisher of *Il Progresso.*[78]

Word soon reached Italy that Sacco, after going on a hunger strike and attempting suicide, was confined to the Bridgewater State Hospital for the Criminally Insane. Deputies Mucci and Costantino Lazzari responded to this news by presenting Mussolini with a harshly worded parliamentary question demanding to know what he had done to help "our fellow countrymen Vanzetti and Sacco." Mussolini wired immediately to Washington for an update on the case and was told that, if the defense motions were turned down, there would be an appeal to the Massachusetts Supreme Judicial Court. "Then there would remain," Caetani noted, "the possibility of asking the governor of the state for a pardon."[79]

That fall Caetani made two direct efforts to influence the case. The ambassador sent Senator Henry Cabot Lodge a "personal" request that he use his influence with Massachusetts officials on behalf of Sacco and Vanzetti. Lodge refused. The next month, Caetani went to the White House; but Coolidge, in a thinly veiled allusion to Thayer, lectured the ambassador on the impropriety of suggesting that Massachusetts' judges were biased. Caetani cautioned Mussolini that Coolidge gave him "to understand that any action by the embassy [in the case] would not be viewed favorably." In any event, Caetani would not have taken either step had he thought Mussolini would object.[80]

When Mussolini answered the parliamentary question in December, he took Mucci and Lazzari to task for not having posed it "in those respectful terms that should be used for a friendly nation such as the United States of America." Failing to mention Caetani's contacts with either Lodge or Coolidge, Mussolini explained that the federal government had no power over state courts, and that any move by Italy in the case would be considered an unwarranted interference in the internal affairs of the United States. He assured parliament, however, that the government would help Sacco and Vanzetti with actions that were "compatible with international usage and [would] be helpful . . . to our fellow countrymen." He also warned against further demonstrations.[81]

For the next two years, public attention died down as the case entered a prolonged phase of legal maneuvers in the Massachusetts courts. These efforts culminated in October 1924 in Judge Thayer's denial of all defense motions and his infamous remark, "Did you see what I did with those anarchistic bastards the other day?" Anxious to know whether the moment had come to ask the governor to grant a pardon, Mussolini telegraphed Washington to learn whether the case would go to the state supreme court. The legal defense, now headed by William G. Thompson, took the case to the Supreme Judicial Court, which did not rule until the spring of 1926.[82]

The same period saw Mussolini faced with major preoccupations at home. The murder of socialist deputy Giacomo Matteotti in the summer of 1924 shook the Fascist regime, leading Mussolini to declare a dictatorship and unleash a new wave of Blackshirt violence against his opposition. The Fascist reign of terror was vividly described to the defense committee by a friend of Felicani living in Italy. In November 1925, after the regime was stabilized, finance minister Giuseppe Volpi di Misurata went to the United States to arrange settlement of Italian war debts and to discuss private loans from American banks. Concerned not to offend American sensibilities, Volpi advised Mussolini, as Caetani had done earlier, to control the Fascists in the United States and abandon efforts to help Sacco and Vanzetti. In January the J. P. Morgan Company announced a $100 million loan to Italy.[83]

The case came back into public focus on May 12, 1926, when the Supreme Judicial Court of Massachusetts denied the defense's appeal. Taking the high ground, Vanzetti wrote to Malatesta that he "not be pained for us: no comrade should fear for our fate; continue the sacred struggle for a truer justice, for liberty. We will know how to face our destiny." In Italy, Sacco and Vanzetti's anarchist comrades joined forces once again with socialists, communists, and republicans in another round of protests, now seeking to obtain signatures on petitions to be sent to the American embassy asking for a new trial. Malatesta, who most likely drafted the petition, suggested that the ambassador not view the request as either a political statement or "an offense against the dignity of the nation you represent," but simply as an act of solidarity with the legal defense in Massachusetts. Nevertheless, when the communist paper L'Unita published appeals for signatures on the petitions, the police confiscated the issue, no doubt in response to American ambassador Henry P. Fietcher's complaints about these activities.[84]

Although Mussolini tightened his grip on the anarchists in 1926, meetings and protests continued throughout the summer. In defiance of the new repression, Malatesta published a portion of Vanzetti's letter in *Pensiero e Volonta'*, a new bimonthly first issued in January 1924. However, the police confiscated the issue before it could be released, along with copies of the petitions. Fascist agents searched Malatesta's apartment and seized both Vanzetti's letter and a bust of Matteotti. Thereafter Malatesta remained virtually under house arrest. The police also began periodic searches of the Vanzetti family home in Villafalletto, and in Torremaggiore Sacco's brother Sabino was placed under surveillance.[85]

Upon learning that the Supreme Judicial Court had turned down the appeal, Giacomo De Martino (who had replaced Caetani as ambassador to Washington in January 1925) advised Mussolini that the radicals had so prejudiced American opinion against Sacco and Vanzetti that even a request for pardon would probably be denied. But Mussolini, pressured by still another deputy and the renewal of protests in Italy, wired back, "let me know if you think it possible to take steps to obtain a pardon for the condemned."[86] De Martino spoke with a State Department official about the matter but was told that it was outside federal jurisdiction. De Martino added that although Massachusetts authorities seemed determined not to give in to the pressure from radicals, he could speak privately with members of the U.S. Supreme Court if the case were appealed to them. Dino Grandi, undersecretary at the foreign ministry, scrawled across the ambassador's report, "Telegraph De Martino to take steps in Boston." Mussolini added his own instructions, authorizing De Martino to contact the U.S. Supreme Court justices if the case went before the federal bench.[87]

But while Mussolini was fully prepared to intervene on behalf of Sacco and Vanzettti, action by the Italian government was now strongly discouraged by defense attorney William Thompson, who feared a reaction from American officials. From Boston, Ferrante reiterated to bleak outlook, citing the "rigid, inflexible character" of Governor Fuller of Massachusetts. In a look meeting on June 26, Thompson told Ferrante that no request should be made for a pardon until legal avenues had been exhausted. When Ferrante asked whether an Italian approach to federal justices would be useful should the case go to the Supreme Court, Thompson warned adamantly against any such effort.

Nevertheless, De Martino seemed anxious for concrete action and advised Mussolini that he was prepared to act in concert with the defense should the need arise for last-minute maneuvers. The next month, while vacationing in Italy, De Martino told a reporter for *L'Impero* that he had been working on behalf of Sacco and Vanzetti because they were Italians and because they were innocent. A career diplomat, De Martino would never have made such a statement except by calculation, knowing full well that his remarks would be monitored by the U.S. embassy in Rome.[88]

Before De Martino returned to Washington, an article in the Paris edition of the *Herald Tribune* announced that Sacco and Vanzetti were to be executed in two days. Mussolini seemed worried until the Washington embassy assured him that the story was untrue, and Grandi rushed a correction to all prefects in order to forestall radical protests.[89] As the date for Thayer's ruling on a defense motion approached, De Martino had one of his deputies speak with Assistant Secretary of State Joseph Grew. Grew was told that, although the Italian government respected the principle of judicial independence, Rome wished to underscore the importance that the case held for Italians, many of whom had long assumed the innocence of the defendants.[90]

Twice during the last months of 1926, anarchists tried to assassinate Mussolini, who responded by intensifying the campaign against them and virtually crushing the movement.[91] He also instituted new mechanisms for repression, including the Special Tribunal for the Defense of the State and the reinstatement of the death penalty for assassination attempts against the king or the head of government.[92] Yet Mussolini still persisted in trying to help Sacco and Vanzetti.

In October, news that Thayer had denied the defense motion was reported in the semiofficial newspapers *Il Popolo di Roma* and *Il Giornale d'Italia*, sparking new protests on both sides of the Atlantic. Radicals in Italy were now under severe restrictions, but in the United States a massive rally was organized in November at New York's Madison Square Garden by the communist Sacco-Vanzetti Emergency Committee. Speakers included Norman Thomas and Arthur Garfield Hays; La Guardia sent a telegram of endorsement but did not attend.[93]

As 1927 opened, the pace of events intensified. In January, Thompson appealed the case once again to the Supreme Judicial Court of Massachusetts. April, however, brought another defeat; on the ninth Thayer sentenced Sacco and Vanzetti to death by electrocution, the

original execution date of July 10 eventually being moved to August 23.
While cries of outrage arose again throughout Europe, Ferrante and De
Martino now believed that the only hope lay with President Coolidge,
who might be able to influence Fuller to grant a pardon. De Martino
suggested that he meet with Coolidge for this purpose, and Mussolini
telegraphed on April 9, "by all means approach the president of the
United States on behalf of Sacco and Vanzetti."[94]

Meanwhile the defense committee—which Ferrante described to
Mussolini for the first time as being full of "ardent anti-Fascists"[95]—
asked Fuller to form a special advisory committee to look into the
conduct of the trial. On June 1, after Vanzetti sent the governor a petition
for clemency, the so-called Lowell Committee was appointed. Ferrante
grew more optimistic, especially when the governor invited him to a
private meeting to discuss the case on July 20. At the end of an hour and
a half, Ferrante left Fuller with the thought that Sacco and Vanzetti had
surely suffered enough during seven years of imprisonment.[96]

Later that same day Ferrante appeared, at the request of the defense
counsel, before the Lowell Committee, where he made an "eloquent, if
unofficial, plea on behalf of Sacco and Vanzetti." After his testimony,
Ferrante invited the governor's secretary, Herman MacDonald, to lunch,
a move that had Thompson and fellow attorney Herbert Ehrmann
wondering whether the consul intended to convey to Fuller a secret
message from Mussolini, but apparently they were unaware of the
meeting earlier that day.[97] In fact, news of Ferrante's meeting with Fuller
encouraged Mussolini, who on July 23 wired instructions that his
personal views should be conveyed to the governor:

> My opinion is that the governor could commute the sentence and
> release our nationals from the terrible circumstance in which they have
> languished for so many years. While I do not believe that clemency
> would mean a victory for the subversives, it is certain that the execution
> of Sacco-Vanzetti would provide the pretext for a vast and continuous
> subversive agitation throughout the world. The Fascist government,
> which is strongly authoritarian and does not give quarter to the
> bolsheviks, very often employs clemency in individual cases. The
> governor of Massachusetts should not lose the opportunity for a
> humanitarian act whose repercussions would be especially positive in
> Italy.

The governor, Ferrante reported to Mussolini, "refrained from making any comment."[98]

Without waiting for a reply either from Fuller or from his earlier telegram to De Martino, Mussolini had already drafted his letter of July 24 to Ambassador Fletcher.[99] Stressing that his plea was "strictly personal." Mussolini authorized Fletcher to make use of it in any way that he thought best. Fletcher, whose private diary speaks of Mussolini as a man "whom I like and admire very much," immediately sent a translation of the letter to Secretary of State Frank Kellogg, and the following morning wired Kellogg for instructions as to a response. Kellogg's answer was stiff: Fletcher was to make only a "personal and entirely informal, oral communication" stating that "the subject matter is one over which the Federal Government has no jurisdiction or control." The prime minister's letter was forwarded to Boston.[100]

As the date for the executions approached, the defense filed further motions and appeals in the Massachusetts courts and a number of writs before justices of the U.S. Supreme Court. In early August, after the Lowell Committee issued its findings, Fuller refused to grant clemency. De Martino detailed for Mussolini the "decisively negative atmosphere" he encountered in the White House and the State Department, reporting that Undersecretary Grew had insisted that the threat of radical agitation could not be allowed to influence the U.S. government. Assistant Secretary of State Castle told De Martino that there was no question of Sacco and Vanzetti's guilt and that the defense counsel had stirred up demonstrations abroad in order to secure financial contributions for their legal fees. In a subsequent talk, Castle argued that the government could not possibly give in to "mob rule" and to the pressure orchestrated from "Moscow." De Martino concluded that there was no hope in "such an irreducibly hostile ambience. Everything possible has been done." In Boston, Ferrante spoke with Fuller's secretary and other "highly placed persons," making it clear that Mussolini would be willing to appeal personally to the governor, but "everyone advised me in no uncertain terms against any further action, which could not fail to encounter a categorical refusal."[101]

Although the efforts of Mussolini and his representatives had been made discreetly, the press detected signs of activity. On August 5, Michele Sacco sent Mussolini a moving appeal to help save his son. Mussolini published the letter in his official newspaper along with his reply. "For some time," he explained, "I have occupied myself assiduously with the situation of Sacco and Vanzetti" and have "done everything possible compatible with international law to save them from execution." Unaware of Mussolini's behind-the-scenes actions, on August 9 a desperate defense committee cabled its own disguised plea to Mussolini: "As head of the Italian nation we address to you an appeal from the depths of our hearts in behalf of our two countrymen. A word from you will do more than that of anyone else to prevent the completion of this tragic injustice and the consequent upsetting of international relations."[102]

In Italy the underground anarchist and communist movements reacted to these events by distributing leaflets attacking the "complicity" of the Fascist regime with "American capitalism" and blaming Mussolini for not registering a formal protest with the U.S. government. Letters, newspaper articles, songs, and other propaganda materials were smuggled into Italy by anarchist comrades in the United States, although much of this material was confiscated by the police. In large industrial cities like Turin and small rural villages, printed handbills and handwritten leaflets were distributed calling for "Death to Governor Fuller," and one handbill purportedly quoted a letter from Vanzetti to Mexican anarchists saying, "I am convinced that any other man at the head of the Italian state would be enough to save us."[103]

Until now, the Italian press, kept under tight control by Mussolini, had been carefully restrained in its reporting of the case. But in a deliberate effort by Mussolini to pressure the Americans, major newspapers began to express what Eugene Lyons called "a curiously muffled excitement." *Il Popolo d'Italia* even sent a reporter to Torremaggiore, where he interviewed Sacco's father and brother Sabino and found the village "confident that Mussolini and the Fascist Government would do all possible to save the condemned men." *La Stampa* of Turin published a favorable interview with a childhood friend of Vanzetti and, while visiting Vanzetti's home in Vallafalletto and Sacco's family in Torremaggiore, the American anti-Fascist journalist Gertrude Winslow found that "we need have no fear of Fascism as far as our errand was concerned—all factions were one in their sympathy for the two condemned Italians." While *Il Giornale d'Italia* printed a statement by Giuseppe Andrower, who had testified that he had seen Sacco in the Italian consulate in Boston on the day he was supposed to have taken part in the South Braintree crime, *La Tribuna* did an interview with Count Ignazio Thaon di Revel, head of the Fascist League of North America. Di Revel asserted that while Fascists were ready to fight to the death against the political ideas of Sacco and Vanzetti, he too had appealed to Governor Fuller. Statements of support also appeared in *Il Tevere and Il Messaggero*. In the United States, an unnamed source revealed to the *New York Times* that Mussolini had written a personal letter on behalf of the defendants, but the embassy "denied emphatically" that it had been instructed to make a formal protest against the execution.[104]

These efforts, together with last-minute legal moves, were to no avail. On August 21, ten thousand protesters gathered in New York's Union Square, while in Boston crowds were dispersed by the police. On August 22, as Fuller refused to stay the execution, the Italian ambassador had a last meeting with Kellogg. De Martino asked the secretary of state about the latest developments and whether the case possibly came within the jurisdiction of the U.S. Supreme Court. When he again raised the specter of radical agitation, Kellogg replied blandly, "if they had not been members of an anarchist group, they would have been hung years ago." Shortly past midnight, Ferrante wired Mussolini, "Execution took place few moments ago."[105]

In Rome, people stood in stunned silence outside newspaper offices,[106] which were now permitted to editorialize about the case and criticize the United States. Some papers attributed "Fuller's crime" to the mechanistic, antihumanistic nature of American civilization[107] and underscored the irony of a Fascist government trying to save the lives of two anarchists.[108] A few blamed the executions on the radical protests,[109] but only the intransigent Roberto Farinacci's *Il Regime Fascista* thought the two anarchists deserved their fate.[110]

Mussolini's personal reaction to the executions is unknown, but Arnaldo Mussolini, editor of *Il Popolo d'Italia*, spoke for his brother when he attacked the "inflexible" American government, contrasting it with the Italian system that had allowed Violet Gibson—the Anglo-Irish woman who had tried to kill Mussolini—to return to her own country.[111]

Political calculation and diplomatic tact had caused Mussolini to vary the intensity of his public support for Sacco and Vanzetti. Between 1920 and 1922, he saw their plight as a useful weapon in his struggle against the socialists and the communists, and when he saw the potential for making them a nationalist symbol, he appropriated for their cause. After coming into office, he believed that support for Sacco and Vanzetti would help bind Italian American loyalties to the Fascist regime, which claimed to act as the protector of Italian emigrants abroad.[112] Yet once in power, Mussolini felt unable to act as decisively as he wished because the case could potentially hinder efforts to establish good relations with the United States and hurt chances for American loans and a more favorable immigration policy.[113] A more strident approach, he feared, would elicit the ire of U.S. authorities, including Governor Fuller, whose presidential aspirations had come to his attention.[114] Even the anarchists recognized his delicate position,[115] and Mussolini himself was embittered by his dilemma.[116]

Raison d'état alone does not explain why Mussolini, even while cracking down on the anarchists at home, strained his ideological credibility as a Fascist and put his prestige at risk by making personal appeals on behalf of Sacco and Vanzetti. The evidence also suggests that a lingering, if perverse, nostalgia for what he identified as his own youthful anarchist impulses remained imbedded in his psyche. His propensity for violence and direct action, along with his inclination to see himself as a rebel who lived in defiance of bourgeois morality, led him to feel a spiritual kinship with the anarchists.[117] The anti-Fascist writer Giuseppe A. Borgese explained Mussolini this way: "He said . . . that every anarchist is a dictator who failed. His road to greatness consisted in making, of the anarchist who failed in him, the dictator who won."[118] As a true anarchist, Malatesta—who never thought of Mussolini as a genuine revolutionary—saw the matter differently. "It's the same old story," he said, "of the brigand who becomes the policeman!"[119]

Notes

1. John Dos Passos, The Big Money, vol. 3 of the trilogy U.S.A. as quoted in John P. Diggins, The Rise and Fall of the American Left (New York and London, 1992), p.143. On Dos Passos's involvement in the Sacco-Vanzetti case see John D. Baker, "Italian Anarchism and the American Dream—the view of John Dos Passos," in Rudolph J. Veccoli (Staten Island, N.Y., 1972), pp. 30-39; and Louis Joughin and Edmund M. Morgan, The Legacy of Sacco and Vanzetti (New York, 1948), pp. 438-44. In 1927 Dos Passos wrote Facing the Chair: Story of Americanization of Two Foreignborn Workmen for the Sacco-Vanzetti Defense Crime Committee.

2. Vanzetti to Alice Stone Blackwell, September 15, 1924, in eds. Marion Denman Frankfuter and Gardner Jackson, *The Letters of Sacco and Vanzetti* (New York, 1930), p. 128.

3. Mussolini is quoted by Yvon De Begnac, *Taccuini Mussolini,* ed. Francesco Perfetti (Bologna, 1990), pp. 612, 413.

4. Gaetano Salvemini, *The Origins of Fascism in Italy,* ed. Roberto Vivarelli (New York, 1973) p.70, and *The Fascist Dictatorship in Italy* (New York, 1927), pp. 10-11. See also Enzo Santarelli, *La revisione del marxismo in Italia: Studi di critica storica,* 2nd ed. (Milan, 1977), p. 263. On the sources of Mussolini's intellectual development, "Socialismo rivoluzionario e 'mussilinismo' alla vigilia del primo conflitto mondiale" in his *Origini del Fascism* (Urbino, 1963), pp. 13-88; Sergio Romano, "Sorel e Mussolini," *Storia Contemporanea* 15 (February 1984): 123-31; Zeev Sternhell, with Mario Sznajder and Maia Asheri, *The Birth of Fascist Ideology: From Cultural Rebellion to Political Revolution,* trans. David Maisel (Princeton, N.J., 1994), pp. 195-232; David Roberts, *The Syndicalist Tradition and Italian Fascism* (Manchester, 1979); A.J. Gregor, *Young Mussolini and the Intellectual Origins of Fascism* (Berkley and Los Angeles, 1979). Italian revolutionary syndicalism should be distinguished from anarco-syndicalism: the former, which arose as an effort to revise Marxism, had a profound influence on Mussolini's thought and provided early Fascism with some of its leading figures, including Edmondo Rossoni, Alceste De Ambris, and Angelo O. Olivetti; the latter, however, arose out of the Bakuninist tradition and was led by anarchists, such as Armando Borghi, who worked for anarchist goals through the syndicalist movement. For the anarchist view of the philosophical and tactical differences among various currents of Italian sydicalism, see Armando Borghi, *Mezzo secolo di anarchia* (1898-1945) (Naples, 1954), pp. 87-96.

5. De Begnac, *Taccuini,* pp. 7-19; Nunzio Pernicone, "Carlo Tresca: Life and Death of a Revolutionary," in *Italian Americans: The Search for a Usable Past,* ed. Richard N. Juliani and Philip V. Cannistraro (New York, 1989), p. 217; Dorothy Gallager, *All the Right Enemies: The Life and Murder of Carlo Tresca* (New Brunswick, N.J., and London, 1988), p. 22; De Felice, *Mussolini il rivoluzionario,* pp. 5-8, 40; Gaudens Megaro, *Mussolini in the Making* (Boston and New York, 1938), p. 102; Gherardo Bozzetti, *Mussolini direttore dell' "Avanti!"* (Milan, 1979), p. 130, n. 16.

6. Edoardo Dusmel and Duilio Susmel, eds., *Opera Omnia di Benito Mussolini,* 37 vols. (Florence, 1951-63), 2:274; 3:136, 141, 148, 286, 4:195 (hereafter cited as *OO*); De Felice, *Mussolini il rivoluzionario,* p.169; Megaro, p. 319; Henri Arvon, "L'actualité de la pensée de Max Stirner," in *Anarchici e anarchia nel mondo contemoraneo* (Turin, 1971), p. 286. Mussolini's translations of Kroptkin's works were for Luigi Bertoni's Swiss anarchist publication, *Reveil.* In 1909 he translated the preface of Elisee Reclus's *La Terre* for *Il Popolo.*

7. Mussolini's references to Bresci are in *OO,* 3:148, 286; and 4:165. Mussolini's remark on royal assassination was a paraphrase of Umberto I's own comment on avoiding the murder attempt by Pietro Acciarito in 1897.

8. Mussolini's articles about Ettor and Giovannitti are in *OO,* 4:146, 180-81, 239-41, 252. See also Megaro, pp. 201-9; Clay C. Burton, "Italian American Relations and the Case of Sacco and Vanzetti," in Vecoli, ed., p. 66; Paul Avrich, *Sacco and Vanzetti: The Anarchist Background* (Princeton, N.J., 1991), p. 26. Mussolini's attitudes toward the United States during his socialist days were typical of those expressed in the newspapers of the Italian left. See Rudolph J. Veccoli, "'Free Country': The American Republic Viewed by the Italian Left, 1880-1920," in *In the Shadow of Liberty: Immigrants, Workers, and Citizens in the American Republic, 1880-1920,* ed. Marianne Debouzy (Paris, 1988), pp. 35-56; and Arnaldo Testi, "L'immagine degli Stati Uniti nella stampa socialista italiana (1886-1914)," in *Italia e America dal settecento all' eta' dell' imperialismo,* ed. Giogio Spini et al. (Padova, 1976), pp. 313-50. Nicola Sacco had worked on behalf of Ettor and Giovannitti's defense in 1912.

9. Raffaele Schiavina, *Sacco e Vanzetti: Cause e fini di delitto di Stato* (Paris, 1927), p. 108; Howard Fast, *The Passion of Sacco and Vanzetti* (New York, 1953), pp. 93-100; interview between Paul Avrich and Spencer Sacco, January 8, 1987. See also "Come Mussolini si e' dis interssato del caso Sacco e Vanzetti," *Il Nuovo Mondo* (New York) (August 12, 1927).

10. Quoted in Salvatore J. La Gumina, *The Immigrants Speak: Italian Americans Tell Their Story* (Staten Island, N.Y., 1979), p. 29.

11. Burton, p. 67; Megaro, p. 209; Ronald Creagh, *Sacco et Vanzetti* (Paris, 1984), p. 190.

12. John P. Diggins, *Mussolini and Fascism: The View from America* (Princeton, N.J., 1972), p. 270; Claudia Damiani, *Mussolini e gli Stati*

Uniti, 1922-1935 (Bologna, 1980), p. 277; remarks by Luisa Cetti, in *Sacco-Vanzetti: Developments and Reconsiderations—1979* (Boston, 1982), pp. 98-99; M. Sylvers, "Sacco, Nicola e Vanzetti, Bartolomeo," in *Il movimento operaio italiamo: Dizionario biografico,* ed. Franco Andreucci and Tommaso Detti, 5 vols. (Rome, 1978), 4:439-40; Gian Giacomo Migone, *gli Stati Uniti e il fasismo: Alle origini dell'egemonica americana in Italia in Italia* (Milan, 1980); and David F. Schmitz, *The United States and Fascist Italy, in Italia 1922-1940* (Chapel Hill, N.C. and London, 1988), do not discuss the case.

13. Mussolini to Fletcher, July 24, 1927, and Fletcher's reply, dated July 25, in the Henry P. Fletcher Papers, General Correspondence, Container 13, Library of Congress; see also Fletcher State Department Decimal File, 1910-29 (hereafter RG 59), 311.6521 Sa 1/556, National Archives, Washington, D.C. (hereafter NA); an undated draft of the letter, with minor changes in Mussolini's hand, is in Servizio Affari Privati (hereafter SaP), 1902-37, b. 9, f 10837/1927, Archivio Storico del Ministero delgli Affari Esteri, Rome (hereafter ASMAE). Renzzo De Felice published the entire text in "Alcuni temi per la storia dell' emigrazione italiana," *Affari Sociali Internazionali* 1 (September 1973): 7-8, having located a copy in *Archivio di Gabinetto,* 1922-1929, pacco 142, ASMAE. Francis Russell published portions of the letter in his *Tragedy in Dedham: The Story of the Sacco-Vanzetti Case* (London, 1963), pp. 380-81; it is mentioned in Joughin and Morgan (n. 1 above), p. 278; Creagh, pp. 223-24; David Felix, *Protest: Sacco-Vanzetti and the Intellectuals* (Bloomington, Ind., and London, 1965), pp. 230-31; and Luigi Botta, *Sacco e Vanzetti: Giustiziata la verita* (Cavallermaggiore, 1978), p. 111.

14. Since the 1870s, Liberal Italy had regularly persecuted the anarchists, employing the full administrative, judicial, and military power of the state against them. See Nunzio Pernicone, *Italian Anarchism, 1864-1926* (Princeton, N.J., 1993); Carl Levy, "Italian Anarchism, 1870-1926" in *For Anarchism: History, Theory and Practice,* ed. David Goodway (London and New York, 1989), pp. 25-35: Richard Bach Jensen, "The Italian and Spanish Governments and the Repression of Anarchist Terrorism, 1890-1914" in *Essays in European History,* ed. June K. Burton (Lanham, Pa., New York and London, 1989), pp. 99-114.

15. There is no adequate treatment of anarchism during the Fascist period. For a general overview, see *Un trentennio di attivita anarchia*

(1914-1945) (Cesena, 1935); Enzo Santarelli, *Il socialismo anarchico in Italia,* 2nd ed. (Milan, 1973), pp. 192-96; Adriana Dada', *L'anarchismo in Italia: Fra moviemento e partito: Storia e documenti dell' anarchismo italiano* (Milan, 1984), pp. 80-101.

16. Mussolini's long-standing animosity for American capitalism reemerged during the period of the Italian Social Republic, 1943-45, when his speeches returned repeatedly to the theme of "American plutocracy." See, e.g., his "Rapporto agli ufficiali della divisone Littorio" (July 18, 1944), p. 104; "Roosevelt e le talpe chiechi" (January 16, 1944), pp. 296-98; "La democrazia dalle pance piene" (May 4, 1944), pp. 355-58; and "Nel gioco delle democrazie" (October 1, 1944), p. 410, all in *OO* (n. 6 above), vol. 31. See also De Begnac, *Taccuni* (n. 3 above), p. 612.

17. On Galleani's influence in the United States see Nunzio Pernicone, "Luigi Galleani and Italian Anarchist Terrorism in the United States," *Studi Emigrazione* 30 (September 1993): 469-88.

18. Avrich (n. 8 above), p. 135; Edward Holton James, "The Story of Mario Buda before the Jury of the World," typescript, dated February 21, 1928 (copy from the Harvard Law School Library provided to the author by Paul Avrich), p. 3. On the Red Scare in the United States see esp. Robert K. Murray, *Red Scare: A Study in National Hysteria, 1919-1920* (Minneapolis, 1955); William Preston, Jr., *Aliens and Dissenters: Federal Suppression of Radicals, 1903-1933* (Cambridge, Mass., 1963); and Julian F. Jaffe, *Crusade against Radicalism: New York during the Red Scare, 1914-1924* (Port Washington, N.Y., 1972). On the revolutionary situation and anarchism in postwar Italy see Vincenzo Mantovani, *Mazurka blu: La strage del Diana* (Milan, 1979), pp. 41-68; Dada', pp. 68070; Giuseppe Maione, *Il bienno rosso: Autonomia e spontaneita' operaia nel 1919-1920* (Bologna, 1975); Albert S. Lindeman, *The "Red Years": European Socialism vs. Bolshevism, 1919-1921* (Berkley, 1974): Giorgio Petracchi, *"La crisi del dopoguerra e la scissione socialista,"* in *Lezioni di Storia del partiti socialista italiano, 1892-1976,* ed. Stefano Caretti, Z. Ciuffoletti, and M. Degl'Innocenti (Florence, 1977), pp. 133-70.

19. The early Fascist movement attracted a number of former anarchists, including Massino Rocca, Mario Gioda, Edmondo Mazzucato, and Edordo Malusardi.

20. Report by Franklin Mott Gunther, counselor to U.S. embassy in Rome, October 1921, *Casellario Politico Centrale,* f. "Galleani, Luigi,"

Archivio Centrale dello Stato (herafter ACS); Ugo Fedeli, *Luigi Galleani: Quarant' anni di lotte revoluzionarie 1891-1931* (Forli, 1956), p. 163; Avrich, p. 208; *Un trentennio*, p. 27.

21. Mussolini, "Inchiodato alla gogna!" (September 5, 1919), *OO*, 14:419-20; see also "Una dichiarazione di anarchici milanesi" (September 2, 1919), in ibid., pp. 420-21. Mussolini was referring to an incident in 1902-3, when Serrati, then editor of *Il Proletario* of New York, publicly exposed Galleani's pseudonym and in so doing allowed the police to arrest Galleani in Barre, Vermont. In 1915, when Mussolini was expelled from the Italian Socialist Party, he resurrected the incident; see *OO*, 7:160-62, 164, 168-69, 177-79, 183-84, 471. On the Galleani-Serati polemic, see esp. Luigi Galleani, *Metodi della lotta socialista* (Sora, 1972); Fedeli, pp. 119-31, 161-62.

22. "Nel vicolo cieco" (April 23, 1920), in *OO*, 14:419-20; Giuseppe Mariani, *Memorie di un ex-terrorista* (Turin, 1953), p. 29. "One can disagree," Mussolini wrote in July with regard to Peter Kroptkin, "with the ideas of the great and irreproachable apostle of anarchism; but his honesty, his probity, his clarity of thought and his faith are beyond question." See Mussolini, "La nota di una illusione" (July 16, 1920), *OO*, 15:98. Mussolini's assessment of the renewed importance of anarchism was shared by socialist Anna Kuliscioff. See Paolo Finzi, *La nota persona: Errico Malatesta in Italia* (dicembre 1919/Luglio 1920) (Ragusa, 1990), pp. 119-20; Santarelli, *Il socialismo anarchicio*, pp. 185-92; Levy, pp. 63-64.

23. "E. Malatesta a Genova ospite di Giuletti," *Il Popolo d' Italia* (December 27, 1919), quoted in Finzi, p. 68; see also Mantovani, pp. 142-59; and De Felice, *Mussolini il rivoluzionario* (n. 4 above), pp. 203-4. Carlo Tresca also raised money for *Umanita' Nova*. See "Apello ai compagni del Nord America," *Il Martello* (November 15, 1920). The money for *Umanita' Nova* was, however, eventually turned over instead to the Sacco-Vanzetti Defense Committee.

24. Eno Mecheri, *Chi ha tradito?* (Milan, 1947), pp. 33-34.

25. Cited in Emilio Gentile, *Le origini dell ideologia fascista* (Rome-Bari, 1975), p. 188, n. 28; see also Mussolini, "Note politiche" (April 20, 1920), in *OO* (n. 6 above), 15:105-7; and *L'ora del fascismo!* (August 21, 1920), in ibid., pp. 271-72, 286.

26. *Un trentennio* (n. 15 above), p. 25; William Young and David E. Kaiser, *Postmortem: New Evidence in the Case of Sacco and Vanzetti* (Amherst, Mass., 1985), p. 137; Finzi, pp. 44, 47; Borghi, p. 210.

27. Mussolini, "Il lamento del pastore" (July 22, 1920), in *OO* (n. 6 above), 15:105-7; and "L'ora del fascismo!" (August 21, 1920), in ibid., pp. 152-54.

28. On the question of a united revolutionary front, see Finzi, pp. 129034, 139; Mantovani (n. 18 above), pp. 88, 98-99; Roberto Vivarelli, *Il dopoguerra in Italia e l'avveno del fascismo (1918-1922)* (Naples, 1967), pp. 437-43 and *Storia delle origini del fascismo* (Bologna, 1991), pp. 515-27; De Felice, *Mussolini il rivoluzionario*, pp. 553-54. Finzi (pp. 145-48) rejects the notion that Malatesta was interested in collaboration with D'Annunzio, while De Felice (*Mussolini il rivoluzionario*, p. 554) and Vivarelli (*Storia*, p. 521) argue that he approved the idea.

29. Enzo Santarelli, *Storia del movimento e del regime fascista*, 2 vols. (Rome, 1967), 1:190-91; *Un trentennio*, pp. 31-36.

30. Avrich (n. 8 above), p. 245, n. 4; the notice appeared in the August 7,1920 issue. See also Italian consul in Boston to Italian embassy in Washington, D.C., July 30, 1920, in *Ambasciata di Washington, 1920-1923,*"Sacco-Vanzetti," Pos. VIII-4 (hereafter *Ambasciata,* followed by the file name), f. "Sacco e Vanzetti," ASMAE. In April, Malateta had spoken at a rally in Milan protesting against the political reaction in the United States.

31. Avrich, pp. 204-6; Buda is quoted in James (n. 18 above), p. 4. Buda remained in contact with his anarchist comrades in the United States, including Sacco, who wrote to him through mutual friends. See Sacco to Giovanni Poggi, July 13, 1925, and prefect report dated September 21, 1925, in *Casellario Politico Centrale*, f. 59729, "Sacco, Nicola," ACS; and Ministero dell' Interno (hereafter MI), 1926, Cat. C-2, f. "Agitazioni pro Sacco e Vanzetti," ACS.

32. *Un trentennio,* pp. 46-48, 57; Avrich, pp. 213-14.

33. *OO,* 15:152-54, 272-73, and (quote) 288.

34. Fred Moore to Francesco Saverio Merlino, October 26, 1920, Aldino Felicani Collection (hereafter AFC), 4A/Fred H. Moore Papers/Correspondence (hereafter 4A), Department of Rare Books and Manuscripts, Boston Public Library; Moore to embassy, February 15, 1921, *Ambasciata,* f. "Sacco e Vanzetti—1921," ASMAE. Eugene Lyons was the pen name of Morris Gebelow.

35. Vanzetti to his father, October 1, 1920, in Bartolomeo Vanzetti, *Non piangete la mia morte: Lettere ai familiari,* ed. Cesare Pillon and Vincenzina Vanzetti (Rome, 1962), p. 64.

36. Mucci had lived in the United States and had worked for Moore in defending Ettor and Giovannitti in 1912. Moore to Musatti, November 30, 1920, and Lyons to Moore, November 26, 1920, AFC/4A; police chief of Rome to director general of public security, April 15, 1921, im MI, 1926, Cat. C-2, f. "Agitazioni pro Sacco e Vanzetti," Acs; Michele Pistillo, "Mucci, Leone" 3:606-7, and Gian Mario Bravo, "Merlino, F.S.," 3:429-38, both in Andreucci and Detti, eds. (n. 12 above), Elia Musatti also assisted Lyons.

37. Sabino Sacco had accompanied Nicola to the United States in 1908 but returned to Italy a year and a half later. During World War I, he deliberately damaged his eyes in order to escape military service, for which he was imprisoned. He was elected to the communal council twice (1914 and 1920) on the socialist ticket. See the documents in *Casellario Politico Centrale,* f. 59728, "Sacco, Sabino," ACS; Avrick, pp. 10-13, 22.

38. Lyons to Moore, December 10, 1920, AFC/4A; Marco Saluzzo di Paesana to embassy, December 3, 1920, and Ferrante to embassy, December 4,1920, *Ambasciata,* f. "Sacco e Vanzetti," ASMAE.

39. On Lyons' activities in Italy and the parliamentary discussion, see Eugene Lyons, *Assignments in Utopia* (New York, 1937), p. 22; Elizabeth Gurley Flynn, *The Rebel Girl: An Autobiography: My Life (1906-1926)* (New York, 1973), pp. 311-12; Avrich, p. 26; Russell (n. 13 above), p. 112; Felix (n. 13 above), p. 108; Sylvers (n. 12 above), pp. 440; Burton (n. 8 above), p. 68; *Atti Parlamentari, Discussioni, Camera dei Deputati,* December 16, 1920, pp. 6670-71; Joughin and Morgan (n. 1 above), p. 201. The Italian ambassador in Washington assisted Moore in obtaining a postponement of the trial in order to secure depositions from witnesses in Italy. Prime minister's secretary to ministry of foreign affairs, December 19, 1920, and attached memo dated January 27, 1921, *Affari Politici,* Stati Uniti, 1920, b. 1594, ASMAE; Ferrante to embassy, January 27, 2921; Moore to embassy, February 15, 1921; and Rolandi-Ricci to Ferrante, February 16, 1921; embassy memorandum to State Department, February 16, 1921; State Department memorandum, February 19, 1921; and State Department to embassy, March 2, 1921, all in *Ambasciata,* f. "Sacco e Vanzetti—1921" ASMAE; Bainbridge Colby to Channing H. Cox, February 18, 1921, RG 59, 311.6521 Sa 1/2, NA; Lyons to Moore December 30, 1920, AFC/4A; Vanzetti to his father, n.d. (but fall 1920), and January 30, 1921, in Vanzetti, *Non piangete,* pp. 66, 69.

40. Copies of the letters and the leaflet, "Giustizia Americana—Il Caso Sacco-Vanzetti," are in MI, 1926, Cat. C-2, f. "Agitazioni pro Sacco e Vanzetti," ACS; Lyons to Moore, April 4, 1921, AFC/4A. Although our contributions were collected in Rome by the anarchist Temistocle Monticlelli, who headed the defense committee there, money continued to be sent to Italy to help finance the campaign. See Irving A. Priest to Aldino Felicani, September 22, 1925, 7A/Aldino Felicani Paper/Correspondence (hereafter 7A), AFC.

41. Avrich (n. 8 above), p. 208; James (n.18 above).

42. "L'attentato organizzato contro Mussolini" (March 24, 1921) in OO (n. 6 above), 16:216-18. Mantovani (n.18 above), pp. 474-77, casts doubt on Mussolini's version of the Masi episode.

43. "Il caso Malatesta" (March 23, 1921), in OO, Appendici, 7 vols. (Rome, 1978-81), 1:252-53; Renzo De Felice, Mussolini il fasicista, 2 vols. (Turin, 1966-68), 1:51, n. 3.

44. Mussolini's Il Popolo d' Italia had supported the purpose of Malatesta's hunger strike, which was to force the government to bring his case to trial. Mantovani, p. 388.

45. "L'orrenda strage anarchica d'ieri sera al Teatro Diana a Milano" (March 24, 1921), in OO, 16:214-15; Mussolini's other reaction are in ibid., pp. 219-28; Giuletti to Mussolini, March 25, 1921, in De Felice, Mussolini il fascista, 1:51-52, n. 3. On the Diana incident see Mantovani, L'attentato al Diana: Processo agli anarchici nell' assise di Milano (Rome, 1973); Un trentennio (n. 15 above), p. 53; Santarelli, Storia del monimento (n. 29 above), 1:59-60; Mariani, Ettore Aguggini, and Giuseppe Boldrini.

46. Director of public security to police chief of Rome, March 25, 1921; police chief to director of public security, April 15, 1921; director of public security to police chief, April 19, 1921; and questura to director of public security, May 28, 1921, all in MI, 1926, Cat. C-2, f. "Agiazioni pro Sacco e Vanzetti," ACS.

47. Ferrante to Rolandi Ricci, May 4, 1921; Rolandi Ricci to Ferrante, May 31, 1921; Ferrant to Rolandi Ricci, ASMAE. Ferrante statement is in Herbert B. Ehrmann, The Case That Will Not Die: Commonwealth vs. Sacco and Vanzetti (Boston, 1969), pp. 462-62. When Judge Thayer saw the statement, he claimed that the consul had assured him that the Italian government "had no interest in this case." In light of Thayer's avowed hatred for Sacco and Vanzetti, it is likely that he willfully misinterpreted Ferrante's remarks.

48. Merlino had told Eugene Lyons that Rolandi Ricci was a personal friend, so the ambassador may have been sympathetic toward the case from the beginning. Lyons to Moore, December 30, 1920, AFC/4A.

49. Ferrante to Rolandi Ricci, July 15, 1921, *Ambasciata,* f. "Sacco e Vanzetti—1921," ASMAR; Joughin and Morgan (n. 1 above), p. 227; Max Schachtman, *Sacco and Vanzetti, Labor's Martyrs* (New York, 1927), pp. 34-35.

50. *Atti Parlamentari, Discussioni, Camera dei Deputati,* July 39, 1921, pp. 961-62; "Appunti per S.E. il Presidente del Consiglio," July 31, 1921, Serie "B," b. 1810, f. 212415/1921, ASMAE; telegram to Harding, August 6, 1921, RG 59, 311.6521 Sal, NA; della Torretta to Rolandi Ricci, August 1, 1921, and Rolandi Ricci to della Toretta, August 11, 1921, *Ambasciatia,* f. "Sacco e Vanzetti—1921," ASMAE. The liberal deputy Paolo Falletti, from Vanzetti's hometown, also sponsored a motion passed by the provincial council of Cuneo on behalf of Vanzetti. See prefect of Cuneo to ministry of interior, August 14, 1921, MI, 1926, Cat. C-2, f. "Agitazioni pro Sacco e Vanzetti," ACS; and Bartolomeo Vanzetti, *Autobiogtafia e lettere inedite,* ed. Alberto Gedda (Florence, 1977), p. 84; petition dated August 5, 1921, in Botta (n. 13 above), pp. 83-84.

51. Errico Malatesta, "Per due innocenti," *Umanita' Nova* (October 1, 1921), now in his *Scritti,* 3 vols. (Geneva-Brussels, 1934-36), 1:245.

52. Errico Malatesta, "Gli italiani all' estero," *Umanita' Nova* (October 6, 1921), in his *Scritti,* 1:249-52; and the following (page numbers refer to Scritti): "Il ministro della Toretta contro Sacco e Vanzetti," *Umanita' Nova* (October 11, 1921), 1:254-56; "Grido di dolore e di vergogna," *Umanita' Nova* (October 11, 1921), 1:258-59; "Liberta', giustizia, umanita'," *Umanita' Nova,* (October 13, 1921), 1:259-61; the entire issue of October 16, 1921; and "Il dovere dello stato," *Umanita' Nova* (October 19, 1921), 1:261-63.

53. Vanzetti to Luigia Vanzetti, September 4, 1921, and the same but no date (October ?), in Vanzetti, *Non piangete* (n. 35 above), pp. 74-76.

54. Prefect of Rome to director of public security, September 20 and September 22, 1921; prefect of Milan to the same, September 29, 1921; prefect of Bergamo to same, September 29, 1921; prefect of Bologna to same, October 2, 1921, all in MI, 1922, f. "Pro Sacco e Vanzetti," ACS. See also *New York Times* (October 4, 1921); and Russell (n. 13 above), pp. 216-17.

55. Ministry of Interior to prefects, October 14, 1921, MI, 1926, Cat. C-2, f. "Agitazioni pro Sacco e Vanzetti," ACS; *Un trentennio* (n. 15 above), pp. 58-59; see the numerous prefect reports in MI, 1922, Cat. C-2, f. "Pro Sacco e Vanzetti," ACS. The Italian committee for Sacco and Vanzetti, which met in Rome under the auspices of *Umanita' Nova,* also asked for a general strike. See questura of Rome to director general public security, December 29, 1921, MI, 1926, Cat. C-2, f. "Agitazioni pro Sacco e Vanzetti," ACS. American Ambassador Richard Washborn Child, in *A Diplomat Looks at Europe* (New York, 1925), p. 163, saw the Italian government's unwillingness to confront the United States over the case as a sign of the weakness that lead to Fascist seizure of power.

56. "Sacco-Vanzetti Case," n.d., in RG 59, 311.6521 Sal, NA.

57. The text of the telegrams to the U.S. embassy, October 1921, and the prefect of Forli to ministry of interior, January 20, 1922, are MI, 1926, Cat. C-2, f. "Agitazioni pro Sacco e Vanzetti," ACS; Child to Department of State, October 13, 1921, RG 59, 311. 6521 Sal/12, NA.

58. Lyons to Moore, March 29, 1921, AFC/4A; see the following articles by Malatesta in *Umanita' Nova,* reproduced in his *Scritti:* "Guerra civile" (September 8, 1921), 1:214-17; "Sulla guerra civile" (September 14, 1921), 1:223-26; "Giuseppe di Vagno assasinato" (September 28, 1921), 1:240-42; "Il partiro fascista" (November 23, 1921), 1:293-94; "Il fascismo e la lagalita'" (March 14, 1922), 1:325-27; see also *Un trentennio,* pp. 57, 63.

59. This paragraph is based on the hundreds of prefect reports for October 1921 in MI, 1922, Cat. C-2, f. "Pro Sacco e Vanzetti," ACS. See also *Un trentennio,* pp. 61-63. Confrontations with Fascists took place in Genoa, Turin, Milan, Bologna, Ancona, Livorno, Rome, Naples, Benevento, Catania, and Agrigento. For events in Massa-Carrara and Pavia, see prefect reports of October 16, 1921, and January 13, 1922.

60. *OO* (n. 6 above), 17:203; Giorgio A. Chiuco, *Storia della rivoluzione fascista,* 5 vols. (Florence, 1929), 3:563; Damiami (n. 12 above), p. 297. Some months later, Mussolini seized the initiative again by lashing out at the socialist and anarchist refusal to protest the trial of some fifty revolutionary socialists about to take place in Communist Russia. "Do your hearts beat," he asked cynically, "only for Sacco and Vanzetti?" See "C'e' una reazione . . ." (March 19, 1922), in *OO,* 18:108.

61. De Felice, *Mussolini il fascista* (n. 43 above), 1:758. On the creation of the Fascist National Party see De Felice, *Mussolini il fascista,*

1:172-91; and Emilioi Gentile, *Storia del Partito Fascisa,* 1919-1922; *Movimento e Milizia* (Rome-Bari, 1989), pp. 314-86. In contrasting the Fascist program with the ideas of Fascism's enemies, Mussolini could not resist one more nod to Malatesta, "saint and prophet, a coherent phenomenon that one can admire." "Il programma fascista," in *OO,* 17:217.

62. Minister of Interior to prefects, October 16, 1921; and Valvassori Peroni to director general of public security, October 19, 1921, MI, 1926, Cat. C-2, f. "Agitazioni pro Sacco e Vanzetti," ACS.

63. Moore to Ferrante, January 18, 1921, AFC/4A; Ferrante to embassy, October, 26, 1921, *Ambasciata,* f. "Sacco e Vanzetti—1921," ASMAE; Rolandi Ricci to ministry of foreign affairs, November 11, 1921, ASMAE, Serie "B," b. 1810, f. 212425/1921; Russell, p. 113; and Joughin and Morgan (n. 1 above), p. 225. Both note that "somehow" Lopez managed to avoid deportation; Valvassori Peroni to Rolandi Ricci, October 27, 1921, and della Torretta to Rolandi Ricci, October 29, 1921, *Ambasciata,* f. "Sacco e Vanzetti—1921," ASMAE. Lopez was finally deported to his native Spain in 1925 but smuggled himself back into the United States, where he lived out his life, during in the 1960s.

64. Prime minister's secretary to foreign ministry, November 24, 1921, "Interpellanza N. 90 [by deputy Michele Maitilasso]," November 18, 1921, and Rolandi Ricci to ministry of foreign affairs, November 29, 1921, Serie "B," b. 1810, f. 212425/1921, ASMAE; Valvassori Peroni to director general of public security, November 24, 1921, and director general to Valvassori Peroni, November 28, 1921, MI, 1926, Cat. C-2, f. "Agitazioni pro Sacco e Vanzetti," ACS.

65. The committee's criticism appeared in its publication *L'Agitazione.* See Ferrante to embassy, October 13, 1921, and December 27, 1921, Serie "B," b. 1810, f. 212425/1921, ASMAE; Ferrante to Rolandi Ricci, February 25, 1922, *Ambasciata,* f. "1922," ASMAE; Vanzetti to his sister, April 4, 1922, in his *Non piangete* (n. 35 above), p. 79; Ferrante to Rolandi Ricc, February 2, 1922, Serie "B," b. 1810, f. 212425/1922, ASMAE. The anarchist Erasmo Abate, one of the founders of the Arditi del Popolo, wrote "the Italian government, while doing nothing for Sacco and Vanzetti, tries hard to stop the agitation in their favor." See "Il proletariato d'Italia per Sacco e Vanzetti," *Il Martello* (May 20, 1922).

66. Ferrante to Rolandi Ricci, March 22, 1922 and April 6, 1922; Rolandi Ricci to Ferrante, March 23, 1922; and Peter F. Tague to

Rolandi Ricci, June 7 and 9, 1922, *Ambasciata,* f. "1922," AASMAE; for approval and denial of funds see Fulco Tosti to Ferrante, August 6, 1922; and Carlo Schanzer to Rolandi Ricci, October 21, 1922, Serie "B," b. 1810, f. 212425/1922, ASMAE; on Mucci in parliament, *Alti parlamentari, Discussioni, Camera dei Deputati,* March 20, 1922, pp. 4-7, "Interrogazione N. 119," Serie "B" b. 1810, f. 212425/1922, ASMAE; transcript of parliamentary debate for same date in AFC/4A; and "Il Caso Sacco-Vanzetti alla Camera," *La Notizia* (May 12, 1922); "Raps Italian Radicals on Sacco and Vanzetti," unidentified newspaper clipping, *Ambasciata,* f. "1922," ASMAE.

67. Rolandi Ricci to Valvassori Peroni, January 19, 1922, *Ambasciata,* f. "1922," ASMAE; and Serie "B," b. 1810, f. 212425/1922, ASMAE; Schmitz (n. 12 above), p. 57; "L'ambasciatore italiano ed i condannati di Dedham," *La Notizia* (January 20, 1922).

68. A week before—probably October 23—Mussolini had visited Ambassador Child at the embassy in Rome.

69. Damiani, pp. 12-19; Schmitz, pp. 46-57; Monte S. Finkelstein, "The Johnson Act, Mussolini and Fascist Emigration Policy; 1921-1930," *Journal of American Ethnic History* 8 (Fall 1988): 38-55; Migone, *Gli Stati Uniti e il fascismo* (n. 12 above) pp. 99-199; Mussolini to Caetani, January 12, 1923, in *Documenti diplomatici italani,* Settima Serie, 16 vols. (Rome 1952), 1:231.

70. *Un trentennio* (n.15 above), p. 76; Santarelli, *Il socialismo anarchico* (n. 15 above), pp. 192-93; Fabbri, "Prefazione," in Malatest's *Scritti* (n. 15 above), 1:26-27. Malatesta's last articles on Mussolini were "Mussolini al potere" (November 25, 1922), 1:198-200; "La situazione," 1:204-6; and *"Umanita' Nova* occupata," 1:209-10, both December 2, 1922, and all in *Scritti.*

71. Fabbri, pp. 10-11.

72. Vassallo to Caetani, December 23, 1922; and Caetani to Ferrante, December 28, 1922, *Ambasciata,* f. "1923," ASMAE. The documents do not make clear which of the McAraney brothers had made the request.

73. Luigi Quintiliano, "Senite De Biasi!" *Il Martello* (August 4, 1923); Diggins, *Mussolini and Fascism* (n. 12 above), pp. 111-12; *Il Carroccio* (July 1921), p. 110, and (May 1927), p. 576; see also Cetti, in *Sacco-Vanzetti; Developments and Reconsiderations* (n. 12 above), p. 98; and Grazia Dore, *La democrazia italiana e l'emigrazione in America* (Brescia, 1964), pp. 342-46, 361-68; Anna Maria Martellone, *Una Little Italy nell'Atene d'America* (Naples, 1973), pp. 434-35.

74. Diggins, *Mussolini and Fascism*, pp. 81-86, 112-19; Giuseppe Fiori, *L'anarhico Schirru condannato a moter per l'intenzione di uccidere Mussolini* (Milan, 1983), pp. 62-63, 77; Cetti, in *Sacco-Vanzetti: Developments and Reconsiderations*, p. 971; Dore, pp. 362-63, 368; Vanzetti to Alice Stone Blackwell, June 13, 1926, in Frankfurter and Jackson, eds. (n. 2 above), pp. 202-3; Enzo Santerelli, "I fasci italiani all' estero," in his *Ricerche sul fascismo* (Urbino, 1971), p. 115.

75. Ferrante to Caetani, March 5, 6, 7; and report by consular official in Lawrence, March 5, 1923, in *Ambasciata*, f. "1923" ASMAE; *Un trentennio*, p. 151.

76. Mussolini to Caetani, April 10, 1923, *Documenti diplomatici italiani*, 1:498; Giorgio Rumi, *Alle origini della politica estera facista (1918-1923)* (Bari, 1968), pp. 243-45; Alan Cassels, *Mussolini's Early Diplomacy* (Princeton, N.J., 1970), pp. 196-98; Migone, *Gli Stati Uniti e il fascismo*, pp. 353-54, and "Il regime fascista e le comunita` italo-americane: La missione di Gelasio Caetani (1922-25)," in his *Problemi di storia nei rapporti tra Italia e Stati Uniti* (Turin, 1971), pp. 25-41; Damiani (n. 12 above), pp. 66-67.

77. Luigi Barzini, "Il Corriere d'America' per Sacco e Vanzetti," *Il Corriere d'America* (June 13, 1923); Sacco-Vanzetti Defense Committee, *News Service* (June 12, 1923); Moore to Barzani, June 11, 1923; Moore to Thompson, June 11, 1923; and Cotillo to Moore, June 16, 1923, all in AFC/4A. Vanzetti thanked Barzini for his support with the words, *"Il Corriere d'America,* by defending us defends the rights and the dignity of the people of Italy." See Quintaliano.

78. The Comitato's president was Giuseppe Vitelli of the Italian Chamber of Commerce of New York; Pasquale L. Simonelli of the Italian Savings Bank of New York was its treasurer. The Comitato held a benefit at the Manhattan Opera House in December that was attended by Carlo Tresca, Luigi Antonini, and Arturo Giovanniti. See Vitelli to embassy, November 24, 1923; and report of June 25, 1923, in *Ambasciata*, f. "1923" ASMAE; Sacco-Vanzetti Defense Committee to Barsotti, July 2, 1923, AFC/2A (Sacco-Vanzetti Defense Committee). Somehow, Barzini learned and made public the fact the Mussolini had been seeking the assistance of federal authorities for Sacco and Vanzetti. See "L'intervento del governo italiano nel caso Sacco-Vanzetti," *La Notizia* (March 16, 1923); Ferrante to Caetani, March 16, 1923, *Ambasciata*, f. "1923," ASMAE.

79. "Interpellanza dell'On. Mucci (Lazzari)," May 26, 1923; Mussolini to Caetani, May 26, 1923; and Caetani to Mussolini, May 30, 1923, all in SAP, 1902-37, b. 9, f. 10837/1923,ASMAE.

80. "Per Sacco e Vanzetti," *Il Progresso Italo-Americano* (June 14, 1923); Ferrante to Caetani, June 14, 1923; Grella to Caetani, September 27, 1923; Caetani to Lodge, September 28, 1923; Lodge to Caetani, September 29, 1923; and Caetani to Mussolini, October 12, 1923, all in *Ambasciata*, f. "1923," ASMAE.

81. Mussolini to Caetani, December 1, 1923; and "Interpellanza dell'On. Mucci (Lazzari)," May 26, 1923, SAP, 1902-37, b. 9, f. 10837/1923, ASMAE.

82. Mussolini to Ferrante, October 3, 1924, SAP, 1902-37, b. 9, f. 10837/1924, ASMAE.

83. Oreste Bianchi to Felicani, June 1, 1924, AFC/7A (Aldino Felicani Papers—Correspondence); on the Morgan loans see Diggins, *Mussolini and Fascism* (n.12 above), pp. 151-56; Schmitz (n. 12 above), pp. 85-110; Migone, *Gli Stati Uniti e il fascismo* (n. 12 above), pp. 116-99; Mussolini's comments are in De Begnac, *Taccuini* (n. 3 above), pp. 376, 518.

84. Maltesta, "Sacco e Vanzetti" (June 1, 1926), in his *Scritti* (n. 51 above), 3:236-37; *Un trentennio* (n. 15 above), p. 87; prefect of Rome to ministry of interior, June 10, 1926, along with the copy of the petition, and prefect of Milan to director general of public security, June 10, 1926, MI. 1926, Cat. C-2, f. "Agitazioni pro Sacco e Vanzetti," ACS; "Agitazione pro Sacco e Vanzetti," *L'Unita`* (June 10, 1926). Fletcher to secretary of state, June 21, 1926; and Fletcher's statement to the Italian press dated June 23, 1926, both in RG 59, 311.6521 Sal/270, NA.

85. Malatesta, "Sacco e Vanzetti"; Fabbri (n. 70 above), p. 17; Malatesta to Giuseppe Tosca, June 12, 1926, in Rosaria Bertolucci, ed., *Errico Malatesta, Episolario: Lettere edite e inedite 1873-1932* (Avenza, 1984), p. 215; Roberta Strauss Feuerlicht, *Justice Crucified: The Story of Sacco and Vanzetti* (New York, 1977), p. x; Cetti, in *Sacco and Vanzetti* (n. 12 above), p. 99. Since the Fascist seizure of power Sabino Sacco had abandoned his socialist political activity and become an admirer of Mussolini. The police dropped him for their subversive list in 1932, and then he requested membership in the Fascist Party. See the documents in Casellario Politico Centrale, f. 59728, "Sacco, Sabino," ACS; Creagh (n. 11 above), pp. 17-18.

86. De Martino to Mussolini, May 19, 1926, and Mussolini to De martino, June 10, 1926, SAP, 1902-1937, b. 9, f. 10837/1926, ASMAE.
87. De Martino to foreign ministry, June 12 and June 19, 1926; Mussolini to De Martino, June 20, 1926,SAP 1902-37, b. 9, f. 10837/1926, ASMAE. In view of the new appeal, Grandi postponed all further responses to parliamentary questions on the case.
88. Ferrante to De Martino, June 24 and 26, 1926; and De Martino to Grandi, July 10, 1926, SAP, 1902-37, b. 9, f. 10837/1926, ASMAE. Grandi showed the reports from De Martino and Ferrante to Mussolini; De Martino's remarks were printed in the July 21, 1926, issue of *L'Impero,* and reported to the State Department by the embassy in a memorandum of July 23, 1926, in RG 59, 856.00/1558, NA, as cited by Burton (n. 8 above), pp. 73-74. See also Botta (n. 13 above), p. 99.
89. Mussolini to De Martino, July 21, Rogers to foreign ministry, July 22, 1926, SAP, 1902-37,b. 9, f. 10837/1926, ASMAE; Fletcher to State Department, July 22, 1926; W. R. Castle, Jr., to governor's office, Boston, July 22, 1926, RG 59, 311.6521 Sal/275, NA; Federzoni to prefects, July 21, 1926; and Grandi to Federzoni, July 24, 1926, MI, 1926, Cat. C-2, f. "Agitazioni pro Sacco e Vanzetti," ACS.
90. DeMartino to ministry of foreign affairs, September 11, 1926, SAP, 1902-37, b. 9, f. 10837/1926, ASMAE; and the document file note regarding memorandum by Grew, September 3, 1926, RG 59, 311. 6521 Sal/311, NA.
91. On September 11, 1926, Gino Lucetti, who had returned to Italy from France for the purpose, flung a bomb at Mussolini; on October 31, Anteo Zamboni was killed after an attempt to shoot Mussolini; see De Felice, *Mussolini il fascista* (n. 43 above), 2:202-8, and *Mussolini il duce,* 2 vols. (Turin, 1974-81), 1:86n., and 122; *Un trentennio,* p. 88; Santarelli, *Il socialismo anarchico* (n. 15 above), p. 193.
92. Charles F. Delzell, *Mussolini's Enemies: the Italian Anti-Fascist Opposition* (Princeton, N.J., 1961), pp. 37-41; De Felice, *Mussolini il fascista,* 2:210-16; Alberto Aquarone, *L'organizzazione dello stato totalitario* (Bologna, 1965), pp. 97-110.
93. Aide memoire by U.S. embassy, October 27, 1926, SAP, 1902-1937, b. 9, f. 10837/1926, ASMAE; prefect reports in MI, 1926, Cat. C-2, f. "Agitazioni pro Sacco e Vanzetti," ACS; Arthur Mann, *La Guardia: A Fighter against His Times,* 1882-1933 (Philadelphia and New York, 1959), p. 259; Schachtman (n. 49 above), pp. 47, 52.

94. Ferrante to foreign ministry, April 6, 1927; De Martino to foreign ministry, April 7 and 8, 1927; De Martino to Mussolini, April 8, 1927; and Mussolini to De Martino, April 9, 1927, all in SAP, 1902-37, b. 9 f. 10837/1927, ASMAE.

95. Ferrante to foreign ministry, April 11, 1927, SAP, 1902-37, b. 9, f. 10837/1927, ASMAE.

96. Ferrante to foreign ministry, July 20, 1927, SAP, 1902-37, b. 9, f. 10837/1927, ASMAE.

97. Ehrmann (n. 47 above), pp. 463-64.

98. Mussolini to Ferrante, July 23, 1927; and Ferrante to foreign ministry, July 28, 1927, SAP, 1902-37, b. 9, f. 10837/1927, ASMAE.

99. See n. 13.

100. Fletcher diary, entry for January 1, 1926, Henry P. Fletcher Papers, box 1, folder "Diary (1915, 1925-26)," Library of Congress; Fletcher to Kellogg, July 25, 1927; and Kellogg to Fletcher, July 25, 1927, 311.6521 Sal/557; Fletcher to Kellogg, July 26, 1927; Kellogg to Fuller, July 27, 1927; and Herman A. MacDonald to Kellogg, July 29, 1927, 311.6521 Sal/560.

101. De Martino to Mussolini, August 5 and 10, 1927; and Ferrante to foreign ministry, August 10, 1927, all in SAP, 1902-37, b. 9, f. 10837/1927, ASMAE. De Martino also went to New York to speak with someone he described as "a person in high finance personally close to the President of the United States who has shown himself a friend of Italy." This could have been Thomas W. Lamont of the House of Morgan, who had been instrumental in the Italian loans. De Martino to Mussolini, August 12, 1927, SAP, 1902-37, b. 9, f. 10837/1927, ASMAE.

102. Michele Sacco to Mussolini, August 5, 1927, MI, 1927, Cat. C-2, "Pro Sacco e Vanzetti," ACS; Michele Sacco's letter and Mussolini's reply are in *OO* (n. 6 above), 23:231-22; see also "Father of Sacco Appeals to Duce," *New York Times* (August 10, 1927); Joughin and Morgan (n. 1 above), p. 291; and Yvon De Begnac, *Palazzo Venezi: Storia di un regime* (Rome, 1950), p. 493. The defense committee's telegram to Mussolini, dated August 9, 1927, was undoubtedly written by Felicani but was signed "La Notizia" and is in AFC/7C (Alsino Felcani Papers-Correspondence).

103. Arturo Bocchini to prefects, August 13, 1927, and the material and prefect reports in MI, 1927, Cat. C-2, "Pro Sacco e Vanzetti," ACS, esp. the leaflets "Salviamo Sacco e Vanzetti!," "Lavoratori Milanesi!," "Operai!," "Confederazione Generale del Lavoro," "Lavoratori!," "Al

popolo italiano perche' sappia ed agisca," and "I sette anni d'orribile agonia di Sacco e Vanzetti."

104. Eugene Lyons, *The Life and Death of Sacco and Vanzetti* (New York, 1927), pp. 176-77; John F. Martin to Kellogg, August 24, 1927, RG 59, 311.6521 Sa 1/841, NA; Vanzetti, *Autobiografia e lettere inedite* (n. 50 above), pp. 119-20; Gertrude L. Winslow, "A Glance at Fascism," *Lantern* (March-April 1928), pp. 21-22; Joughin and Morgan, pp. 290-91; "Family of Sacco Sure He's Innocent," and "Mussolini Wrote to the State Department Personal Plea on Behalf of Condemned Men," both in *New York Times* (August 11, 1927).

105. "Conversation with the Italian Ambassador," August 23, 1927, RG 59, 311.6521 Sa 1/747, NA; Ferrante to Ministry for foreign affairs, August 22, 1927, SAP, 1902-37, b. 9, f. 10837/1927, ASMAE.

106. Eugene Lyons, *Vita e morte di Sacco e Vanzetti* (Ragusa, 1966), p. 4.

107. "Fuller il 'puritano,'" *L'Impero* (August 24, 1927); "Senza nobilita'," *Il Lavoro d' Italia* (August 24, 1927). Mussolini seems to have harbored a similar view about American "conservatism" to the end. See "La democrazia dalle pance piene" (May 4, 1944), in *OO*, 31:357.

108. "Constazioni," *Il Messaggero* (August 24, 1927); "Il dramma di Boston nel giudizio del mondo," *Il Corriere della Sera* (August 25, 1927).

109. "Il vero volto dell'agitazione per Sacco e Vanzetti," *La Tribuna* (August 26, 1927); "Bassifondi messianici," *Il Giornale d'Italia* (August 30, 1927).

110. "A Farinacci," *L'Impero* (August 27, 1927). On the reaction of the Fascist press, see also "Il fascismo e il caso Sacco e Vanzetti," *Il Nuovo Mondo* (New York), (August 6, 1927).

111. "L'esempio dell'Italia," *Il Popolo d'Italia* (Rome) (August 30, 1927), and the Milan edition of August 25, 1927. See also Michael Musmanno, *After Twelve Years* (New York and London, 1939), p. 333. Malatesta was stunned by the execution. From his closely watched apartment in Rome, he wrote to a friend, "I was convinced that Sacco and Vanzetti, if not freed, would at least not be killed; the blow has struck me terribly." See Malatesta to Virgilia D'Andrea, September 1927, in *Errico Malatesta Episolario* (n. 85 above), p. 259.

112. De Felice, "Alcuni temi per la storia dell'emigrazzione italiana" (n. 13 above), p. 7.

113. Burton (n. 8 above), p. 68.

114. When the journalist Edward H. Jones interviewed Mussolini in 1928, Mussolini asked him, "Do you think that Fuller will be the next president of the United States?" See Creighton Hill, "Alvan T. Fuller—Failure," *Lantern* (July-August 1928), pp. 7-8; and "Cio` che narra un americano che visito` Mussolini per il caso Sacco e Vanzetti," *Il Progresso Italo-Americano* (August 1, 1928).

115. Schiavina (n. 9 above), p. 108.

116. "I am no longer," Mussolini exclaimed in 1934, "the head of government who, between 1925 and 1927, had to limit himself to asking for the salvation of Sacco and Vanzetti. I no longer have American creditors who impose their will. Now I have my hands free." De Begnac, *Taccuini* (n. 3 above), p. 376.

117. Gentile, *Le origini dell'ideologia fascista* (n. 25 above), pp. 2-6, 133, 136.

118. Giuseppe A. Borgese, *Goliath: The March of Fascism* (New York, 1938), p. 192.

119. Errico Malatesta, "Mussolini al potere," *Umanita' Nova* (November 25, 1922), in his *Scritti* (n. 51 above), 2:198 (quote); De Felice, *Mussolini il rivoluzionario* (n. 4 above), p. 173, n. 4.

Chapter 6

Concord and Discord: Italians and Ethnic Interactions in Tampa, Florida, 1886-1930

Gary R. Mormino and George E. Pozzetta

During the past twenty years our knowledge of the Italian immigrant experience has greatly expanded. We now have at hand a variety of community studies, more specialized examinations of selected aspects of Italian migration (the family, crime, mobility, etc.), and analyses which provide a conceptual framework to assist in understanding the wider implications of this great folk movement. What we should like to examine today is one aspect of this tapestry that perhaps has not received the scholarly attention it deserves. We are referring to the interactional dimensions of the immigrant experience in America. Using the Italian community in Tampa, Florida as a case study, this preliminary exploration suggests some of the questions present in an inquiry of this sort and proposes some hypotheses that may be useful to other community studies.

With some notable exceptions, scholars have not addressed in a systematic way questions dealing with the adaptations and interrelationships resulting from the coming together of diverse immigrant groups in North American urban centers. This is true despite the fact that immigrants often came into initial and most immediate contact with other immigrant groups, rather than with some idealized "American" society. As one important study of ethnic interactions pointed out,[1] most scholarly analysis has been conducted "in terms of majority-minority relations" or, more recently, along the lines of comparative group experiences (Juliani and Hutter, 1975, p. 42).

Although these efforts have resulted in important advances, gaps remain in our understanding of how groups interact with one another. This is particularly true of the nonconfrontational, more ordinary patterns of life in multiethnic neighborhoods. An examination of such interactional situations, sociologists Richard Juliani and Mark Hutter remind us, is necessary "to understand minority-minority relations as another normal and enduring part of the social structure of complex, pluralistic societies" such as our own. Moreover, it is important to see how these relationships related to the wider urban context and how they evolve over time.

Our brief remarks will deal with Tampa, Florida, an important manufacturing center situated along the Gulf Coast of Florida. More specifically, they will focus on Ybor City, a multiethnic, multiracial enclave located in the northeast sector of the city. Ethnicity in Ybor City was shaped in important ways by the interactions taking place among four distinct groups (Italians, Cubans, Spaniards, and Afro-Cubans), and on a different level, by the relationships existing between these immigrants and the host society. The nature of these relationships, both structural and social, changed over time and place, but they remained central to defining what it meant to be "immigrant" (and later "ethnic") in Tampa.[2] By examining the nature of these contact points we can perhaps gain insight into the processes by which groups in such multi-ethnic situations sorted out their New World Orders for themselves. There exists also the opportunity to explore the dynamics by which the wider context of ethnicity was arranged in a bustling, urban-industrial center.[3]

Tampa played a key role in the history of the Florida frontier, first as a fort and later as a trading post and commercial hub of a region open to exploration in the 1840s. Change came slowly to South Florida, and as late as the 1870s, economic stagnation, political paralysis, and yellow fever forestalled growth. As in other areas of the "new South," city fathers in the late nineteenth century combined an aggressive entrepreneurial spirit with buoyant boosterism to spur development. Yet, almost unique in the southern experience, Tampa's expansion was powerfully linked to the inflow of foreign immigration (Mormino and Pizzo, 1983, pp. 60-76; Long, 1971, pp. 31-44).

Numbering only 720 residents in 1880, Tampa awakened from its economic slumber in 1884 when railroad magnate Henry Bradley Plant wove the city into his transportation network. Small discoveries of phosphate near the city added to the commercial activity, which, up to that point, had consisted mainly of the sale of fish, cattle, and citrus from the hinterland. By 1885 Tampa contained fewer than 1,000 inhabitants (U.S. Census, 1900, p. 214; Long, 1971, pp. 333-345).

This equilibrium was profoundly altered when an enterprising Spanish industrialist, Don Vincente Martinez Ybor, decided to move his cigar manufacturing operations to Tampa in the same year. Embroiled in bitter labor disputes with his fractious workforce and seeking a more competitive location, Ybor was attracted to Tampa. The newly formed Tampa Board of Trade lured him with free grants of land and pledges to protect the cigar industry from disturbances. In a section of unincorporated land to the northeast of Tampa, Ybor laid out an industrial community with workers' homes, factories, streets, and wooden sidewalks (Westfall, 1977, pp. 55-75; Muniz, 1976, pp. 6-14). Native Tampans welcomed this addition to their municipal fortunes, but very early exhibited a set of ambivalent attitudes toward the cigar workforce, which was comprised almost entirely of Cubans, Afro-Cubans, Spaniards, and later Italians. They quickly employed the word "Latin," a term of generalized ethnicity when referring to these immigrant workmen, a label that simplified for them a confusing blend of peoples and cultures. Immigrants countered with the equally inclusive, but more accurate, term of "Anglo" when referring to Tampans (the notable exception here being American blacks, who were given specific identities by each immigrant group) [Federal Writer's Project, n.d., p. 186; American Guide Series, p. 42].

The economic fortunes of Tampa soared as more and more cigar factories relocated to this emerging cigar manufacturing center. "The cigar industry is to this city what the iron industry is to Pittsburgh," exclaimed the *Tampa Morning Tribune* (July 30, 1896). By Ybor City's first anniversary, some 3,000 immigrants were settled into the community and engaged in producing high quality, hand rolled cigars. By 1890 the city counted 5,500 individuals, with more than 50 percent of the population comprised of foreign-born immigrants connected in some capacity with the cigar industry. Census takers in 1900 listed over 15,000 residents (almost surely an undercount), 5,000 of whom were cigarmakers. By 1910 the city numbered nearly 40,000 inhabitants, including almost 21,000 foreign-born. Ethnic development followed almost parallel lines in West Tampa (incorporated in 1895 but remaining separate from Tampa until 1925, which, by the end of the new century's first decade possessed more than 8,000 residents, only 626 of whom were native born, of native parentage [U.S. Census, 1910, Washington, 1912, pp. 330-332; Muniz, 1963, pp. 335-336; Long, p. 341].

During the period 1886-1910, the cigar industry accounted for 75 percent of the city's entire payroll and the percentage of foreign-born employed in the industry never dipped below 70 percent. By 1895 Tampa had some 130 factories of various sizes, with more constructed monthly, and in 1909 the value of tobacco products accounted for nearly 82 percent of the city's manufacturing effort. The cigar trades and ancillary industries, therefore, dominated the economic structure of Ybor City (U.S. Senate, pt. 14, 1911, p. 87; *Tampa Morning Tribune*, Dec. 18, 1911; Rerrick, 1902, p. 222). It should be mentioned, however, that though Tampa was a one-industry town, it was not a one company town. This fact allowed for a substantial amount of diversity within the ranks of owners and it also encouraged the efforts of enterprising immigrants to begin small-scale *chinchales*, operations employing a handful of individuals (Rabb, 1938; Scaglione, 1933, pp. 7-10).

The cigar industry arriving in Tampa in 1886 was characterized by skilled workers who possessed a special work ethos. Dominated by a pre-modern craft mentality and possessing a full complement of artisan work styles and outlooks, it created an industrial environment governed by the rhythms of the individual. There existed within factories a clear occupational hierarchy, which in the early years was organized along ethnic lines. The first major division existed between salaried and piecework employees. The former category included foremen, managers, skilled clerical staff, salesmen, and accountants, most of whom typically were Spaniards. The salaried staff also included *selectores* (selectors), trained men who selected the tobacco on the basis of color, maturity, and texture. Spaniards filled these ranks exclusively. Below this level were skilled cigarmakers, who ordered themselves by status in relation to the size, complexity, and particularly the rate of return attached to the type of cigar produced. Next in the hierarchy were banders, strippers, box makers and packers, and the like. Here the Spanish generally held the higher level positions of skilled craftsmen, with Cubans ranking below. At the bottom of the occupational ladder rested those individuals who did not work directly with tobacco, but merely dealt with the physical tasks of sweeping, hauling, portering, etc. Cubans and early arriving Italians usually filled these positions (Campbell and McLendon, 1939; Leon, 1962, pp. 76-83).

Skilled cigar workers followed distinctive work styles. Cigarmakers typically had no formal schedule. They came and went as they pleased, often taking extended coffee breaks at neighboring cafes catering to immigrant artisans. Cigarmakers also enjoyed the privileges of taking home free cigars at day's end, and of smoking as many cigars during work hours as they desired.[4] A complicated system of apprenticeship also served to order the workplace, with its own panoply of relationships, privileges, and perquisites. In general, Spanish owners maintained a set of pre-modern, *Patron* attitudes toward their workers, reflective of an older style of work management. Ybor exemplified this tradition by providing kitchen utensils for workers' homes at his expense and sponsoring numerous banquets and musical performances for his factory staff (Westfall, pp. 118,130; Federal Writer's Project, Tampa, p. 18; del Rio, Tampa, 1950, p. 11).

Most symbolic of the special *ambiente* of the industry was the presence of *el lectore*, the reader. The practice of reading from a raised platform (the *tribuna*) in the workroom had been a Cuban tradition. Cigarmakers paid the lector's fee and also selected the items to read. During the course of a typical day, the lectors read selections from the labor press and excerpts from the great radical masters (Marx, Kropotkin, Malatests, Fanelli, etc.). Among the works of fiction read, those featuring proletarian themes of the class struggle found particular favor (Hugo, Gorky, Zola, etc.) (Perez, 1975, pp. 443-444; Gallo, 1936; Interview with Coniglio, May 2, 1976). "When in 1902 I landed in Tampa," reminisced Angelo Massari (who became a banker), "I found myself in a world of radicals." The lectura, therefore, provided an underpinning for a militant labor movement that took root in Ybor City. This fact was not lost on the owners, who waged an unremitting war to abolish the system of reading and gain control of the workforce and workplace (Massari, New York, 1965, p. 107; New York, 1959; Stelzner and Bazo, 1965, pp. 124-131).

The importance of the reader extended beyond factory walls, as the information disseminated from the tribuna filtered outward into the wider immigrant community through a series of informal networks. Family and friends at the evening meal discussed readings of the day, thus extending the range of contacts. Early Italian arrivals established a loose system of meetings among fellow immigrants to allow those few who had gained access to factories to pass on news gleaned from the daily readings (Interview with Provenzano, Tampa, March 13, 1982; Interview with Longo, June 1, 1979).

The cigar industry also influenced residential patterns. The groupings of factories close by each other—and the constellation of workers' homes about them—resulted in a high degree of residential concentration (but relatively low density because of a relative absence of multifamily units). Remarkably for a city rooted in the deep South, Afro-Cubans resided in integrated neighborhoods in Ybor City.[5] In the early years, the very low cost of housing and rentals, coupled with the frontier-like quality of the surrounding area, limited the possibilities for wider dispersal. The mere clustering of housing, of course, did not in itself make for social contact as even close neighbors can be invisible. Yet individual and group contacts appear to have been frequent and fervent.[6]

The topography of the enclave added its own distinctive flavor to the evolving immigrant society. The land lay very flat and few buildings were more than one story in height (the exception being the factories and the club buildings). Hence, the opportunities for mutual sharing of such functions as parades, picnics, and festivals were enhanced. Unlike residents of the canyons of New York's lower East Side, few individuals in Ybor City could avoid notice of their neighbors' public lives.

It is impossible in this short space to do more than suggest the differences characterizing the migration streams that flowed into Tampa. These divergent patterns, however, did play important community roles in determining the nature and extent of the interactions that followed.

Spaniards

The Spanish community consisted almost entirely of immigrants who came from the three northern provinces of Asturias, Galicia, and Catalonia (areas of Spain long noted for traditions of migration and immigration). The great majority had spent time in Cuba working in the cigar industry centered in the capital city of Havana. Generally, they followed a pattern of migration which was characterized by the flow of skilled labor and mercantile activity and long periods of sojourner status. Indeed, many Spaniards in the New World "commuted" between Spain and the Americas for extended time periods, maintaining separate households on both sides of the Atlantic. Persistently high ratios of males to females characterized the Spanish presence, as did the heavy use of boarding houses, very low rates of English language usage, and a continued adherence to regional identifications until well into the twentieth century. Also indicative of the strength of the Old World connective tissues were the unusually large numbers of Spanish radicals (especially anarchists) who found Tampa a congenial home. Yet, because of the large number of wealthy factory owners among Spaniards, they occupied, as a group, the apex of the immigrant status pyramid (Gomez, 1962, pp. 59-77; Federal Writer's Project, Tampa, pp. 2-50).

Cubans

Above all, the geographic proximity of Ybor City to Cuba facilitated the process of migration and the peripatetic nature of Cuban movement. The continuing struggle for independence on the island also profoundly shaped the Cuban community. For the most part, Cubans regarded themselves as exiles, long awaiting *Cuba Libre*. Movement most commonly involved families, in large part due to the unsettled conditions in Cuba. Depending on the fortunes of the cigar industry and the revolution, Cubans shifted between the island and the mainland. After 1898 they diverted their energies to labor militancy and radical activities (Perez, 1979, pp. 129-140; Steffy, *Tampa Morning Tribune*, June 23, 1895).

Afro-Cubans

Afro-Cubans tended to live on the periphery of Tampa and Ybor City. They similarly occupied marginal positions in the economic structure of the community, although Afro-Cuban women appear to have been engaged in a relatively wide range of jobs. They followed essentially the same migration patterns as white Cubans, who courted them during the patriotic struggle against Spain. After 1898, however, Afro-Cubans increasingly assumed separate identities. They constituted roughly 10 percent of the Cuban population throughout the period under review (*Tampa Times*, Sept. 14, 1977; Muniz, 1982; Cordero, 1982).

Italians

Italian immigrants initially followed classic sojourning patterns, featuring single males seeking seasonal employment. Five Old World villages in west central Sicily supplied the migrants who made their way to Florida. Two streams branching through New Orleans and St. Cloud, a sugar plantation in east central Florida, brought individuals first to

Tampa. The sojourner stage was very short, however, as the lynching incident in New Orleans (1891) and the suppression of the *fasci* in Sicily (1894) forced a rapid movement into the family stage.[7] Although the latest of the immigrant groups to arrive, by 1894-95 the Italian community already possessed a rough institutional framework and numerous family groups.

Interactions during the initial years of settlement and community formation were principally shaped by events surrounding the struggles in Cuba. The independence movement among Cubans spawned intense organizing movements in Ybor City and West Tampa in support of *Cuba libre* and splintered the city's Spanish-speaking population. Only the Spanish anarchists broke ranks to denounce Spanish colonial policies and support Cuban demands for independence. As the 1898 war approached, relations deteriorated badly and there were frequent shootings, knifings, and fights between the two groups. Even such a respected figure as Ignazio Haya, an early Spanish industrialist active in the founding of Ybor City, was stoned by Cubans while walking with his wife (Federal Writer's Project, Tampa, p. 177; Steffy, pp. 66-67; *Tampa Morning Tribune*, Dec. 27, 1895; Westfall, p. 119). Indeed, it was Haya who played a key role in forming *Centro Espanol* (the first major immigrant club of Ybor City) as a place of refuge (Interview with Balbontin, Tampa, 1939, pp. 48-54; Bagley, 1948; Middleton, pp. 288-289).

Cubans were the most volatile element of the Latin community as they struggled with the problems of independence and conflicts generated by the local labor movement. They came most often into direct confrontation with other Ybor City groups and the host society. For their part, the Native Americans often experienced conflicting pulls as they attempted to relate to the Cuban presence. Americans generally supported ideals of freedom and independence, but they feared any disruption of the cigar industry that Cuban activism might bring. Their attitudes, therefore, tended to whipsaw widely.[8]

Within the Cuban immigrant group, the independence movement eroded color distinctions and generated numerous occasions for interracial contact. One must be cautious with easy generalizations about racial harmony, however, as conflicting evidence exists suggesting that racial distinctions remained important throughout.[9] Similar doubts surrounded the opinions Anglos had of Afro-Cubans. At times natives were clearly confused by the curious mix of color and culture that Afro-Cubans possessed, but they usually solved any dilemmas by simply referring to them as niggers or "Cuban" niggers. The fact that Afro-Cubans' residences tended to border these sections of the city normally occupied by native blacks seemed to give validity to the characterizations (Middleton, p. 290; *Tampa Morning Tribune*, Oct. 29, 1895; September 14, 1977; Steffy, pp. 46, 143).

The first large-scale arrival of Italians occurred in an atmosphere of conflict and confrontation existed between Cubans and Spaniards. This situation affected the multilayered adaptations Italians faced. On an economic level, Italians encountered obstacles to an easy entry into the cigar factories. Lack of skills and the hostility of Spanish owners and foremen emerged as the most important impediments (U.S. Senate, 1911, pp. 204-205; Westfall, pp. 116-117). Cubans tended to have ambivalent attitudes. They sensed the new economic threat that Italians posed, but they were anxious to use these new arrivals as challenges to the Spanish. Hence, they often taught Italians cigarmaking skills and frequently patronized Italian stores and shops (Ginesta, Tampa).

Italians squeezed into areas of the occupational structure where vacuums existed and competitive advantages could be forged. Such a strategy, at least in the initial years, promised less overt conflict with immigrant neighbors. Thus, Italians gravitated to street trades, small shops, truck farming, and dairying. One 1909 report detailing street trades, for example, found that of 115 licenses granted, 102 were given to Italians.[10] Yet, these immigrants were not blind actors on the stage of economic structure; there was a range of choice and individual initiative.

Many Italian shop owners went into small businesses that served groups of *paesani*. Others supplied services that aimed at different clienteles. Each large cigar factory spawned a satellite formation of small cafes, shops, and stores. Italians quickly delved into the potential markets existing in this situation and learned to supply the necessary services. They opened cafes that specialized in Cuban coffee, others that featured Spanish pastries and meats, etc. These shops were often used to expand the range of contracts for entry into factory jobs and to forge the linguistic tools needed for entry into the wider Ybor City society. Italians appear also to have almost exclusively shown an inclination to open small groceries in Tampa's Afro-American community (Interview with Scaglione, Tampa, 1980; with Longo, 1979).

A wide variety of middlemen arose in the Italian community to provide the brand of services mandated by Tampa's pluralistic society. Individuals to teach Spanish, contact persons to supply the right types of foods for small cafes and groceries, intermediaries to interact with the Anglo community, etc. all found ample need for their services. This pattern was clearly seen in the nature of the early community leadership—the men who guided the destinies of Italian Tampa came heavily from this adaptable element.[11]

Just as Italians adeptly shaped their small businesses to the demands of the wider ethnic landscape, so too did they manipulate the variety of ethnic labels available in Ybor City to their advantage. The Cuban war crystallized national identities in Tampa and energized them with significance. The strong sense of "Cubanness" and "Spanishness" existing in Ybor City pushed later-arriving Italians to shape an identity for themselves. Italians defined themselves according to context and contest. In family and kin situations, individuals embraced the security of *campanilismo*; thus one grasped the exclusivity of Stefanesi or Alessandrini. In the wider neighborhood, residents preferred "Sicilian," a label which served the purpose of separating the small non-Sicilian contingent of the Italian population (Interviews with Cacciatore, March 2, 1982; Palermo, March 6, 1982; Grimaldi, Nov. 9, 1978, Tampa). To immigrant Tampa, the term "Italian" was most used because this was the designation most familiar to non-Italians and it carried with it possible rewards to Sicilians (e.g., the exploitation of favorable stereotypes regarding Italians' expertise as fruit peddlers and merchandisers). In reference to cigar manufacturers from New York City who transferred to Tampa after 1900 and often did not distinguish between different kinds of "Latins," Spanish-speaking Italians sometimes utilized that designation to gain factory employment (Interviews with Adamo, April 19, 1980, Palermo and March 23, 1979, Tampa; *Tampa Morning Tribune*, July 4, 1897).

Italians did make concessions to local conditions (they learned Spanish, accepted Latin labels, participated in Spanish medical programs, and acquired cigarmaking skills), but they continued to manifest their own particular cultural preferences. In work choices, for example, men typically used factories as springboards to other occupational niches, not as permanent choices. Italian women entered cigar factories in greater numbers than men, usually starting work in the stripping rooms. Males normally worked a few years, built nest eggs for investment in business or property, and left the cigar trades. Women, and to a lesser degree children, provided steady wages until these ventures matured. By 1909 cigar industry reports showed that Italian women actually earned more than Italian men on average.[12] Because of their greater presence in factories, they also learned Spanish quicker, English slower, and participated slightly more often in militant unions. Though Spanish and Cuban families were not adverse to allowing women to work in factories, male cigarworkers always predominated among them (Interview with Italiano, April 16, 1980, Tampa; U.S. Senate, 1911, Table 150, p. 218).

Italian men tended to view the cigar industry as too volatile to suit their conservative family goals. As cigarmaker-turned-grocer Frank Setticasi explained, "the cigarworkers were too crazy—too many radicals, too many strikes" (Interview with Setticasi, July 1, 1979, Tampa). Italian strategies made them more able to survive the disruptions recurring strikes brought to Tampa. Indeed, for Italians these occasions often brought opportunities, as Cubans often left Tampa in search of employment and sold their possessions at a loss. Italians also readily shifted employment in strike situations as they probed the area economy for job possibilities. Using the family as a collective producer, strike-bound cigar workers could be found engaged in tenant farming, phosphate mining, citrus harvesting, and truck gardening (Interview with Provenzano, March 13, 1982, Tampa; U.S. Senate, 1911, pp. 433-435; *Kissimmee Valley*, Nov. 11, 25, 1896; *Tampa Morning Tribune*, April 1, 12, 1908).

The early associative life of these groups also owed much to the collective presence of immigrant neighborhoods. The first clubs formed in the Spanish and Cuban communities clearly reflected the fissures created by the island struggle. Italians borrowed from both sides to forge an early, broad-based association (*L'Unione Italiana*, 1894).[13] A process of sharing and cross-fertilization similarly existed in the structuring of Ybor City's radical subsociety. Each of the immigrant group possessed a leftist element, although the Spanish always were most active and numerous. By the early years of the twentieth century, there existed a network of speaking clubs, debating societies, and cultural centers representing the full spectrum of radical ideologies. Some were open to freethinkers of all nationalities; others were restricted to individual immigrant groups. The *Centro Obrero*, the Labor Temple, served as a flagship center for immigrant workers. The cooperative effects of this phenomenon extended to the sharing of club libraries, the pooling of resources to finance visits of radical luminaries, occasional efforts to enter the local political arena, and the frequent sponsoring of public debates.[14] The possible integrative effects of this cooperation were diluted by the fact that the radical subsociety never constituted more than a small minority of the population and the long-term trend was toward factionalism rather than increasing accord. Radicals served as lightning rods for the Anglo community, which attributed many of Ybor City's problems to them, often with violent consequences (*El Internacional*, March 24, 1911; *Tampa Weekly Tribune*, June 22, 1899; March 5, 1903; *Tampa Journal*, Jan. 26, 1887).

As the twentieth century dawned, immigrants in Tampa faced a transitional period. The settlement of the struggle in Cuba, the trends toward consolidation in the cigar industry (as seen in the formation of a Manufacturer's Trust and broad-based workers' unions), and the "coming of age" of second generation ethnics called forth a different set of adaptations. This period also witnessed the Anglo community and greater American society play a more decisive role in shaping the social environment of Ybor City as both the intensity and frequency of their intrusions increased dramatically. The evolving ethnic community created a powerful set of institutions to cope with these changed conditions.

Union development reflected the new realities. With the war in Cuba ended, long deferred working-class issues gained priority in the cigar workforce. Starting with the immigrant-created and -led union, *La Resistencia*, cigarworkers moved toward consolidation within the folds of the AFL locals of the Cigar Makers International Union (CMIU). These unions led workers in a series of protracted general strikes occurring in 1901, 1910, and 1920-21 which became benchmarks in the lives of the Ybor City's residents.[15] The local orientation of AFL structures, coupled with the presence of effective ethnic leaders and the continuing influence on the lector, led to the creation of a labor consciousness of such a broad and malleable nature that a disparate membership found common ground. That ethnic workers were able to stay out on protracted strikes and maintain their solidarity in the face of manufacturer opposition, vigilante justice, and economic deprivation attested, at least in part, to the effectiveness of union organization.[16]

Residents of Ybor City realized, however, that the most powerful institutions shaping their community were the ethnic clubs, not radical groups or unions. The Roman Catholic Church, which nominally claimed the allegiances of many residents, failed to play a significant role. Church leadership responded ineptly to immigrant needs, in part because it was forced to battle against strongly entrenched, Old World anti-clerical attitudes.[17] More importantly, each of the major groups formed an ethnic club which, in addition to providing the usual range of services, added the unique benefits of a cooperative medical program. The first private hospitals in the state of Florida were begun by these Latin associations (Bryan, Tampa, p. 5; Long, Nov. 1965, pp. 217-234; Federal Writer's Project, Tampa). The foundation provided by these shared medical programs underwrote a vibrant and enduring club life that, in somewhat altered form, survives today.

The club provides Latins with opportunities to interact with their Anglo neighbors in other than conflict situations. This was particularly true of the contacts generated by various political campaigns, parades, club picnics, theater performances, and sporting events, which typically attracted elements of the Anglo population.[18] Within Ybor City the clubs worked to sort out and solidify the various ethnic identities present in the community. The magnificent club buildings themselves illustrated this point. The construction of these multistory, marble and granite structures (in the period 1897-1919) generated an element of rivalry between groups, each one of which attempted to outdo the other in terms of ostentation and display. Club construction became another legitimate expression of ethnic difference, rivalry, and status.[19]

At the same time as the clubs worked to bring Anglo and Latin Tampa together, they served counter purposes. By drawing ethnic groups inward toward a congenial local environment they insulated Latins from more open social contacts with others. There remained a tangible chasm between Anglo and Latin Tampa, as evident in, among other things, signs prominently displayed at Anglo bathing spots proclaiming "No dogs, Niggers or Latins allowed."[20] During periods of crisis, of course, these gaps became even wider and the vigilante practices so often resorted to by native Tampans dramatically reminded Latins of both their composite identities in the eyes of the city's power structure and the common problems this generated. In the early years, native Tampa generally welcomed immigrants as a skilled labor force underwriting the city's most important industry. Yet, they also exhibited rabid misgivings over the leftist ideologies finding favor in Ybor City and the popularity of labor militancy. In this context, the possibilities for harmonious relations between native and immigrant remained problematic.

The internal social relations of the Latin community itself were often characterized by disharmony. Points of division persisted and ethnic

162 Gary R. Mormino and George E. Pozzetta

difference remain an important part of daily life. As Italians in greater numbers moved into the cigar industry, for example (even if for brief periods of employment), they increasingly clashed with Cubans. The growing commercial and political power of Spaniards and Italians served to separate Cubans further within immigrant ranks and often underwrote the forging of sharply negative stereotypes of them (Interview with Maella and Diaz, August 1, 1983, Marti-Maceo Club, Tampa; "Life history of Fernando Lemos," p. 4; Ginesta, p. 3). Afro-Cubans experienced a greater degree of segregation as the Jim Crow system expanded and pushed them further to the periphery of Ybor City Society. Indeed, southern mores came to exert an increasing hold on the community as seen, for example, in the decision of *Cirulo Cubano* to ban blacks from society ranks in 1902 (an action taken, in part, because of strident demands made by Anglo Tampans) (*Tampa Morning Tribune*, May 5, 1903 and January 20, 1905; "History of Circulo Cubano"; Muniz, *Los cubanos*, p. 116).

Divisions based upon subjective views of group difference also divided the immigrant population. For years intermarriage between Cubans and Italians was extremely rare and families on both sides strictly regulated dating (Interviews with Grimaldi, Nov. 9, 1978; Antinori, March 5, 1982; Interviews by Pollato and Kennedy, Tampa, 1939). Among other things, Cubans complained of Italian ungratefulness for past assistance in breaking into the cigar trades and derided their propensity for keeping cows, chickens, and goats in their backyards. They also decried Italian frugality and abstention, seeing in these qualities the worst kind of parsimony. Cubans saw themselves as the true builders of Ybor City because of their cigarmaking skills, and their free spending, Havana-oriented folkways. Italians and Spaniards, on the other hand, perceived Cubans as lazy spendthrifts who failed to share their values of thrift and industry, and the pursuit of property ownership (Middleton, p. 297; *Tampa Morning Tribune*, May 2, 1903, Sept. 20, 1905, and Oct. 28, 1902; U.S. Senate, 1911, pp. 192, 204-205). Occupying the bottom of the status hierarchy, Cubans were the pariahs of immigrant Ybor City.

Even the growth and the resiliency of the ethnic clubs played a paradoxical role within the ethnic community. In one sense this signaled a move toward homogenization as each club became structurally similar, but the process also worked to isolate each group within its own bailiwick. As each segment carved out its own niche, responsive to its own specific needs, and as Ybor City evolved into self-sufficient neighborhoods, the range of contacts reduced rather than increased. The chances for more diffused and intensive intergroup contact lessened, particularly so after factors pushing the groups together began to disintegrate (the decline of union strength after 1920, the collapse of the radical subsociety by World War I, the diminishing vigilante violence, etc.). As a result each group developed its own solidarity. This meant that by 1920 points of contact tended to be more confined to the workplace, schools, recreational areas, and the great main street for walks and parades, 7th avenue.[21] Contacts were most often made at the secondary rather than primary level—important distinctions for such a compact community as Ybor City.

By the 1920s the city had undergone other profound changes. The Ten-Month Strike of 1920-21 seriously weakened the competitive advantage of Tampa factories in wider markets and the industry, including the introduction of tin molds to make cigars, followed soon by the use of cigar-making machines. The cigar machines were often operated by unskilled and unorganized American women who were recruited from small communities around Tampa.[22] The workforce changed as the workplace itself was transformed. When Latin workers rallied for one last major challenge to their deteriorating world and precipitated a general strike in 1931 (led by the Tobacco Workers International Union, an affiliate of the Communist party), they were completely crushed in little more than one week (Ingalls, Westport, CT, 1981, pp. 44-57; *Tampa Morning Tribune*, Dec. 7, 8, 1931). Owners then abolished the readers, replacing them with radios. The radical subsociety had been seriously weakened earlier after the 1910 strike and the repression of the World War I-Red Scare Era. With the defeat in 1931, whatever lingering influence it enjoyed passed away.

Native Tampa was making vigorous efforts to redirect the economic foundations of the city, looking toward a future based upon tourism and a diversified economy. The Great Depression destroyed any immediate hopes of these dreams. It also destroyed the cigar industry. Customers could no longer afford the high-priced, hand-rolled cigars that had made Tampa famous. Factory after factory filed for bankruptcy and went out of business (Campbell, pp. 5-12). Cuban cigarworkers felt the pressure of these combined forces most acutely and began to desert the city for Havana, New York, and elsewhere in search for work. Italians meanwhile had been moving outside the confines of Ybor City in increasing numbers as their commercial strength in small businesses, trades, and farming permitted. Only the clubs remained strong because of the unique range of services offered. For the most part, however, the Latin community was feeling the transforming effects of these profound changes occurring in its occupational structure, its residential patterns, and its institutional completeness. [23]

What followed was a new era and a new set of interactive situations structured on very different foundations. When second and third generation Latins rediscovered the Catholic Church, for example, it ironically occurred in the suburbs, devoid of past meaning.

The immigrant groups of Ybor City and Tampa were influenced by sets of centripetal and centrifugal forces, alternately driving them apart and pulling them together. Unfolding over time was a measure of sharing and rivalry, of cooperation and conflict, of contacts and social distancing. These dynamics operated along both formal and informal social and institutional lines, some drawn in the Old World, others sketched in the New World setting. Although these forces were at work during all periods under review, they existed in various combinations and intensities depending on various factors. The Tampa experience suggests that there was not a simple continuum at work, stretching from, on the one side, a less unified, more balkanized cluster of groups moving to a more unified, more "modern," and "Americanized" group existing at the other end. What happened was much more complex than that, with many smaller dramas acted out within the larger sweep. Yet, the long-term trend, at least to 1930, suggests that, if anything, the reverse is true. That is, once intrusions from the outside diminished and groups followed different routes to social mobility and group acculturation, they tended to grow further apart. During the early years, the groups possessed a set of common problems and enemies and, in some cases, a cluster of integrative institutions which by 1930 had largely fallen away. By the end of the period in question the groups were, in some important ways, more different from when they had first come together. [24]

With reference to the Italian experience in Tampa, the collective presence of other immigrant groups profoundly influenced the adaptations that took place. An economic structure essentially created by Cuban and Spanish immigrants largely shaped initial Italian work adjustments. Once settled, Italians often used Spaniards as their role models in the immigrant community, aiming at their status levels and finding many of their values compatible with their own. They desired the easy entrees that Spaniards possessed into Anglo society, believing that these were the roads to ultimate political and social position.

Italian institutional life also owed much to immigrant neighbors. Spanish club organization provided the model for *L'Unione Italiana*, a critically important institution for the community. Italian language newspapers frequently included Spanish language sections, a concession to the multiethnic environments in which they circulated. Immigrant unions, to which large numbers of Italians belonged, recognized fully the need for ethnic accord to achieve worker unity. Although Italians often devised their own strategies to cope with strikes and union policies, they learned the art of compromise and borrowed from the experiences of their fellow union members. Tampa's radical subsociety similarly reflected the heterogeneous qualities of life in the city as it created organizations (some Italian) which aimed at pan-ethnic memberships and featured ideologies which accommodated different national backgrounds.

Italian social and recreational life was responsive to these wider trends as well. Ranging from drama programs offered by ethnic clubs to Italian linguistic adaptations, the cross-currents of differing immigrant cultures were evident. Religion did not escape the influence of interactive forces. Anticlericalism, which remained a minor current in many Italian American settlements, flourished in Ybor City, due in no small part to shared attitudes on those issues existing among Spanish and Cuban co-residents. Space limits further details which document similar development at work in the realms of politics, crime, and education. As Italians intersected with other immigrant groups, they found that their private and public lives were changed. Over time these various contact points proved to be important occasions for shaping loyalties, expanding relationships, and defining the different contexts of social intercourse.

What resulted from the coming together of these particular immigrant streams in Tampa was the creation of a distinctive community with a cultural landscape uniquely its own. To understand how it came to take the forms it did requires something more than an examination of each of its parts. In the case of this settlement—and presumably other multiethnic communities as well—the sum of its parts did not equal the whole. What must be added is recognition of the role played by the broader, interactive qualities of group life.

Notes

1. Richard Juliani and Mark Hutter, "Research Problems in the Study of Italian and Jewish Interaction in Community Settings," in Jean A. Scarpaci, ed., *The Interaction of Italians and Jews in America* (American Italian Historical Association, 1975), pp. 42, 43. Ronald Bayor, *Neighbors in Conflict: The Irish, Germans, Jews, and Italians of New York City, 1929-1941* (Baltimore, 1978) deals primarily with conflict situations, but does have material on neighborhood developments.

2. Gary R. Mormino, "Tampa and the New Urban South: The Weight Strike of 1899," *Florida Historical Quarterly*, 60, January, 1982, pp. 337-356. A very insightful essay by D. R. Middleton, "The Organization of Ethnicity in Tampa," *Ethnic Groups*, 3, 1981, pp. 281-306, has informed the arguments of this paper.

3. We should add here that each group possessed an interior history of its own that could be investigated with profit and pleasure. Thus, this essay is not to deny that there were aspects of each groups' adaptations that belonged very much to its own inner strategies, cultural imperatives, and personalities.

4. Interview with Fermin Souto, Federal Writer's Project (Tampa, n.d.), pp. 3-5; Muniz, *Los cubanos*, p. 89. A short strike was occasioned by an effort to deny workers free cigars. See *Tampa Morning Tribune*, September 23, 28, 29, 30, 1911.

5. Interview with Juan Maella, August 1, 1983, Tampa; Interview with Francesco Rodriguez, July 15, 1983, Tampa; Tampa City Directories, 1900-1930, Special collections, USF Library, Tampa. The remarkable insurance maps of the Sanborn Company show the clustering effect. They are available for Tampa from 1884 onward (with some missing years) and are located at the University of Florida.

6. Joan Marie Steffy, "The Cuban Immigration to Tampa, Florida, 1886-1898" (unpublished M.A. thesis, University of South Florida, 1975), pp. 14-15; Westfall, pp. 82-85. Ybor owned the Ybor City Land and Improvement Company, which controlled much of the early housing.

7. Interview with Rosalia Cannella Ferlita, May 18, 1980, Tampa; Interview with Philip Spoto, June 30, 1979; Interview with Joe Valenti, April 18, 1980; Calogero Messina, *S. Stefano Quisquina: Studio critico* (Palermo, 1977). The villages were Santo Stefano Quisquina, Allessandria della Rocca, Bivona, Cianciana, and Contessa Entellina.

8. Strike situations most often brought out the widest variations in attitudes. See *Tampa Morning Tribune*, December 20, 1910 and January 26, 1911, for during-strike and post-strike opinions.

9. Interview with Jose Ramon Sanfeliz, Federal Writer's Project (Tampa, 1939), 7; Steffy, pp. 44-45, 46-49. Sanfeliz claimed that the early Cuban Club was characterized as being like "rice and black beans" (with whites and blacks).

10. *Immigrants in Industries*, p. 205. Among the trades, Italians totally dominated fruits and vegetables, ice cream, peanut vending, oyster and clam sales, and street bear exhibitions.

11. Interview with John Grimaldi, November 9, 1978; Interview with Nick Nuccio, June 10, 1979, Tampa. Leaders of radical groups and labor unions did not come from this element.

12. A more extended discussion is in Gary R. Mormino and G. E. Pozzetta, "Immigrant Women in Tampa: The Italian Experience," *Florida Historical Quarterly*, 61, January, 1983, pp. 303-307. The 1900 and 1910 manuscript census schedules for Hillsborough County also reveal numerous instances of the employment pattern described above.

13. The first president of *L'Unione Italiana* was Bartolomeo Filogamo, the bookkeeper of Pendas and Alverez cigar factory. When Pendas, a Spaniard, organized *Cenrto Espanol*, Filogamo assisted him, and the Spanish club served as a model for the 1894 creation of the Italian club. Messari, *La comunita*, pp. 149-152.

14. *La Federacion*, February 16, 1900, describes a visit of Errico Malatesta; for evidence of various sharing activities, see *El Internacional*, February 19, 1915, March 3, 10, 1916, October 6, 1916.

15. Durward Long, "Labor Relations in the Tampa Cigar Industry, 1885-1911," *Labor History*, 12, Fall, 1971, pp. 551-559; Long, "The Open-Closed Shop Battle in Tampa's Cigar Industry, 1919-21," *Florida Historical Quarterly*, 47, October, 1968, pp. 101-121; *Tampa Morning Tribune*, January 31, 1899. In each instance of a major strike, Anglo Tampa responded with vigilant activity, including deportations, lynchings, and a widespread physical intimidation.

16. Interview with Jose Vega Diaz, August 24, 1980, Tampa. A reading of the columns of the major union newspapers of Tampa, *El Internacional* during the period 1904-1930 will also verify the observations.

17. Interview with Sister Norberta, Sister Mary Lourdes, and Sister Mary Edith Mallard, September 13, 1982, St. Augustine. St. Augustine

diocese records contain voluminous correspondence between the Bishop and various clerics working in Ybor City. One letter written to Amleto Giovanni Cicognani, Apostolic Delegate in 1935 concluded, "For 50 years and more, zealous, unselfish priests and sisters have exhausted themselves in trying to save these people, but their reward must be sought in heaven for they receive no earthly one." Bishop to Cicognani, August 25, 1935, St. Augustine Diocese Archives, St. Augustine.

18. Middleton, p. 295; Interview with Manuel la Rosa, July 30, 1983, Tampa; *Tampa Morning Tribune*, May 21, 1927; *El Internacional*, May 3, 1902 and March 26, 1920. By the early 1900s Latin baseball teams sponsored by the clubs were playing in city leagues and track teams were competing in races. The clubs were regular stops for Anglo politicians.

19. Interview with Joe Maniscalco, April 3, 1980; Interview with Nina Ferlita, April 25, 1980; Interview with Angelina Comescone, July 18, 1979, Tampa. Many Italians described the erection of the Italian Club thusly, "Oh, when that [building] was going up! We were all so excited, so thrilled. Most everybody didn't work because we'd go out and stand around and watch the building go up."

20. Interview with John Pizzo, July 30, 1983, Tampa; "History of Ybor City as narrated by M. Jose Garcia," Federal Writer's Project, Tampa, 1936, p. 11. Garcia, a pioneer Cuban cigarworker, bitterly described old cigarworkers in 1936 refusing to attend a 50th anniversary banquet given in their honor by Tampa Mayor D. B. McKay. He did not go because for years Cubans were "considered little more than dogs by McKay and many others in prominent positions."

21. "Life History of John Cacciatore," Federal Writer's Project, Tampa, n.d. See Juliani, pp. 51-52, for a discussion focusing on Italian-Jewish interactions at this stage.

22. Scaglione, pp. 26, 33-34, 63-64; Campbell, pp. 8, 10-11, 66-67. Long-time cigarworkers greeted all of these changes with consternation. Their protests fill the pages of *El Internacional*, the major cigarworker newspaper.

23. Yancey et al., pp. 391-392, relate these variables to expressions of the ethnicity in community settings.

24. Melvyn Dubofsky, "Comment on Education and the Italian and Jewish Community Experience," in Scarpaci, *Interaction*, 59, hypothesizes that Jews and Italians in northeastern urban centers tended, over time, to follow similar lines.

Chapter 7

From Urban to Suburban: Italian Americans in Transition

Salvatore J. LaGumina
Nassau Community College

Long Island, New York, suburban communities had an early attraction for people who loved being close to the land, people who yearned to raise their families in hospitable physical environments in their own homes. Among these people were small groups of turn of the century Italian Americans who, in the mid-twentieth century, were joined by large numbers of their ethnic group and currently form the largest single nationality bloc (approximately 700,000) in proportion to the area's population. The way they shaped their lives in the midst of a suburban setting and were, in turn, influenced by their surroundings, helps illuminate an issue of contemporary relevance—the question of whether the suburban experience has proven to be a less harsh, less difficult place to ascend from the bottom to the uppermost rungs of the socioeconomic success ladder. Has the suburban environment been a boon or an obstacle in the quest for acceptance on the part of Italian Americans and their descendants? Have they been truly accepted? What strategies did they employ to render their suburban residency viable? Does this have meaning regarding the acceptance of other, newer Latin Catholic immigrants?

What unfolded on Long Island may tell us much about what was experienced by new immigrant peoples in other parts of the country whose suburban growth in effect paralleled this area. To aver that this review of Long Island's Italian Americans provides us with valuable insights into the workings of suburban communities or immigrant peoples in the period under review is not to claim that Long Island was representative in any statistical sense. Rather, it is to say that these suburban communities were undergoing a process of transformation that eventually affected all American suburbs to one or another degree, and it is likely that there were important uniformities in the social consequences of suburbanization.

The purpose of this review was to uncover and narrate the history of Italian Americans on Long Island by concentrating on several selected communities of long standing. I use "community" in the sense that it refers to a social group whose members live in close proximity and who share a cultural and historical heritage. On the other hand the unitary view that all of the people studied were impoverished, "proud of their heritage," and tightly organized would be an exaggeration of the interactions, feelings and perceptions encompassed. An analysis of their social history serves a number of useful purposes such as that of dispelling certain myths or confirming widely held views about ethnic groups in suburbia. This case study helps us discern differences between the dynamics of life in the city ethnic enclaves—the fast-paced, congested and stressful environment—and their more peaceful, relaxed and serene counterparts in suburbia, which affirms Handlin's observation regarding the less alienating confrontation awaiting immigrants in small towns. The study also renders it possible to trace and evaluate the process of assimilation in these demographic settings, to conceptualize pluralism as a vital entity outside of the archetypical urban neighborhoods, and to understand the dynamics of interaction within ethnic institutions which played a role in making the transition from one culture to another. This study should further explicate how economic forces influenced occupational choices, residential choices, schooling, lifestyles, etc. It should encourage us to evaluate success on the part of the immigrants, to acknowledge the immigrants' contributions to the larger society and, finally, to assess the status of the ethnic group in our times.

One truism that emerges from surveying the totality of the Long Island Italian American experience is the role of choice, that is the exercise of the option regarding settlement outside of congested city neighborhoods. Coming at the height of immigration and in contradistinction to the masses who sought their destinies in the cities, a small but significant minority of Italian immigrants chose the suburbs. Those who opted for the suburbs exercised a conscious effort to satisfy an overwhelming desire to own their own homes. The decision also represented an effort to live in residential environments which more closely resembled the lands from which they came, and thus helped to appease a yearning to live in familiar circumstances insofar as they could, and till the soil—although few became permanent, full-time farmers. Most Long Island Italians worked their lands to supplement meager incomes and to accommodate that innate desire to maintain connections with the past. In growing vegetables and fruit, in raising chickens, fowls and pigs they practiced a self-sufficiency which afforded them the comfort of recalling and comparing their present life with that of their youth in the old country.

The overwhelming majority of Italians on Long Island emigrated from small towns and villages, rather than large Italian cities. They were, for the most part, from southern Italy or Sicily—the exception of being the founding families of Marconiville (Copiague). The chain migration phenomenon which immigration historians have documented elsewhere pertained here as well; in fact in many respects it is startling to realize how insular and provincial this migration has been. The relatively closed Italian-Albanian community in Inwood, the equally tight Durazzano settlement in Westbury, and the heavy Calabrian migration to Patchogue and environs were so powerful that decades later other Italian Americans moving into those areas experienced resistance even to the point of exclusion. Coming from small towns in Italy and settling in familiar sized communities on Long Island enabled them to cushion the shock of resettlement in the new country without having to endure the physical and psychological strains of big city life. The development of small to mid-sized ethnic communities in Long Island towns also rendered more palatable the transition. The importance of settlement choices in suburbia is attested to by repeated responses elicited from informants as well as an awareness of the staying power that characterizes residential patterns. It is striking to realize how many of the "first families" remained rooted in homes they or their ancestors built early in the century. It is also manifested by continuing immigration from places of origin in Italy, as in Westbury. That so many of their descendants have settled in or near the original enclaves is further affirmation of their positive regard for the settlement choices of their ancestors.

The preeminence of economic factors finds validation among Long Island Italian Americans and is reflected in a number of ways. First, in virtually all the communities studied, finding employment in town or nearby played a fairly decisive role. Only in Marconiville did one find Italian Americans of the first generation engaged in extensive travel of an hour or more for employment. In the other locations, work opportunities locally such as in nurseries and estates in Westbury, Glen Cove and Inwood, the sand mines in Port Washington, the lace mill in Patchogue proved indispensable. They offered work opportunities, moreover, for semi-skilled laboring classes which, in the main, Italian immigrants were. They also constituted possibilities for employment for their offspring, especially males. The only Long Island town in which Italian American females of the first generation were employed extensively was Patchogue. In this sense the Micaela di Leonardo thesis that in evaluating ethnic mobility "we should consider the encounter between different ethnic economic strategies and the ethnic mix of particular region of settlement," might seem to pertain.[1] Having said that, however, it would be too strong a statement to invoke materialist preoccupation as the sole determinant of the ethnic group life. As Joseph Lopreato has shown the causes of emigration were many, but

> perhaps more important than all these factors, however, was the cruel social and psychological punishment of the peasant middle class and its satellites, to the point where a peasant, a contadino, in southern Italy was to be a stupid and despicable earthworm, an image accepted even by the peasant himself.[2]

Thus, while material circumstances of immigrant settlement choices were significant, they formed part of a larger mosaic of factors which entered the decision, i.e., reuniting of families, connections with paesani, perceived opportunities to enter the petit bourgeoisie world, health-related considerations, abandonment of a rigid way of life, the perception of suburbia as intrinsically more desirable than the city. It was not as if they lacked choices regarding the workplace; there were options. "We can not ignore the role of choices, as applied to determinism, in human actions, immigrants or otherwise," writes Andrew Rolle.[3] Donna R. Gabbacia, in her recent study on Sicilian immigration, is close to the mark in analyzing the causes of migration.

The dissatisfaction of ordinary peasant men and women with their Sicilian social relationships is the background against which migration and life in the United States must be interpreted. Migrants left Italy not to establish familiar social ties elsewhere but to build lives both economically and socially more satisfying that the ones they left behind.[4]

Furthermore, if we look at the second and third generation who left the cities, we find that here too it is inadequate to locate economics as the sole cause for movement. Donald Tricarico, in his 1984 volume, *The Italians of Greenwich Village*, confirms as much: "The exodus of Italians to the suburbs was more than the result of favorable material conditions. There was an eagerness to leave the small world of the neighborhood and enter the mainstream of American life."[5]

A second lesson to be gleaned is that to relocate to the suburbs required possession of some capital, however small, as usually was the case. The fortunate few did indeed have some funds—generally savings accumulated from earnings in the city's Little Italies where they lived briefly before relocating. But it would be erroneous to suggest that the first generation of Italian settlers on Long Island were middle class; rather they were in lower class economic circumstances, although not at the very bottom of the economic ladder. As members of the lower middle class, they occupied a position which was potentially revolutionary, that is, they experienced enough success and failure to make them discontent with the status quo. Locations were determined by pursuing the chain migration model of seeking out places where relatives and friends were already ensconced. The usual process of home ownership was to purchase land in inexpensive Long Island areas by placing a small down payment and paying off the remainder over a period of time. As financial circumstances and time permitted they built their own homes with the aid of family members. In many instances permanent settlement was preceded by frequenting places in the summertime and gradually finding the wherewithal to make the move.

A third lesson is that suburban Italian Americans, because they were confronted with lesser degrees of discrimination than their counterparts in the large cities, often enjoyed the option of choosing among alternatives. They could opt for rapid assimilation including a negation of their ethnic roots, or they could choose to gain acceptance as Americans of Italian descent, fully conscious of a particular heritage. For the most part, the latter was the choice although there was variety. Many perceived themselves as Americans of Italian ancestry pursuing the *via vecchia* (old way) in the new country. For over four generations the family remained the principal socializing institution as well as the major transmitter of its own culture. However, it was not an exclusive family preoccupation model which characterized these transplanted people; rather it was a sense of interaction with fellow ethnics, whether kinfolk or paesani, who settled nearby.

Still another important lesson taught by a study of the suburban ethnic experience is that ethnic group life demonstrated considerable utilization and interaction with other institutions beginning with the church. With respect to the Catholic Church, to which the overwhelming number of Italian Americans belonged, it is significant to note that no single pattern was followed. In Westbury they were accommodated by the existing Hibernicized parish as they were in Port Washington. In Inwood the Italian immigrants became parishioners of a new Catholic Church created primarily but not exclusively for them. On the other hand in Copiague, Hagerman and Patchogue they helped create Italian national parishes which eventually were transformed into regular territorial parishes. Only in Glen Cove did Italians originate a parish which continues as a national ethnic church.

The history of the suburban ethnic parishes truly deserves to be better studied. It is surprising how total is the ignorance of their history even on the part of contemporary scholars of Italian American life. Joseph Crispino, for example, in his recent book, *The Assimilation of Ethnic Groups: The Italian Case,* completely ignores their role when analyzing the decline of the national parish. His conclusion regarding the decline may have some validity for the old ethnic parishes which either barely survive or no longer function in the old, changing and decaying urban neighborhoods. This, however, is not the entire story regarding such institutions because, as the Long Island experience demonstrates, they either continue to operate as originally envisioned as in Glen Cove, or have been modified to accommodate larger growing heterogeneous parishes as in the instances of Inwood, Copiague, Patchogue, and Hagerman. Where the truly ethnic enterprise endures as in Glen Cove, the result is a greater tendency to perpetuate the "via vecchia," although not exclusively.

Italian immigrants and their progeny also interacted with mutual aid societies and fraternal organizations. Indeed the rapid proliferation of voluntary groups was one of the most striking features of social life in the ethnic enclaves of Long Island. The formation, within a short span of years, of dozens of voluntary organizations in response to social needs, should give lie to the "amoral familism" thesis propounded by Edward Banfield, which posits the view that because of their dedication to the interests of the nuclear family, south Italians could not cooperate with others. Clearly one must come to the conclusion that the "amoral familism" label must be abandoned when referring to Italians in America. Likewise the view that stems from that thesis, that Italian Americans were not joiners and refused to collaborate with each other to advance their interests, must also be rejected with respect to Long Island Italians. Thus, sociologist Joseph Lopresato's assertion that "cooperative ethnic activity comes hard to Italian Americans" finds much contradiction in numerous civic, social and political organizations that flourished in Port Washington during the 1930s. For example, this does not mean that these organizations necessarily worked together, although there were significant efforts to unify. One wonders, in fact, that had it not been for the interruption of the Second World War, ethnic group activity might have been even more pronounced. When it came to suburban Italians, from the earliest days of their residency in the communities examined, one finds strong evidence of a disposition to organize along ethnic lines into voluntary self-help, social, political and religious associations, maintaining them for decades and with some still functioning. One sees also an inclination on the part of succeeding generations to join in non-ethnic organizations as well. Participation in civic bodies such as school boards, fire departments, civic, community, fraternal, service clubs and hospital boards reflects a willingness to assume their share of community responsibilities.

The vaunted reputation Italian Americans had for creating and developing strong, vibrant neighborhoods in cities found verification in suburbia and therefore serves as another lesson of this study. Interestingly, even as many of the urban Italian city neighborhoods have weakened or disappeared, their suburban counterparts have demonstrated remarkable staying power as is evidenced by the Italian communities of Westbury, Glen Cove, Inwood and East Patchogue. Scholars continue to debate the virtues of ethnic group homogeneity and its role as a barrier to assimilation. Stephen Steinberg in his 1982 volume, *The Ethnic Myth*, is extremely critical. "The history of ethnic groups in America is a history of institutional resistance to assimilating forces, and the ethnic revival is only the latest chapter." I must take sharp issue with this conclusion especially with respect to the experience of Long Island's Italian Americans. The history of these ethnic "colonies" is not a history of rigid, inflexible separatism and resistance, rather right from the outset there were manifestations of interaction and intermingling not only within the ethnic group but with the larger society—in employment, education, marketing, and political activity. Although one can cite Italian community after community in which the ethnic group interacted beyond the enclave early in the century, a couple of examples will suffice. The degree of such involvement by Glen Cove's Italians in the First World War, a time during which they entered military service in large numbers and were integrated into units outside of an ethnic environment, is such a case in point. Another instance of this involvement is supplied by the activities of first generation Joseph Cardamone in Patchogue and second generation Dominick Posillico in Westbury, both unquestionably products of the Italian hubris, yet both were eager to assume active political leadership roles in their communities. Thus, these examples, it could be argued, indicate instances of how individuals from the ethnic community worked to bridge the gap between cultures and to promote civic and political responsibility among newcomers.

Still another lesson revealed by this study is that Italian Americans of first and second generation in large numbers have helped transform Long Island political life. Within two generations they have moved from the periphery of political activity to a prominent place in current politics serving in various capacities such as: Alphonse D'Amato, United States Senator; Ralph Case, Nassau County Executive; and numerous members of the New York State Legislature, town supervisors, town board members and village mayors. Italian Americans are extremely conspicuous within the structure of Democratic and Republican parties in Suffolk County and chairmen of the Republican Party in Nassau County. Indeed in the latter instance Italian Americans have headed the party continuously for almost a quarter of a century. As the largest single nationality bloc on Long Island, major political parties cannot afford to ignore them.

Another important lesson yielded should serve to dispel myths about the impact of Italian immigrants and organized labor circles. Coming at a time when the organized labor movement in this country was in its infancy, and working both within organized labor circles and on ad hoc bases, these newcomers made important contributions toward the improvement of the lot of working people on Long Island. Their leadership role proved indispensable in improving working conditions in the nurseries of Westbury, the sand mines of Port Washington, the garment factories of Copiague and the Long Island Railroad, all prior to the First World War. Accordingly, these examples should render mistaken the notion that adumbrates Italian immigrants as inimical to organized labor. Clearly a revision of this traditional reading of labor history at the turn of the century is required.

What does a study about Italian American community life tell us about the issue of crime—the phenomenon which so engrossed Americans about the ethnic group and which rendered organized crime virtually synonymous with Italian immigrants? Comprehensive examination of the communities under study in this volume suggests that criminal activity was not a natural sequence of the existence of Italian enclaves. Of the several Long Island Italian American neighborhoods which were flourishing in the pre-World War I era—the period when crime in the form of the Mafia or, even more, the Black Hand (La Mano Nero) was the preoccupation of urban Italian colonies, there was, with the exception of Inwood, no such focus. Inwood presented a singular case wherein public concern over organized criminal activity among the Italian element approached hysteria. Why this was so requires further scrutiny, however; perhaps its proximity to New York City offers an explanation, although this is, frankly, speculation. The conclusion one draws is that given the excessive and protracted fixation with Italian crime in large cities such as New York and Chicago, its near absence in the suburbs constitutes a remarkable contrast. With the unique exception of Inwood, the bottom line conclusion is that organized crime did not play a major role insofar as Long Island Italians were concerned.

Closely connected with the crime issue is the evolution of law enforcement in Long Island Italian neighborhoods. Specifically, the early and extensive use of indigenous ethnic community people to enforce laws locally is worthy of comment. It was more than mere coincidence that found Vincent Zavatt, Dominick Posillico, John Stephani and Charles Barcellona to elevated deputy sheriffs or, as in the case of Barcellona, elected to town constable. What is evident is the degree of prescience on the part of local political chieftains, virtually all Republicans, in selecting leaders within the ethnic community to their first public posts. Indeed these would be the first public positions that members of the ethnic group achieved. By this calculated move, the political power brokers extended recognition to the individuals of standing within the ethnic community and by association sowed the seeds of partisan political incubation within the group.

The 1980 United States census, by addressing itself to the questions regarding ethnic background, provides extremely useful data on issues of self-perceptions. The data yields information that about twelve million persons claimed Italian ancestry in the United States, or approximately 5.4 percent of the total population. For Italian Americans on Long Island this data is especially significant in that it reveals that almost 25 percent (24.56) of the residents of the two counties identify themselves as of Italian ancestry—the city figures which show 1,132,861, or 16 percent of the city's total population are Italian Americans. On Long Island, Italian American represent at least 40 percent of the total population in six individual towns or hamlets (Franklin Square 42.5 percent; Deer Park 41.6; Elmont 41; Shirley 40.1; North Lindenhurst 40.1; and Inwood 40). Large numbers speak Italian at home: Elmont 3,149; Franklin Square 2,367; West Babylon 2,415; Valley Stream 1,915; Deer Park 1,974; Westbury 1,763. With respect to the selected communities under study in this volume the 1980 population is as follows: Inwood 40.0 percent; Copiague 38.0; North Patchogue 32.5.; Glen Cove 31.2; Westbury 29.7; East Patchogue 28.6; Port Washington 24.9; Patchogue Village 24.9; and North Bellport 20.1. These statistics confirm a continuing attachment to the Long Island communities which first attracted Italian immigrants approximately a century ago.

Given the large number of Americans of Italian descent, one can conclude that they do not reflect a monolithic, clone-like people all of whom manifest identical characteristics, interests and outlooks as is repeated so frequently as to become stereotypes. We are reminded by Andrew Rolle whose penetrating psychological history, *The Italian Americans, Troubled Roots,* says that "In their search for selfhood the immigrants assumed no single identity. Each worked out an accommodation in unique ways, realigning the personality to fit new realities. The idea that we historians can homogenize the ethnics into one national experience has become ridiculous."[6] While the first and second generation were heavily represented in the laboring, unskilled or semi-skilled classes, for example, the third and fourth generations span the occupational ladder and are represented in every economic sphere. Although precise data on the following is wanting, the impression gleaned from years of research and observation is that they attend and complete educational goals on a level with the Long Island population at large, have significant representation in the various professions of law, medicine, education, dentistry, etc., and are involved in business activities as entrepreneurs in numbers approximating their percentage of the population. Their representation among the Catholic clergy of Rockville Centre is probably below their proportion of the Catholic population of the diocese; however, increased percentages of Italian names seem to have appeared in recent years among the younger clergy. Overt discrimination of the type practiced in the early part of the century and as exemplified in the real estate broadside excluding Italians from purchasing Long Island property in one community is, fortunately, a thing of the past. Unfortunately, discrimination of a more subtle type is still possible, as some of examples in the 1960s indicate. Subtle discrimination is of course more difficult to document, but a feeling exists among many of the informants that it is not altogether a thing of the past.

The question of success is an intriguing one. American mythology and folklore have always emphasized an Horatio Alger theme of this country as a place of unquestioned opportunity leading toward upward mobility, a land wherein people of impoverished background could rise to the uppermost rungs of the social and economic ladder, a nation where opportunity abounded and hard toil paid handsome dividends. It would be the height of naiveté to generalize that Long Island Italian Americans have "made it" and that the heady dream of American success has in fact been realized—obviously such an assertion would be exaggeration and misrepresentation. Yet in a number of respects these sons and daughters from Italy can be said definitely to have improved their collective status over the past few generations. As Richard Alba has written, "Given the socioeconomic advances of the Italians, it was only natural that they should participate in the suburban pilgrimage."[7] There are two definitions of success, Thernstrom reminds us. One revolves around the commonly held view that success is measured as mobility away from the status of manual laborer and into positions of supervision such as foreman, clerks, managers, professionals, or business owners. The second definition of success has as its criterion property ownership, which obviously presupposes the ability to save money with which to negotiate this type of proprietorship.[8] Arguably these models of success may not be accepted as sufficiently inclusive, thereby overlooking large areas of action, thought and feeling. Be that as it may, within the parameters of Thernstrom's definitions, Long Island Italian Americans enjoy modest success.

By any measure these unskilled or semi-skilled manual laborers, who formed the vast majority of Italian newcomers to the area, stood at the bottom of the social ladder, but it was not to a permanent underclass status and in the course of a relatively short period—one or two generations—a significant degree of mobility was discernible in improved occupational and homeownership categories. Other researchers use the term "social mobility" rather than success. Richard Alba, for instance, chooses to single out two indicators of social position: education and occupation to measure mobility. Using WASPs (descendants from the British Isles) for comparison, he concludes that in certain categories such as all members of an ethnic group who have attended college, Italians are behind British Americans. Likewise they trail British Americans when it comes to representation on the upper end of the occupational spectrum. However, differences in the lower end are not so great so that even if Italians are more represented in blue collar jobs, presently there are virtually no Italians in the ranks of the unskilled, which in itself reflects a significant change from a few decades ago. Further, when one considers the more recent generations, much of the disparity between British Americans and Italian Americans disappears: "The third and fourth generations, those born after World War II, and those of mixed background have either caught up or are about to do so."[9]

The Italian-descended population of Long Island is, then, a variegated people, a many-dimensioned populace who offer a wide variety of ethnic behavioral patterns. There are those who have retained much of their Italian culture including strong family attachment based on blood kinship; their married children live in close proximity, the Italian language is spoken in the home, there is a love for working the land, a high priority accorded to home ownership, support for old ethnic organizations such as the now resurgent Sons of Italy lodges, or for new ethnic-based organizations such as the Italian American Service Club of Brookhaven. This group of Italian Americans, furthermore, tends to identify itself unhesitatingly as of Italian background, and travels to Italy extensively to either visit family or absorb the culture of their ancestors. Having said that, one also notices Long Island Italian Americans living lifestyles, enjoying family incomes, aspiring to professions, attending schools, joining civic organizations, becoming involved in politics, and entering the entrepreneurial world in patterns not too dissimilar from the prevailing culture. They are, if you will, to a considerable extent assimilated, but not altogether. Even when studying the complacent 1950s when ethnicity seemed to have receded, scholars have found that it nonetheless prevailed in the suburbs. Richard Polenberg, in *One Nation Divisible*, found that just as class distinctions persisted, "so too, did distinctions based on ethnicity." When one can point to a rebound of ethnic organizations, to an increase in the numbers studying Italian in schools, to large attendance at feast-day celebrations, in sum, when one can point to a continuity of ethnic practices, then one concludes that despite apparent assimilation, the ethnic past is not wholly blotted out; it endures, altered in shape and format from the ethnic style of yesteryear, but distinct enough for participants to acknowledge that they are of Italian background and that others in society identify them as such. It is as if the words of anthropologist Milton Gordon were designed for them.

My essential thesis here is that the sense of ethnicity has proven to be hardy. As though with a wily cunning of its own, as though there were some essential element in man's nature that demanded it—something that compelled him to merge his lonely individual identity in some ancestral group of fellows smaller by far than the whole human race, smaller often the nation—the sense of ethnic belonging has survived. It has survived in various forms and with various names, but it has not perished, and twentieth-century man is closer to his stone-age ancestors than he knows.[10]

There is a need to be reminded that intergroup relations revolve around a number of social forces among which ethnicity has played and continues to play an important part. It functions as a basis for the social life of people not only in urban centers but also in the nation's suburbs. The history of Long Island Italian Americans, it is hoped, provides a strong argument for the incorporation of the ethnic dimension in any understanding of the past history of a group as well as in assessing the social record of an area. It is hoped also that this history will help develop a better appreciation for the dynamics of ethnic group life in suburbia.

Notes

1. Micaela di Leoardo, *The Varieties of Ethnic Experiences*, Ithaca, 1984, p. 107.

2. Joseph Lopreato, *Italian Americans*, New York, 1970, p. 3.

3. Andrew F. Rolle, *Italian Americans, Troubled Roots*, New York, 1980, p. 182.

4. Donna R. Gabbaccia, *From Sicily to Elizabeth Street*, Albany, 1984, p. 52.

5. Donald Tricarico, *The Italians of Greenwich Village*, New York, 1984, p. 74.

6. Rolle, p. 180.

7. Richard Alba, *Italian Americans: Into the Twilight of Ethnicity*, Englewood Cliffs, New Jersey, 1985, p. 88.

8. Stephen Thernstrom, *Poverty and Progress, Social Mobility in a Nineteenth Century City*, New York, 1975, pp. 8-9.

9. Alba, p. 130.

10. Milton Gordon, *Assimilation in American Life*, New York, 1955, p. 245.

Chapter 8

Italian Immigrant Women in Comparative Perspective

Donna R. Gabaccia
University of North Carolina at Charlotte

In 1977, when the American Italian Historical Association and the Canadian Italian Historical Association jointly sponsored a conference on the historical study of women in Italian migrations the topic seemed well launched.[1] Virginia Yans-McLaughlin's exciting (1977) study of Buffalo had just opened many questions about the lives of immigrant women. The published proceedings of the Toronto conference and Luciano Iorizzo's preface to it conveyed the optimistic sense of beginning apparent at the conference itself (Caroli et al., 1978).

Measured quantitatively, the conference was indeed an important beginning. Study of Italian immigrant women continues to this day. Recent bibliographies of U.S. immigrant women point to roughly one hundred published works on Italians (exclusive of biography and autobiography)—about half have appeared since 1970 (Cordasco, 1985; Gabaccia, 1989).

Still, this growing literature on Italian immigrant women in the U.S. is not widely cited, nor is it integrated into general accounts of immigrant and ethnic life in the U.S. (Gabaccia, 1987). George Pozzetta's (1989) otherwise very helpful and complete review directs those interested in women's lives only to Caroli et al. (1978). Similarly, women's historians rarely cite more than one or two works on Italian immigrants when discussing the ethnicity of working-class women (Hewitt, 1985).

Scholarship on Italian women seems "nowhere at home" (Gabaccia, 1991).

Because I want research on Italian women to find the home it deserves, I will pursue two related topics in this paper. First, I will trace the marginality of research on Italian immigrant women to methodological choices. Second, I will argue that comparative methods, when carefully chosen, can help scholars find a home for their research. Scholars must recognize that women's history and immigration offer conflicting home addresses. Different types of comparisons open doors to each, and usually we can enter through only one.

I will begin by rejecting one obvious but too simple explanation for the invisibility of Italian women as immigrants. While historians of other immigrant groups produced monographs on the women of those groups, no monograph or synthesis appeared on the experience of Italian women as migrants, immigrants or women "left behind" by male migration. For the U.S., we have no equivalent of Hasia Diner's *Erin's Daughters* (1983) or Sydney Weinberg's *World of Our Mothers* (1988). In Canada, too, research focuses on particular periods and particular cities (Iacovetta, 1991 and 1992; Dubinsky, 1991).

With no synthesis, most scholars in women's and immigration history treat Virginia Yans-McLaughlin's early work as the main (and usually the only) source on Italian immigrant women. McLaughlin portrayed Buffalo's Italians as submissive women, with lives narrowly confined to the home and family by the dictates of Italian patriarchy. Italian women worked for wages outside the home only when they could avoid contacts with strange men; when they earned money at home, they and their families did not recognize their contributions (Yans-McLaughlin, 1971, 1974, 1977a, 1977b).

The early influence of Yans-McLaughlin's work is not surprising. Her interpretation paralleled much early women's history research that focused on the victimization of women by patriarchal traditions, and by the men of their own groups. What is surprising is the continued influence of Yans-McLaughlin's work. Recently, both women's history generally and research on Italian women instead emphasize women's agency in confronting and modifying male dominance. It is these newer interpretations, not Yans-McLaughlin's work, that are not cited in women's history and immigration history.

Miriam Cohen first (1977) disagreed with Yans-McLaughlin, when she found high rates of wage-earning among unmarried and married

Italian women in New York City. (See also Mormino and Pozzetta, 1982; Vecchio, 1989). Colomba F. Furio (1980) and Jean Scarpaci (1980) documented conditions under which Italian immigrant women were active as labor organizers. I attempted to revise notions of Italian familism and to portray Italian misogyny as a compensatory ideology rather than an everyday practice (Gabaccia, 1982 and Gabaccia, 1984). Lucia Chiavola Birnbaum (1980, 1983) portrayed powerful Italian "godmothers and earthmothers." These interpretations have influenced Italian scholars (Cetti, 1984; Vezzosi, 1984, 1986; Tirabassi, 1982, 1990a, 1990b; Parrino, 1988) but their work remains unknown to most U.S. women's and immigration historians.

U.S. women's historians continue to portray Italian women as family-bound, and to use Italian families as examples of extreme patriarchal control over women (Bloom, 1985; Gordon, 1988). Their preference for "oppressed" Italian women stands out with particular starkness because portraits of other Latin and immigrant women, especially Mexicanas and Chicanas, have been significantly revised to acknowledge women's activism and agency (Ruiz, 1987; Zavella, 1987). Immigration historians do not especially emphasize the oppression of Italian women within families, yet they agree in seeing family concerns dominating the lives of women.[2]

Why has the portrait of the submissive or family-bound Italian woman persisted in the face of repeated challenges? I will explore here only the simplest—and least judgmental—of explanations, one emphasizing methodology.

Unlike Yans-McLaughlin, later students of Italian immigrant women rarely followed the one-group case study methodology popular in immigration history in the 1970s and 1980s. Instead, most compared immigrant women of several backgrounds. Maxine Seller's *Immigrant Women* (1981), for example, challenged stereotypes of passive women, but did so by presenting documents on the lives of immigrant women of many backgrounds, Italians among them. Corinne Krause (1977, 1978a, 1978b, 1981), Judy Smith (1978, 1985), Elizabeth Ewen (1980, 1985), Ardis Cameron (1985), Kathy Peiss (1986), Laura Anker (1988), Miriam Cohen (1977), Thomas Kessner and Betty Boyd Caroli (1978) compared Italian to Jewish, Polish, and South Slav women.

Comparative studies of immigrant women either emphasized broad similarities between Italian and other female immigrants' experiences, or they identified distinctive Italian patterns in women's educational, recreational, and courtship behavior. Scholars of Italian migrations seem to have found little of interest in comparative studies that revealed no significant differences between Italian and other immigrant women.[3] Comparisons which revealed differences described Italian immigrant women as less "emancipated," educated or autonomous than other women. Yans-McLaughlin's research better explained this outcome than newer research on active, resourceful women.

To complicate matters further, many early studies of Italian migrants focused on gender—comparing Italian men and women, and analyzing their relations among themselves and with each other—rather than utilizing the women-centered method (studying women separately from men) that dominated women's history throughout the 1970s. Yans-McLaughlin and Judy Smith (1980, 1985) analyzed men and women within Italian families and communities. I examined gender in the migration process, family, kinship and neighborhood socializing in changing urban environments, and old and new world protest traditions (Gabaccia 1982, 1984a, 1984b, 1988). Published in the mid-1980s, Smith's and my work appeared at a time when women's historians had become skeptical of studying women in their families (considered by then "the seat of their oppression," see Hartmann, 1979). Although the women of Smith's and my work are neither submissive, male-dominated nor limited strictly to household duties, their lives remain centered in families and ethnic communities; they do not venture into the English-speaking "public" world, where Anglo-American women sought autonomy and independence. Thus, from the perspective of women's history, they appeared no different from the women Yans-McLaughlin had described ten years earlier.

Work on gender in immigrant life also appeared at a time when immigration historians had recognized the centrality of families to immigrants (Bodnar, 1985). By stressing family solidarities shared by men and women, immigration historians rarely showed much interest in gender differences. They assumed they satisfactorily summarized women's lives by describing the family as a unit (Weinberg, 1992). Immigration historians ignored evidence on women within families, although gendered accounts had highlighted precisely this topic. Information on childbirth, housework or consumption did not fit easily into accounts that defined confrontation with capitalism as men had experienced it—in the workplace, the fraternal club, and the union (Gabaccia, 1987).

As these examples suggest, I have concluded that the main challenge facing scholars of Italian immigrant women is a methodological one. Escaping marginality requires recognition that women's history and immigration history diverge methodologically. It requires us to recognize that each field has its own, unique research agenda. This is an ideal time for scholars interested in Italian women as migrants to take stock. Both women's history and immigration history are undergoing methodological transformation. If the study of Italian immigrant women is to proceed and to receive the attention it deserves, it must be formulated with a clear sense of which audiences we want to address, and what their new methodological and topical concerns will be.

It may seem ironic to call my paper "Italian Immigrant Women in Comparative Perspective" since I have argued that comparative work contributed to women's marginality. But I remain firmly convinced that the answer to finding an academic home is more comparison, not less. Breaking with the past, many of our colleagues in immigration history and women's history now embrace some type of comparative method. Methodological choices remain the key to finding our audience.

Comparison is arguably the most complex of historical methods. In migration studies, Samuel Baily (1983, 1985) and Nancy Green (1990) have urged us to define our "units of analysis" carefully or risk careless conclusions. Green (1991) has argued further that the type of comparison chosen inevitably shapes the conclusions drawn. A promising alternative to case studies, the comparative method nevertheless demands careful choices. What is true in the comparative study of any social group is doubly true when the subject is women, for whom the possibilities for comparison emerge in two scholarly fields.

However unintentionally, *The Italian Immigrant Woman in North America* outlined the types of comparisons which still await scholars of Italian women as migrants. The articles in this collection represented a wide variety of approaches, demonstrating that Italian women could sensibly be compared to others in at least five ways.

They could be compared, first, among themselves, as immigrant women. Articles by Strom, Smith, and Krase (Caroli et al., 1978) compared Italian women of differing generations in the U.S. The very title of the Toronto conference suggested comparing Italian immigrant women in North American receiving nations, or—by implication at least—in other receiving nations, whether Australia and Canada or Argentina and Switzerland. Second, female migrants could be compared to women in Italy (see articles by Noether, Howard, Gibson, LaVigna and Eshelman in Caroli et al., 1978). Third, they could be compared to immigrant women of other backgrounds (see articles by Krause and Collecchia in Caroli et al., 1978), and fourth, to the native-born American or other women with whom immigrants interacted in social welfare settings, especially settlement houses, and in public schools (see articles by Juliani, Seller, Batinich, and Pozzetta in Caroli et al, 1978). Finally, Italian immigrant women could sensibly be compared to Italian immigrant men (see articles by Harney, Pautasso, and Sturino in Caroli et al., 1978).

The options for comparison outlined by this 1978 publication remain exhaustive and worthy of consideration today. Most point to women-centered research, comparing Italian women to each other or to other women. The fifth points to methodologies which instead focus on gender. Either approach can be formulated in ways that would be interesting and central to women's history or immigration history. But only a few approaches will be simultaneously interesting to both fields.

Reviewing these five comparative methods reminds us that research on Italian immigrant women up until now has compared Italian immigrant women primarily to other immigrant women and usually in one place—the United States—and in one period of time—the years before 1914. Women-centered comparative studies rarely gained the attention of Italianists in the 1980s but they received somewhat more attention from women's historians. Will women's history continue to be the logical home for such comparisons?

Perhaps not. Women's historians (Amott and Matthaei, 1991) currently view Italians and many other immigrant women of the nineteenth century as "Euro-Americans." Assuming cultural homogeneity among Europeans leaves little room for interest in comparisons among them. Studies which compare Italian immigrant women to Asian or Latin immigrants or to native-born minority groups (African and Native Americans and Chicanas) might be of greater interest. Comparisons which focus on religious differences among Europeans hold promise too, as women's historians rarely recognize how religion simultaneously divides Italians from, say, Norwegians, while linking them to Hispanics.

Studies which compare Italian women to other immigrant and native-born women need to confront head-on the difficult issue of defining female autonomy and emancipation cross-culturally. The native-born woman of the Anglo-American middle classes, and the family in which she has lived have typically been the implicit standard against which the autonomy of immigrant and minority women of many backgrounds have been measured. The more like their Anglo-American or middle-class sisters, the more emancipated women are claimed to be; the less like them, the less emancipated. Measures of emancipation like these should be recognized for what they are: measures of cultural assimilation—no more. Again, comparisons of the family loyalties and community activism of Italian and native-born racial minorities might make this point most explicitly.

Comparisons of Italians to other immigrant and minority women will be of interest to women's historians writing a women-centered "multicultural history" of the United States (DuBois and Ruiz 1990). But they will be of less interest to women's historians who argue instead for research on gender rather than women-centered history (Blewett 1991).

Sydney Weinberg (1992) has argued recently that immigration historians, too, have a great need for gendered histories of immigration and immigrant life; she argues for including gender in studies of immigrant families and communities. It strikes me as unlikely that immigration historians—having just completed twenty years of case studies of particular communities, including Italian ones—will pursue case studies merely to compensate for past neglect of gender. Instead, historians of gender will be receptive to studies of particular immigrant communities in the future. These historians are particularly concerned at present with the construction of masculinity and femininity; women's historians like Mary Blewett (1991) and Nancy Hewitt (1991) demonstrate that the social construction of gender must be studied in particular communities and in particular times.

Linkages between the new concerns of gender historians and traditional topics in immigration and ethnic history—particularly generational change and ethnic identity—may provide historians of immigrant women with a unique opportunity to reach both audiences. Both studies of gender and studies of ethnicity now focus on their creation, or construction. Suzanne Sinke (1992) has recently called for attention to the reproduction of ethnicity as an important dimension of immigrant women's work. Sinke's concept of social reproduction opens new opportunities for rethinking the powerlessness of "submissive" or "family-oriented" Italian immigrant women, for it was their work as child-rearers and kinswomen that guaranteed or demolished group and individual ethnic identity into the second or third generation. Attention to the reproduction of ethnicity and gender will be particularly interesting to women' historians if it is sensitive to language. Few deconstructionists have yet confronted the complexities of language and bilingualism in creating gender or ethnicity.

Gendered approaches focus on immigrant life in one country, usually (still) the U.S., but the construction of ethnicity and gender already has competitors in U.S. historiography. These demand a different methodology. James Barrett has recently called for studies of interactions among immigrants of many backgrounds and generations; Barrett argues that our focus on immigrants of particular backgrounds has kept us from describing or understanding the consequences of a process he calls "Americanization from the Bottom Up"—the creation of a working-class culture that was as much a product of successive generations of immigrants interacting with each other as with a mainstream "American" culture. Rather than comparing immigrant women to women of other backgrounds, whether foreign- and native-born, a new generation of scholarship on Italian women might focus instead on the places where Italian women came together with girls and women of other backgrounds—in schools, workplaces, domestic science classes, dances, neighborhoods, church sodalities and the like, to create working-class and ethnic versions of "American womanhood."

In striking contrast to comparative studies of immigrants in any one nation, Italianists have led the way in developing international, comparative and "diaspora" methodologies that wrench the study of migration out of the historiographical context of any one nation (Harney, 1977; Baily and Ramella, 1988; Gabaccia 1988; Ramirez, 1991; Pozzetta and Ramirez 1992). A strong argument for diaspora studies of Italians globally is that they use Italian-language sources. (In strong contrast, comparisons of Italians to immigrants or natives of other backgrounds in one nation typically depend exclusively on sources of the receiving country—limiting their reliability.)

Still, in studying Italians "everywhere," scholars are moving onto terrain where the study of women and gender are both quite undeveloped. Study of Italian immigrant women in countries other than the U.S., Canada (Iacovetta, 1986, 1991, 1992; Dubinsky 1991) and Australia (Pesman, 1989; Diana, 1988; Vasta, 1990; Vasta, 1992) has only just begun. (For Argentina, see Gandolfo, 1990.) I know of no studies that compare Italian women in several receiving nations (although Susanna Garroni's [1988] study of Italian women in many U.S. locations points to an interesting method for doing so). Worse, the "internationalist" and "world-systems" approaches from which migration historians increasingly borrow are not known for their sensitivity to gender (see Simon and Brettell, 1986; Pedraza, 1991). If women are not to be excluded from a new generation of innovative studies, then the time to think about integrative strategies is now.

My own guess is that integration can best be achieved through attention to gender studies, not a series of parallel international comparisons of Italian women separate from men. We all know that the international labor market for Italians was deeply divided by sex and that Italian labor migrant "birds of passage" or "golondrine" were almost all male. Migrations to Europe, Africa and South America were even more male-dominated than migrations to the U.S. and Canada.

The male domination of labor migrations itself should call our attention to gender. The separation of men from women during migration is in no sense natural—as wide variations in migrant sex ratios easily demonstrate. Robert Harney pointed out in his early and influential article, "Men without Women" (in Caroli et al., 1978) that the separation of the sexes through migration and their strategies for reunion are themselves worthy of study. Harney's article has been praised for many things, but I do not think anyone has ever identified it as an early study in the history of masculinity—a topic of considerable interest to gender historians today.

Greater attention to Italian women left behind could also help us explain both the male migrations and Italian patterns of settlement—which clearly differed from country to country internationally and from Italian province to province—in the nineteenth and early twentieth century. We badly need to think about the function of women "left behind" in the international division of labor emerging of years. Men migrated to accumulate capital and save money, but they could not always send home regular remittances. Either other men had to feed the women left behind, or women had to feed themselves. We have evidence for both patterns. Women came to dominate subsistence agriculture in many parts of Italy during the mass migrations. The consequences of that feminization have barely been mentioned, let alone explored. Women's takeover of subsistence agriculture at home might be seen as a structural explanation for male migrants' willingness to accept low wages: men's wages in the new world did not have to support reproduction; women paid those costs by laboring at home. At the same time, women's ability to feed themselves and their children during men's absences set a bottom line for men's wages abroad.

Women's work shaped migration patterns. It is very clear, for example, that in areas where women had little access to land for subsistence or to local wage-earning jobs (e.g., Sicily), sex ratios among migrants were far more balanced than they were in other areas (e.g., the northwest) where women took over subsistence production from men (Gabaccia, 1986). Attention to the decline of rural cottage industries, especially textile production in the south, may also shed light on the differing migration patterns of Italian men and women to many destinations.[4]

Still, in recommending gendered approaches to the study of the Italian diaspora, I would caution scholars with a concluding observation. International, diaspora and comparative studies are often undertaken to determine what—if anything—is particularly *Italian* about Italian immigrants or about Italian immigrant women. Nancy Green (1991) has argued that differing comparative strategies inevitably result in differing conclusions about the influence of culture. Comparing an immigrant group to many others in one location will focus attention on the differences introduced by cultural particularities, while comparing that group as it migrates to many locations will as inevitably reveal the enormous variation every culture subsumes. We tend to see the primordial depths of cultural difference with the first approach, and the shallowness of culture's influence with the second.

When discussing women, this relationship between method and conclusion is especially complex. Differing types of comparisons reveal not only the strengths or the limits of culture but also the strengths and limits of "sisterhood" based on gender. By comparing Italian women to men as they migrate around the globe, we reveal the strength of gender divisions, not the power of Italianita. But when we compare Italian women to women of other backgrounds in the U.S., we will instead be impressed with the power of culture or ethnicity to divide (or even undermine) sisterhood. The choice of comparative method then, cannot be a completely objective one. It reveals much of our own identities and desires. In choosing our method we identify the group from which we wish to differentiate ourselves. Comparison, in this sense, may never provide for a scholarly home based purely on identity—whether of gender or ethnicity.

Notes

1. I'd like to thank Diane Vecchio and Nancy Green who alerted me to important questions I might otherwise have left aside. Thanks also to Thomas Kozak for his editing help with this and other projects.
2. One difference is that authors like Bodnar (1985) believe family concerns equally dominated men's lives.
3. Pozzetta (1978), for example, cites only Smith's 1985 book in his influential review essay, and then in reference to family pattern's more than women's lives.
4. See chapter 3 in Gabaccia (forthcoming).

References

Amott, T. and J. Matthaei. 1991. *Race, Gender, and Work: a Multicultural Economic History of Women in the United States*. Boston: South End Press.

Anker, L. 1988. "Women, Work and Family: Polish, Italian and Eastern European Immigrants in Industrial Connecticut, 1890-1940." *Polish American Studies* 45 (Autumn): 23-49.

Baily, S. L. 1983. "The Adjustment of Italian Immigrants in Buenos Aires and New York, 1870-1914." *American Historical Review* 88 (April): 281-305. 1985.

————. "The Future of Italian American Studies: An Historian's Approach to Research in the Coming Decade." Pp. 193-201 in *Italian Americans: New Perspectives in Italian Immigration and Ethnicity*, ed. L. Tomasi. Staten Island: Center for Migration Studies of New York.

Baily, S. and F. Ramella, eds. 1988. *One Family, Two Worlds: An Italian Family's Correspondence Across the Atlantic, 1901-1922*. New Brunswick: Rutgers University Press.

Barrett, J. R. Forthcoming. "Americanization from the Bottom Up: Immigration and Remaking of the American Working Class, 1880-1940."

Birnbaum, L. C. 1980. "Earthmothers, Godmothers, and Radicals: The Inheritance of Sicilian American Women." *Marxist Perspectives* 3 (Spring): 128-141.

————. 1983. "Education for Conformity: The Case of Sicilian American Women Professionals." Pp. 243-252. *Italian Americans in the Professions*, ed. R. U. Pane. New York: American Italian Historical Association.

Blewett, M. H. 1991. "Manhood and the Market: The Politics of Gender and Class among the Textile Workers of Fall River, Massachusetts, 1870-1880." Pp. 92-113 in *Work Engendered: Toward a New History of American Labor*, ed. A. Baron. Ithaca: Cornell University Press.

Bloom, F. T. 1985. "Struggling and Surviving—the Life Style of European Immigrant Breadwinning Mothers in American Industrial Cities, 1900-1930." *Women's Studies International Forum* 8 (6): 609-620.

Bodnar, J. 1985. *The Transplanted: A History of Immigrants in Urban America.* Bloomington: Indiana University Press.

Cameron, A. 1985. "Bread and Roses Revisited: Women's Culture and Working-Class Activism in the Lawrence Strike of 1912." Pp. 42-61 in *Women's Work and Protest: A Century of U.S. Women's Labor History*, ed. R. Milkman. Boston: Routledge and Kegan Paul.

Caroli, B. et al. 1978. *The Italian Immigrant Woman in North America.* Toronto: Multicultural History Society of Ontario.

Cetti, L. 1984. "Donne Italiane a New York e Lavoro a Domicilio (1910-1925)." *Movimento Operaio e Socialista* 7(3): 291-303.

———. 1984-85. "Work Experience among Italian Women in New York, 1900-1930." *Rivista di Studi Anglo Americani* 3(4-5): 493-505.

Cohen, M. 1977. "Italian American Women in New York City, 1900-1950: Work and School." Pp. 138-157 in *Class, Sex, and the Woman Worker*, ed. M. Cantor and B. Laurie. Westport, Conn.: Greenwood Press.

Cordasco, F. 1985. *The Immigrant Woman in North America: An Annotated Bibliography of Selected References.* Metuchen, N.J.: The Scarecrow Press.

Diana, A. 1988. "Italian Women in Australia." *Affari Sociali Internazionali* 2.

Diner, H. R. 1983. *Erin's Daughters in America: Irish Immigrant Women in the Nineteenth Century.* Baltimore: The Johns Hopkins University Press.

Dubinsky, K. 1991. "Murder, Womanly Virtue, and Motherhood: The Case of Angelina Napolitana." *Canadian Historical Review* (December).

DuBois, E. C. and V. L. 1990. *Unequal Sisters, A Multi-Cultural Reader in U.S. Women's History.* New York: Routledge.

Ewen, E. 1980. "City Lights: Immigrant Women and the Rise of the Movies." *SIGNS* 5: 545-565.

———. 1985. *Immigrant Women in the Land of Dollars: Life and Culture on the Lower East Side, 1890-1925.* New York: Monthly Review Press.

Furio, C. 1980. "Immigrant Women and Industry." In *Pane e Lavoro: The Italian American Working Class*, ed. G. Pozzetta. Staten Island: American Italian Historical Association.

Gabaccia, D. 1982. "Sicilians in Space: Environmental Change and Family Geography." *Journal of Social History* 16(2): 53-66.

———. 1984a. "Kinship, Culture and Migration: A Sicilian Example." *Journal of American Ethnic History* 3(2): 39-53.

———. 1984b. *From Sicily to Elizabeth Street: Housing and Social Change among Italian Immigrants, 1880-1930.* Albany: State University of New York Press.

———. 1987a. "In the Shadows of the Periphery: Italian Women in the Nineteenth Century." Pp. 166-176 in *Connecting Spheres: Women in the*

Western World, 1500 to the Present, ed. M. J. Boxer and J. H. Quataert. New York: Oxford University Press.

———. 1987b. *"The Transplanted*: Women and Family in Immigrant America." *Social Science History* 11(3): 243-253.

———. 1988. *Militants and Migrants: Rural Sicilians Become American Workers*. New Brunswick: Rutgers University Press.

———. 1989. *Immigrant Women in the United States: A Selectively Annotated Multidisciplinary Bibliography*. Westport, Conn.: Greenwood Press.

———. 1991. "Immigrant Women: Nowhere at Home?" *Journal of American Ethnic History* 10(4): 61-87.

———. Forthcoming. *From the Other Side: Women and Gender in American Immigrant Life, 1820-1990*. Bloomington: Indiana University Press.

Gandolfo, R. 1990. "Dall'alto Molise al centro di Buenos Aires: le donne agnonesi e la prima emigrazione transatlantica (1870-1900)." Paper presented at the Conference for the Historical Study of Women in the Italian Countryside, Conselice/Ravenna.

Garroni, M. S. 1988. "Coal Mines, Farm and Quarry Frontiers: The Different Americas of Italian Immigrant Women." *Studia Nordamericana* 5(2): 115-136.

Gordon, L. 1988. *Heroines of Their Own Lives: The Politics and History of Family Violence*. New York: Viking Press.

Green, N. L. 1990. "L'Histoire Comparative et le Champ des Etudes Migratoires." *Annales, Economies, Societes, Civilisations* 6 (Nov.-Dec.): 1335-1350.

———. 1991. "La Methode Comparative en Histoire: Elements pour une Theorie et une Pratique." Unpublished paper in possession of author.

Harney, R. F. 1977. "The Commerce of Migration." *Canadian Ethnic Studies* 9(1): 42-53.

Hartmann, H. 1979. "The Family as a Locus of Gender, Class, and Political Struggle: The Example of Housework." *SIGNS* 6(3): 366-394.

Hewitt, N. A. 1985. "Beyond the Search for Sisterhood: American Women's History in the 1980's." *Social History* 10(October): 299-321.

———. 1991. "'The Voice of Virile Labor': Labor Militancy, Community Solidarity, and Gender Identity among Tampa's Latin Workers, 188-1921." Pp. 142-167 in *Work Engendered: Toward a New History of American Labor*, ed. A. Baron. Ithaca: Cornell University Press.

Iacovetta, F. 1986. "From *Contadina* to Worker: Southern Italian Working Women in Toronto, 1947-63." Pp. 195-22 in *Looking Into My Sister's Eyes*, ed. J. Burnet. Toronto: The Multicultural History Society of Ontario.

———. 1991. "Ordering in Bulk: Canadian Immigration Policy and the Recruitment of Workers from Italy." *Journal of American Ethnic History* 11,1 (Fall).

————. 1992. *Such Hardworking People: Italian Immigrants in Postwar Toronto*. Kingston and Montreal: McGill-Queens University Press.

Kessner, T. and B. B. Caroli. 1978. "New Immigrant Women at Work: Italians and Jews in New York City." *Journal of Ethnic Studies* 5 (Winter): 19-32.

Krause, C. 1977. "Italian, Jewish and Slavic Grandmothers in Pittsburgh: Their Economic Roles." *Frontiers* 2 (Summer): 18-28.

————. 1978a. *Grandmothers, Mothers and Daughters: An Oral History Study of Ethnicity, Mental Health, and Continuity of Three Generations of Jewish, Italian, and Slavic-American Women*. New York: American Jewish Committee Institute on Pluralism and Group Identity.

————. 1978b. "Urbanization Without Breakdown: Italian, Jewish and Slavic Women in Pittsburgh, 1900 to 1945." *Journal of Urban History* 4 (May): 291-305.

————. 1991. *Grandmothers, Mothers and Daughters: Oral Histories of Three Generations of Ethnic American Women*. Boston: Twayne Publishers.

Mormino, G. R. and G. E. Pozzetta. 1982. "Immigrant Women in Tampa: The Italian Experience, 1890-1930." *Florida Historical Quarterly* 61(July): 296-312.

Parrino, M. 1988. "Breaking the Silence: Autobiographies of Italian Immigrant Women." *Studi Nordamericana* 5(2): 137-158.

Pedraza, S. 1991. "Women and Migration: The Social Consequences of Gender." *Annual Review of Sociology* 17: 303-325.

Peiss, K. 1986. *Cheap Amusements; Working Women and Leisure in Turn-of-the-Century New York*. Philadelphia: Temple University Press.

Pesman, R. 1989. "Beyond Victims. Agendas for the History of Italian Women Immigrants to Australia." Unpublished paper in personal possession of author.

Pozzetta, G. 1989 "Immigrants and Ethnics: The State of Italian American Historiography." *Journal of American Ethnic History* 9(1): 67-95.

Pozzetta, G. and B. Ramirez. 1992. *The Italian Diaspora: Migration Across the Globe*. Toronto: Multicultural History Society of Ontario.

Ramirez, B. 1991. *On the Move: French-Canadian and Italian Migrants in the North Atlantic Economy, 1860-1914*. Toronto: McClelland & Stewart.

Ruiz, V. L. 1987. *Cannery Women, Cannery Lives: Mexican Women, Unionization, and the California Food Processing Industry, 1930-1950*. Albuquerque: University of New Mexico Press.

Scarpaci, J. 1980. "Angela Bambace and the International Ladies Garment Workers Union: The Search for an Elusive Activist." In *Pane e Lavoro: The Italian American Working Class*, ed. G. Pozzetta. Staten Island: American Italian Historical Association.

Seller, M. 1981. *Immigrant Women*. Philadelphia: Temple University Press.

Simon, R. and C. B. Brettell, eds. 1986. *International Migration: The Female Experience*. Totowa: Rowman and Allanheld.

Sinke, S. 1992. "The International Marriage Market and the Sphere of Social Reproduction: A German Case Study." In *Seeking Common Ground, Multidisciplinary Studies of Immigrant Women*, ed. D. Gabaccia. Westport, Conn.: Greenwood Press.

Smith, J. 1978. "Our Own Kind: Family and Community Networks in Providence." *Radical History Review* 17 (Spring): 99-120.

—. 1985. *Family Connections: A History of Italian and Jewish Immigrant Lives in Providence, Rhode Island, 1900-1940*. Albany: State University of New York Press.

Tirabassi, M. 1982. "Prima le Donne e Bambini: gli International Institutes e l'Americanizzazione degli Immigrati." *Quaderni Storici* 51: 853-880.

—. 1990a. "The Meaning of 'Americanization' for Italian Immigrant Women." Pp. 195-200 in *Looking Inward-Looking Outward, From the 1930s through the 1940s*, ed. S. Ickringill. Amsterdam: VU University Press.

—. 1990b. *Il faro di Beacon Street. Social Workers e immigrate negli Stati Uniti (1910-1939)*. Milano: Franco Angeli.

—. 1992. "Bringing Life to History: Italian Ethnic Women in the United States." Pp. 135-54 in *The Italian Diaspora, Migration Across the Globe*, ed. G. E. Pozzetta and B. Ramirez. Toronto: Multicultural History Society of Ontario.

Vasta, E. 1990. "Gender, Class and Ethnic Relations: The Domestic and Work Experiences of Italian Migrant Women in Australia." *Migration* 7.

—. 1992. "Italian Migrant Women." In *Australia's Italians: Culture and Community in a Changing Society*, ed. S. Castles et al. Sydney: Allen & Unwin.

Vecchio, D. C. 1989. "Italian Women in Industry: The Shoeworkers of Endicott, New York, 1914-1935." *Journal of American Ethnic History* 8 (Spring): 60-86.

Vezzosi, E. 1984. "L'immigrata italiana: alla ricerca di una identita femminile nell'America del primo novecento." *Movimento Operaio e Socialista* 7(3): 305-319.

—. 1986. "The Dilemma of the Ethnic Community: The Italian Immigrant Woman Between 'Preservation' and 'Americanization.'" In *Support and Struggle: Italians and Italian Americans in a Comparative Perspective*, ed. J. Tropea et al. Staten Island: American Italian Historical Association.

Weinberg, S. S. 1988. *The World of Our Mothers: Lives of Jewish Immigrant Women*. Chapel Hill: University of North Carolina Press.

—. 1992. "The Treatment of Women in Immigration History: A Call for Change." In *Seeking Common Ground, Multidisciplinary Studies of Immigrant Women*, ed. D. Gabaccia. Westport, Conn.: Greenwood Press.

Yans-McLaughlin, V. 1971. "Patterns of Work and Family Organization: Buffalo's Italians." *Journal of Interdisciplinary History* 2: 299-314.

———. 1974. "A Flexible Tradition: South Italian Immigrants Confront a New Work Experience." *Journal of Social History* 7: 429-445.

———. 1977a. *Family and Community, Italian Immigrants in Buffalo, 1880-1930.* Ithaca: Cornell University Press.

———. 1977b. "Italian Women and Work: Experience and Perception." Pp. 101-119 in *Class, Sex, and the Woman Worker,* ed. M. Cantor and B. Laurie. Westport, Conn.: Greenwood Press.

Zavella, P. 1987. *Women's Work and Chicano Families: Cannery Workers of the Santa Clara Valley.* Ithaca: Cornell University Press.

Chapter 9

Columbus, Whitman, and the Italian American Connection

Frank Cavioli

Though centuries apart, a meaningful connection can be made between Christopher Columbus, the Italian explorer, 1451-1506, and Walt Whitman, 1819-1892, the American poet. Both sought a new world without physical and spiritual barriers in their quest to alter long-held concepts of the universe. Emerging social, economic, and political forces, evident in fifteenth-century Europe and nineteenth-century America, respectively, shaped these two men. Shifting social institutions, scientific advances, commercial expansion, emergence of capitalism, intellectual emancipation, and religious stirrings evoked creative mental impulses leading to revolutionary change in an emerging modern civilization.

By 1492, the European situation had provided ample opportunity to mold the world through cultural and imperial expansion. The eventual far-reaching effects of Columbus's discoveries allowed Europe to dominate world civilization for more than four hundred years. The mariner explorer's impact was profound and permanent. What had preceded seemed insignificant as Columbus transcended the bonds of contemporary Renaissance Europe. His fierce ambition, originality, and daring courage shaped an inner will characteristic of great historical figures. Columbus internalized the strong belief that God had chosen him to spread the Gospel to those people ignorant of the Christian faith, and that it was his destiny to endure suffering because God willed it. In this sense he was a mystic, a deeply religious man who, when imploring aid for his enterprise from King Ferdinand and Queen Isabella, stated he was "a man sent from God. The Holy Trinity moved me to come with this message into your royal presence."[1]

In a similar sense, and expanding on this premise, the poetry and thought of Walt Whitman profoundly advanced the American national consciousness in the nineteenth century. His celebration of democracy, political union, and the common man and woman as heroes diverted attention from a fractious society and contributed to a spiritual faith in the American community. Nearing his death in 1892, he could proudly survey a vibrant nation more united in its values and common goals. This spirit of unity occurred at a critical juncture in United States history in the post-Civil War era and at the beginning of mass immigration.

Walt Whitman, the good grey poet of American democracy, was born in Huntington, Long Island, in 1819, of English and Dutch parents. He worked as a carpenter and typesetter, taught school, and wrote for, and edited, newspapers. Essentially self-educated, he studied the Bible, Shakespeare, and translations of great Greek and Roman classics.

It is appropriate at this point to identify an Italian influence on Whitman. As he matured, he attended plays and operas in cosmopolitan New York. Whitman delighted in the "opera's vocalism of sun-bright Italy."[2] He drew inspiration and pleasure from grand opera, an art form claimed and perfected by Italians. He attended operatic performances faithfully in New York. The beautiful music, superb voices, and emotional plots stirred his creative imagination. Throughout his poetry there appear numerous musical images, as in "Song of Myself":

I hear the chorus, it is a grand opera,
Ah this indeed is music—this suits me.[3]

Whitman's passion for opera greatly influenced his poetry in contributing to its structure. In his memorable poem, "Out of the Cradle Endlessly Rocking," can be seen the touches of operatic references. The lyrical language of his free-verse poetry parallel the music and form of Italian opera.[4] Even toward the end of his life in Camden, New Jersey, Whitman would bathe daily while his dinner grew cold, but at the same time he enjoyed himself singing "broken arias from the Italian operas that were the passions of his life." Whitman enjoyed performances of tenor Alessandro Bettini singing Donizetti's *LaFavorita* at Castle Garden and Italian prima donna Marietta Alboni singing the principal roles in ten different operas. Whitman himself stated the opera inspired him to write *Leaves of Grass*. By extracting the rich vocabulary from opera and foreign languages, he was able to bring American poetry to a new level of excellence.[5]

His early writings were mediocre at best. However, at the age of thirty-six, in 1855, he produced *Leaves of Grass* which contained twelve poems which were largely ignored by critics, or the collection was damned for its egotism and revolutionary language: "I am the poet of the Body and I am the Poet of the Soul."[6] Only Ralph Waldo Emerson praised it for its originality. Nevertheless, throughout his life Whitman produced nine editions of *Leaves of Grass*, constantly revising and adding new poems.

During the Civil War, Whitman became a nurse in the Union Army in 1862 and remained in this capacity until after the war. Afterwards he took a government job as a clerk but was dismissed because his book, *Leaves of Grass*, was considered immoral. Whitman obtained another government clerkship until 1873 when he suffered a paralytic stroke which forced him to retire. He settled in Camden, New Jersey, where he lived until his death in 1892.

He matured "as poet and a prophet with a message for his countrymen." He also experienced a kind of religious conversion in 1855 with his composition of *Leaves of Grass*. Whitman shared the idea with Emerson and others that American literature should embrace domestic themes that reflected the American spirit. This was not a novel idea, since it had been cultivated during the period of the American Revolution. What was new was Whitman's effective implementation of that agenda.[7] He demanded American literary independence; Americans should not imitate foreign models; and writers should war against narrow provincialism. The poet according to Whitman "must first be cosmic before he can be American."[8]

The United States underwent a massive expansion of wealth in the last half of the nineteenth century. Growth seemed limitless. Anything was possible. Such energies demanded a compression into a national poetic spirit to articulate national uniqueness, to render true meaning to the American experiment. Whitman believed the ideal poet to be a "seer" who possessed transcendent power who could combine the past, present, and future, and by eliciting elements from nature could reveal the universal cosmic plan. In the preface to the 1855 edition of *Leaves of Grass* he stated,

Past and present and future are not disjoined
but joined. The greatest poet forms the consistence
of what is to be from what has been and is . . . he
places himself where the future becomes the present.[9]

Thus, Whitman, the poet, had special powers to speak for and
represent the mass:

I hear American singing, the varied carols I hear.[10]

By abandoning the restrictions of rhymed meters, he symbolically
emancipated himself from the conventions of history, just as Americans
had freed themselves from the constraints of feudal Europe. Moreover,
his message extolled all the people:

The Female equally with the Male I sing.[11]

Whitman's best defense of his poetry appeared in the May 19, 1860,
issue of the *Saturday Evening Post* when he presented himself as the
"Poet of the American Republic." His rejection of established poetic
forms and his exultation of democracy signaled to the world a new
American art, coupled with the growth of a free society. "I shall use the
words America and democracy as convertible terms," he proclaimed in
Democratic Vistas (1871).[12] Here, then, is America's poet, identifying
with the common person, who is "large," "containing multitudes," who is
"not a bit tamed," but who will sound his "barbaric yawp over the roofs
of the world." The world had never witnessed anything quite like this.[13]

Although both Whitman and Columbus are complex and are
centuries apart, a parallel relationship can be discerned between them as
both experienced triumph and agony in their search for change.
Columbus's monumental achievements served to inspire Whitman's
imagination in four of his poems: "Spain, 1873-74" (1874), "Passage to
India" (1871), "A Prayer of Columbus" (1874), and "A Thought of
Columbus" (1891).

The first, "Spain, 1873-74," was a brief poem of fourteen lines of
free verse. It contained the name *Columbia*, a term used to honor
Christopher Columbus as a dignified personification of America or the
United States. The use of the name *Columbia* by American writers and
poets had its origin in the colonial period and was popularized during the
American Revolution when the need for national unity and symbols was

imperative. Alluding to Spain and to the archaic feudal institutions of Europe, Whitman wrote:

> Out of the murk of heaviest clouds,
> Out of the feudal wrecks and heap'd-up skeletons of kings,
> Out of that odd entire European debris, the shatter'd mummeries,
> Ruin'd cathedrals, crumble of palaces, tombs of priests,
> Lo, Freedom's features fresh undimm'd look forth—the same immortal
>   face looks forth;
> (A glimpse as of thy Mother's face Columbia,
> A flash significant as of a sword, Beaming towards thee.)[14]

It is in Whitman's masterpiece, "Passage to India," however, where his philosophy of poetry and his attempt to combine the natural with the supernatural to transcend the physical world can be seen and appreciated. Moreover, his references to Columbus demonstrate a reverence for the great Admiral. Whitman, the poet as the "true son of God," possessed the special power to understand and explain God's plan. He believed that scientific knowledge had achieved progress through the ages, but it also led to faith. The poem began by celebrating the "works of engineers," such as the Suez Canal, America's transcontinental railroad, and the transatlantic cable. These achievements, made possible by the explorers of an earlier age, unified the world. But as he sang "the achievements of the present," he also acknowledged:

> The past—the infinite greatness of the past!
> For what is the present after all but a growth out of the past.[15]

The failures of the past led to success in the present, and this enabled Whitman to see a purpose in history and in God's plan.

> Passage to India!
> Lo, soul, seest thou not God's purpose for the first?
> The earth to be spann'd, connected by network,
> The races, neighbors, to marry and be given in marriage,
> The oceans to be cross'd, the distant brought near,
> The lands to be welded together . . .
> A worship new I sing
> You captains, voyagers, explorers, yours,
> You engineers, you architects, machinists, yours,

You, not for trade or transportation only,
But in God's name, and for thy sake O soul.[16]

In section three of "Passage to India" Whitman presented a catalogue
of scenes depicting natural beauty, traveling across his own continent,
"through the grandest scenery in the world," across mountains, plains,
rivers, forests, desert. He then turned to Columbus in affirmation of his
daring discovery.

Tying the Eastern to the Western Sea,
The Roads between Europe and Asia . . .
(Ah Genoese thy dream! thy dream!
Centuries after thou art laid in thy grave,
The shore thou foundest verifies thy dream.)[17]

In section four of the poem, again with Columbus in mind, Whitman
hailed the many captains and sailors, who, though failing to achieve
passage to India, made possible

Lands found and nations born, thou born America,
For purpose vast, man's long probation fill'd,
Thou rondure of the world at last accomplish'd.[18]

Throughout history, explorers such as Columbus dared to dream
through "ceaseless thought" to strive against all obstacles. The spirit
would not die in the souls of the daring.
    In section six of "Passage to India" Whitman presented a series of
images from the ancient past that culminated in Columbus's epochal
event. The poet intoned:

The mediaeval navigators rise before me,
The world of 1492, with its awaken'd enterprise,
Something swelling in humanity now like the sap of
the earth in spring,
The sunset splendor of chivalry declining.[19]

Columbus arrived on the scene, "gigantic, visionary . . . with pious
beaming eyes. . . ." With the Admiral in mind, Whitman continued:

As the chief histrion,
Down to the footlights walks in some great scena,

Dominating the rest I see the Admiral himself,
(History's type of courage, action, faith,)
Behold him sail from Palos leading his little fleet,
His voyage behold, his return, his great fame,
His misfortunes, calumniators, behold him a prisoner, chain'd,
Behold his dejection, poverty, death.
(Curious in time I stand, noting the efforts of heroes,
Is the deferment long? bitter the slander, poverty, death?
Lies the seed unwreck'd for centuries in the ground?
lo, to God's due occasion,
Uprising in the night, it sprouts, blooms,
And fills the earth with use and beauty.)[20]

Whitman saw Columbus as a courageous figure who set in motion great forces in history through his discoveries. Yet his hero is rejected by contemporaries who slander, chain, and deprive him of his rightful reward. Recognition is deferred, however, as the seed that was planted would produce a more advanced civilization as part of the flow of events.

The final section of "Passage to India" deals with Whitman's mysticism, his search for a spiritual self, his probing for religious and intellectual meaning, his attempt at union of the soul and the physical, and his wonder of approaching death. The rite of passage is a passage to "more than India"; rather, it is a passage to where no mariner-explorer has ever traveled.[21]

"Passage to India" was initially published in 1871 as the title poem of a separate volume. Later, during the 1870s, it was included as a supplement to three editions of *Leaves of Grass*. Finally, it was incorporated into the body of the book in the 1881 edition. Whitman identified with Columbus at this stage of his life because of the similarities between them. Columbus was the explorer seeking a new route to the Indies, while Whitman explored the realm of literature and life. Both men were slandered in life and their achievements rejected by contemporaries.[22]

Honoring Columbus as a heroic figure had been established during the American Revolution when patriotic writers used the lyrical term *Columbia* to symbolize national unity and democratic progress.[23] The research of Salvatore J. LaGumina has demonstrated how important it is for members of an ethnic group to have one of its own honored in society, especially with a national holiday.[24] So it has been with Italian Americans who, over time, have joined and led the movement to celebrate Christopher Columbus's arrival in America. Few Italians lived in the United States when the nation's capital was designated the District of Columbia. The first actual celebration of Columbus's arrival took place October 12, 1792, in New York City, and was conducted by the Society of St. Tammany, or the Columbian Order as it was also known. Later that month the Massachusetts Historical Society led a procession in Boston to honor the three-hundredth anniversary of the event.

By 1892, mass emigration from Italy had begun to shape the nation as impressive ceremonies highlighted the Quadricentennial. Prominent Italian Americans led the way with enthusiastic cooperation within the ethnic communities of such cities as New York, Brooklyn, Buffalo, Chicago, Detroit, Utica, Philadelphia, Paterson, Elizabeth, Baltimore, Providence, New Haven, and New Orleans. Honoring Columbus provided the catalyst that awakened Italian American ethnic pride. The celebrations, and those who participated in them, expanded into the twentieth century.

Remarkably, Washington Irving, the prominent nineteenth-century American writer, contributed toward establishing Columbus as a modern icon. His comprehensive three-volume study, *The Life and Voyages of Christopher Columbus,* published in 1828, elevated the mariner to heroic proportions. A briefer volume appeared the next year. The biographies became so popular that by 1859, when Irving died, they had gone through fifty-one foreign language editions. By 1900, 175 editions and abridgments had appeared, and Irving's interpretation of Columbus remained the standard view throughout the period.

Irving's three-year research in Spain produced an image of a man who was a visionary, impelled by God and driven by idealism, who sought to open new routes to Asia to advance the cross and western civilization. He saw in Columbus an indomitable spirit that could not be crushed. Irving judged Columbus by contemporary values which seemed reasonable for his time. Remarkably, Irving's biography was largely forgotten in the twentieth century, and it played a minimal role in the Quincentennial debate.[25]

Irving's biographical study of Columbus excited Whitman's imagination when the latter's life took a dramatic turn in 1873 when he suffered a paralytic stroke. Whitman was forced to resign his government post and moved to Camden, where he lived till his death in 1892. Paralyzed, drained of vitality, his creative work under criticism, he suffered a further setback when his mother died in 1873. Having read and been impressed with Irving's biography of Columbus, Whitman saw analogies between the Admiral's life and his own as he sought strength to overcome his depressed condition. The elements in Columbus' life—achievement, rejection, slander, vilification—were now being internalized by Whitman. Both explorer and poet searched for new worlds and new truths, causing the poet to compare himself with his hero.[26]

Attaching this identification to his imagination, thus strengthening his personal well-being, Whitman composed "Prayer of Columbus." This poem may be viewed as a continuation of "Passage to India." Whitman, however, became totally absorbed in the symbolic embodiment of Columbus's life, and the poem contained the elements of a dramatic soliloquy. Considering these factors, it is understandable that Whitman's inspiration would lead to a lyrical poem quite distinct from, say, "Song of Myself" in *Leaves of Grass*. In "Prayer of Columbus" the mariner is

> A batter'd, wreck'd old man,
> Thrown on this savage shore, far, far from home,
> Pent by sea and dark rebellious brows, twelve
>   dreary months,
> Sore, stiff with many toils, sicken'd and nigh to death.[27]

Now Columbus is "too full of woe" and "old, poor, and paralyzed." Yet Whitman does not catalogue the deeds of the Admiral, but lays out feelings of frustration and pain suffered by ordinary people. The poet has the explorer appealing to God, resigning himself to what will befall him.

> Thou knowest my years entire, my life,
> My long and crowded life of active work, not
>   adoration merely;
> Thou knowest the prayers and vigils of my youth,
> Thou knowest my manhood's solemn and visionary
>   meditations,
> Thou knowest how before I commenced I devoted all
>   to come to Thee,
> Thou knowest I have in age ratified all those vows
> and strictly kept them,
> Thou knowest I have not once lost nor faith nor
>   ecstacy in Thee,
> In shackles, prison'd, in disgrace, repining not,
> Accepting all from Thee, as duly come from Thee.

It is clear that in describing the passion of Columbus, the poet was thinking of himself. His dominant mood of resignation is coupled with a deep faith.

The end I know not, it is in Thee.

Discouraged, the Admiral acknowledged the concluding chapter of his life, a life that been challenged and forfeited.

My terminus near,
The clouds already closing in upon me,
The voyage balk'd, the course disputed, lost,
I yield my ships to Thee.

The Columbus persona is joined by Whitman as the realities of life take hold and as spiritual grace is sought to sustain that persona. As one approached the altar of God, Columbus and Whitman reach for true meaning of life and divine sanction for life's work. Divine sanction is generated by a religious transformation. According to poet Walt Whitman, understanding this experience justified human existence. The most compelling lines follow in "Prayer of Columbus."

My hands, my limbs grow nerveless,
My brain feels rack'd, bewilder'd,
Let the old timbers part, I will not part,
I will cling fast to Thee, O God, though the
    waves buffet me,
Thee, Thee at least I know.

Finally, as if to reward Columbus's deep faith, Whitman concluded the "Prayer of Columbus" on an optimistic note as "new tongues" uplift him and "salute" him.

And these things I see suddenly, what mean they?
As if some miracle, some hand divine unseal'd my eyes,
Shadowy vast shapes smile through the air and sky,
And on the distant waves sail countless ships,
And anthems in new tongues I hear saluting me.[28]

When "Prayer of Columbus" was published in 1874 by *Harper's New Monthly Magazine*, Whitman indicated that he had put an "autobiographical dash in it." One of his admirers, Anne Gilchrist, recognized the similarity and she noted in a letter to the poet,

> You too have sailed over stormy seas to your
> goal—surrounded with mocking disbelievers—you
> have paid the great price of health—over Columbus.[29]

In an earlier period, Whitman had turned to another heroic figure to help him in another personal crisis: Abraham Lincoln. The 1860 edition of *Leaves of Grass* revealed conflicts within himself that contributed to a spiritual demise when he even contemplated suicide. As he experienced a division within himself, symbolically, a divided nation moved closer to civil war over slavery. Whitman advocated a strong union and recognized President Lincoln as the saviour of that union. Later, in 1865, he mourned Lincoln's death with lyrical passages of deep compassion. One scholar assessed the poet's emotional experience in this way: "Lincoln saved the union and he probably saved Whitman spiritually and practically." In 1873, following the Washington period, Whitman turned to Columbus to sustain him. After suffering a paralytic stroke and having his poetic soul slandered, he perceived a similarity in the Admiral as a "batter'd, wreck'd old man." "Prayer of Columbus" provided literary and spiritual nourishment in this time of stress.[30]

The strong relationship between Whitman and Columbus, transcending time and place, continued to the time of the poet's death. Conscious of the four-hundredth anniversary of the discovery of America, Whitman wrote his very last poem, "A Thought of Columbus," in early 1892. Whitman died on March 26, 1892. The poem appropriately honored the martyred explorer to whom he had turned in his time of depression when he wrote "Prayer of Columbus."[31] Now with death near, his reverent prayer to his hero furnished the nourishment to uplift him. This poet-son of God wrote,

> The mystery of mysteries, the crude and hurried
> flame, spontaneous, bearing on itself.
> A breath of Deity, as thence the bulging
> universe unfolding!

Whitman sensed a divine hand guiding the "bulging universe unfolding" and ushering forth "farthest evolutions of the world and man." Reason provided the justification for four hundred years of progress.

> A thought! a definite thought works out in shape.
> Four hundred years roll on.
> The rapid cumulus—trade, navigation, war, peace,
>   democracy, roll on;

As life closed around him, Whitman saluted history's greatest explorer with these final lines, the last he was to compose:

> (An added word yet to my song, far Discoverer, as
> ne're before sent back to son of earth—
> If still thou hearest, hear me,
> Voices as now—lands, races, arts, bravas to thee,
> O'er the long backward path to thee—one vast
> consensus north, south, east, west,
> Soul plaudits! acclamation, reverent echoes!
> One manifold, huge memory to thee, oceans and lands!
> The modern world to thee and thought of thee!)[32]

Thus, Walt Whitman the poet, as seer of truth, employing Columbus as symbol, joined past with present to make explicit the unfolding of historical forces. The many references to Columbus by Whitman continued a long literary-historical tradition that supplied inspiration, introspection, and meaning in the progression from a simpler American civilization to a more advanced, complex one.

In summary, the pattern of honoring Christopher Columbus as an heroic figure was instituted during the American Revolution when patriotic writers used the name *Columbia*, as derived from the great Italian explorer, to signify democracy and national unity. Reflecting the concept of the dignified personification of the United States, *Columbia* served the national needs by embracing an earlier period of western European exploration. It also furnished an opportunity for American poets (and others) to articulate national self-definition, so necessary for the foundation of nationhood.

Americans, throughout their history, striving to fulfill their destiny, created the image of *Columbia* as a metaphor to overcome a divided multicultural society. Walt Whitman contributed dramatically in this line of national development. Within the nine lifetime editions of *Leaves of Grass* can be seen the growth and maturity of one of the most original

American poets whose work may be measured in epic proportion. In his long narrative poetic style Whitman celebrated the deeds of the common man and woman, his heroes, in a period of progressive democracy and economic growth. He is expansive; he elevated that practical growth to a higher level of culture and spirituality through the implementation of linguistic and lyrical technique. *Leaves of Grass* broke new ground. For Whitman the poetry of the past was unsuited for modern American civilization. He instinctively sensed the greatness of the United States and its special mission in the world. In referring to another of his masterpieces, "Song of Myself," in *Leaves of Grass*, it "does make for a new kind of heroic poetry. In it, the hero comes into being, as realizing the full creative force of the self. . . ." This new heroic poem contained the power of creative energy.[33]

The connection between Walt Whitman and Christopher Columbus is indeed considerable. In four poems Whitman turned to the great explorer, drawing inspiration and comfort from him: "Spain, 1873-74," "Passage to India," "Prayer of Columbus," and "A Thought of Columbus." It was not unusual that Whitman empathized so eloquently with Columbus. As a Long Islander, Whitman was influenced by the rolling waves of the Atlantic Ocean, the calm of the Long Island Sound and its endless sandy shorelines. He fished, swam, and dug for clams. The many sea stories narrated by old timers helped shape his poetry. In a similar sense, the sea shaped the career of Columbus.[34] Moreover, water imagery was used in his poetry to convey powerful feelings and meanings.[35] Whitman internalized Columbus's suffering; Whitman endured as Columbus endured; Whitman's search for new literary frontiers matched Columbus's search for new physical boundaries. In a simpler age of the nineteenth century the hero could be accepted for his obvious achievements without reservation. In celebrating Columbus, and the common man and woman, Whitman commemorated the American nation.

Notes

1. Marvin Lunenfeld, *1492: Discovery, Invasion, Encounter* (Lexington, MA: D. C. Heath, 1991), p. 53.

2. James D. Hart, "Walt Whitman," *Atlantic Brief Lives*, ed. by Louis Kronenberger (Boston: Little, Brown, 1971), p. 870.

3. Walt Whitman, *Leaves of Grass* (New York: Barnes & Noble, 1992), p. 48. All quotations from Whitman's poetry are taken from this collection.

4. James E. Miller, Jr., *Walt Whitman* (Boston: Twayne, 1962), p. 20; Cf.: Robert D. Faner, *Walt Whitman and Opera* (Philadelphia, 1951).

5. Justin Kaplan, *Walt Whitman, A Life* (New York: Simon & Schuster, 1980), pp. 13, 178.

6. W. Whitman, p. 42.

7. Jay B. Hubbell, *American Life in Literature*, vol. 2 (New York: Harper & Brothers, 1949), pp. 21-23.

8. J. E. Miller, Jr., p. 58.

9. J. E. Miller, Jr., p. 66.

10. W. Whitman, p. 10.

11. W. Whitman, p. 1.

12. J. B. Hubbell, pp. 23-24, 69.

13. W. Whitman, p. 76.

14. W. Whitman, p. 401.

15. W. Whitman, p. 342.

16. W. Whitman, p. 343.

17. W. Whitman, p. 344.

18. W. Whitman, p. 344.

19. W. Whitman, p. 346.

20. W. Whitman, p. 347.

21. J. E. Miller, Jr., pp. 58-66, 150-157; Gay Wilson Allen, *A Reader's Guide to Walt Whitman* (New York: Octagon Books, 1984), pp. 202-210; Andrew J. Angyal, *A Critical Survey of Poetry*, rev. ed., vol. 7, ed. by Frank N. Magill (Pasadena, CA: Salem Press, 1992), pp. 3549-3561; Stanley K. Coffman, Jr., "Form and Meaning in Whitman's 'Passage to India,'" 69 *PMLA* (1955): 337-349.

22. Ronald Gottesman et al., *The Norton Anthology of American Literature*, vol. 1 (New York: W. W. Norton, 1979), pp. 1962-1964.

23. Cf. Frank J. Cavioli, "Columbus and the Name Columbia," *Italian Americana* 11 (Fall/Winter 1992): 6-17.

24. Salvatore J. LaGumina, *In Honor of Columbus: Places, Organizations and Celebrations*, paper presented at the 25th Annual Conference of the American Italian Historical Association, Washington, D. C., November 13, 1992.

25. James Finn Cotter, "How Americans Discovered Columbus: Irving's *The Life and Voyages of Christopher Columbus*," *The Italian American Review* 1 (October 12, 1992): 19-26.

26. J. E. Miller, Jr., pp. 33-34.

27. W. Whitman, p. 351; the quotes from "Prayer of Columbus" are taken from pp. 351-353.

28. G. W. Allen, pp. 206-207; Joseph Tusiani, "Christopher Columbus and Joel Barlow," *Italian Americana* 3 (Autumn 1976): 30-44.

29. J. Kaplan, p. 348. Anne Gilchrist was the widow of Alexander Gilchrist, biographer of William Blake.

30. Gay Wilson Allen, *The New Whitman Handbook* (New York: NYU Press, 1975), pp. 42-43.

31. G. W. Allen, *The New Whitman Handbook*, p. 159.

32. W. Whitman, pp. 464-465.

33. Roy Harvey Pearce, "Toward an American Epic," *Hudson Review* 12 (1959): 362-377.

34. J. Kaplan, p. 61.

35. S. K. Coffman, Jr., pp. 340-341.

Part III

Italian American Community

Introduction

The Italian American Community

Jerome Krase
Brooklyn College of The City University of New York

The four essays in this section on the Italian American community display an extremely wide range of the various ways by which the term "community" is used in describing and analyzing Americans of Italian descent. Prior to the 1970s, in more or less "classical" anthropological, sociological and historical studies, Italian Americans were seen most broadly as being tied together by relatively objective social structures such as economic, political, and kinship systems, and the more subjective cultural systems of ideas, values, and beliefs. The major paradigms in use at the time were those of assimilation and urban ecology. To these earliest studies were added others which looked at Italians through the theoretical and methodological lenses of social scientists trained in more phenomenological schools of symbolic interaction and social construction. Looking at Italian America from these newer perspectives scholars produced many works on ethnic stereotypes and self images. The most recent model for studying the community, political economy, looks at the Italian American experience through the lenses of gender, race, and class.

In her seminal essay "Involved and 'There': The Activities of Italian American Women in Urban Neighborhoods," Judith N. DeSena informs the reader that although women as a topic of sociological inquiry had been given increased attention in recent years their role had not been a specific focus in most studies of urban neighborhoods. She argues that studies on Italian American neighborhoods, like other sociological works, have traditionally taken a male perspective and treat women as merely being "there." That is, "they are part of the scene, but are not part of the action."

As a segment of a larger study on the defense of urban neighborhoods by their residents, DeSena looked closely at the activities of women in Greenpoint—a blue collar neighborhood in Brooklyn, New York—as they participated in, and indeed created, many of the multiethnic neighborhood's informal, yet influential structures. She interviewed female community residents most of whom were of Italian, Irish, and Polish descent. Instead of concentrating only on formal, local community structures, the focus of her innovative investigation was on more informal activities. Among other findings she concluded that the involvement of women in general, and Italian American women in particular, in neighborhood activities was evident by such things as the existence and operation of informal housing networks and local civilian anti-crime surveillance.

My own contribution to this section is "Bensonhurst, Brooklyn: Italian American Victims and Victimizers." The article is a fusion of two columns written for an alternative newspaper, *The Free Press,* and was a response to the most infamous in a series of tragic "incidents" which had a major impact on the reality and image of Italian America. Between 1982 and 1989 three racially motivated homicides took place in neighborhoods described as Italian American. As a result Gravesend's Avenue X, Howard Beach, and Bensonhurst received worldwide media attention.

I must admit here that among the many different, often competing, perspectives my own preference for defining the Italian American "community" has been for the neighborhood community that connects people because of shared residential space. Italian Americans are especially seen as "neighborhood" people. A central issue addressed in the essay was the role played by those who study the Italian community in presenting an accurate picture of the various and diverse segments of the Italian American population in response to even distasteful situations. There are many ways by which Italian Americans are defined or stereotyped. Here we see an incident which occurred in a particular neighborhood defining the entire ethnic group as "racist." It is argued strongly here that ethnic defamation cannot be effectively dealt with by mere denial; it must be countered with accurate information. Both reality and fiction impact on the "community" of persons of Italian descent.

Therefore, to better anchor the Italian American experience in America's racial history the "Bensonhurst incident" is connected to the lynching of Italian Americans in New Orleans a century earlier.

In "Community and Identity in Italian American Life," Salvatore Primeggia and Joseph Varacalli provide a social constructionist theoretical framework for Italian American studies in which human beings are assumed to be active, creative, and reflective, and yet operating within certain structural and cultural restraints. For them, Italian American ethnicity is socially reconstructed from one generation to the next in light of changing structural and sociohistorical realities. In their paper special attention is paid to the powerful notion of "symbolic ethnicity" by which socially mobile and quite assimilated American ethnics are viewed by some commentators as merely attempting to maintain some psychological connection with their real and imagined origins. By this way they retain some ethnic affective quality in their identity and social life.

Primeggia and Varacalli stress that although they have no trouble with the phrase "symbolic ethnicity," they strongly disagreed with the interpretation of the term which was given to it by some assimilation theorists and claim that Italian Americans continue to be an "authentic" ethnic group. Symbolic ethnicity can be voluntary and self-conscious and still be real. Italian American ethnicity is not restricted to leisure-time activities or other limited, situational, intermittent, and undemanding pursuits. From a constructionist perspective, people choose from alternatives provided by the society in which they live; therefore, Italian Americans can be Italian American by "consciously drawing on the Italian American components of their community attachments and fashioning both new and authentic variations of both Italian American community and identity."

Angela Danzi's contribution to our discussion of the Italian American community is an insightful interpretation of findings concerning a significant, but little noticed, cultural practice. Her study of Italian American midwifes contrasted the mass immigration of eastern European Jews and Italians to urban centers during the late nineteenth and early twentieth centuries in the United States. This was also a period of the medicalization of childbirth. She notes that immigrants were a challenge to medical practitioners in general and the newly emerging specialty of obstetrics in particular. Both Jews and Italians, for example, preferred midwife-assisted home birth. By 1940, however, the role of the midwife was effectively taken over by trained male medical professionals connected to expanding urban hospital systems.

Danzi argues that home birth was an option still available to women in an era of rapid change. She discusses how some women consistently selected home birth through these years and how these choices in turn suggest how social subgroups can shield themselves from some of the effects of powerful structural forces. In comparison to Jewish families, Italian families had an inward focus with few ties to outside structures. Each woman, embedded in her own family and neighborhood relationships, did what made individual sense to her, but collectively such decisions show how and why apparently powerless people can resist the plans which were made for them by others. Home birth was not an isolated decision, but part of an ongoing way of life. Today, developments have come full circle as American women, deeply dissatisfied with the impersonal and often alienating experience of hospital birth, are rediscovering home birth and thereby expanding the role of the midwife in America.

Chapter 10

Involved and "There": The Activities of Italian American Women in Urban Neighborhoods

Judith N. DeSena
St. John's University

Women as a topic of sociological inquiry have been given increasing attention over the past decade. However, women have not been a focus in studies on urban neighborhoods. More specifically, research on urban neighborhoods has not included an examination of the role of women. Furthermore, studies on Italian American neighborhoods[1] have been based on a male perspective and treat women as merely "there,"[2]—they are part of the scene, but are not part of the action.

This chapter focuses on the activities of women in a blue-collar neighborhood in Brooklyn called Greenpoint. It examines the role of women in general and Italian American women in particular as they participate in and create many of Greenpoint's informal structures. This research is part of a larger study on neighborhood defense in Greenpoint. The data presented are from interviews with twenty-eight women who were residents of Greenpoint and of Italian, Irish, and Polish descent. The focus is on informal activities instead of formal structures. The involvement of women in general and Italian American women in particular in neighborhood activities is evident by the existence of an informal housing network and local surveillance by civilians in Greenpoint.

This chapter begins with a description of Greenpoint, followed by a review of literature. Women's activities in Greenpoint are then presented. This includes a discussion of an informal housing network previously mentioned and local surveillance. Finally, the implications of this research for theory are examined, since neighborhood women are involved in a variety of local dynamics.

Description of Greenpoint

Greenpoint is a peninsula at the northermost tip of Brooklyn. It is bounded on the north and the east by Newtown Creek, and on the west by the East River. The Brooklyn-Queens Expressway (Meeker Avenue) and North 7th Street are Greenpoint's southern boundary (this is the boundary cited by the New York City Planning Commission in 1969).

Greenpoint lies across the river from Manhattan. In fact, the Citicorp building is visible from Greenpoint's main shopping strip (Manhattan Avenue). Its waterfront overlooks Manhattan's east side. Manhattan is easily accessible from Greenpoint by car. Greenpoint is also connected to neighborhoods in Queens, namely Long Island City, Sunnyside, and Maspeth by the Pulaski Bridge, the Greenpoint Avenue Bridge, and the Kosciuszko Bridge, respectively.

Greenpoint has been described as a working class neighborhood. In 1980, the population of Greenpoint was approximately 39,310. Like the population of the city that it is part of, Greenpoint's has been declining. Between 1970 and 1980, Greenpoint lost approximately 11,900 residents. Since the early 1900s Greenpoint has been a white ethnic neighborhood comprised mostly of Irish, Italian, and Polish families. The Irish were the largest group through the 1920s. A significant influx of Polish immigrants occurred in Greenpoint after World War II.[3] More recently there has been an additional wave of Polish refugees who fled martial law in Poland.

In 1980, residents of non-Hispanic, white ethnicities made up 75 percent of Greenpoint's population.[4] Since 1950, however, northern Greenpoint has seen an influx of Hispanic residents, who in 1980 comprised 21 percent of the neighborhood's population. Although the Hispanic population increased between 1970 and 1980, the Puerto Rican population grew very slightly in this ten-year period.[5] In 1970 there were 5,014 Puerto Ricans living in Greenpoint. In 1980, the Puerto Rican population was 5,166, the largest Hispanic group in Greenpoint (63% of

Hispanics). The increase in Greenpoint's Hispanic population has been among Latin Americans, Colombians, and Ecuardorians. The remaining 4 percent of Greenpoint's population was made up of Asian (2.5%) and black (.5%) individuals. One percent identified themselves as "other." Therefore in 1980, 75 percent of Greenpoint's population was made up of whites (non-Hispanic), while the remaining 25 percent was made up of minority residents.

In 1980, 44 percent of Greenpoint's population were high school graduates.[6] The proportion of graduates in Greenpoint is much lower than that of Brooklyn as a whole, and substantially lower than the proportion of high school graduates in New York City.

Average median family income in 1979 in Greenpoint was $14,464. In 1980, Greenpoint residents held a variety of occupations. The largest group was in technical and sales occupations (32%), and only 9 percent held professional or managerial occupations.

While a majority of Greenpoint's housing was built before 1939, many structures were built before 1900. More than 60 percent of the residential buildings are made of wood.[7] There are a few streets in Greenpoint made up of brownstones and brick townhouses, remnants of Dutch settlement from the seventeenth century. Residential structures in Greenpoint are not higher than six stories, and 71 percent of them contain four or fewer dwelling units per structure.[8] The percentage of owner-occupied buildings with rental units is unusually high.

The Role of Neighborhood Women

Urban sociology has ignored women.[9] Research on Italian American neighborhoods, in particular, is based on a male perspective and focuses primarily on men.

Whyte's study of Cornerville, an Italian slum in the North End of Boston, is an example.[10] Whyte selected Cornerville because he was interested in studying a slum district, and Cornerville best fitted his sense of what a slum district should look like. He focussed on the interaction of "corner boys" (The Nortons), "college boys" (the Italian Community Club), "racketeers," and "politicians. "

The intensive examinations of these groups enabled Whyte to uncover the status of group members and the social structure of Cornerville, which held individual members in their places. This study also helped to dispel a widely held idea that slums were disorganized. The area's physical decay did not reflect its social structure.

Whyte notes in response to a critique of his research that, because of local customs, he could not become involved with young women in Cornerville. He would have been expected to marry a woman whom he dated steadily.[11]

Like Whyte, Gans studied an Italian American community in Boston.[12] Gans studied the West End, which was bulldozed between 1958 and 1960 and replaced by luxury housing, in contrast to Whyte's North End which still exists as an Italian American area. Gans' research began in an effort to test the validity of the approach used by professionals to help low income populations improve their living conditions. He argued that professional "caretakers" (city planners, social workers, etc.) impose their middle class values on low-income populations by making policy decisions regarding the future existence of slum districts. His research, therefore, focused on the lifestyles of a working class Italian American subculture in West End, a Boston neighborhood that had been previously declared a slum. Gans concludes from his study that "caretakers" were wrong about the West End, since it was not really a slum. The West Enders' way of life constituted a distinct, complex, and independent working class subculture. Thus, for Gans, the values and lifestyles of this population should first be understood and considered by "caretakers" before policy decisions are made. These conclusions, however, were too late to have an impact on the West End, for it has been redeveloped under the federal urban renewal program, and no longer exists in the way that Gans studied it. Like Whyte in the North End, Gans found a viable social structure in the West End and not a disorganized slum. Furthermore, like Whyte, Gans also collected more of his data from men than women. Gans states that he was unable to gain access to women's groups.

Suttles also examined Italians as well as Mexicans, Puerto Ricans, and Blacks in the Addams area of Chicago.[13] Territory has been divided among these four groups and residents are fragmented. In the Addams area an "ordered segmentation" has been created that allows for orderly relationships among groups. Turf is clearly defined. Groups only combine in instances of opposition to outside threats. Ethnic groups are separated by location, institutional arrangements (religion, recreation), and communicative devices (language, clothing). Street corner gangs maintain ethnic boundaries. Like Whyte and Gans, Suttles also focuses on men.

Lofland argues that, in studies on urban sociology, women are merely "there."[14] They are part of the background, but are not included in the action. Lofland points to the emphasis on formal elements of community as a model of social organization and as a factor in creating the "thereness of women." Lofland argues that the use of this model moves researchers away from women's activities. This study on Greenpoint captures the activities of women because of its focus on informal practices.

Moreover, most researchers have been men. This creates a problem of access into various research situations. Gans notes, for example, that communication between the sexes is limited in a working class neighborhood. Thus, gaining access to women's groups and obtaining interviews with women are difficult tasks for male researchers. Women will be the focus of urban research when more urban researchers are women, or when male urban researchers realize the possibility of "taking the role of the other." According to Daniels, researchers can penetrate a social setting even when they do not fit into roles that are traditionally acceptable.[15] In her study of U.S. army subgroups, Daniels describes the tactics and strategies she employed in order to overcome the resistance of military officers to a sociologist, a civilian, and a woman. Howell, in his study of Clay Street, spent a great deal of time with two respondents who were women, Bobbi Jean Shackelford and June Moseby.[16] He attributes his being married and having a child as a major factor which enabled him to gain access to women neighbors. Howell lived in the neighborhood and his wife and child were often with him when he visited Bobbi Jean and June. As Howell explains, his family was friendly with their families.

In addition, Horowitz's study of a Chicano community in Chicago suggests that being a women is advantageous in field work.[17] She frequented street corners and park benches with male gang members in order to understand their process of growing up. She gained access to these gangs because, as a women, she did not threaten them. Because of her sex, she also had access to the young women.

Criticisms have been made by professionals from other fields who rely on this literature. Wekerle notes that detailed research on women in urban settings might provide information for planners and designers, which would enable them to create environments that are more responsive to women's needs.[18]

Greenpoint's Informal Housing Network

It is difficult to rent an apartment or purchase a house in Greenpoint. Local realtors have said that "there isn't a one, two or three family house available." The local newspaper lists only a few apartments and houses for sale, while the length of its "APTS. WANTED" and "HOUSES WANTED" column increase. It seems that residents are particularly cautious about renting their vacant apartments. Not only do they want to control rigidly the type of tenant they may get, but they also want to determine who will be informed about the availability of an apartment.

It appears that women play a major role in Greenpoint's informal housing network. They seem to "pass along the word," regarding the availability of housing to family, friends, and neighbors. Women have replaced the role of realtors. The following anecdote reported by a local woman illustrates this point:

> I was in a butcher one day and we were talking, and I just happen to mention that my niece was looking for rooms, and this woman says, "Hello," she told me who she was, and that she had rooms. So there right in the butcher shop, not that I ever got the rooms. But (if I wanted) rooms for a friend of mine or for anybody I would spread the word around in the society (a woman's religious organization). That would be the first place, right I's say, "Girls, anybody hears of rooms let me know." They would tell someone.

This account suggests that women's activities are largely informal and occur in places like a butcher shop. It further suggests that when women are members of formal organizations, the organizations tend to be made up of mostly women. Male researchers are therefore unable to reach them. Moreover, it supports the idea that women's activities are "behind the scenes." Greenpoint's informal housing network is a sound example.

Surveillance

Another way that women are involved in Greenpoint is through local surveillance. Surveillance in Greenpoint can be divided into two categories, informal and formal.

Informal surveillance refers to activities where individuals "watch" the block. These individuals are not sanctioned by any authority to "block watch," nor are they tied to any local organization for this purpose. Formal surveillance, on the other hand, operates by a Civilian Observation Patrol (COP). The Civilian Observation Patrol is a local organization whose purpose is to train and coordinate individual block or small area (a number of blocks) patrols. In both cases, the objective is to protect the neighborhood (i.e., neighbors, children, property, etc.) from criminal disturbances.

Neighborhood women, particularly Italian American women, act as informal surveillants, witnessing and reporting suspicious events and crimes to the police. As one woman described,

I walked up Calyer Street towards Manhattan Avenue, I got as far as Guernsey Street and I'm crossing Guernsey Street and I see these two men coming, and one with a television on his shoulder, and I said, "Gee, they could have robbed that television." So I turned around to see if I could get the license plate number. There was no license plate number on the front of the car. So I make believe I forgot something and turned around like that, (as if I were) the cop, and I walked back, and I crossed Guernsey Street back again, and I turned around just as they were pulling away. And I got the license plate number of the car, and it was a Bonneville, and I forgot about it. I did write it down but I forgot about it. But later on in the evening a neighbor, now I happened to be walking up the Avenue again and I saw (a neighbor) sitting and few other people sitting on the stoop down Guernsey Street. And they called to me there to ask me a question of some kind. When I was leaving I said, "By the way if anybody lost a television on this block I know where it is, I'm a detective." The next morning (the neighbor) calls me, she says, "Do you still have the license plate number," she said. "The lady across the street was robbed yesterday and they took her television." So the two of them went around to the police station and I understand they did get them.

Women in Greenpoint are also involved in formal surveillance. They are members of an organized civilian patrol. The Civilian Observation

Patrol (COP) is a voluntary organization in Greenpoint which first began as part of a block association. It developed in response to numerous complaints by members of block associations about auto thefts and break-ins. The result was a system in which two residents ride around a particular segment of the neighborhood in their own cars which are equipped with CB radios. If they encounter any criminal activity or any event which appears suspicious, they relay the event to their "base station." A base station consists of a CB radio in someone's home and a resident to respond to calls. If a call is relayed to the base station, the base station operator responds by alerting police to the incident. According to a COP member, most base station operators are women, while most car patrols are made up by men. Patrol members do not become directly involved with neighborhood disturbances. They act as additional "eyes and ears" for the local police. Patrols usually operate on weekend nights and follow a schedule that was developed by members.

In Greenpoint, women are important members of the civilian patrols. As mentioned earlier most operate base stations, as opposed to policing the area in cars at night. However, it was reported that one of the active patrols included a day patrol which is made up of local women. The day patrol is a foot patrol. Teams of women walk around the area with CB radios and relay reports of disturbances to their base station. They patrol an area around the Greenpoint Savings Bank on the first few days of each month, during which time senior citizens receive and cash their Social Security checks. This patrol tries to prevent robberies. Moreover, there is an organization in Greenpoint called Friends of McGolrick Park, whose membership is mostly female. The major objective of this group was to restore and beautify McGolrick Park. The group encountered some problems with drug addicts congregating in the park. To help alleviate this problem they formed a day patrol which is comprised solely of women. The patrol is called Park Anti-Crime Teams (PACT). PACT was originally a member of a larger COP which acted as an umbrella organization for smaller COPs, but withdrew its membership. This group felt that they were being discriminated against because they were women.

> They took almost a year in training us before we could get out on patrol. They didn't like the idea of two women in a car; they wanted a man. And I always felt that they had no right to make a decision. (Then at a fundraising event they wanted us) to sell raffles . . . and all hell broke loose and my whole group left and we formed our own (patrol).

Conclusion

In Greenpoint, Italian American women appear to be local power brokers. They make decisions regarding who is informed about available housing. They also negotiate between tenants and landlords and essentially decide who lives in Greenpoint. Moreover, women are disproportionately represented in all forms of civic, religious, and neighborhood improvement organizations. They are also much more likely than men, to actively participate in grassroots protests or efforts of pressure aimed at government or elected officials. As this research indicates, the role of Italian American women continues to expand. Their involvement in neighborhood activities persists even though they are assuming more responsibilities outside the home, such as seizing educational opportunities and/or entering the labor force.

The neighborhood has traditionally been viewed by Italians as an extension of the home.[19] Italians in urban neighborhoods create symbolic boundaries which define their turf and engage in block watching activities. Street festivals, such as the "festa," are quite common in Italian neighborhoods, as well as the practice of neighbors gathering on steps and sidewalks in front of their homes. However, as Italian American women continue to enter the labor force and to achieve success and social mobility by increasing their levels of education[20] they will experience greater pressures. Competing issues of work, home, and family, combined with constraints of time, will lead to a re-ordering of responsibility for domestic tasks within the household. Involvement in neighborhood activities is among these tasks. The decisions made by Italian American households are crucial to the future of the "Italian Village." The viability of ethnic neighborhoods in general will be decided by "choice." Households can choose to give up the neighborhood by not participating in activities and by ignoring local practices, such as an informal housing network. On the other hand, they may organize their domestic tasks in such a way that neighborhood activities are viewed as important. This decision will help to maintain the existence of ethnic neighborhoods.

Given the crucial role that women play in ethnic neighborhoods, you would expect them to be a major focus of studies on urban neighborhoods. However, this is not the case. The stereotype of Italian American women views them as being "indoors."[21] Unfortunately scholars have adopted and promoted this view, which helps to explain why women's activities have not been included in studies on urban neighborhoods. Scholars begin their research with the idea that women are indoors and, therefore, not visible. Their research is directed away from women from the outset. This paper suggests the opposite. Women of Italian descent are active participants in neighborhood life. Scholars must look past stereotypes, traditional roles, and formal organizations in order to recognize the importance of women.

The role of Italian American women will continue to expand. In many ways their heritage has been conducive to a modern role because Italian culture provides support for women through the family and religion.[22] Scholars must recognize their expanding role and realize that women have power in neighborhoods and with regard to the future of neighborhoods. They can no longer be disregarded or not seriously considered in research on urban neighborhoods.

Notes

1. William Foote Whyte, *Street Corner Society* (Chicago: University of Chicago Press, 1955); Herbert Gans, *The Urban Villagers* (New York: The Free Press, 1962); Gerald Suttles, *The Social Order of the Slum* (Chicago: University of Chicago Press, 1968).

2. Lynn Lofland, "The Thereness of Women," in *Another Voice,* eds. Marcia Millman and Rosabeth Moss Kanter (New York: Anchor Books, 1975).

3. Ida Susser, *Norman Street* (New York: Oxford University Press, 1982).

4. Information on total population and race were obtained from block data from the 1980 census. The white and black counts do not include Hispanic persons. Hispanics were counted as a separate category.

5. This was obtained by examining tract data from the 1970 census on Puerto Rican birth or parentage.

6. Information on education refers to person over twenty-five years old. It was obtained from the 1980 census.

7. *Greenpoint: Striking a Balance Between Industry and Housing* (New York: New York City Planning Commission, 1974).

8. *Greenpoint: Striking a Balance Between Industry and Housing.*

9. Sylvia Fleis Fava, Janet Abu-Lughod, and Noel Gist, *Urban Society,* 7th edition (New York: Harper and Row Publishers, forthcoming).

10. Whyte, *Street Corner Society*, 1955.

11. William Foote Whyte, "Comments on Robert E. Washington's Review *on Street Corner Society*," in *Reviews in Anthropology 5*, 1978.

12. Gans, *The Urban Villagers*, 1962.

13. Suttles, *The Social Order of the Slum.*

14. Lofland, "The Thereness of Women."

15. Arlene Kaplan Daniels, "The Law Caste Stranger in Social Research," in *Ethnics, Politics and Social Research*, ed. Gideon Sjorberg (Cambridge, Mass.: Schenkman Publishing Company, 1967).

16. Joseph T. Howell, *Hard Living on Clay Street* (New York: Anchor Books, 1973).

17. Ruth Horowitz, *Honor and the American Dream* (New Brunswick, N.J.: Rutgers University Press, 1983).

18. Gerda Wekerle, "Women in the Urban Environment," *Signs: Journal of Women in Culture and Society, 5* (1980).

19. Donald Tricarico, "The Italians of Greenwich Village: The Restructuring of Ethnic Community," in *The Family and Community Life of Italian Americans*, ed. Richard N. Juliani (New York: American Italian Historical Association, 1983).

20. Jerome Krase, "Italian American Female College Students: A New Generation Connected to the Old," in *The Italian Immigrant Women in North America*, ed. Betty Boyd Caroli, Robert F. Harney, and Lydio F. Tomasi (Toronto: The Multicultural History Society of Ontario, 1978).

21. Jerome Krase, "The Italian American Community: An Essay on Multiple Social Realities, " in *The Family and Community Life of Italian Americans*, ed. Richard N. Juliani (New York: American Italian Historical Association, 1983).

22. Venetta-Marie D'Andrea, "The Social Role Identity of Italian American Women: An Analysis and Comparison of Families," in *The Family and Community Life of Italian Americans*, ed. Richard N. Juliani (New York: American Italian Historical Association, 1983).

Chapter 11

Bensonhurst, Brooklyn: Italian American Victims and Victimizers

Jerome Krase
Brooklyn College of The City University of New York

This chapter addresses a number of interrelated issues which have emanated from a series of recent tragic "incidents" which have seriously affected the reality as well as the image of Italian Americans. The incidents in question were racially motivated assaults and homicides involving Italian Americans or taking place in a neighborhood described as Italian American. These events have received national as well as international media attention. As a result, the three New York neighborhoods—Gravesend's Avenue X, Howard Beach and Bensonhurst—have been added to the American urban lexicon of infamous places. In these places three black men—Willie Turks (1982), Michael Griffith (1987), and Yusuf Hawkins (1989)—were murdered.

A central issue addressed here, and seldom discussed elsewhere, is the role played by Italian American professionals, and those others who study the Italian community, in helping to present to the general public an accurate picture of the various and diverse segments of the Italian American population. This must be done without reservation and without apology even when the situation, such as instances of intergroup violence, is distasteful. Equally important to Italians in America is the issue of ethnic defamation. Defamation, however, cannot be effectively dealt with by mere denial; it must be countered with accurate information.

Italians in the United States, as elsewhere in the world, have long suffered from a "bad press." Works such as Salvatore J. La Gumina's *WOP: A Documentary History of Anti-Italian Discrimination in the United States* (1973), for example, have clearly demonstrated this symbolic historical reality on the American scene through an examination of text and illustrations concerning Italians in newspapers and other periodical literature. As I had noted in a previously published article on "The Italian American Community: An Essay on Multiple Social Realities," the negative images produced and disseminated in the various media have persisted despite the presentations and protestations of more or less objective scholars and ethnic group spokespersons. The three organizations which have been most active in the area of combating the negative stereotyping of Italian Americans in recent years have been the American Italian Historical Association, the National Italian American Foundation and the Commission for Social Justice of the Order Sons of Italy in America. Groups such as these have been exceptionally forceful regarding the "criminal" and "mafia" stereotyping of Italian Americans.

Since the liberal social activism of the 1960s, two new, and perhaps even more dangerous, negative images have been added to the historical repertoire of nocuous and innocuous organ grinders, old ladies in black dresses, birds of passage, stiletto wielders, mindless madonnas, mafia dons, wise guys, spaghetti sauce makers and disco dancers who have been held up as images of Italian Americans; these new images are of social "reactionary" and racial "bigot."

A major threat presented by this contemporary stereotype is the potential that the Italian American community can be easily scapegoated for the economic and other failures of low-income minority groups in the United States, making intergroup cooperation even more difficult. On the political side, this would also make it less likely for Italian Americans leaders to serve as interethnic bridges in American politics as they have frequently done in the past. One could note in this vein, for example, Vito Marcantonio, Fiorello LaGuardia and Mario Cuomo and many others, who promoted better intergroup relations.

The reputation of Italian Americans and Italian American neighborhood groups as vocal opponents of racial integration is not undeserved. The question in this essay is not *whether* some Italian

Americans are biased but *why* they are perceived as being so much more so than other ethnic groups, and *what* can and should be done about it. It is not merely that the reputation of Italians in American is at stake; the establishment of better intergroup relations is an especially critical problem in large American cities and their near suburbs today.

Not since the turbulent 1950s have cities been faced with such rapid demographic transitions. The United States in the 1980s is experiencing a new, almost tidal, wave of Hispanic, Black and Asian immigration which is virtually swamping older urban areas, such as the New York-New Jersey Metropolitan Area. Given that working class Italian American populations occupy residential territories which are directly in the path of minority group expansion, they are also the most likely to experience interracial and interethnic conflict on a local level between themselves and other ethnic minorities. As noted by Robert C. Freeman in his recent article on "The Development and Maintenance of New York City's Italian American Neighborhoods, "the cultural propensity of Italians toward residential stability has resulted in their being, in many cases, the last white ethnic group in changing urban communities."

The recent history of bias-related criminal incidents in Brooklyn, New York presents glaring evidence of the reality of intergroup fear, hostility and ever-present potential for violence. These incidents have been by no means limited to those between Italian Americans and others. No ethnic group, either as victim or perpetrator, has been immune to this plague. In researching New York City newspapers for stories concerning interethnic violence not involving Italian Americans over the past two years, the following polarities of victim and perpetrator represent only a partial listing: Black-Korean, Asian-Black, Black-Jewish, Jewish-Black, Jewish-Hispanic, Hispanic-Jewish, Indian-White as well as intra-Caribbean, Asian, and Hispanic.

Despite the participation of a broad spectrum of ethnic groups in the troubling reality of interethnic violence, the Italian American community has received the greatest press attention. Why has this happened? I believe that a major reason for the focus upon Italian Americans as epitomizing racial bigotry among white Americans is the reluctance of most Italian American organizations and their leaders to honestly address the problem of racial and ethnic bias. In most cases Italian American spokespersons have tended to deny the extent or degree of the problem or to make defensive statements when bias incidents in the community occur. This has resulted in an even greater focus on the community because it projects an appearance of lack of remorse or sympathy for victims of bias-related violence.

The following are two articles written by the author following the most recent highly publicized interracial homicide involving Italian Americans or a neighborhood identified as Italian American. They were published in *The Brooklyn Free Press*, a bi-monthly local newspaper. Being a professional sociologist, I have studied community problems in many different ethnic contexts. These pieces combine a direct, no excuses aproach to the incident with some historical and sociological "understanding" of the Italian American experience. Rather than excuses, influenced by ethnic pride or shame, they offer an alternative and more effective approach to explaining the problem of interethnic violence to the public. A new approach is needed because it is certain that intergroup violence will continue in urban America and elsewhere. As an American of Italian descent, I believe that the Italian American scholarly and professional community has an "ethnical" responsibility to offer its sensitive and informed opinions and advice in the service of better intergroup relations in an increasingly volatile urban environment.

As the reader will easily notice, this first article was written with a great deal of anger. It was composed immediately after the slaying of a black teenager in a predominately first and second generation working-class Italian American section of Bensonhurst, Brooklyn. The stereotypical "Italianness" of the area was highlighted in all the major press accounts of the homicide.

Although I was consulted as an "expert" by many reporters and widely quoted in a number of the resulting stories, my own reaction to the slaying was focused on the political and economic, not the ethnic aspects of the tragedy. Simply stated, the various media were doing a story about a homicide of an African American by Italian Americans.

"Yusuf Hawkins and The Closing of the American Mind" by Jerry Krase
The Brooklyn Free Press, September 1, 1989

To hear some people talk, it appears that 16 year-old Yusuf Hawkins made a couple of ultimately fatal mistakes. One mistake was in biology and the other in geography. According to the rules of the game in the U.S., he committed a serious violation by being born black. At least this error was not his fault. His second and most grievous fault was geographical. He assumed that a ride on the "N" subway train to Bensonhurst, Brooklyn, U.S.A. would not stop in Soweto, South Afrika. For this misreading he had to be punished. And punished he was! It was like a Moslem or a Christian in Beirut crossing the Green Line. In Lebanon they hurl artillery shells at one another. In American Cities we throw teenagers.

Those who laid down the law to Mr. Hawkins feel they should be absolved of any guilt in his execution because of his (the victim's) and their own unfortunate, but understandable, miscalculations. Some witnesses claim it took about thirty punks wielding baseball bats and at least one loaded pistol to put Mr. Hawkins to rest. Remnants of this rabid mob of miscreants claim absolution for their conduct based on the doctrine of mistaken identity. Undoubtably someone will also claim that they "didn't know the gun was loaded." Besides, they swear, they mistook Mr. Hawkins for another dark-skinned African-American whom they had also never met. According to a lot of people young Yusuf was just unlucky and the assassinators had made an honest error in staunchly defending the crumbling walls of their sacred neighborhood against the barbarian hordes. This honorable "duty" is even fun to do when the barbarians are unarmed and vastly outnumbered.

Academically speaking, these young hoodlums are Allan Bloom's kind of people. They obviously have been saved from the horror of the liberal American educational system which produces the "democratic personality." Professor Bloom's widely acclaimed best selling book, "The Closing of the American Mind," is a stirring indictment of America's schools which practice "education of openness" and other subversive anti-absolutist doctrines. Bloom laments that this system has created citizens who are unfortunately open to "all kinds of men, all kinds of life styles, all ideologies." According to this Professor in the Committee on Social Thought and the College and Co-director of the John M. Olin Center for Inquiry into the Theory and Practice of Democracy at the prestigious University of Chicago, America is in danger because too many educated people think that "everything is relative." To Bloom and his colleagues on 20th Avenue, absolutism is a virtue and certainly not everyone is a relative.

Bloom *et al.* claim that the founders of their version of American society considered minorities to be a bad thing—"selfish groups who have no concern as such for the common good." According to this

University of Chicago-20th Avenue view, as a result of misinterpretation of the founding fathers (or perhaps evil design?) Americans have been educated not only to accept differences but to exhalt them. The Professor has travelled all over the world and most notably has translated Plato's *Republic* as well as Rousseau's *Emile*. He also wrote an excellent book on Shakespeare's politics. I didn't know that Skakespeare even had any politics and I wonder what he thought of minorities.

One can conclude from all this that the ivory tower and the medieval neighborhood fashion similar kinds of bigotry. Intellectual bigots however are much more fashionable than those who yell "nigger go home" and hold up watermelons during civil rights marches. Both groups frequently rail about Affirmative Action. In fact, one local source interviewed about the murder of Yusef Hawkins last week in Bensonhurst cited anger about affirmative action policies which residents believe have taken away job opportunities for neighborhood youths as a major reason for the hostility that led up to the killing. Blacks and other minorities are seen by unsuccessful people as the cause of their failures. This claim of victimization is a worrisome echo of times past. I remember once reading the heading of a German Newspaper in the Ann Frank House in Amsterdam about fifteen years ago—"Die Juden Sind Unser Unglueck."—The Jews are our Misfortune. Millions of Jews were murdered *en masse*. In New York City we murder our misfortunes one at a time.

There are lots of excuses which have or will be offered for the murder of Yusef Hawkins. I don't think his death can be excused but it can be easily explained. Like other young men who have killed, maimed, raped and simply terrorized people because they are "different" and therefore "less then" themselves, the mob on 20th Avenue is reflecting the behavior and attitudes of the most powerful of people in our society. They emulate their leaders—the people they look up to and fear. Neighborhood gangs also have an unfortunately accurate sense that no one is looking out for their interests and that they have to defend themselves against any and everyone. They want to be feared by others. Blacks are easy targets for those on 20th Avenue because blacks are easier to spot on their own, reasonably white, turf. The other enemies are hidden from view or protected by powerful institutions. 20th Avenue in Bensonhurst, Brooklyn differs from other neighborhoods only by on the surface characteristics. This community of struggling people is simply another place that is off limits to "outsiders."

When I was a teenager in the 1950's I was living in a neighborhood under seige in Prospect Heights. My family had an apartment on the third floor over Love's Meat Market which catered to the rapidly diminishing population of wealthy WASP's on the once elegant Eastern Parkway across the street from the Brooklyn Museum. We were the janitor-family ("supers") of the building. The Mafia, the 80th Precinct, and the Grand Avenue "Boys" were the neighborhood's first lines of defense against the imperial growth of black Bedford/Stuyvesant and their teenage gangs— the "Bishops" and the "Chaplins." It was a war mentality and the children played war games.

One warm summer evening my friends (a mix of working class Irish and Italian Catholics, one Jew and one WASP) decided to have a race around the block—Sterling Street to Underhill Avenue to Park Place to Washington Avenue and the Sterling Street finish line by Lewne's Ice Cream Parlor. The winner would got a few bucks in prize money from those who ran and those who bet on the race. I needed the money badly so I ran like a deer. I was way ahead on Park Place when two guys jumped in front of me and forced me into the space between the high Brownstone stoops. The space was dark but some light penetrated from the street lamp down the block. Three black kids, about my size and age were preparing to rob me of all my worldly goods. They didn't know I had nothing to my name. One held what felt like a knife to my side.

I am certain that the dim light from the lamp post saved me as one of the crew said to his friends, "Let him go. I know him from school." Indeed, he was a friend of mine from P.S. 9 which billed itself as the "Brotherhood School." I came in last in the race. Yusef Hawkins didn't find a friendly face in the crowd.

Some powerful people in New York City have fostered an atmosphere of intense paranoia and we have all become its victim. Our paranoia benefits them. It keeps us from looking for and finding the things we have in common and things we all need. Each group in the city has a unique history before they got here, but once here they fall into the same pattern of intergroup hostility, the volume and violence level of which rises and falls like the tide. The hostility is seldom addressed except as lip service at the anniversaries of the deaths of fallen heroes. For many politicians the violence is measured first as to who benefits most by it, themselves or their opponent. The greatest sadness which I can contemplate after Mr. Hawkins' death, and the greatest insult to his family, is that some people will soon be receiving campaign literature with the subliminal message "Vote for Me, I'm Not Black" or "Vote for Me, I'm Not White." Yusuf Hawkins will eventually become a "Statistical Bump" in an election year public opinion poll.

This second article was written after it become increasingly obvious that the press had decided to make the "Italian" aspect of the murder of Yusuf Hawkins and the neighborhood reaction to provocative marches through the community a continuing story. The Italian *versus* Black "angle" tied in nicely to the fact that Italian American Rudolf Giuliani, a Republican, was to face African American David Dinkins, a Democrat, in the upcoming New York City general election for mayor. I felt it necessary to express in my own writing and in my subsequent interviews with the media not only the non-ethnic aspects of the homicide but the common experiences of all of America's minorities as exemplified in the infamous lynching of eleven Italian Americans in New Orleans almost a century ago.

"Lest We Forget: Racism Will Make Victims of Us All" by Jerry Krase
The Brooklyn Free Press, September 22, 1989

On August 23, 1989 an African-American man by the name of Yusuf Hawkins was murdered in a predominately Italian neighborhood in Brooklyn. He was killed by a person, or persons, who were part of a mob of young men who some excuse because they acted in defense of their "turf." Since this racist murder by a monstrous few has taken place, the wider racism and bigotry of the society at large has been prominently, and at times proudly, displayed. It was not unlike a lynching—murder by a hateful mob. It was not the first. Let's try to make it the last.

Not unexpectedly many of those who are most responsible for the problems in our social and physical environment—our political leaders— have absolved themselves of guilt for the generally hostile intergroup climate in our city. Our politicians now claim they have been "unifiers"; their opponents have been the "dividers." Editorialists and academics have done their part by blaming a particular neighborhood (Bensonhurst) or a particular ethnic group (Italian Americans)—in effect scapegoating working-class ethnics for the continued discrimination and episodic violence against nonwhite Americans.

As a sociologist and "expert" on urban affairs I was quoted in the papers and appeared on television explaining how the centuries-old Southern Italian culture of family and village defense makes Italian American neighborhoods especially suspicious and fearful of outsiders. In every case however I emphasized that such communities are by no means more racist or discriminatory than any other "American" community. In working-class, white ethnic enclaves battles to keep "them" out of the neighborhood are just more likely to be fought in the street by residents. Other, more advantaged, people for example use co-op boards or "color-blind" economic criteria and rely on private security and closed circuit television for protection against those they don't like.

Pitting people who should be working together against each other is a long-standing American tradition. Putting the blame on Italian Americans for American racism is not unlike blaming Irish Americans for anti-Catholicism or Jews for anti-Semitism. Not too long ago—and to many, still today—Italians (especially Southern Italians) were (are) considered members of an inferior race. The idiots who held up watermelons while black protesters marched near the site of Hawkins death haven't the faintest idea that watermelons, racism and Southern Italians have a lot in common.

First of all my grandfather, from Palermo, Sicily, Gerolomino Cangelosi worked his way up from selling watermelon by the slice on New York City street corners and had to endure the anti-Italian bias of America society. Being a victim, however, gives no one a right to victimize others.

Recently, Assemblyman Frank Barbaro led a contingent of Italian American community leaders and members of FIERE, an Italian American student group, who met with a group of African-American protest-marchers at the site of Yusuf Hawkins murder as part of what should be a continuing dialogue. Barbaro and others have courageously spoken out against the violence committed by a small minority in the community and stand in marked contrast to the silent embarrassment and sympathy of a much larger group of local residents. The difference between those who speak out and those who are silent is that, like the members of FIERE, those Italian Americans who confront and try to correct the problems in their own community rather than ignore or deny them are proudly aware of their own group's suffering as well as their accomplishments and heritage. They know that Italians are not simply racist "guido's" and Mafia Don's and they know that Italians, as many other "Euro-American" immigrants were the victims of poverty and the focus of racist attention in past decades.

Parallels between the African-American and Italian American experiences are numerous and should be the source of cooperation rather than conflict. All of the historical events which follow should seem familiar to the reader as they are the plagues visited upon wave after wave of poor American migrants and immigrants. In 1906, speaking on "The Immigration Problem" Robert DeCourcy Ward warned that Slavs, Italians and Jews because of their high birth rates would "degrade" the "American race." Other contemporary critics of Southern Italian immigration warned that Italians were a threat to America because they were not "white." In fact it has been argued by some experts that the epithet "guinea" was "derived from a name attached to slaves from part of the western African coast." The poverty of Southern Italy was so great during the latter part of the 19th Century that a trans-oceanic traffic was created for "Italian Slave Children." *The New York Herald* reported on one of many "raids" on Italian *padrones* who either through contractual arrangements with parents or kidnapping sent hordes of juvenile minstrels out to beg in the streets of New York and Philadelphia. In one cellar "home" for the children the police and reporters found "an abominable place, the breeding ground of disease and the abode of roaches and vermin." In 1870 there was a "Riot in Mamaroneck." Irish and Italian laborers clashed over jobs. The end result of the battle as reported in *The New York Sun* was: "The Italian population of Grand Park was Driven Out—The Women and Children Sheltered in the Town Hall of Morrisania—Our Home War of Races." In many cases Italian laborers were paid lower wages than "native whites" or "negroes," making them more desirable employees. This fact of life was the justification for many riots against Italian workers who also were eager to work as "scabs" during strikes. Poor Southern Italian peasants were viewed by Dixie plantation owners as potential replacements for freed black slaves. The Italian government even cooperated in several "experiments" at population transfers which were unsuccessful. The major problem for the plantation owners was that Italian peasants were too difficult to control.

Late 19th and early 20th Century American press accounts and descriptions of Italians conveyed the message that "dagoes" were "dangerous," "lazy," "filthy," "cruel," "ferocious," and bloodthirsty." One Irish-American critic in the 1880's noted that "The Italian was all too ready to ask for public assistance." And that the absence of "manly qualities" separated the Italian immigrants from others in America.

As with African-Americans, the best indicator of racial hatred is the American custom of "lynching." Although there are many incidents of Italians being lynched by racist mobs, the most (in)famous took place in New Orleans on March 14, 1891 when, as related by historian Patrick Gallo: "a mob of six thousand to eight thousand people, led by prominent citizens, descended on the parish jail to get the 'Dagoes.' State and local law officers, and the governor who was in the city at the time, stood by and did nothing, the mob hanged two of the suspects from lampposts, and lined nine of them up in front of the prison wall and blasted their bodies with rifles, pistols and shotguns, taking less than twenty minutes for their grim work." The victims of the mob had been accused of killing the New Orleans Superintendent of Police whose dying words were "The Dagoes shot me . . . the Dagoes did it." He did not recognize his killers. Neither did any other witnesses. The Mayor of New Orleans therefore ordered the police "to arrest every Italian you come across." About 150 were arrested. When the courts began to find them innocent, the New Orleans *Times-Democrat* called for "All good citizens . . . to attend a mass meeting . . . to take steps to remedy the failure of justice . . .," resulting in the largest mass lynching in American history. Reaction to the lynchings were as good as could be expected considering the general stereotype of Italians. Theodore Roosevelt considered the lynching of eleven "rather a good thing." and *The New York Times* agreed that "the Lynch Law was the only course open to the people of New Orleans." To preserve American honor President Benjamin Harrison apologized to the Italian government for the slaughter of these and other Italians in America and gave a $25,000 indemnity to the families of 18 victims.

I imagine that some poor Italian back in the 1890s, maybe even my grandfather, when he read about the lynchings, shivered and prayed that racial violence would someday end.

*Note: This paper is a revised version of that presented at the American Italian Historical Association 22nd Annual Conference, held on November 9, 1989, in San Francisco, California.

References

Freeman, Robert C. "The Development and Maintenance of New York City's Italian American Neighborhoods," in Jerome Krase and

William Egelman, eds., *The Melting Pot and Beyond: Italian Americans in the Year 2000*. Staten Island: American Italian Historical Association, 1987, 223-235.

Gallo, Patrick J. *Old Bread, New Wine*. Chicago: Nelson Hall, 1981.

Krase, Jerome "The Italian American Community: An Essay on Multiple Social Realities," in Richard N. Juliani, ed. *The Family and Community Life of Italian Americans*. Staten Island: American Italian Historical Association, 1983, 95-108.

La Gumina, Salvatore J. *WOP: A Documentary History of Anti-Italian Discrimination in the United States*. San Francisco: Straight Arrow Books, 1973.

Tomasi, Lydio F., ed. *The Italians in America: The Progressive View, 1891-1914*. New York: Center for Migration Studies, 1978.

Chapter 12

Community and Identity in Italian American Life

Salvatore Primeggia and Joseph A. Varacalli

Introduction

The purpose of this paper is twofold. The first is to describe the present state of community attachments and individual identity of Americans of Italian ancestry. The second is to analyze both the sociological and social-psychological processes at work that account for the historical development, maintenance, and evolution of community and identity in Italian American life. This study utilizes appropriate data from a wide range of existing sources including those from the social sciences, history, and the humanities.

Definitions

The concepts of "community" and "identity" are related but not identical. The former is a macrolevel social phenomenon, not necessarily spatial in nature, that is synonymous with the ideas of "environment" and "frame of reference." The latter is a microlevel social-psychological phenomenon describing the prioritizing of role commitments in human consciousness and the processes that lead to the formation, continuity, and change of an individual worldview. Communities provide the background social matrix within which identities are forged. A certain range of identities is plausible and likely to be socially constructed from within the social parameters set by a community. However, the relationship between these micro- and macrophenomena is not merely one-sided. It can best be described as dialectical: that a given constellation of identities influences the nature of community and vice versa.

Theory

This paper operates, with certain qualifications to be noted, from the theoretical framework of the social construction of reality as developed by Peter Berger and Thomas Luckmann (1966), among other like-minded theorists. The dialectical sociology employed is one which, following Vidich and Lyman, speaks "of an open-ended world, of existential phenomena, of the contingencies of history, and of the individual located somewhere between freedom and determinism" (1985, p. 307). As such, the image of the human being assumed in this work is one who is active, creative, and reflective, and yet operates within certain structural and cultural restraints.

Ethnicity is socially reconstructed from one generation to the next in light of changing structural and socio-historical realities, consistent with the perspectives of such scholars as Glazer and Moynihan (1970), Tricarico (1984), Juliani (1987), and LaRuffa (1988). The interpretation offered here, conversely, stands in opposition to straight-line assimilation theorists of Italian American ethnicity such as Herbert Gans (1979), James Crispino (1980), and Richard Alba (1985), who view the present importance of ethnicity to most Italian Americans as peripheral in both thought and activity. As Tricarico puts it, "The emphasis on assimilation . . . (tends) to preclude a concern with, and an awareness of, the transformation or internal development of the ethnic community" (1984, p. xv). On this score, Juliani not only agrees with Tricarico but points out that the very culture and society into which Italian Americans are assimilating is a social reality that is constantly being regenerated. As Juliani states:

> It also seems that . . . (assimilation theorists) fail to recognize the extent to which the core culture of American society and the social patterns of the dominant group are not ethnically neutral, but clearly reflect the ethnic origins of earlier arrivals to the United States. In short, upward mobility may not necessarily eradicate ethnicity, but generate newer

forms of it, and we must be alert and imaginative enough to recognize these possibilities. (1987, pp. 69-70)

While Tricarico is correct in pointing out the "shortcomings of . . . (an assimilation) perspective that . . . generally regards ethnic community as . . . (merely) an artifact of the immigrant experience" (1984, p. 164), it must also be recognized that there are broad limits to any adaptation of Italian American ethnicity. As Varacalli has stated:

To say that there is a range of thought and behavior to being Italian American does admit of pluralism, but it is a pluralism that operates within parameters set by the tradition. In the case of Italian Americans, this means that parameters are set by the tradition of south Italy at the turn of the twentieth century. . . . It was this moment in time and space that served as the "launching pad" for the subsequent evolution in Italian American belief and practice. . . . Traditions, of course, do change. They change in light of new historical developments, newly developing social-structural conditions, and emerging cultural innovations. However, it is crucial to point out that if any "innovation" is to be successfully grafted into existing tradition, that innovation must be "organically" related to tradition. That is, the innovation must either arise from, be connected in a logical way to, be a diffuse specification of, and be compatible with, tradition. Any creation "de novo" that is so foreign as to radically subvert the tradition must be considered an illegitimate contender for the title "Italian American." (1987, pp. 4-5)

Tricarico's assertion, then, that "a more fruitful approach would recognize ethnic community as capable of assuming new forms and shapes in response to the socialhistorical context" (1984, p. 164) should be slightly modified to include the idea that those forms and shapes must stand in an organic relationship to the southern Italian/Italian American heritage, if they are to be considered true variations. Indeed, as LaRuffa argues correctly:

The Italian Americans as an ethnic population share a similar culture that includes language, values, beliefs, cuisine, recreational and aesthetic preferences, material items, and a common history. The latter may be broadly interpreted to mean the past life-styles of the southern region of Italy. The regional society with its culture and subcultures provided the backdrop for the ethnic process in a new context. This process involves adaptations to changing circumstances resulting in variations within the ethnic population. (1988, p. 40)

Italian Americans today constitute a distinctive and authentic ethnic group. Whether in the private sphere existence of the family, neighborhood, church, or voluntary association, or in the public sphere of economics, politics, and education, Italian Americans have maintained a vital sense of their Italianicity. This is so despite the many factors and considerations that affect and mediate the social construction of Italian American life: *historical considerations, generational cohorts, the impact of the Mafia, the developmental nature of ethnicity, ecology/geography, and culture.* Although a certain degree and type of assimilation into the outer American culture and society are a distinct reality for virtually all modern-day Italian Americans, it has not been complete. Empirically, it is the case that Italian American traditions endure by continually being reconstructed socially. It is the contention of the authors that Italian Americans have authentically adapted their ethnicity to fit the ever-evolving social contexts in which they find themselves. Put into the terminology of this essay, Italian American identity is—and will continue to be—constantly generated as long as various elements of the Italian American community are empirically available to be appropriated in human consciousness. It is crucial to stress that the constant reconstruction of Italian American identity does not require that the individual's community attachments be completely Italian American.

Italian American Community and Identity: The Present Situation

Family

The centrality of the family for Americans of Italian heritage is an undisputed reality in both the common public mind and in the scholarly literature. Whether originally depicted as "amoral familists" (Banfield, 1958) in the impoverished south of the Italian nation-state, as members of working-class ethnic enclaves, or as participants in the modified extended families of the middle-class suburbs, the Italian American has had the family as the primary frame of reference. The continuing family-centered nature of present-day Italian Americans is a reality despite the increasing needs of the highly educated, socially mobile middle class to balance other commitments with that of the family. Modern means of transportation and communication, in conjunction with a willingness to trade off some upward social mobility, make this possible. Contemporary authority patterns in the modem Italian American family have no doubt evolved organically along egalitarian lines. This development, however, has stopped short of the modern utopian vision of a complete and radical democratization. The average middle-class husband and wife probably would not assent publically to the age-old Italian adage that "the father is at the head of the family and the mother is at the center," but with egalitarian modifications, this is still the empirical reality. Likewise, middle-class Italian American parents may raise their children in a progressively more child-centered way, but they show few signs of abandoning the realism and practicality that lies behind adult-centered childrearing. For instance, corporal punishment is no stranger to the middle-class Italian American child. The offering of *rispetto* (respect) by children to their parents and grandparents is still an essential article of faith in Italian American homes. Moreover, parents expect that their children will learn the meaning of *la bella figura* (to cut a good figure) or, at the very least, not to exhibit *la mal'figura* (to present a bad image). This expectation is tied to the belief that children are extensions of their parents and therefore reflect the honor of the family name.

Modern Italian Americans may no longer completely distrust *stranieri* (strangers) or *forestieri* (outsiders), but the principle that "the only one you can really count on is the family" is still heartily endorsed. Modern-day Italian Americans definitely hold different sets of expectations and different sets of rules for different groups as they extend centrifugally away from the family (*paese*, neighbors, other Italians, Americans, and so forth). Distrust has been generalized at a higher level of abstraction and only somewhat moderated. Figures of importance are *compares* (godfathers) and *comares* (godmothers)—the institutionalized mechanism which draws nonblood family members into the family/clan. Like all close family members, godparents, in assuming this status, acquire very serious duties as well as receive generous benefits. It is impressed upon Italian American children at an early age that all family business stays within the family. Gossiping with outsiders is prohibited. Psychiatrists and other family-oriented professionals are regarded with indifference and even amusement.

Key to the Italian American family is the social role of food ("food is love," "as good as bread"), especially the integrating and unifying function of the Sunday meal. The latter has brought many an Italian American son and daughter to travel impressive distances once a week or at least several times a month. Family gatherings—attenuated to a small degree with the death of family patriarchs and matriarchs—are still part of Italian American life. They serve both manifest and latent functions. Regarding the former, they are enjoyed for their own sake—for the food, conviviality, and general celebratory mood they engender. Regarding the latter, they keep the family together. These gatherings are the vehicles through which family members commit themselves to future economic and social exchanges. The family, it is often said, will always take care of its own.

The most effective type of social control is the successful internalization of norms; guilt plays an important role in Italian American families. Those who violate their Italianicity usually suffer the consequences of a conscience forged out of the experience of Italian American family living. Un-self-consciously or not, Italian American mothers lavish attention and concern on their children with the expectation that, come old age and possible future dependency, the children will reciprocate. It is also common for children to pledge periodically to keep the family together after the death of their parents. Italian Americans are also notorious in the rejection of group homes for the elderly; for them this is the option of last resort.

Probably the most important issue regarding the Italian American family is socialization. Is the family still an effective agent of socialization or have other, more powerful, institutions gained control of this function? Is the socializing message—regardless of its effectiveness—still Italian American? Based on disparate, but convincing, evidence, the answer appears to be yes to both questions.

Italian Americans, even the more affluent, remain in inner-city enclaves more than other groups do. When Italian Americans do move, many times two or more generations are involved in the exodus to a new suburban residence. If they do not relocate together, Italian American family members find residences within short distances of one another. When upwardly mobile children leave their inner-city parents for the suburbs, they visit them more than any other group (Lopreato, 1970). When leaving the extended family, Italian Americans most often move into some modified extended family arrangement characterized by continual economic and social exchanges. Similarly, Italian American middle- and working-class children are more likely to take geographical proximity to the family into account when considering college attendance. Contemporary Italian American youth spread their wings, but not too far.

Although crude survey data indicate that Italian Americans are increasingly intermarrying, these measures miss the reality that many times it is the non-Italian marriage partner who is drawn into the powerful magnet of the Italian American family. In addition, intermarriage need not diminish the ethnicity of the Italian American partner nor does it mean necessarily that the offspring will not be reared in the Italian American way. Italian Americans are more entrepreneurial than most; family businesses, by definition, provide not only income and independence from outsiders but also keep the family together (Battistella, 1989). Socially mobile Italian Americans are willing to sacrifice some career and employment opportunities in order to stay within the orbit of family life. Middle-class Italian American women have moved into the labor force but with a distinct difference from other groupings of women: for the most part, they accept employment that assists the family and meets its needs and are therefore underrepresented in the career-women category. Italian American families are more apt to be dual worker than dual career families.

Neighborhood

Since their arrival on American shores, Italian Americans have been an urban and, after World War II, suburban people. The 1980 census indicates that only 12.8 percent of people of Italian ancestry live in rural areas as compared to 26.3 percent of the U.S. population (Velikonja, 1989, p. 25). The heaviest areas of population continue to be in the Northeast, with strong Italian American representation in such locations as Boston, Providence, New Haven, Newark, Jersey City, Trenton, and New York City. Other traditional and continuing strongholds are to be found in south Philadelphia, Chicago, Cleveland, St. Louis, New Orleans, and San Francisco. Some Italian Americans have followed the general population movement to such newly emergent urban centers as San Diego, San Jose, Houston, and Phoenix (Velikonja, 1987, pp. 27-28). Italian Americans, an aging population, now reside in certain sections of Florida. Given their present middle-class status and following the general exodus to the suburbs, Italian Americans can be found in significant numbers in locations around the great cities. In New York, for example, Italian Americans are to be found in such areas as Westbury,

252 Salvatore Primeggia and Joseph A. Varacalli

Glen Cove, Deer Park, Port Washington, Franklin Square, Elmont, Inwood, Copiague (Marconiville), Lindenhurst, Island Park, and West Babylon (LaGumina, 1988). In New Jersey, large concentrations can be found in such suburban locations as Bloomfield, Belleville, and Elmwood Park (Starr, 1985). The embourgeoisement and sub-urbanization of the third and subsequent generations, however, do not necessarily entail any simple assimilation. Neighborhood-centered Italianness has been socially reconstructed into nonspatial forms of Italian American identification. In this regard, we generally agree with LaRuffa, who argues:

> Data on residential preferences of Italian Americans in the (New York) metropolitan area compel us to seriously question the views of the class assimilationists who argue that as Italian Americans move into the "mainstream" of American society the glow of ethnicity dims. It appears to me that something very different occurs. Italian Americans as an ethnic population change and as they change they display a resplendent array of varying colors embedded in a matrix of history, symbols, residence, and social ties. (1988, p. xvi)

Historically, Italian Americans have viewed the ethnic neighborhood as an extension of the family and home (DeSena, 1987, p. 246; Tricarico, 1984). This attachment to the neighborhood, however, did not develop overnight. Despite the reality of chain migration, in which members of a village would follow each other across the sea to a particular neighborhood, these "little Italies" were rarely populated solely by Italian immigrants. Also, they would contain Italian immigrants from different provinces and villages who did not identify with being Italian and who felt little or no bond of sympathy for one another. These ethnic communities attempted to replicate old world village life, started the slow process of forging a common Italian identification (Femminella and Quadagno, 1976), and introduced outside American and modern elements. Strong attachments to the neighborhood did eventually develop as Italian Americans carved out symbolic boundaries and a distinctive set of institutional allegiances (clubs, cafes, associations, feasts, parishes, local gangs) (Gans, 1962; Nelli, 1983; Suttles, 1968; Whyte, 1943).

The relative weakening of a neighborhood-centered Italian Americanness was a result, as with all migrations, of a combination of push and pull factors. Italian Americans, especially after World War II and spurred on by the benefits of the GI Bill, fully accepted the

American dream and the status symbol of a suburban home. Italian Americans, who have historically faced the reality of racial and ethnic succession, have often been in conflict with blacks (Rieder, 1985), and have contended with the destructiveness of liberal urban reformers who destroyed their communities in the name of progress (Gans, 1962). More recently, Italian American communities also have had to deal with yuppies and other gentrifiers (Freeman, 1987, p. 228) who attempt to buy out homeowners. In many instances, the urban planners, ethnic and racial minorities, or gentrifiers have won out. (East New York, for instance, no longer has any identifiable Italian population.) However, Italian Americans have a strong record of fighting and opposing these forces.

Any demise of the Italian American urban ethnic neighborhood is far from complete, since many Italian Americans still choose to remain together, despite impressive gains in income, education, and status. Moreover, many urban ethnic institutions are transferred and adapted to the suburbs (restaurants, feasts, and family gatherings). As Tricarico states, "While the old neighborhood is in eclipse, certain institutions have managed to adjust to new settings" (1984, p. 165). Additionally, the middle-class suburban Italian American has created many new forms of ethnic attachment that are indicative of contemporary Italian American vitality. In this regard Tricarico states:

> At the same time, new forms of ethnic identification and association are evident outside of the neighborhood. They are based on common interest, as well as the satisfaction of primordial or affective needs. Thus, there are associations of Italian American businessmen and professionals, advocacy groups, as well as symposiums on the ethnic experience, . . . (and) specialized ethnic networks are kept in touch by mass circulation techniques. (1984, p. 165)

While both are basically antiassimilationist theorists, Tricarico and LaRuffa debate one final important issue regarding the role of the contemporary Italian American urban enclave: Is the latter necessary to keep ethnicity alive for the suburbanized Italian? Tricarico basically answers in the negative:

> Although a powerful focus of ethnic identification and expression, the old neighborhood may not be indispensible. The principle "festa in the heart of New York" now has an out-of-town run in a New Jersey suburb. Although the parking lot of a sprawling shopping center that served as the site lacked the ambiance of Mulberry Street, the movable

feast points to the changing nonspatial character of Italian American life. This is important if only because the old neighborhoods have new residents: even Little Italy is predominantly Chinese. (1984, p. 166)

Speaking of an important Italian urban area in the Bronx, LaRuffa basically answers in the affirmative:

Nevertheless, its status as an Italian American enclave contributes to the maintenance of Italian American ethnicity in areas beyond its borders. Italian Americans living in other communities in the Bronx, in New Jersey, Westchester County, Long Island, and Connecticut drive to Monte Carmelo to shop; to visit relatives; to eat at restaurants; to participate in club activities; to attend hometown association meetings and community organization meetings; to hear mass in Italian; to celebrate a wedding; to mourn a friend or kinsperson; to hang out; and to enjoy the feasts, street festivals, and cultural events at the Monte Carmelo Cultural Center. (1988, p. 122)

Theoretically, LaRuffa has the better argument—similar to Edward A. Shils' claim (1975) that, if social "peripheries" are to maintain continuity with the past, they require social "centers" that provide at least some minimal form and articulation. For LaRuffa:

Some, like Monte Carmelo and the North End of Boston have become enclaves sustaining their role as symbols of ethnicity for large numbers of Italian Americans both near and far. . . . New space and old space become part of an ever-changing pattern of ethnic symbolism. The symbolic character of the particular space called "Monte Carmelo" transcends the boundaries of the community, linking up with other Italian Americans in other spaces, and thus serving as a spatial centerpiece of Italian American ethnicity. (1988, p. 123)

If LaRuffa is correct that existing Italian American ethnic enclaves serve a vital function in the protection and constant regenerating of new Italian American ethnic variations, the question then becomes: Will the enclaves survive? On one hand, Battistella's demographic analysis (1989) indicating a diminishing new immigration of Italians from Italy is not heartening in this regard. However, this finding may not be decisive given what LaRuffa says of both urban and suburban Italian Americans: "Italian Americans have demonstrated a preference for living in neighborhoods where their co-ethnics comprise either majorities or significant proportions of the population" (1988, p. 135).

Religion

Distinctions are necessary in order to analyze the issue of the religion of Italian Americans. Varacalli (1986), for instance, makes distinctions among the "sacred," "religious," and "Catholic" attachments of Italian Americans. The first, derived from Durkheim (1947), refers to whatever symbols an individual or a group holds as ultimate or extraordinary, whether those symbols are secular or involve some supernatural referent. The second is defined in terms of allegiances that are primarily "supernatural," while the third refers to a specific ideational and organizational interpretation of the supernatural. Using these distinctions, one can argue that the most "sacred" attachment of Italian Americans remains the family, although its spatial location has moved from the urban enclave to the suburbs and its cultural inspiration and social-structural support from the southern Italian village to an Italian American version of the American dream. Regarding "religious" attachments, belief in the supernatural remains a reality for contemporary Italian Americans, although the processes of what Berger (1969) calls a "compartmentalization" in human consciousness lessens the degree to which supernatural conceptions infiltrate all spheres of thought and activity. Regarding "Catholic" attachments, Orsi (1985) argues that immigrant and working-class Italian Americans have been very selective in their attachment. For Orsi these mostly urban-based Italian Americans are "domus-centered"; they mediate their religion through the frame of reference of the family and neighborhood. Italian immigrants and their working-class children have been

> involved in Church activities only when those activities coincided with the concerns of family/neighborhood. They were "good" Catholics when it came to baptisms, weddings, and funerals; they were "bad" Catholics when it came to attending Sunday Mass, going to Catholic schools, making financial contributions, and offering their sons and daughters for the religious life. (Varacalli, 1988, p. 76)

Since their post-World War II trek to the suburbs, some second- and many third-generation Italian Americans have modified significantly their anticlerical feelings and indifferences toward an "official"

Catholicism (Glazer and Moynihan, 1970; Lenski, 1961; Russo, 1977). However, the fourth-generation children of Italian American suburbanites, now twice removed from the immigrant experience, seem to be fully involved in the general secularization of Catholicism in the United States (Varacalli,1986). In this regard, Gambino states:

> The old inheritance's strong pragmatic preoccupation with this-world combines with a similar American attitude in the young people, making a turn toward organized religion even less likely. Thus, young Italian Americans might give up their energies to the secular values which function in place of orthodox religious lives—education and work, recreation and family. In short, this view sees the young people evolving new forms of the old preoccupations of their grandparents with a distinctly American twist. (1974, p. 242)

The Feast

Bridging our previous discussion of the family, neighborhood, and religion is an analysis of the Italian American feast. As most feasts center on the honoring of a southern Italian town or village saint, they are mechanisms that connect the old world to the new. For instance, the *Giglio* feast of Williamsburg, Brooklyn, is, to this day, celebrated simultaneously in the town of its origin, Nola, Italy (Primeggia and Primeggia, 1983). Feasts also serve as a way by which Italian Americans continue to sacralize neighborhoods. Former residents of a particular neighborhood return annually to visit family, friends, restaurants, and other neighborhood institutions while they engage in the celebration of the feast. Feasts are also significant watersheds within the rhythms of each year as is indicated by the title of Primeggia and Primeggia's article, "Every Year, the Feast" (1983). It is a truism for many Italians that each year contains only three important religious celebrations: Christmas, Easter, and the Feast.

Mention should be made of the high recognition and status that are given to those who organize the feast. In many neighborhoods, certain elite families assume this yearly responsibility and garner its symbolic rewards. The feast is a magnet, introducing many non-Italians to Italian American culture, yet at the same time, it serves as a boundary-maintaining device. Members of the feast committee, long-time residents of the neighborhood, and those with continuing contacts in the neighborhood are easily able to differentiate the *paesani* from the *stranieri*. The social or religious nature of the feast and its relationship to Roman Catholicism are subjects long debated in both the scholarly literature and by Italian Americans themselves. Orsi (1985), for instance, sees the feast as an expression of a "people's religion" while Varacalli (1986) sees the feast as primarily social and as a mechanism to maintain the "sacredness" of *la via vecchia* (the old way). Regarding the relationship of the feast to Roman Catholicism, Tricarico (1984) sees a developmental process at work; originally the feast, with its semipagan celebrations, operated outside the parish and as an alternative to it. Later, the feast became coopted by the local parish. As Tricarico states:

> Although the parish was introduced on a more inclusive basis (i.e., nationality), it does not seem to have been a replacement for *paesani* frameworks and loyalties. . . . The *feste* of the madonna and saints then continued to be sponsored by the societies, independent of the Italian parish. (1984, p. 14)

He notes, however, that

> as the number of parishioners dwindled, however, it became a critical device for keeping the parish solvent. Previous objections were now suspended with the tempering of its folk-religious ceremonies and the procession of devotees were no longer sacriligious; parish priests escorted the statue of the saint past parishioners who occasionally left their place on the sidewalks to affix dollar bills to the image for a special intention. (1984, p. 114)

La Ruffa argues correctly that "feasts and street festivals— combining old and new characteristics—continue to provide an important dimension to a perduring Italian American ethnicity" (1988, p. 130). Primeggia and Varacalli (1990) note the intermingling of early immigrant humor and entertainment with modern Italian American and Italian forms that are evident in the many feasts that take place today. The idea that feasts continue to be a very important cultural—and perhaps, religious—factor in the lives of contemporary Italian Americans is made clear by LaRuffa:

> Despite the fact that many old neighborhoods change and feasts honoring the Madonna or a patron saint are discontinued, similar

religious and secular festivities have been inaugurated in other neighborhoods which contain substantial numbers of Italian Americans. . . . The Italian American feast complex consists of a socio-cultural inventory of traits which has undergone changes over the years but, nevertheless, continues to provide a paradigm for the emergence of variations of feasts and street festivals. (1988, pp. 130-131)

Voluntary Associations

Jonathan Rieder's claim that "Italians never achieved the leverage that comes from belonging to organizations that recruit members on other than personal criteria" (1985, p. 33) was certainly true for the immigrant and working-class Italian American. The almost total commitment that most early Italian Americans had to the circles of family, friends, neighborhood, and fellow *paesani* (countrymen) severely limited their participation in various voluntary associations. To the degree that these formally uneducated Italian Americans did participate in voluntary groupings, it was in those associations which supported and surrounded family life. In terms of Max Weber's "communal-associative" distinction (1947), early Italian American voluntary groups were more "communal" (mutual aid societies, hometown clubs, feast committees) as compared to the contemporary situation, in which these groups coexist with those more "associative" in nature (academic, political, business, literary).

Battistella's important demographic analysis (1989, p. x) points out that approximately half the 1,500 Italian American organizations in existence were created since the 1970s. This explosion of Italian American organizations is supported, in part, as Glazer and Moynihan point out (1970), by the recent politicization of Italian Americans. Italian Americans today are more apt to demand their share of the political and economic pie; the creation of Italian American interest groups is one way to secure this. The National Italian American Foundation should be mentioned in this regard. This politicization is not merely an outgrowth of embourgeoisment but also a reaction to the organizing activities of blacks, feminists, and other minorities, which started in the 1960s.

It is also important to acknowledge the status needs of a rising middle class. In this regard, the explosion of voluntary life among Italian Americans is also part and parcel of a "symbolic crusade" (Gusfield,

1976), as Italian Americans increasingly are demanding various forms of status recognition. In a similar vein, LaRuffa states:

> County, regional, and national Italian American organizations are plentiful. . . . A significant portion of the organizations . . . consists of middle-class Italian Americans, many of whom would fit into Gans' category of "upper middle class professional." These associations— along with many others representing a wide range of ethnic types within the Italian American population—are a constant reminder of the viability and changing styles of Italian American ethnicity. (1988, pp. 132-133)

Economics

Berger and Berger postulate (1972, p. 156) that money, marriage, education, politics, and impression management are the five major mechanisms of upward social mobility. Clearly, until very recently, Italian Americans have taken the first route. As Karl Bonutti observes, for instance, "the economic attainments of Italian Americans far exceed their educational achievements" (1989, p. 78). Indeed, as Juliani states, "Since the 1950's, the Italian American level of income has increased more than that of any other white ethnic groups except the Jews. The level of Italian American income today exceeds the national average" (1987, p. 64). In his statistical analysis, Andrew Greeley (1977, p. 30) goes even further, noting that Italian Americans under forty earn more per capita income than does any other ethnic or religious group in the United States other than American Jews.

Interestingly, Greeley (1977, p. 63) suggests that a subtle bias exists against Italian Americans (and Eastern European groups) because their income level is significantly higher than their corresponding "occupational prestige" level. Although bias against Italian Americans does exist in American society, a simpler reason accounts for at least part of this discrepancy. Italian Americans are still a very family-oriented people. As Bonutti notes, for Italian Americans, the "preference is for well-paying jobs rather than for prestigious positions" (1989, pp. 65-66). Put another way, Italian Americans, relatively immune to the status symbols of the greater collectivity, will give first priority to income earning as a way to support the family.

The economic gains of Italian Americans in recent decades has been well documented.[1] This has led Bonutti, for instance, to a broad conclusion:

> Based upon their economic success, one would conclude that the assimilation process for Italian Americans has been completed. Although, we further suggest, economic assimilation is but one aspect of a complex process and that the cultural and social assimilation processes advance at a different pace. (1989, pp. 78-79)

While it is certainly true that cultural and social assimilation may proceed at a different pace than that of economic assimilation, we take sharp exception if by "economic assimilation" Bonutti means that thought and behavior in the business sphere is devoid of traditional or ethnic considerations. Furthermore, the fact that Italian Americans have made it financially and in terms of occupational status says nothing about whether they have been economically assimilated. There is no reason to assume that a prominent Italian American businessman or -woman— even in a bureaucratic private enterprise setting—cannot be both successful and authentically Italian American in the way he/she thinks and conducts business.

There are other indicators that economic success and maintaining a sense of Italianicity are not in a zero-sum relationship. As Bonutti notes, for instance, "there are relatively few employees of Italian extraction in Federal and State government. Only at the local level, their presence is still strong" (1989, p. 66). Employment within local government is more conducive to family and neighborhood life because it allows the individual to support his/her family without having to consider the issue of relocation. Although it is clear that many Italian Americans have moved up professionally, many other contemporary Italian Americans are willing to sacrifice socioeconomic mobility by not leaving their ethnic enclaves. As Juliani reports, "Despite this newer pattern of upward mobility, Italian Americans are still more concentrated in the working-class than most other white groups" (1987, p. 64). While a bit dated and a little less true, Gambino still speaks for many Italian Americans today when he argues:

> Because of their general distaste for abstractions and abstracted values, their ambivalent attitude toward formal schooling, and their desire to

remain close to the family roots, Italian Americans have gone into blue-collar rather than white collar work. (1974, p. 82)

Italian Americans, relative to other American groupings, are not ashamed of either their blue-collar or urban village designations as long as their occupations and neighborhoods provide a secure and comfortable family existence. As Gary Mormino notes, "Success is more often measured not by mobility through white collar suburbia, but by preservation of family and community. By this standard, Italian Americans have succeeded, making their way to the mainstream via different routes" (1986, p. 8).

Education

For Italian Americans, formal education has been viewed pragmatically; primarily it has been supported in those cases in which it assisted the family. For immigrant and working-class Italian Americans, remunerative work simply overpowered education as a means of survival and upward social mobility. While Femminella's assertion (1989, p. 47) that "among Italian Americans, education was not . . . the major means of upward mobility" is true, one must also note, following Juliani (1987, p. 64), that "the great increase in the years of schooling completed by the third and fourth generation of Italian Americans places them at almost the same levels as other white ethnic groups."

The fact that Italian Americans have caught up with many other American groupings does not automatically entail a lessening of individual Italianicity. For one thing, Italian Americans seem to carry over their pragmatism into their choice of educational careers. They tend to major in the more practical fields that are economically lucrative, such as law, business, medicine, and engineering. Conversely, Italian Americans are underrepresented in those fields that are more intellectual and speculative such as philosophy, history, social sciences, and the humanities. Following Peter and Brigitte Berger's argument (1971), while the sons and daughters of many Jews and WASPs rejected American society by majoring in "soft," "critical" fields during the 1960s and 1970s, Italian Americans (and other white ethnic groups) continued to major in the "hard" sciences and in business. While the hippies and semi-hippies "greened" (Reich 1970), to a certain degree, America was "blued" as the children of the working-class advanced up the social ladder.

As a matter of fact, participation in the system of higher education may not be deleterious to a continued ethnic attachment, as indicated by the proliferation of well-attended courses in Italian American (and Italian) culture in many colleges and universities. In New York State, for example, both the CUNY and SUNY systems offer many programs, courses, and special seminars and events dealing with the heritage.

Finally, many third- and fourth-generation Italian Americans demonstrate a willingness to attend colleges and universities close to home out of family loyalty. The response of one Canarsie working-class Italian American father is suggestive of the possibility of both emotional and social conflict between generations: "And I don't believe in those coed dorms. My daughter wanted to go away to college, but I put my foot down" (Rieder 1985, p. 143). This attempt to utilize the formal educational process and yet remain Italian is a task that causes much soul-searching among Italian American youth. As Gambino tellingly puts it:

> They are bewildered by the seemingly conflicting desires their parents communicate to them. Get an education but don't change. Enter the larger world but don't become part of it. Grow but remain within the mode of the tradition. . . . In short, maintain that difficult balance of conflicts which is the life style of the second generation. The problem has become an enormous one as third and fourth generation youngsters are entering college in large numbers in the 1970's. (1974, p. 241)

The potential for identity crisis and emotional conflict has been exacerbated for Italian American women, especially with the changing definitions of womanhood that began to emerge in the 1960s.

Politics

As Andrew Rolle (1980, p. 141) has observed, historically Italian Americans have lacked any united political front. Old World regional loyalties, invidious intra-ethnic jealousies, and a willingness to cut a deal for the benefit of one's immediate family are among the most cited reasons for this political individualism. To a certain degree, this has changed since the 1960s in the reaction of Italian Americans both to the political organization of other minority groups and to the changes in the direction of the national leadership of the Democratic party. Also, the recent embourgeoisement of Italian Americans is a factor in their recent increased political consciousness.

In general, it can be plausibly argued that Italian Americans are public sphere liberals and private sphere conservatives. That is, they tend to be conservative on those issues that most immediately affect the family and neighborhood, such as crime, forced busing, urban redevelopment, perceived welfare abuses, and racial quotas. Italian Americans tend to be liberal on socioeconomic issues such as social security, unemployment insurance, education, and unionism.

Until the 1972 presidential campaign of George McGovern, Italian Americans generally felt comfortable within the Democratic party. However, with the ascendency of an ultra-left wing to its leadership position, this has changed. Italian Americans now perceive that the national Democratic party no longer countenances any private sphere conservatism while favoring certain interest groups (feminists, blacks, homosexuals) at their own expense. As Italian Americans have increasingly become involved in both racial antagonisms and class conflict with a progressive "new class" consisting of scholars, governmental bureaucrats, the mass media, and others involved in the therapeutic helping professions (Berger and Berger 1984), they have realigned themselves to become an independent swing vote or have moved to the Republican party. As Rieder (1985) reports, many Italian Americans felt that the Democratic party betrayed them, not that they abandoned it. Speaking at least for the working-class Italian Americans of Canarsie, Rieder continues:

> Since 1960 the . . . Italians of Canarsie have embellished and modified the meaning of liberalism, associating it with profligacy, spinelessness, malevolence, masochism, elitism, fantasy, anarchy, idealism, softness, irresponsibility, and sanctimoniousness. The term conservative acquired connotations of pragmatism, character, reciprocity, truthfulness, stoicism, manliness, realism, hardness, vengeance, strictness, and responsibility. (1985, p. 6)

Pragmatism best describes the historical Italian American attitude toward, and involvement with, politics (Varacalli, 1985a). Where Democrats rule, and respect Italian American needs, Italian Americans have supported Democrats. If, on the other hand, Democrats refuse to satisfactorily incorporate their needs, Italian Americans have demonstrated a willingness to switch to the Republican party. In rural and suburban areas where many times Republicans are the reigning power, Italian Americans have, for the most part, gone along with the main political current. The pragmatism of the Italian American goes hand in hand with a politics that is people centered and distinctly non-ideological. Italian Americans show no strong interest in defending the abstract principles that undergird both capitalist and socialist philosophies (Varacalli, 1985b). Their range of political involvement is usually no wider than that of moderate conservative to moderate liberal. Italian Americans are willing to work with anyone, as long as the needs of the family, neighborhood, and general lifestyle are not adversely affected (Rieder, 1985; Varacalli, 1985a). This is further supported by Gambino, who states:

> Italian Americans as a group are neither liberal nor conservative, radical nor reactionary. They are reactive. They ignore politics until and unless their ethnically originated values are accosted. . . . [They] align themselves politically according to their own ethnic values rather than to political parties or ideologies. (1974, pp. 294, 297)

Key Factors in the Social Construction of Italian American Life

The argument hitherto presented is that both contemporary Italian American community and identity are alive and well. This argument, however, must be modified somewhat by an awareness that there are many historical, social-structural, and cultural factors that impact upon the development of Italian American ethnicity.

Historical Considerations

There are several key historical considerations that are important in our discussion of Italian American community and identity, all of which focus on the concept of the two Italies. Hitherto, northern and southern Italy have represented two very different social structural worlds. Northern Italy was more industrialized, urbanized, cosmopolitan, affluent, and perceived to be within the orbit of mainstream European society. Southern Italy, on the other hand, was hardly touched by the political national unification that occurred in 1870 and was set apart from northern developments. *Il Sud* (the South) was pre-modern, agricultural, and impoverished. *Il problema di Mezzogiorno* (the problem of southern existence) also involved the issues of northern political, economic, cultural, and racial discrimination toward the south. It is no exaggeration to claim that northern Italians viewed most southern Italians in a way analogous to the way American whites historically have looked at American blacks.

The first Italian migration to the United States started during the colonial period and lasted through to the Civil War. Coming almost exclusively from northern Italy, it was numerically small and not charactistic of the later mass migration of southern Italians. Most of the northern migrants were lower middle-class merchants, shopkeepers, and artisans (Iorizzo and Mondello, 1980). These European Italians were, for the most part, well received by American society. They posed no cultural/religious threat to Protestant hegemony or any economic threat to the host population. This group underwent a gradual, unforced Americanization. An absence of large numbers, combined with a relative lack of discrimination and a high degree of geographical dispersion, negated a strong sense of Italian community. The lack of significant elements of Italian American community, both spatial and nonspatial, made the maintenance of an Italian American identity difficult.

The second wave of immigrants, overwhelmingly from south Italy, started to flood America in the 1890s and continued until the introduction of the tightened, and essentially racist, immigration laws of the 1920s. Unlike the previous migration, in which the lure of America— the pull factor—was the primary consideration, southern Italians were pushed out of their villages by severe economic depression and overpopulation. Illiterate, poor, and unskilled, the immigrants sought out countries in which industrialization required large numbers of unskilled laborers. The United States was one such country. Most of the original migrants were men who did not intend to settle in the United States. The goal of these "birds of passage" (Lopreato, 1967) was to earn enough money to be able to resettle on more favorable terms back in Italy.

Despite their separation from the Old World, both the community attachments and identity formation of these potential returnees were, in this particular case, synonomous with and centered on the ideal of southern Italian life. Southern Italian life was a classic example of how an individual identity became a direct reflection of the community. The relevant term here is that of *campanilismo*, which suggests that the locus of meaningful life extends only so far as the sound of the village bell. Spatial community, moral community, and identity were coterminous for the southern Italian peasant, living in a basically premodern, *Gemeinschaft* (Toennies, 1957) southern Italian setting.

The hearts and minds of the southern Italian immigrant slowly and torturously shifted to America and to those ethnic enclaves in the northeastern cities in which they settled. Eventually, a coherent sense of Italian American community developed in the immigrant. The possibility of a pluralization and individualization of identity, however, would have to await a second generation in conflict (Child, 1943), a generation in which the neighborhood involvements or "liability" (Janowitz, 1952) might be more "limited."

Generational Cohorts

The fact that certain groups of individuals are born into a given social context during the same historical period means that these groups tend to share the same set of social experiences (Riley, Foner, and Johnson, 1972). Put into the terminology of this essay, different generational cohorts tend to be influenced by distinct forms of community and are, as such, characterized by different identity formations (Mannheim, 1952).

As for the mass migration of individuals from a turn-of-the-century southern Italy, certain generalizations can be made regarding the different generations of Italian Americans vis-à-vis community and identity. First, the immigrant brought over a distinct set of community allegiances and identities that were formed in the Old World but that could be adapted only within narrow limits by the first generation in the New World. For *i contadini del Mezzogiorno* (the peasants of the South), the social circles (Simmel, 1971) in which the peasant participated alternated between the family (Banfield, 1958) and, more inclusively, the village (Lopreato, 1967). In terms of identity, the peasant ranged from being an "amoral familist" (Banfield, 1958) who evidenced no concern for anything outside the nuclear family to an individual whose civic participation did not extend beyond the community (Lopreato, 1967). The first-generation immigrant initially transplanted, then adapted, his Old World allegiances to a neighborhood commitment that was "institutionally complete" (Breton, 1964). For Tomasi, "the institutional completeness of the ethnic community is correlated to its degree of ability to perform all the services requested by its members" (1975, p. 8). James Crispino summarizes what might be called the neighborhood/ethnic-centered stage of community and identity for most first-generation immigrants:

> For early generation Italians, the neighborhood was the spatial equivalent of the social structure. Its boundaries, and those of one's social circle, were in many instances coterminous and circumscribed a geographic and social space with which one could feel secure in the knowledge that he was surrounded by persons he could trust. The neighborhood provided a haven to which one could retreat to avoid contacts with strangers and to shut out the influence of the outside world which threatened to intrude on or even destroy the social fabric of the community. Thus, the congregation of Italians into "Little Italies" was the result of both an attempt to preserve the "ethnic way" and a defense against out-group hostility. The neighborhood, as an insulating agent, worked well for first-generation ethnics. (1980, pp. 89-92)

With the emergence of the second generation, there was an expansion of moral community, in part through dependence on a more Americanized peer group (Whyte, 1964) and, concomitantly, a wider range of identity formations. The second generation could choose to be either American, Italian, or some variation of the two (Child, 1943). By adapting Child's typology, we can offer four identity possibilities especially salient for the second generation. The first is the in-group reaction affirming one's Italianicity. The second is the out-group or rebel reaction emphasizing a quick assimilation into the outer American culture. Third is the apathetic response, indicating either an unwillingness or inability to decide between or synthesize the two allegiances; social-psychologically, the path of least resistance is almost always chosen. Finally, and ignored by Child, is the creative solution in which the attempt is made to forge a *via media* (middle way) between the first two identity responses (Gambino, 1974).

Existing interpretations by various assimilationist theorists (Lopreato, Gans, Crispino, Alba) argue that the third generation is moving toward complete assimilation. However, alternative interpretations that suggest the evolution of Italian American ethnicity are possible. In short, the creative solution of continually synthesizing elements of southern Italian and American cultures across the generations has been de-emphasized or ignored by the assimilationist theorists.

The Impact of the Mafia

Another key consideration in the social construction of Italian American life is the various responses of Italian Americans to the myths and realities surrounding the Mafia. Utilizing the modified typology of Irvin Child, we may discern four different reactions. The first, or in-group, response manifests itself in two widely divergent modes, that of denial and acceptance. In the former, the reaction is fundamentally defensive in the reluctance of the Italian American to give any credence whatsoever to the existence of the Mafia. Denial becomes the mechanism through which the individual defends his ethnic allegiance in the face of widespread societal discrimination. The latter response (acceptance), in contrast, takes vicarious pleasure and even pride in the economic and power achievements of Italian Americans involved in organized crime. For such individuals, noted crime figures represent startling success in an American society that at one time provided little opportunity for Italian American upward social mobility. In the past, these Mafia "folk heroes" provided a psychological vehicle by which some immigrant and working-class Italian Americans struck back at a hostile host society. With the increasing embourgeoisement of Italian Americans, this reaction is less prevalent but can still be found among those who have not been able or willing to transfer mentally to more mainstream Italian American symbols.

The second or out-group response is to acknowledge the Mafia label as an obvious negative symbol and source of embarrassment in the quest for respectability. For such individuals, the Mafia stigma only accelerates the assimilation process as an attempt is made to distance oneself from the negative connotations of Italian American life.

The third or apathetic and the fourth or creative reactions also perceive the Mafia association in negative terms. In the apathetic response, however, the resources to effectively deal, in some way, with the stigma are lacking. The creative response, however, honestly accounts for the existence of an undesirable criminal subculture within the Italian American community, but understands well that this subculture is not representative of the values and behavior of a vast percentage of Italian Americans. This response is creative in that it realistically addresses or synthesizes the relative merits of all sides of the controversy surrounding the Mafia.

The Developmental Nature of Ethnicity

Regarding the central issue of this essay the question is: what is the significance of a certain amount of cultural, and more important, structural assimilation for Italian American community and identity? Joseph Lopreato expresses one version of the structuralist fallacy of straight-line assimilation thinking in equating assimilation with socioeconomic achievement. For Lopreato, "The degree to which Italians have adapted to American society and culture is best exemplified by their . . . (high) achievement with respect to the holy trinity of Modern Graces: Education, Job, Income" (1970, p. 141). Referring to Milton Gordon's definition of structural assimilation as "large-scale participation in the cliques, clubs, and institutions of the host society at a primary-group level" (1970, p. 181), Lopreato concludes that "what has been observed about Italian Americans suggests that . . . (future) studies will reveal rising rates of structural assimilation. Nothing we know says that there is a point beyond which no more assimilation will occur" (1970, p. 186). We acknowledge that the position of contemporary Italian Americans has improved dramatically in terms of income, education, and to a lesser degree, occupational prestige. However, Lopreato's emphasis on structural variables ignores the ability of contemporary Italian Americans to socially reconstruct an authentic Italian American identity and to exhibit Italian American behavior in communities that are not fully ethnic.

James Crispino demonstrates another version of the structuralist fallacy by defining assimilation in terms of how far away, in thought and behavior, contemporary Italian Americans are from their immigrant roots. As Crispino puts it, "The perspective from which assimilation is viewed is not that of the extent to which Italian Americans become similar to other groups in America, but of the degree to which they depart from a specifically Italian way of life" (1980, p. xxiii). Only by ignoring, again, the developmental nature of ethnicity and by overstating the importance of structural factors can Crispino argue that "generally, the findings support the straight-line hypothesis, although there is some evidence of an ethnic resurgence in the form of increased Italian self-identity among young, later generation ethnics" (1980, p. xxiii).

Crispino's failure to capture the regenerative nature of Italian American ethnicity is intimately tied to his definition of assimilation as simply a falling away from the immigrant experience. New forms of Italian American ethnicity, the authors contend, are constantly being created in light of changing social contexts.

Despite this limited definition, Crispino is certainly correct in asserting:

> Today . . . continuous involvement in the cultural and social life of the community is not required to maintain ethnic awareness. . . . Because of the emphasis on the subjective aspect of ethnicity, the objective condition of being of ethnic descent is less important. What is more significant is the social-psychological component: a mind-set stressing ethnic pride and placing a positive valuation on in-group membership. (1980, p. 159)

He is fundamentally incorrect when he concludes:

> Since there is little need to interact today on an ethnic basis, ethnic identity is neither deeply engrained nor long lasting and its present form may more correctly be termed a "label" than an "identity." . . . Rather than being a strongly felt psychological need, ethnicity and ethnic identification are particularly subject to exogenous influences and may be expected to wax and wane as external circumstances require. (1980, p. 159)

Similarly, one can agree that what Crispino calls the New Ethnicity "is much more conscious, voluntary, and rationalistic than the earlier ethnicity" while dissenting from his claim that "it is transitory and manifested in activities requiring little commitment" (1980, p. 158). Indeed, adapting Gordon Allport's terminology (1950) describing religious commitment, one could assert that an intrinsic or a mature ethnicity is more authentic than an extrinsic or immature one.

Ecology/Geography

In his valuable study *Members of Two Worlds* (1971), Jon Galtung reported that there is significant variability in social-psychological orientations to the world and in social behavior which is influenced by their different ecological settings. Galtung's analysis involved three Sicilian villages: one by the sea, a second in the hills, and a third in the mountains. A relevant question is: to what degree do different ecological or geographical settings influence different forms of Italian American community and identity?

One basic ecological division used by sociologists is the tripartite distinction among urban, suburban, and rural settings. As previously mentioned, Italian Americans have historically congregated in urban settings, mostly in the Northeast. Given the highly concentrated and populated nature of Italian American urban community settings, the effect on maintaining an authentic Italian American identity is highly favorable. Consistent with the mobility patterns in America, Italian Americans have moved into the suburbs, where community life is more heterogeneous and they increasingly find themselves interacting socially with many non-Italian neighbors.

Theoretically, the more pluralistic nature of suburban community should translate into a weakening of Italian American identity; however, the Long Island Italian American experience (LaGumina, 1988) indicates this is not necessarily the case. Several points should be made immediately. First of all, the distance from New York City to Long Island is not great. When inner-city Italians move, they do not move far, indicating a desire to stay close to their original "little Italy" enclaves. Such is the case, as LaRuffa (1988) reports, of ex-Bronx Italians who move to adjacent Westchester County. Second, when they do move—and Italian Americans stay in their urban neighborhood long after other groups of similar status leave—they often migrate together as an extended family unit. Third, when they leave, they tend to congregate in the same areas, thus creating new suburban Italian American enclaves. As LaGumina reports, for instance, on Long Island there are distinctive Italian American communities founded by recent migrants from Manhattan, Brooklyn, and Queens who have relocated in such areas as Franklin Square, Elmont, Westbury, Port Jefferson, and Glen Cove. Finally, even those Italian Americans who live on Long Island in other than Italian concentrations can easily avail themselves of things and ideas Italian American. A community setting need not be predominantly Italian American to produce the option of identifying as an Italian American.

Italian Americans do not have a long tradition of living in more rural and frontier environments. Whether or not a rural environment negates the possibility of maintaining authentic Italian American community and identity depends on the degree to which the environment incorporates important components of Italian American culture. The northern Italians who founded Italian American communities along unpopulated regions of the north shore of California point to the possibility that those in rural environments can maintain their own form of ethnicity.

Culture

As previously argued (Varacalli, 1987), there is a distinctive southern Italian worldview that has been dialectically modified by the American experience, yet is organically linked to the past. This worldview is a "social fact" (in the Durkheimian sense) that is continually being reappropriated by most contemporary Italian Americans. This cultural perspective consists of six themes or orientations to the world: *cynicism, traditionalism, marginality, personalism, familism,* and *work* (Primeggia, Primeggia, and Varacalli, 1989). It is important to point out that it is the constellation of six themes which constitutes this southern Italian and Italian American worldview. Empirically, these themes overlap, are interdependent, mutually reinforce one another, and are perceived by the Italian American to be part and parcel of a total perspective.

Regarding *cynicism,* it has been argued that typical of the southern Italian American mentality is a propensity to "debunk" (Berger 1963) the claims of those who occupy official authority positions in any society. Italian Americans, for instance, continue to show disdain toward the insensitivity of urban planners regarding neighborhoods. The political apathy of Italian Americans, likewise, is connected to their disbelief in the claims of assorted reformers and utopian thinkers of all ideological stripes. The anticlerical and anti-institutional Church postures of the descendants of *Il Sud* are a matter of historical record. Given the history of oppression to which the group in question has been subject, it is no surprise that a strong comedic tradition with this debunking motif has developed which spans from the immigrant era of Eduardo *"Farfariello"* Migliaccio to that of the contemporary "Uncle Floyd" Vivino.

Consistent with Max Weber's understanding, the *traditionalist* is someone who manifests a respect for events, activities, symbols, and individuals that emanate from the past and are perceived to be relevant to the present and future. Faithful attendance and participation at feasts and pilgrimages to the Old World are but two ways by which the contemporary Italian American looks back in an attempt to construct a meaningful existence. Others would include the maintenance of southern Italian cuisine, the sustaining of neighborhood institutions, the perpetuation of sacred holidays, and a continuation of gardening that produces vegetables and fruits for the distinctive Italian American table. More subtle indicators for the present use of custom can be found in the utilization of body language, gestures, and certain linguistic formulations (dialect, "Italglish," adages).

Marginality has also been a theme of the southern Italian and Italian American experience with its attendant characteristics of creativity, entrepreneurialism, risk taking, and resentment. Generally speaking, Italian Americans have been peripheral to mainstream public life in politics, business, education, and the Catholic Church in terms of both participation and access to power. Significantly, their creativity has been evident especially in the arts, fashion, entertainment, and food industries. Italian Americans are more likely than other groups to start their own businesses and endeavors. A feeling of resentment has arisen from the outsider status afforded the Italian immigrants and their heirs. Perhaps this is most manifest politically as Italian Americans perceive such social policies as affirmative action, busing, and urban renewal to be specifically directed against them.

Personalism refers to a belief in the essential honor, sincerity, trustworthiness, and basic importance of those individuals and symbols within one's circle; it can be contrasted with the more modern contractual mentality, which has faith only in the law and written rules. Religiously, this is illustrated by the intimate bond that the Italian American has with the feast, individual saints, and the neighborhood itself. Politically, this trait is manifest in the reliance on the local committee member or ward leader to serve as a mediator to and protector from the more powerful and distant powers that be. The symbolic interaction occurring between neighborhood peers is characterized for Italian Americans as being infused with almost mythic qualities. This involves such things as the individual's reputation, the exaggeration of peculiar traits (flattering and otherwise), the utilization of nicknames, and the employment of in-group jargon. Most generally, the quality of Italian American interpersonal relationships tends to be concrete, intense, and diffuse. Above all, the concept of personalism is realized in the idea that an individual's word is his bond.

The belief that all other social involvements and considerations are subordinate to the health, happiness, and welfare of the family can be

termed *familism*. This phenomenon has both intra- and inter-family
dimensions. The former involves the celebration of all aspects of family
life: cuisine, holidays, gatherings, loyalty, intimacy, sharing, and
reliance. The latter involves the willingness to significantly shape
educational, political, economic, geographical, and other important social
considerations from the vantage point of maintaining the cohesiveness
and continuity of family life. In essence, there is nothing more significant
for Italian Americans than attachment to the family.

A great deal of importance is placed on the value of *work* as a
vocation or calling by Italian American women and men. The job, apart
from any financial reward, is seen as a worthwhile endeavor from which
satisfaction and pleasure are derived. Traditionally, for the Italian
American, the society-wide status of an occupation is not critical; what is
important is the pride a person takes in work and the fact that it provides
for the family welfare. Work, for the adult, in the public sphere is seen
usually as an extension of one's creativity, potentiality, and worth. In the
private sphere and in the female domain, the special care given in the
preparation of meals, the maintenance of the interior of the home, and the
raising of children are of paramount concern. For children, work is
viewed as crucial for the development of character, the engendering of
responsibility, and, fundamentally, as preparation for adult roles. Italian
American males, for their part, derive great satisfaction from the
repairing extension, and most generally, beautification of home exteriors.

Conclusion: "Symbolic Ethnicity"—An Authentic Identity for Many Contemporary Italian Americans

The class assimilationist theorist Richard Alba summarizes what Herbert
Gans means by the concept of "symbolic ethnicity":

> There is even room for ethnic identity in a muted form in this melting
> pot. As Herbert Gans has observed, many mobile ethnics attempt to
> maintain some psychological connection with their origins, as a way of
> retaining some ethnic "spice" in their identity. But such a link must be
> compatible with their integration into middle-class society; in
> particular, it must not prevent them from mixing freely with others of
> different backgrounds. Hence, this ethnic identity must be intermittent
> and undemanding in nature; and for this reason, it focuses on symbols
> of ethnic cultures rather than the cultures themselves, and it tends to be
> expressed in leisure-time activities rather than in the fabric for

everyday life. . . . . Symbolic ethnicity is vastly different from the ethnicity of the past, which was a taken-for-granted part of everyday life, communal, and at the same time imposed on the individual by the very fact of being born into the group. The ethnicity that survives in the melting pot is private and voluntary. The depth of change is profound. (1985, p. 173)

Surprisingly, Donald Tricarico, who so well understands the developmental nature by which ethnicity is transformed, agrees with Gans, Alba, and Crispino that the Italian American identity of the third and fourth generations is less than authentic. As he states:

In contrast to the "24 hours a day" ethnicity (Ibson, 1981) of the urban village, . . . developments signify an ethnicity that is circumscribed by nonethnic roles and identities. The social and psychological investment in ethnicity is limited and "situational." (Etzioni, 1959;1984, p. 165)

Although having no trouble with the phrase "symbolic ethnicity," we disagree with the interpretation and significance of the phrase imputed to it by the assimilation theorists. Rather, we support the contention of Richard Juliani that "it is not clear that membership in the middle-class precludes serious and meaningful expressions of ethnic group membership, that is, personal values, patterns of behavior, and interpersonal relationships that go beyond merely 'symbolic ethnicity'" (1987, p. 69). It is central to the overall argument of this essay to recall, at this point, the previous distinction we made between community and identity. That is, while it is true that, in terms of community, middle-class, fourth-generation Italian Americans are not twenty-four-hour-a-day Italians, it is quite possible, in terms of identity, that the middle-class, fourth-generation ethnic is authentically Italian American twenty-four hours a day in the way he/she thinks and acts. Put another way, the fact that the present-day Italian American confronts an environment or frame of reference that is not completely Italian American by no means precludes consistently being Italian American in such a context.

While symbolic ethnicity may be more voluntary and self-conscious, it need not be any less real. It need not be restricted to leisure-time activities or be limited and situational or intermittent and undemanding. Just as the contemporary comedian Uncle Floyd Vivino—who appeals in part to a non-Italian audience—is both consciously and unselfconsciously influenced in his work by his southern Italian and Italian

American past (Primeggia et al., 1989), so may be the teacher, nurse, sociologist, or police officer, as well as the mother, father, and daughter. Human beings are free to choose from among the various alternatives provided by the cultural and social-structural environment; Italian Americans are free, therefore, to continue to be Italian American by consciously drawing on the Italian American components of their community attachments and fashioning both new and authentic variations of both Italian American community and identity.

Note

1. The following information, provided by Bonutti, offers a useful overview of the impressive economic situation of most contemporary Italian Americans:

> Of the 3.5 million Italian Americans who are employed in eleven major industries, the largest percentage is found in service occupations. This percentage is lower than the national average (28.6% national vs. 26.7% Italian), because few Italian Americans are now found in low paying service jobs. For instance, few Italians are employed in household services: domestics, servants, etc., representing not more than one-third of the national average (2.5% national vs. 0.8% Italian). On the other hand, over ten percent more than the national average are found in various business fields (9.7% national vs. 11.0% Italian), in personal services (8.5% national vs. 11.7% Italian), entertainment and recreation (3.6% national vs. 4.7% Italian), and repair services (4.8% national vs. 5.3% Italian). Even higher is their representation in the higher paid professional fields, especially legal and engineering, where their participation is twenty percent higher than the national average (10.4% national vs. 12.2% Italian). . . . In the lower paid professions their participation is below the national averages. For instance, in social service and religious fields they are all well below the national averages (10.7% national vs. 9.0% Italian); in hospital jobs they are ten percent lower (22.3% national vs. 20.1% Italian). The only exception is in the medical profession where their participation ratio is close to the national average. Another good indication of the Italian upward mobility is found in the declining industries (which seventy years ago were the most prosperous and promising employment fields), where Italian participation rates are lower than the national averages. In mining, their participation is at 35% of the national average, in forestry, 50 percent of the national average. Additional comparisons in lumber and furniture (9.1% national vs. 4.3% Italian), in transportation

equipment (18.5% national vs. 15% Italian), in railroads (8.1% national vs. 6.6% Italian) confirm the same trends. Equally interesting is their lower than average participation in sanitary services (19.4% national vs. 15.4% Italian) where, incidentally, many Italians hold supervisory positions. In the retail trade, the only areas with greater than average participation rates for Italian Americans are in the food, bakery, and dairy products and especially in grocery stores, with a fifteen percent vs. nineteen percent participation. . . . The most convincing evidence of successful upward mobility by Italian Americans can be observed by their income levels. (1989, pp. 69, 71-72)

References

Alba, R. 1985. *Italian Americans: Into the Twilight of Ethnicity*. Englewood Cliffs, N.J.: Prentice-Hall.

Allport, G. 1950. *The Individual and His Religion*. New York: Macmillan.

Banfield, E. C. 1958. *The Moral Basis of a Backward Society*. New York: Free Press.

Battistella, G., ed. 1989. *Italian Americans in the '80s: A Sociodemographic Profile*. Staten Island, N.Y.: Center for Migration Studies.

Berger, B. and P. Berger. 1984. *The War Over The Family*. New York: Anchor Books.

Berger, P. 1963. *Invitation to Sociology*. Garden City, N.Y.: Doubleday.

———. 1969. *The Sacred Canopy*. Garden City, N.Y.: Doubleday.

Berger, P. and B. Berger. 1971. "The Bluing of America," in *New Republic*, April 3.

———. 1972. *Sociology: A Biographical Approach*. New York: Basic Books.

Berger, P. and T. Luckmann. 1966. *The Social Construction of Reality*. New York: Doubleday.

Bonutti, K. 1989. "Economic Characteristics of Italian Americans." Pp. 62-79 in *Italian Americans in the '80s: A Sociodemographic Profile*, ed. by G. Battistella. Staten Island, N.Y.: Center for Migration Studies.

Breton, R. 1964. "Institutional Completeness of Ethnic Communities and the Personal Relations of Immigrants." *American Journal of Sociology* 70, No. 2:193-205.

Child, I. 1943. *Italian or American? The Second Generation in Conflict*. New Haven: Yale University Press.

Crispino, J. A. 1980. *The Assimilation of Ethnic Groups: The Italian Case*. Staten Island, N.Y.: Center for Migration Studies.

DeSena, J. 1987. "Involved and 'There': The Activities of Italian American Women in Urban Neighborhoods." In *The Melting Pot and Beyond: Italian*

Americans in the Year 2000, ed. J. Krase and W. Engelman. Staten Island, N.Y.: American Italian Historical Association.

Durkheim, E. 1947. *The Elementary Forms of the Religious Life.* New York: Free Press.

Femminella, F. X. 1989. "Italian Americans and Education." Pp. 36-48 in *Italian Americans in the '80's,* ed. G. Batistella. Staten Island, N.Y.: Center for Migration Studies.

Femminella, F. X. and J. S. Quadagno. 1976. "The Italian American Family." In *Ethnic Families in America,* ed. C. H. Mindel and R. W. Habenstein. New York: Elsevier.

Freeman, R. C. 1987. "The Development and Maintenance of New York City's Italian American Neighborhoods." In *The Melting Pot and Beyond: Italian Americans in the Year 2000,* ed. J. Krase and W. Engelman. Staten Island, N.Y.: American Italian Historical Association.

Galtung, J. 1971. *Members of Two Worlds.* New York: Columbia University Press.

Gambino, R. 1974. *Blood of My Blood: The Dilemma of the Italian Americans.* Garden City, N.Y.: Doubleday.

Gans, H. 1962. *The Urban Villagers.* New York: Free Press.

———. 1979. "Symbolic Ethnicity: The Future of Ethnic Groups and Cultures in America." In *On the Making of Americans: Essays in Honor of David Riesman,* ed. H. Gans, H. Glazer, J. Gusfield, and C. Jencks. Philadelphia: University of Pennsylvania Press.

Glazer, N. and D. P. Moynihan. 1970. *Beyond the Melting Pot: The Negroes, Puerto Ricans, Jews, Italians, and Irish of New York City,* 2nd ed. Cambridge, Mass.: MIT Press.

Greeley, A. M. 1977. *The American Catholic: A Social Portrait.* New York: Basic Books.

Gusfield, J. 1976. *Symbolic Crusade.* Chicago: University of Illinois Press.

Iorizzo, L. J. and S. Mondello. 1980. *The Italian Americans.* Boston: Twayne Publishers.

Janowitz, M. 1952. *The Community Press in an Urban Setting.* Chicago: University of Chicago Press.

Juliani, R. 1987. "The Position of Italian Americans in Contemporary Society." In *The Melting Pot and Beyond: Italian Americans in the Year 2000,* ed. J. Krase and W. Engelman. Staten Island, N.Y.: American Italian HistoricalAssociation

LaGumina, S. J. 1988. *From Steerage to Suburb: Long Island Italians.* Staten Island, N.Y.: Center for Migration Studies.

LaRuffa, A. L. 1988. *Monte Carmelo: An Italian American Community in the Bronx.* New York: Gordon and Breach Science Publishers.

Lenski, G. 1961. *The Religious Factor.* Garden City, N.Y.: Doubleday.

LoPreato, J. 1967. *Peasants No More.* San Francisco: Chandler.

―――. 1970. *Italian Americans.* New York: Random House.

Mannheim, K. 1952. "The Problem of Generations." In *Essays in the Sociology of Knowledge*, ed. and trans. P. Kecskemeti. London: Routledge and Kegan Paul.

Mormino, G. R. 1986. *Immigrants on the Hill: Italian Americans in St. Louis, 1882-1982.* Urbana and Chicago: University of Illinois Press.

Nelli, H. 1983. *From Immigrants to Ethnics: The Italian Americans.* New York: Oxford University Press.

Orsi, R. A. 1985. *The Madonna of 115th Street: Faith and Community in Italian Harlem, 1880-1950.* New Haven: Yale University Press.

Primeggia, S. and P. R. Primeggia. 1983. "Every Year, The Feast." *Italian Americana* 7, No. 2 (Spring/Summer): 4-12.

Primeggia, S., P. R. Primeggia, and J. A. Varacalli. 1989. "Uncle Floyd Vivino: An Italian American Comic." *New Jersey History* 107, Nos. 3 and 4: 1-19.

Primeggia, S. and J. A. Varacalli. 1990. "Southern Italian Comedy: Old to New Worlds." Pp. 241-252 in *Proceedings of the Twenty First Annual Conference of the American Italian Historical Association.* Staten Island, N.Y.: Center for Migration Studies.

Reich, C. 1970. *The Greening of America.* New York: Random House.

Rieder, J. 1985. *Canarsie: The Jews and Italians of Brooklyn Against Liberalism.* Cambridge, Mass.: Harvard University Press.

Riley, M. W., A. Foner, and M. Johnson, eds. 1972. *Aging and Society*, Vol. 3. New York: Russell Sage Foundation.

Rolle, A. 1980. *The Italian Americans: Troubled Roots.* New York: Free Press.

Russo, N. J. 1977. "Three Generations of Italians in New York City: Their Religious Acculturation." In *The Italian Experience in the United States*, ed. by S. M. Tomasi and M. H. Engel. Staten Island, N.Y.: Center for Migration Studies.

Shils, E. A. 1975. *Center and Periphery.* Chicago: University of Chicago Press.

Simmel, G. 1971. *On Individuality and Social Forms*, ed. and with an introduction by D. Levine. Chicago: University of Chicago Press.

Starr, D. J. 1985. *The Italians of New Jersey.* Newark: New Jersey Historical Society.

Suttles, G. D. 1968. *The Social Order of the Slum: Ethnicity and Territory in the Inner City.* Chicago: University of Chicago Press.

Toennies, F. 1957. *Community and Society.* East Lansing: Michigan State University Press.

Tomasi, S. 1975. *Piety and Power.* Staten Island, N.Y.: Center for Migration Studies.

Tricarico, D. 1984. *The Italians of Greenwich Village: The Social Structure and Transformation of an Ethnic Community.* Staten Island, N.Y.: Center for Migration Studies.

Varacalli, J. A. 1985a. "Ethnic Politics in Jersey City: The Changing Nature of Irish-Italian Relations, 1917-1981." In *Italians and Irish in America*, ed. F. X. Femminella. Staten Island, N.Y.: American Italian Historical Association.

___. 1985b. "Toward the Italian American Moment: In Praise of the Tortoise." Paper presented at the Fifth Annual Conference of the National Italian American Foundation, New Haven, Conn., April 20.

___. 1986. "The Changing Nature of the 'Italian Problem' in the Catholic Church of the United States." *Faith and Reason* 12, No. 1 (March): 38-72.

___. 1987. "What It Means to be an Italian American: Initial Reflections." Paper presented at American Italian Historical Association Conference, Chicago, November 13.

___. 1988. "Review of Anthony Orsi's The Madonna of 115th Street: Faith and Community in Italian Harlem, 1880-1950." New Haven: Yale University Press, in *Sociological Analysis* 49, No. 1 (Spring): 76-77.

Velikonja, J. 1989. "Demographic and Cultural Aspects of Italian Americans." In *Italian Americans in the 80s: A Sociodemographic Profile*, ed. G. Battistella. Staten Island, N.Y.: Center for Migration Studies, 1989.

Vidich, A. and S. Lyman. 1985. *American Sociology: Worldly Rejections of Religion and Their Directions.* New Haven, Conn.: Yale University Press.

Weber, M. 1947. *The Theory of Social and Economic Organization.* New York: Oxford University Press.

___. 1958. *From Max Weber.* Ed. H. H. Gerth and C. W. Mills. New York: Oxford University Press.

Whyte, W. F. 1943. *Street Corner Society: The Social Structure of an Italian Slum.* Chicago: University of Chicago Press.

Chapter 13

Jewish and Italian American Women's Childbirth Choices in the United States, 1920-1940: An Examination of Home Birth

Angela D. Danzi
State University of New York at Farmingdale

This chapter juxtaposes two important social processes that occurred in the late nineteenth and early twentieth centuries in the United States: the mass immigration of east European Jews and Italians to the urban centers, and the medicalization of childbirth. Immigrants presented many challenges for the medical practitioner and the newly emerging specialty of obstetrics, not the least of which was their preference for midwife-assisted home birth. Yet by 1940, the role of the midwife was effectively eclipsed by the trained male medical professional affiliated with the expanding urban hospital.

The shift away from midwives and home births occurred in two stages. By 1920 most native-born middle class women were electing to have their children in the hospital with a medical professional in attendance. But immigrant women and their daughters were still in a period of change (New York Academy of Medicine, 1924, 1933; Wertz and Wertz, 1990; Devitt, 1977). While second-generation Jewish women generally preferred birth in a hospital with a private doctor in attendance, Italian woman were more varied in their choices. Some continued to prefer home birth, others used a hospital clinic, and others moved from home to hospital over the course of their childbirth careers. What explains these varied responses to childbirth? How and why did some women accept innovation while others continued to practice established cultural routines?

The women whose lives and experiences are highlighted here were caught up in an important process of social change. Their lives were dramatically affected by outside forces and pressures; nevertheless they were not so constrained that they could not exercise some important choices and refashion their own circumstances. What follows here represents only a partial summary of a larger research undertaking that examines the various decisions or pathways these women took in dealing with childbirth over their birth careers (see Danzi, 1997). While we are concerned here with a particular transformation at a particular time—the shift from home to hospital birth in New York City between 1920 and 1940—and the influence of ethnicity in this process, there are far larger implications. Our discussion can also shed light on the complex question of how individuals and groups accept, reject, or refashion innovative ideas and behaviors.

We will first discuss the theoretical perspectives that can explain this variation in childbirth practice. Next we will highlight the experiences of the women—mostly Italian American—who through this period were able to exercise their preference for home birth at a time when it was becoming increasingly difficult to do so. Our discussion of shifting childbirth practices is based on eighty in-depth interviews with Jewish and Italian second generation women born in the United States of foreign-born parents who had children in New York City before 1940. These interviews explored women's decisions about childbirth care over the course of their birth careers.

Theoretical Perspectives

Two substantive bodies of sociological research can be applied to the question at hand. The first has investigated the relative assimilation of immigrant groups, and the second has been interested in understanding how and why individuals seek out medical care. We will briefly discuss each of these subfields in turn, and then synthesize their common themes.

Assimilation Theory

As first proposed by Robert Park and others of the Chicago School, the classic assimilation perspective posits that when divergent cultures interact in urban environments, a cycle of contact, accommodation, and assimilation is set into motion. Each of these stages involves different degrees of absorption. The final or assimilation stage is reached when immigrants adopt significant aspects of the dominant culture (Park, 1950; Park and Burgess, 1925). Milton Gordon (1964) later modified Park's ideas, acknowledging the multidimensional nature of modern life by noting that groups can take on American behaviors and values (acculturate) yet retain ethnic family or religious patterns.

Assimilation theorists have long been interested in the so-called "New Immigration"—arrivals to the United States from east, central, and south Europe from 1880 to 1920. From the beginning, the physical characteristics, languages, and religious and political traditions of these peoples created much anxiety about their ability to be resocialized as members of American society (Higham, 1972). Jews and Italians were the largest groups within this migration, and comparisons with respect to their rates and degrees of economic and social success were logical and inevitable. By 1920 it was apparent that Jews were acculturating rapidly, and were moving into higher education and professional positions, while Italian educational and occupational attainment remained low (Covello, 1967; Glazer, 1955, 1958).

Explanations for this difference relied on either cultural or structural factors. Cultural explanations emphasized the utility of Jewish values and beliefs, like the importance given to formal schooling, in accounting for Jewish success. Italian parents, in contrast, valued practical knowledge and placed a low value on formal schooling. Parenthetically, there is a well-developed body of literature that examines Italian American culture as problematic, even pathological, providing its members with few mechanisms or strategies that could have legitimate payoffs in terms of economic and social mobility in a modern setting (see for example Adams, 1881; Speranza, 1908; Price, 1917; Cordasco and Buccioni, 1974; Foerster, 1919, 1969; Williams, 1938; Ware, 1935; Child, 1943; Whyte, 1947; Banfield, 1958; Gans, 1962).

Structural explanations for the varying economic and social success of Jews and Italians focused on the match between pre-migration characteristics and features of American society. Jews meant to be permanent settlers, while Italians were birds of passage. In Europe, Jews were predominantly urban entrepreneurs while Italians were largely rural agriculturalists. These differences gave Jews an advantage. They were better equipped from the outset to succeed in the American urban-industrial milieu. In sum, both cultural and structural attributes were seen as positive forces in Jewish educational and occupational achievement, but were considered barriers for Italians. Seen in this light, Jewish women's fairly rapid acceptance of medical innovation in childbirth may be viewed as simply another example of Jewish success in the acculturation process, while Italian women's resistance to medical assistance and preference for home birth may be interpreted as an inability or unwillingness to abandon familiar but inferior practices.

A more recent theme in the assimilation literature is the relative importance of coercion versus personal agency and the degree to which groups could manipulate their circumstances. While earlier work portrayed immigrants as helpless victims, newer interpretations found that they could choose options that could refashion both traditional values and the structural limitations of their new situations (Hareven, 1980; Morawska, 1985). This new emphasis on personal and group agency recast both structure and culture. Structures were not unyielding, while cultural traditions were malleable and sometimes helped groups to endure and survive. Seen in this light, both Jewish women's rapid acceptance of doctor-assisted hospital birth and Italian women's more varied responses to childbirth may be interpreted as a more deliberate appropriation by both groups of available options to suit their own preferences and requirements. This newer scholarship helps us to realize Weber's worthy goal of *verstehen:* to understand human activity from the point of view of the actors, and to recognize that actions spring from the subjective meanings groups and individuals attach to them.

The assimilation perspective is still the dominant approach, but for our purposes, we are left with questions and problems. While this perspective names an outcome, it says little about the process of change. Further, debates about assimilation or acculturation have concentrated on male domains and institutions, and have focused on processes and developments rather distant from women's lives. Ethnic women were more embedded in family and neighborhood, and their process of change must be conceptualized as more socially grounded, and must place more emphasis on social relationships.

Theories of Medical Utilization

We next turn to a brief look at medical utilization theory. This body of literature is concerned with providing explanations for how and why clients understand illness and either seek out or reject medical treatment. The earliest work in medical sociology focused on the social definition of sickness and the examination of social variables as they related to the acceptance or rejection of the sick role (Parsons, 1951, 1958). The Health Belief Model, developed over a generation or more, posits a fairly complex interaction of personal and social variables that affect how individuals recognize symptoms and seek medical assistance (Rosenstock, 1966; Becker, 1979; Janz and Becker, 1984). Sociocultural and demographic factors have also been found to influence health action (Koos, 1954; Twaddle, 1987; Aday, Anderson, and Fleming, 1980; Freidson, 1961; Zborowski, 1952; Graham, 1957; Blackwell, 1967; Blaxter, 1976). These approaches have been criticized as atomizing individuals by placing too much emphasis on a rational/cost-benefit model of decision making (Pescosolido, 1992).

More helpful is the concept of the lay-referral system (Freidson, 1988). In this model, individuals are grounded in family and friendship networks, and medical utilization is conceptualized as a series of widening consultations with family, friends, neighbors, co-workers, and others. This approach requires a more subjective look at the sick, their everyday concerns and relationships, and the ways in which families are pivotal actors in health behavior. The lay referral system acknowledges that social interaction and social relationships predate and provide the context for utilization and health behavior (Freidson, 1988; Conrad, 1987).

Theoretical Synthesis

Theories about immigrant/ethnic assimilation on the one hand and illness behavior and the utilization of medical systems on the other both provide assistance in understanding ethnic women's childbirth experiences. Each has begun to redirect attention away from individuals and toward collectives in understanding change or stability. Each has devoted promising but underdeveloped attention to networks and to the layers of interpersonal connections between primary and secondary groups. Each has also become more interested in understanding the subjective experiences of the ethnic and the patient.

Both, however, display a tendency to regard what is modern or innovative as the most desirable or effective mode of action. With respect to medical innovation, this bias or uncritical stance obscures the fact that medical treatments often did not produce more satisfying or healthier outcomes. Additionally, in each of these literatures, women's lives and experiences are underdeveloped. Childbirth is a central human event, yet neither branch of literature has devoted much attention to it.

Our synthesis and further development of these research traditions requires that we first acknowledge the inherently social nature of life and human experience. Women are not atomized individuals, but active members of families and friendship groups, making purposive decisions in a social context.

We conceptualize the causal chain as follows: both cultural and structural variables shape social networks, and social networks in turn provide social supports for and personal links with childbirth caregivers. Our intent is to go beyond conventional observations of cultural or structural differences among these women, and examine the mechanisms by which these factors operated to produce different ideas and behaviors.

The Home Birth Experience Before 1940

We now turn to consider the experiences of women who were able to select home birth exclusively and explore the question of why they made this atypical choice. Data from personal interviews indicate that fully 25 percent of Italian women but only 3 percent of Jewish women gave birth to all their children at home. These births spanned the years 1916 through 1936, and took place in the context of the decreasing availability of home birth attendants. My focus will be on Italian Americans; the experience of Jewish women will be used here as comparison and contrast.

It was widely assumed during this era that hospital birth was superior but, medical propaganda notwithstanding, women who chose home birth were exercising the safest birth option. Contemporary studies confirmed that infant and maternal mortality were lower in midwife-attended home births (New York Academy of Medicine, 1933). Home birth was fundamentally different from hospital birth because control over the extrinsic arrangements remained for the most part in the hands of the parturient woman and her family, not in the hands of medical personnel. Three factors influenced the home birth decision: preferences based on values and ideas about childbirth; the availability of birth attendants; and the economic and social costs of the various options.

Italian women who selected home birth were heavily dependent on an older generation of women for ideas about birth. They believed in the legitimacy and worth of their mother's, mother-in-law's, or aunt's ideas and preferences, and assumed that she had the knowledge necessary to guide them. This assumption can be traced to two important influences of their pre-marriage and adolescent years which operated together to restrict knowledge and the flow of new information about the various dimensions of the birth process. These were, first, low levels of education, and second, strict parental supervision of young girls from their earliest years through their courtships and marriages.

Italian American women left school, often unwillingly, at or before eighth grade to join the paid labor force. Families actively encouraged daughters to begin to contribute to the family economy. Low levels of education restricted knowledge about childbirth by narrowing their exposure to modern, scientific notions about the world in general and biological processes in particular. Additionally, low levels of education channeled women into the protected and homogeneous environment of the neighborhood factory. In contrast, Jewish women were far more likely to attend high school, and/or to train as typists or bookkeepers, work that took them out of local enclaves and into the diversity of the downtown office.

Mothers and fathers of Italian home birth women tried to shelter and protect their unmarried daughters by arranging employment nearer to home and among relatives or neighbors. Families also promoted marriages between their sons and daughters, and kept a close, sometimes claustrophobic watch over courting couples. Again, there is a sharp contrast here to Jewish women, who had more personal freedom and autonomy, and who generally met husbands through peer, not parental connections.

After marriage, Italian couples maintained a high degree of residential continuity, often living on the same block or in the same apartment house as parents.

Italian women knew little about sexuality, and had very little opportunity to inform themselves about the birth process. After marriage and as they began having children, they continued to be dependent on one or several older women to help them manage childbirth. They believed that mothers had the knowledge and judgment required to provide assistance. This dependency carried forward a feature of premodern life—the continuity and validity of the knowledge base of the older generation. Jewish women more often felt their mothers to be hopelessly old-fashioned; mother's way of doing things had little relevance for daughters.

Home birth women adopted mother's negative attitudes toward the hospital. Hospitals were believed to be dangerous places and their personnel were considered incompetent or conspiratorial. Some women were convinced that hospitals routinely sent women home with the wrong baby. Overall, they believed that hospitals were for the sick, while childbirth was an every day event that did not require medical intervention.

Preference for home birth was also a preference for a midwife, although doctors were also called in from time to time. Most women who wanted a home birth assumed that the attendant would be a midwife, but a doctor was also acceptable.

Through their generational positions, mothers and mothers-in-law could help their daughters find a suitable midwife by tapping into neighborhood and family networks. After the first birth, midwives and their patients considered themselves to be *comare* in acknowledgement of the quasi-family relationship that now existed between them.

Religious belief and practice also helped to maintain continuity between mothers and daughters. Many women practiced the same devotions to the saints or to the Blessed Virgin as did their mothers, fervently lighting candles, offering prayers, and marching in religious processions to receive a blessing or favor (see Orsi, 1989). This was in sharp contrast to Jewish young women who often firmly rejected a mother's religious observances and rituals because they found no solace or meaning in them.

While the number of practicing midwives dropped sharply during this period because of immigration restrictions after 1921, and because of new licensing requirements in New York City, these women were consistently able to find a midwife. Their residential stability and the concentrated timing of their births ensured that personal links to midwives remained active. Often, Italian mothers' and daughters' childbirth careers overlapped, and daughters could employ the same midwife used by their mother. Additionally, the short-lived, municipally sponsored Bellevue School, operating from 1912 to 1930, graduated small numbers of women who often practiced in the Italian enclaves of New York City (Baker, 1911).

Cost was another important consideration. Home birth consistently was less expensive than hospital birth. A midwife's fee was generally the equivalent of a working man's weekly salary, but doctor and hospital fees were nearly double this figure.

Home birth did however have other social costs. Older children had to be sent out of the house to stay with relatives. Home birth was labor intensive and required a great deal of laundering, meal preparation, and cleaning. Living near relatives, especially one's mother, mother-in-law, or sisters, meant that women relatives would be available to provide this assistance on a reciprocal basis.

Women generally appreciated the help of mothers and relatives but objected to the presence of overbearing, unhelpful, or overly curious relatives. Even when they were unhappy with some aspect of assistance, women felt that they had no choice but to accept some loss of control over their households in exchange for assistance, and as part of the complex web of give and take among families and neighbors.

There was a very high degree of satisfaction with the care they received from midwives, and women often spoke of them with affection. Midwives did not intervene in the process or use any intrusive measures. They simply allowed nature to take its course. Women who continued to select home birth generally experienced safe, routine, and uncomplicated deliveries. In all cases, the health of the mother and child was sustained.

Husbands were generally available and often present as observers and comfort-givers, but for the most part they did not take any active role in the proceedings.

Preparations in the home were often rudimentary, glancing, and last-minute. It was indeed a woman's sphere, and women went about the business at hand with a degree of matter-of-factness and informality. Women were responding to events rather than shaping them. All present—midwife and women relatives—watched and waited and assisted the parturient woman.

In sum, women's preference for home birth, at first largely borrowed from a trusted older woman and later more firmly their own, remained fixed throughout their birth careers. Residential stability and the timing of their pregnancies allowed them to carry forward this preference in the selection of a home birth attendant who often became someone they admired and in whom they placed great trust and confidence. Their relative health and the absence of complications at birth, as well as on-going availability of relatives and friends to assist, also ensured their continued satisfaction. Overall, they experienced the home birth decision as reflecting what their own families and communities considered to be right and proper. They felt themselves to be doing what everyone else was doing.

Early observers of Italian communities in New York City noted some Italian American women's acceptance of medical assistance in childbirth as a marker of assimilation (Ware, 1935; Campisi, 1947). Implicit in their analysis was an evaluation and approval of groups or aspects of group life that had moved in this direction. But childbirth in a hospital with a doctor in attendance was far less safe, and more fraught with danger for both mother and infant than the old-country way of having babies at home in one's own bed.

Home birth was one pathway available to women in an era of rapid change. In delineating the mechanisms by which some women were able to consistently select home birth through these years we have also begun to suggest how it is that social subgroups may protect themselves, at least for a while, from the effects of larger structural forces. Each of these women, embedded in her own family and neighborhood relationships, was doing what made sense to her, but taken together, these actions represent an important example of how and why subordinates can resist superordinates' plans for them.

Our analysis is consistent with recent observations about the structure of Jewish and Italian networks (Coser, 1991). Italian families are seen as having an inward-focus with few ties to outside structures, at least in comparison with Jewish families. The Jewish family had more members with higher educational and occupational achievement; this opened connections to the world at large, especially to social agencies and health systems. Italians, in contrast, were able to carry forward their settled routines and cultural habits longer because challenges from alternative ideas and modes of action were slow to penetrate their personal networks. Additionally, peer networks—or connections *within* a generation—were important alliances for Jewish women in seeking out medical assistance. Italian women's networks were more likely to be rich in contacts *across* generations. Italian mothers and daughters, unlike Jewish mothers and daughters, were not separated by differences in their levels of education, work experience, or religious practice.

Home birth women were living "settled lives" (Swidler, 1988). They were practicing routines and habits so taken-for-granted that they appeared inevitable. This is not to say that women were not aware of other ways of managing childbirth, only that their resources best equipped them to make the choice they did. Home birth was not an isolated decision, but a highly contextualized episode in an ongoing way of life. Women made these decisions not as individual actors but as members of stable intergenerational networks.

Developments have come full circle. Today, contemporary American women are deeply dissatisfied with the impersonal and often alienating experience of hospital birth. Many have begun to rediscover home birth and to expand the professional role of the midwife in the United States (Danzi, 1995). In an interesting process of reevaluation, we can now reconsider Italian women's preference for home birth long after most women had abandoned it, not as a sign of their backwardness, but as an opportunity to maintain and reaffirm a safe and satisfying cultural routine.

References

Aday, L., R. Andersen, and G. Fleming. 1980. *Health Care in the United States: Equitable for Whom.* Beverly Hills, Calif.: Sage.

Baker, S. J., M. D. 1911. "School for Midwives," *American Journal of Obstetrics and Diseases of Women and Children* Vol. LXIII, Jan., No. 1: 256-270.

Banfield, E. C. 1958. *The Moral Basis of a Backward Society.* New York: The Free Press.

Becker, M. H. 1979. "Psychosocial Aspects of Health-Related Behavior," in S. Levine and L. Reeder, *Handbook of Medical Sociology.* Englewood Cliffs, N.J.: Prentice-Hall.

Blackwell, B. J. 1967. "Upper middle class expectations for entering the sick role for physical and psychiatric dysfunctions," *Journal of Health and Human Behavior* 8 (June): 83-95.

Blaxter, M. 1976. *The Meaning of Disability.* New York: Neale Watson.

Burgess, E. W. 1925. *The City.* Chicago: University of Chicago Press.

Campisi, P. 1948. "Ethnic Family Patterns: The Italian Family in the United States," *American Journal of Sociology* 53 (May): 443-449.

Child, I. L. 1970. *American or Italian: The Second Generation in Conflict.* New York: Russell and Russell.

Conrad, P. 1987. "The Experience of Illness: Recent and New Directions," *Research in the Sociology of Health Care* 6: 1-31.

Cordasco, F. and E. Bucchioni. 1974. *The Italians: Social Backgrounds of an American Group.* Clifton, N.J.: Augustus M. Kelley.

Coser, R. L. 1991. *In Defense of Modernity: Role Complexity and Individual Autonomy.* Stanford, Calif.: Stanford University Press.

Covello, L. 1967. *The Social Background of the Italo-American School Child.* Lieden, The Netherlands: E. J. Brill.

Danzi, A. D. 1997. *From Home to Hospital: Jewish and Italian American Women and Childbirth, 1920-1940.* Lanham, Md.: University Press of America.

———. 1995. "Taking Back Childbirth: A Preliminary Analysis of Birth Wisdom and Its Membership." Paper presented at the Eastern Sociological Society Meetings, Philadelphia, Penn., April 1-3.

Devitt, N. 1977. "The Transition from Home to Hospital Birth in the United States, 1930-1960," *Birth and the Family Journal* Vol. 4:2 (Summer).

Friedson, E. 1961. *Patients' Views of Medical Practice.* New York: Russell Sage Foundation.

———. 1988. *Profession of Medicine: A Study of the Sociology of Applied Knowledge.* Chicago: University of Chicago Press.

Foerster, R. F. 1969 (1919). *The Italian Emigration of Our Times.* New York: Arno Press.

Gans, Herbert. 1962. *The Urban Villagers.* New York: The Free Press.

Glazer, N. 1955. "Social Characteristics of American Jews, 1654-1954." *American Jewish Yearbook* 56, no. 1.

————. 1958. "The American Jew and the Attainment of Middle Class Rank: Some Trends and Explanations," in Marshall Sklare, ed., *The Jews.* New York: Free Press.

Gordon, M. M. 1964. *Assimilation in American Life.* New York: Oxford University Press.

Graham, S. 1957. "Socioeconomic Status, Illness and the Use of Medical Services," *Millbank Memorial Fund Quarterly* 25 (January): 58-66.

Hareven, T. K. and J. Modell. 1980. "Ethnic Families," in S. Thernstrom, ed., *Harvard Encyclopedia of American Ethnic Groups.* Cambridge: Harvard University Press.

Higham, J. 1972. *Strangers in the Land:* New York: Atheneum.

Janz, N. K. and M. Blecker. 1984. "The Health Belief Model," *Health Education Quarterly* 11: 1-14.

Kessner, T. 1977. *The Golden Door: Italian and Jewish Immigrant Mobility in New York City, 1880-1915.* New York.

Koos, E. L. 1954. *The Health of Regionville.* New York: Columbia University Press.

Levine, S. and L. Reeder. *Handbook of Medical Sociology.* Englewood Cliffs, N.J.: Prentice-Hall.

Morawska, E. 1985. *For Bread with Butter: Life-Worlds of East Central Europeans in Johnstown, Pennsylvania, 1890-1940.* New York: Cambridge University Press.

New York Academy of Medicine. 1924. *The Hospital Situation in Greater New York: Report of a Survey of Hospitals in New York City.* New York: G. P. Putnam & Sons.

————. 1933. *Maternal Mortality in New York City: A Study of All Puerperal Deaths, 1930-1932.* New York: Oxford University Press.

Orsi, R. A. 1989. "What did women think they were doing when they prayed to St. Jude?" *U.S. Catholic Historian* 8 (Winter-Spring): 67-79.

Park, R. E. 1950. *Race and Culture.* New York: Free Press.

Park, R. E. and E. W. Burgess. 1925. *The City.* Chicago: University of Chicago Press.

Parsons, T. 1951. *The Social System.* New York: The Free Press.

————. 1958. "Definitions of Health and Illness in Light of American Values and Social Structure," in E. G. Jaco, ed., *Patients, Physicians and Illness.* Glencoe, Ill.: The Free Press.

Pescosolido, B. A. 1992. "Beyond Rational Choice: The Social Dynamics of How People Seek Help," *American Journal of Sociology* 97, No. 4 (January): 1096-1138.

Rosenstock, I. M. 1966. "Why people use health services," *Millbank Memorial Fund Quarterly* 44: 94-127.

Swidler, A. 1986. "Culture in Action: Symbols and Strategies," *American Sociological Review* 51 (April): 273-286.

Twaddle, A. and R. M. Hessler. 1987. A *Sociology of Health.* New York: Macmillan.

Ware, C. F. 1935. *Greenwich Village: A Comment on American Civilization in the Post-War Years.* New York: Harper and Row.

Wertz, R. W. and C. Dorothy. 1990. *Lying-In: A History of Childbirth in America.* New York: The Free Press.

Williams, P. A. 1938. *South Italian Folkways in Europe and America.* New Haven: Yale University Press.

Whyte, W. F. 1943. *Street Corner Society.* Chicago: University of Chicago Press.

Zborowski, M. 1952. "Cultural Components in Response to Pain," *Journal of Social Issues* 8: 16-30.

Part IV

Italian Americans and Literature

Introduction

Italian Americans and Literature

Jerome Krase
Brooklyn College of The City University of New York

In this final section, "Italian Americans and Literature," we have assembled some of the most notable scholars in a field most broadly described today as "literary criticism." Although this discipline has been defined in many ways, as a social scientist my own preference is to see these studies of content and contextual analysis as a vital bridge between the humanities and sciences. It is the careful study of writings *by* Italian Americans and *about* Italian Americans as subject matter that has become one of the most fruitful and exciting areas of Italian American studies today. The attention to Italian American literature by an assortment of scholars in the humanities, for example, has assumed prominence as Italian Americans have become less interesting to social scientists whose instincts lead them to study the more recent and "exotic" immigrant groups.

We begin this section with Robert Viscusi's *"De Vulgari Eloquentia*: An Approach to the Language of Italian American Fiction." Viscusi tells us that Dante Alighieri's goal was to "enhance the speech of vernacular speakers" and that this monumental endeavor was not very different from that which faces many Italian American writers today. He cautions that if, like Dante, contemporary writers want to use the speech learned "without any rules [from] our nurse," then they will be required to also create a rhetoric in which it becomes a tool for "self-conscious literary art." In doing so, the language of the successful writer will transcend the particular, perhaps even peculiar, local or parochial usage without becoming merely a "grammar."

According to Viscusi, Italian American writers look for an English that comprehends and welcomes the language of their parents. When starting out on a project all writers face similar problems. However, because language varies so much the art of writing requires innovative solutions. The writers he discusses shared a common situation and dealt with it in similar ways. Looking at how they overcame their difficulties and measuring the degree of their success he finds a "common eloquence" in the Italian spoken in the United States. There may be a common language among American Italians with its own *vulgari eloquentia*. However, although English is to some degree "Latin," the English employed by Italians in America creates a challenge perhaps more complex than was Dante's. Viscusi suggests that if Italian American writers can discover methods for mediating between Italian and English then it will be possible to maintain both.

Fred Gardaphe's contribution is both an essay and an informed directive. "The Evolution of Italian American Literary Studies" outlines three aspects of Italian American literary studies: first, by recounting the neglect of Italian American culture by mainstream America's cultural institutions; second, by describing what happened when Italian Americans read, write, and act; and third, by offering a sense of future directions for the field.

Gardaphe claims that during "The Unused Past" a history of the Italian American intellectual was not written, but when it is, "It will present a gallery of rogue scholars whose voices are vulgar and vital and whose place in American culture has never been stabilized by political lobbies, cultural foundations, or endowed chairs." Next he informs us about "The Unknown Present" during which some critics of Italian American narrative have produced exciting and vital works by looking toward the future. These Italian American ethnic scholars represent the development of an indigenous criticism. Finally, there is "The Uncertain Future" when it is necessary to create a climate for scholarly cooperation in Italian American literary studies.

Gardaphe concludes his instructive essay with a number of practical suggestions such as increased Italian American "presence" in academic programs to encourage and direct graduate students. We are told that the key word for the future is collaboration, especially since governmental funding, never very supportive of Italian American projects, is being further diminished. On the bright side, Italian American intellectuals have many more outlets for their work today, but there is still a great need for these publications to interact with each other, cooperate, and provide mutual support.

In John Paul Russo's "From Italophilia to Italophobia: Representations of Italian Americans in the Early Gilded Age," from loving to fearing Italians is an apt description of the journey of what I might call the imagining of Italians in America. "Never before or since has American writing been so absorbed with the Italian as it is during the Gilded Age," wrote Richard Brodhead. The larger part of this fascination reflected a yearning for high culture and gentility. This "aesthetic-touristic" attitude towards Italy resulted in a flood of travelogues, guidebooks, antiquarian studies, translations, drama, poems, and historical novels, which reached their height at the turn of the twentieth century and declined after The Great War.

This essay, however, focuses upon the Italian immigrant as "alien-intruder." Travel writing's golden age corresponded exactly with the period of greatest Italian emigration to the United States. The causes of this change to a more negative attitude go back several generations before the arrival of the mass of Italian immigrants. Powerful economic forces which began in the 1830s had produced, by the mid-1880s, a general sense of impending crisis in America. The newest and most "foreign" immigrants of the 1880s were easily identified as the cause of the painful adjustments which wrenched American society.

Russo notes that, shortly after the American Civil War, Italian immigrants began appearing on the margins of American fiction. Their representation would change dramatically, and toward the negative, with each passing decade as the presence of Italians become more pronounced. In the works of William Dean Howells (*Suburban Sketches*) and Arlo Bates (*The Pagans*) set in Boston, Massachusetts, we are able to see how both familiarity with and fondness for Italians can be contrasted to less sympathetic treatments which in turn illustrate the ideological and social conflicts filling the void between italophilia and italophobia. Then in a surprising Epilogue, Russo considers two books that had an impact on 1950s "urban renewal" in Boston's Italian North and West End, the settings for Howells' and Bates' work during the Gilded Age.

Mary Jo Bona's essay, "*Mater Dolorosa* No More? Mothers and Writers in Italian American Literary Tradition," examines the position of

300 Jerome Krase

mothers of Italian ancestry, women who traditionally define themselves according to the needs of their families. One of the most persistent images of Italian cultural history and Western iconography was the figure of the *mater dolorosa*, the eternally suffering and beseeching mother. The writers discussed by Bona neither reduce Italian women to a stereotypical image of a suffering servant, nor exclude that particular image as a vital and complex aspect of their identity. Instead they explore the relationship between the role of Italian women and their definition within *la famiglia* and the figure of Mary. One of Mary's manifestations is the *mater dolorosa* which reveals an insistent social reality for women from Southern Italian culture. Later generations of Italian Americans continue to be fascinated by this image, incorporating, negotiating, and interrogating the figure of the pining mother in poetry and in prose.

According to Bona, the recurring image of the *mater dolorosa* might be a symbol of the Italian American writer's allegiance to an insistent social reality not only for the women in the family, but for the Italian-descended family at large. By recalling the image of the suffering mother (father, grandparents, children), Italian American writers simultaneously examine the fate of the Italian American family. Without a doubt they find a family which is as diverse and complex as any other contemporary American family. An important part of that social reality is the idea of the *mater dolorosa* which is grounded in a richly meaningful religious and cultural history. Writers who have dealt with the boundary between the *mater dolorosa* and the Italian family in America have produced creative works that reveal complex ideas about the relationship between nurturing and suffering. Bona concludes that, in doing so, these writers construct themselves and their relationship to Italian American identity.

The capstone of this section is Anthony Julian Tamburri's "In Recognition of the Italian American Writer: Definitions and Categories," which reminds us that in ethnic studies ethnicity is used as a primary yardstick and does not necessarily provide a satisfactory correction to the America's ethnic myopia. The history of the United States of America is written upon lines of diversity. Because factional diversity has often resulted in tragedy, it is necessary to understand the origins of the differences that characterize the many groups which constitute the American kaleidoscope. According to Tamburri, by accepting literature as a societal mirror we come to see that ethnic literature can address the negative stereotypes of group members who are not part of the dominant culture.

He defines ethnic literature as a kind of writing dealing "with customs and behavioral patterns that the North American mindset may consider different from what it perceives as mainstream." As ethnic writers may not follow accepted conventions, they might not be recognized for producing *good* literature.

One of the goals of ethnic literature is undermining negative stereotypes. Another is to impart knowledge of the customs, characteristics, language, etc. of the various groups in this country. It is also a process of analytical inquiry. Ethnic groups are compared with one another, and also with the dominant culture. Through this process we learn how differences between groups may not be as great as they initially seem. Interestingly, cultural differences not only can co-exist but even overlap with those of the dominant society. Finally, Tamburri puts part of the blame for the lack of validity in ethnic literatures to the critics and theorists who may have limited themselves to "the invention of another mode of reading."

Chapter 14

De Vulgari Eloquentia: An Approach to the Language of Italian American Fiction

Robert Viscusi
Brooklyn College of The City University of New York

Dante Alighieri, finding that no one before him had "treated systematically the doctrines of eloquence in the vernacular" and seeing "that such eloquence [was] needed by almost everyone," set out to "enhance the speech of vernacular speakers."[1] It was a difficult, even a bewildering, task. And it bears resemblance to the task that faces the Italian American writer. For his language, like Dante's, is a confusing array of dialects and "grammars" (in Dante's sense of a secondary, acquired language). If, like Dante, he wishes to employ the vernacular, the "speech . . . which we learn without any rules [from] our nurse,"[2] then he must do as Dante did: set out deliberately to devise a rhetoric that can employ the vernacular as the tool of a self-conscious literary art. If he succeeds, his language will rise above the idiosyncratic usage of his home town without becoming merely "grammar."

Every writer, of course, must to some degree face the same problem when setting out. Language is so various that the art of writing demands of each practitioner a fresh solution, a new rule for the making of choices. The writer, however, whose ancestral tongue differs altogether from the language of his book has difficulties which are especially acute. Each writer whose work we shall examine here has his own resolution of these difficulties and his own degree of success in the endeavor. But it is also true that all of the writers we shall discuss share a common situation, and it will come as no surprise that they have dealt with it in ways that have striking similarities.

If Dante was able to hunt down his panther by imagining wider and wider categories of speech, till he arrived at the "illustrious, cardinal, courtly, and curial vernacular of Latium . . . which belongs to all the Latian cities against which all the Latin municipal vernaculars are measured, weighed, and compared,"[3] we may ask whether the American Italian may not do some similar thing. If he attempts to locate a common eloquence in the Italian spoken all over the United States, he may meet some success. There are, at least, those who claim that an American Italian *koine* exists,[4] and this language may possess its own *vulgari eloquentia.* But when he seeks a vernacular eloquence that will employ the English spoken and written by Italians in America, he faces a great task, in some ways more complex even than the one which confronted Dante. For the American Italian seeks an English that will somehow comprehend and welcome the language of his fathers. English has enough of Latin in it to make such a rapprochement conceivable but scarcely enough to make it easy. Then there is the unpleasant fact that the language of his fathers is scarcely the "illustrious, cardinal, courtly, and curial vernacular" of Dante, nor is it any descendant thereof. It is, rather, much more likely to be the distant and fugitive heir of one of the many dialects that Dante merely waves away with a single gesture as irrelevant to the purposes of a vernacular eloquence. Can the dialect of the immigrant, damned and derided in Italy, join itself to the demotic American speech that the immigrant's children acquire, and can it, having done so, rise by easy stages—or by any stages—to the eloquence of the general vernacular of Hawthorne or James or Faulkner? Can the American Italian find a category of speech wide enough to accommodate such purposes?

Some possibilities of *rapprochement* between English and Italian come readily to hand but fail to serve the purpose. Of all such, the easiest is merely to record the immigrant's broken English. But this language, filled as it is with signs of his oppression and shame, has generally not attracted the Italian American writer. Indeed, its best-known writer has been a member of the dominant language group, T. A. Daly, who was able to find broken English colorful and pathetic without needing, as an Italian American would have needed, to portray in it any color or pathos of his own.[5] At the other end of the scale, it has often seemed attractive simply to Latinize English eloquence, making it yet more "illustrious, cardinal, courtly, and curial" than it was already. But this is a dangerous inflation in a Germanic dialect which for centuries has been devising eloquence with rich mixtures of Latin and French and Italian. It has tempted largely the young, the pedantic, and the incurably grandiose.[6] But they have not met success. Latinity has transfigured and elevated English writing. But Italian Americans have not needed to do so for their English what Tasso did for Milton's or Virgil did for Tennyson's. Indeed, to attempt this is in effect to kiss the toe of the King's English, laying down its tribute his own ancestral dialect, a severed tongue, an embarrassing token of late arrival and immemorial social marginality. He must find an English eloquence that does not follow an English model.

This eloquence must be able to change English in a way that will look Italian, that will in some way *be* Italian, no less indelibly than the writer's own name. It requires this property because of a purpose it shares with Dante's vernacular eloquence: it aims to suit the dignity of a nation that does not exist. Dante, indeed, hoped to bring Italy into being by giving it a tongue fitted for the deliberations of its princes and judges. Such was his "illustrious, cardinal, courtly, and curial" vernacular. The Italian American writer, too, speaks for a nation whose absence he feels. Italian America is even more remote from him than a unified Italy was from Dante, for it is a mythical place compounded of other myths—false memories of Italy and passionate dreams of America. Dante's Italian needed to be illustrious and cardinal and courtly and curial because it would thereby give sovereign attributes to a nation which might then be induced to claim its sovereignty. The American Italian's Italian American eloquence has aims that are slightly more diffuse. It does not wish to call a nation to sovereignty. Rather, it wishes to awaken Italian America to a sense of self, and then to console, to encourage, and to locate for this mythical nation a secure place that no one can confuse with its lost homeland or its fabulous landfall.

This language then must, like Dante's, possess appropriate qualities. It must be liturgical, to call up the power of lost Italy. It must be patriarchal, to emphasize a continuity that often seems to have been broken. It must be heroic, to reflect the nature of the immigrant enterprise. It must, finally, be diplomatic, to negotiate the terms on which Italian America can exist—exist, not as a mere political convenience, not as the object of some altruism, but as a culture, a state of mind, and a system of referents rich enough to generate works of art in a tongue that, howsoever American or Italian any of its parts may be, remains irreducibly Italian American.

Liturgical, patriarchal, heroic, diplomatic: these four terms, like Dante's "illustrious, cardinal, courtly, curial," are not so much attributes of *language* as they are of *parole*. They apply, that is, less to how the language is made and more to what it means to accomplish when someone uses it. My four terms, like Dante's, are interdependent and have all the same goal. But their order is of rising importance and difficulty. And the whole sequence is necessary. Only in its diplomatic abilities does this language begin to fulfill the possibilities of Italian American expression. For the sake of clarity, I begin with the simplest and work toward the most complex term; the explanations and exemplifications will be cumulative, so that when we see how this vernacular is diplomatic, we shall also see how it is liturgical and patriarchal and heroic.

Liturgical

By this I mean that the Italian American writer fills his English with Italian that serves the ritual purpose of invoking and celebrating the power of a mythical Italy. By *mythical* I mean that this Italy has exchanged physical for psychological presence. Though the actual place be absent, the mythical Italy is a universal presence that Italian American writers devote themselves to, sometimes unconsciously. They invoke it by using Italian as an almost magical tongue that has power to bless, to afflict, even to create a world.

In Lou D'Angelo's *What the Ancients Said,* for example, the narrator opens the novel with this sentence: "My brother Vinnie and I were brought up on Sicilian proverbs, most of them enigmatic."[7] Then he devotes a whole chapter to outlining how these proverbs created, within the confines of his immigrant family in East Harlem, a world filled with puzzles, fear, and doubt. Of these gnomic sayings, the most typical, he tells us, was the following: "*King Solomon, for all his sapience, died without assistance.*"[8] "I gave a good deal of thought to that one," he says, and we contemplate the puzzlement of a young American boy who must learn to negotiate his surroundings in terms of such antique distillations. We only begin, however, to estimate their full power when he tells us how his grandfather finally explained this to him:

The meaning is that King Solomon was a very wise man of whom many people, including, and especially, his sister, were jealous. And for all his majestic learning, he died without help, with a spoon stuck in his ass. The ancients said, *"Things there are, but we are not obliged to believe them."*

My grandfather had ended his explanation with the most quoted Sicilian proverb of all. What the ancients probably had in mind was authenticating Sicilian beliefs in witchcraft, ghosts, and evil omens, while noting their lack of ecclesiastical approbation. In our corner of the New World, this pronouncement served as an all-purpose comment on everything from small pleasures to major catastrophes. My grandmother, particularly, repeated it several times a day.[9]

In subsequent chapters, D'Angelo writes in a similar fashion about the use of names—both the given name and the cruel nickname, la ngiuria[10]—as well as the use of maledictions to create a state of terror, even of insanity; he associates this state with both his (or his narrator's) mother and with the presence of Italy in America. The mother tongue is the tongue of a lunatic mother in this novel, one that threatens to swallow into the darkness of her terrors even her own children.

D'Angelo rarely cites any of his proverbs or nicknames except in English. This seems part of a general policy in his works, a policy of keeping Italian at a distance, usually through irony, sometimes through outright burlesque.[11] The fear of the mother that runs through *What the Ancients Said* and his subsequent *A Circle of Friends* provides the plausible motive for this distancing. The distance is not comfortable, however; and the satyr's mask that D'Angelo likes to wear is not always appropriate as a mouthpiece for the difficult things he wishes to say.

Some writers employ Italian to invoke a more benign power. In DiDonato's *Christ in Concrete*, the characters speak an English that either suggests Italian word order or seems to translate Italian locutions literally. With the peculiar idiom that results, DiDonato portrays the emotional and spiritual stature of this novel's immigrant protagonists. When Luigi is lying in hospital after an amputation, he says to his sister, "Ah, the sheets are clean but God only knows how many Christians have decayed on this mattress, for the lice have grown big and bold in my hair and walk down my face. They do keep me awake, sister."[12] Italian presses through the surface of this English. "Christians" is a standard synecdoche for "human beings" in Italian, not in English. "They do keep

me awake, sister," is an artificial locution, meant to sound like a literal
rendering of Italian and not like American idiom at all. At moments of
great agony—and there arc many, for this novel is built around ritually
repeated crucifixions, life unfolding as innumerable sacrifices that follow
one another like priests to the altar of daily mass—this artificial manner
is likely to disappear, and the characters will call out, as Luigi does
during the amputation, in the sacred language: "Jesu-Giuseppe-
Marieee*eeeeeeee*. . . ."[13]

One might multiply examples freely here. It would, indeed, be
difficult to find an Italian American novel that completely refrains from
using Italian in this liturgical sense, though few do so as successfully as
Christ in Concrete. Tag lines in Italian, proverbs in Italian, catalogues of
names and litanies of love in Italian—these are the commonplaces of
Italian American fiction. It will, for the moment, be enough to say why
this liturgical use parallels Dante's sense of the illustrious quality of his
vernacular, which, he says, means that this eloquence is "exalted both in
instruction and power, and itself exalts its followers with honor and
glory."[14] I replace *illustrious* with liturgical because, in Italian America,
Italian may not bring "honor and glory" but seems always at least to
carry "instruction and power"—"power," because it calls up Italy,
always a strong presence, if sometimes an equivocal one; "instruction,"
because Italian is the medium, often enough, that brings the traditional
wisdom of the old country into the discourse of the new world.

Of course, there is more to be done than merely to invoke the old
gods and gospels. But to do so has proved tempting and even inevitable
for many Italian American writers. In truth, the liturgical use of Italian in
English is the most unmediated, and therefore the most powerful, way to
join the languages. Also, consequently, it is the easiest way, and the most
dangerous, the readiest to the hand of the sentimentalist, the demogogue,
the fraud. Literature must use liturgy, but it must add, it must examine, it
must dismantle, it must surround liturgy with other powers, and the
Italian American vernacular eloquence does this.

Patriarchal

By this I mean that the Italian American writer fills his English with
signs of the patriarchal structure of the Italian family. Whether, indeed,
the patriarchate or the matriarchate dominates in the Italian family is a
question I do not pretend to decide, as I am discussing households not of

the world but of the novel, where the patriarchal nomenclature of Italy has assumed in America what may, admittedly, be a disproportionate significance. *Names* are the only Italian words that find their way into some Italian American novels. They appear, if nowhere else, on the title page, where the Italian American's insistence upon keeping unaltered his inconvenient patronym establishes a clear line to Italy.[15] In many novels, too, the importance of patronyms shows itself from the outset, where a novelist is likely to define his world in terms of them. Here, as a particularly apt example, is the first sentence of Garibaldi La Polla's *The Grand Gennaro*:

> The singularly narrow house, three stories high, in which the destinies of the Accuci, the Dauri, and the Monterano families became hopelessly entangled, still throws its late afternoon shadow into the East River.[16]

Names, important as they are, only begin to suggest the place that the language of patriarchy fills in Italian American fiction. To find a way of identifying American son with Italian father is one of the main purposes that Italian serves in these works. Robert Canzoneri's *A Highly Ramified Tree* invites us to follow the narrator, who is an Italian American professor of English, and his father, who is a Sicilian immigrant turned Southern Baptist preacher, as they return to the father's home town of Palazzo Adriani. We follow the narrator, too, into his own childhood in the American South, where his father has married an American woman. But when they are in Sicily, we suddenly enter with the narrator a boyhood in Sicily that he has never had:

> "Roberto! Venecca!" It is my grandmother, calling from the other room. She sits all day in the chair, dark and short; her little arms can reach out and grab me no matter how far around her I try to pass, pull me to her to be examined, scolded, hugged. "Come kiss your nanna good morning. It is a beautiful day, a very special day. . . ." Her voice chokes. She begins to cry. "Oh," she is wailing. "Oh, San Giuseppe be praised. . . ."

> "Mamma, mamma," my mother says. "He does not understand."

> "So papa," my grandmother cries. "He will get to see his father at last. He will not remember him."[17]

Two elements are crucial here. First, the opening phrase, "Roberto! Venecca!" This is a ritual motif that recurs several times in the novel always to call forth the Italian hidden within the American man. Second, the grandmother's speech about the boy's father. For in this fantasy, Canzoneri has imagined a boyhood in Sicily during the thirties where his father has been imprisoned for three years by Mussolini; when the father returns to his village, he immediately plans to leave for America and writes to his prosperous relatives there (who include, by the way, Tony Canzoneri, then lightweight boxing champion of the world); they send a check to pay for passage to America, but at the last moment the narrator's father gives in to the pleadings of his wife and son and decides to remain in Italy. The fantasy fulfills in a complex way the narrator's desire to be one with his father. Complex, because it moves in two directions: while the narrator and his father are joined in Sicily, still they are separated by Mussolini's prison, and so the fantasy makes the break between them seem inevitable, almost a kind of original sin. We see its importance when the narrator shows the father's desire to escape to America as a temptation to break the male chain of generation, a temptation that in the fantasy the father rejects.

Desire to mend the broken link runs through the language of Canzoneri's novel from beginning to end. In Chapter 1, he arrives in Sicily, and the opening of the first paragraph recounts how his cousin greets him: "In black Sicilian suits and caps they sit in the sun like a flock of blackbirds far across the plaza. One is drawn stiffly from his chair as I approach. 'Roberto?'"[18] With one word, the cousin calls up an entire inner body of feelings, and the narrator says, "He is my cousin, old enough to be my father; the look of him, the smell and feel of him I know from my father, my dead and dying uncles, myself."[19] Thus, from the start, the narrator moves among a tribe of Sicilian men to which he does and does not belong. His need to resolve the contradictions of his own nature produces some striking results. Towards the end of the novel, travelling through Italy and seeing little of it because his mind is on a woman back in the States for whom he is about to leave his wife, feeling the American in him tearing away from both his father the Sicilian patriarch and his father the American preacher, the narrator writes a short story which becomes a chapter in his narrative: its hero is an American just like himself who tries to join himself to Italy by having the whole cycle of paintings from the vault of the Sistine chapel tattooed to his bald head and by then arranging to have himself murdered and to have his body hung in the catacombs. This hero's mute eloquence never finds expression. There are several reasons. For one, he cannot find an assassin willing to take part. But fundamentally, his plot is ephemeral because the narrator wants not to be one with Italy but to be united with his father. This means he must accept not only his own "crimes" against the old order but his father's transgressions as well: for it is the father who has left Italy and brought the family to America. In the final scene, the son with his new wife and his father and his American mother visits Vicksburg on a sightseeing pilgrimage. He concludes his narrative by reporting what his father says:

> When I get back to the driver's seat, my father turns to me; the senility seems fully taken into consideration, the flow of blood to the brain. Out of nothing, yesterday, he has said to me with this same clear look, I may be old but I'm still here. This time he says, "We going home now?"[20]

The father's imperfect English, American speech despite its Sicilian echoes, suggests how highly ramified the Canzoneri tree has become; and it points, at the same time, to a home that is neither fully America nor fully Italy but, whatever it is, is where father and son are joined.

I am using *patriarchal* where Dante uses *cardinal*, by which he means that his vernacular will be the *pivot* of a hinge, whose movement will affect all other vernaculars. I observe that the patriarchal impulse has a pivotal importance in the rhetoric of Italian American fiction. Many of the works where the tradition tries to define itself are structured, as is Canzoneri's more successful novel, around the continuity of the male line. Luigi Forgione's *The River Between,* a very early example, deals with the struggle for mutual acceptance between a father and son. Joseph Arleo's *The Grand Street Collector,*[21] though nominally "about" the murder of Carlo Tresca, follows the search of an American son for his Italian father. Rocco Fumento's *Tree of Dark Reflection*[22] has a narrator who struggles mightily with his immigrant father and can resolve his conflicts only after he learns in Italy the secrets of the old man's character. Even in *The Fortunate Pilgrim,*[23] the strength of the matriarch Lucia Santa develops only because her two husbands have failed her; further, it is her only male-bonded son, Larry Angeluzzi, who has the sterling masculinity that enables his to acquire a "godfather" and so can manage to bring the family out of bondage of the West Side and into the Canaan of Long Island. We might consider the importance of this theme

in the plot of *Christ in Concrete,* where Paul's need to replace his father
gives the book much of its shape—or in *The Godfather,* where Don Vito
Corleone and his sons show us a wide range of the forms that father-son
relationships can assume.[24] But the patriarchal themes of Italian
American fiction are presupposed by our subsequent categories; and it
will be appropriate, accordingly, to move on to these.

Heroic

Put this where Dante uses *courtly,* which he finds appropriate
because "if . . . Italians had a royal court, this vernacular would be
spoken in the palace."[25] The courtliness, in Dante's sense of the work, of
his eloquent vernacular is a sign both of Italy's greatness and of her
agony. One feels, reading *De Vulgari Eloquentia,* that it is almost the
very lack of a court—that is, of a unified and potent Italy—which
requires so elevated a tongue: the language must stand for all that is
missing. For similar reasons, Italian American novelists employ a
language that is *heroic:* their words give stature and dignity to those
whom there is no nation to ennoble. These novelists wish to create
alternative versions of a world only too frequently discussed in the
dialects of the immigration officer, the social worker, the landlord, and
the politician. Garibaldi La Polla, by profession an elementary school
principal, was thoroughly familiar with the language of the oppressor. In
this passage from the first chapter of his novel *The Grand Gennaro,* he
specifically aims to revise the vocabulary of the social science:

> The depression that really had its beginnings in 1890 but delayed the
> full force of its fury until 1893 had registered in Europe before it had
> become fully admitted into the United States. A stream of immigration
> began to pour into New York City. Especially from the southern
> portion of Italy great masses of people, for all the world like an ancient
> migration, braved the terrors of slow, weather-beaten streamer, and,
> once landed in New York, pooled into scattered communities
> throughout Manhattan.[26]

The simile *for all the world like an ancient migration* is a gesture in the
direction of historical dignity. Unfortunately, it amounts to little more
than a grace note in a paragraph otherwise composed largely in the
dialect of the settlement house and the newspaper. The novel as a whole
is a similarly incomplete attempt to show how these immigrants recreate,

surrounded though they are by American power and American bureaucrats, the intricate glories of an irrecoverable Italy.

A similar program—carried out this time, however, with professional thoroughness—underlies Mario Puzo's *The Godfather.* Here, liturgical and patriarchal elements combine in a sustained effort to reinvent the notion of *mafia,* to make it mean, not *criminal world,* but *refuge* and *heroic world.* Puso uses names with blunt allegorical intent. The first character to appear is the undertaker Amerigo Bonasera, the man who tried to be "American," who was denied justice by the New York courts and has now, consequently, bidding America goodnight, decided to go on his knees to Don Corleone. *Lionheart,* the great Don, lives up to his name. To his world of relatives and allies, he is nothing less—leader, man of respect, dispenser of justice, arranger of high matters, Lord Godfather Lionheart. Puzo keeps all this afloat not only by labelling everyone carefully but also keeping persistently present an Italian diction, which, literally translated into English and made part of discourse, becomes in effect a heroic language. Don Corleone, we are told, refers to Santino as his "first-born, masculine son."[27] The redundant epithet in English is in Italian, *figlio maschio,* idiomatic for *son.* The translated phrase becomes a key expression in the novel, which elevates maleness to a level of heroic mystery. This heroic maleness enters, as it were, literally, during the wedding scene in Chapter 1, with its description of Santino Corleone's massive sexual organ: after Sonny made love to the maid of honor, the singers Johnny Fontane and Nino Valenti sing what Puzo calls "an obscene Sicilian love song" with a "sly double-meaning tag line that finished each stanza."[28] This can only be *"La luna mezzu o mari,"* where the daughter learns that a baker husband will always be putting his loaf in her oven, a fisherman his fish, and so on.[29] All this phallic celebration received echoes in the ordinary language of characters, who call important people big *shots* or *pezzonovanti (pezzi di novanta,* ninety-caliber pieces).

Puzo best succeeds at making this maleness seem the force of a heroic enterprise in those parts of the novel where the Don plays a major role, and the most notably in his speech to the assembled Dons, which begins, "What manner of men are we then, if we do not have our reason?"[30] Puzo tells us that Don Corleone is speaking Sicilian here, and the English is stilted in a way that hints at literal translation (but is not, since *avere ragione* does not mean "to have reason") and moves with a marked stateliness. Later in the same speech, the Don offers this well-known defense of his world:

> "As for our deed, we are not responsible to the .90 calibers, the *pezzonovants* who take it upon themselves to divide what we shall do with our lives, who declare wars they wish us to fight in to protect what they own. Who is to say we should obey the laws they make for their own interest and to our hurt? And who are they then to meddle when we look after our own interests? *Sonna cosa nostra,"* Don Corleone said, "these are our own affairs. We will manage our world for ourselves because it is our world, *cosa nostra.* And we have to stick together to guard against outside meddlers. Otherwise they will put the ring in our nose as they have put the ring in the nose of all the millions of Neapolitans and other Italians in this country."[31]

This is bravura writing. Puzo takes the newspaper term *cosa nostra* and turns its meaning inside out. Rather than sinister, he implies, these men are admirable: not outlaws but heroes, crusaders, guerillas, proud and lion-hearted men. The idea is not new. To make heroic the excluded—the outlawed no less than the humble and the dispossessed—is a standard operation in folklore and can sustain varieties of revolutionary art. Little wonder, then, that it should find a place in Italian American fiction.

Puzo's very rhetorical success has troubled many readers who, considering the complexity of American Italian reality, find the heroic mode misleadingly simple and, in Puzo's skillful work, dangerously seductive. It is useful in this connection to consider a more modest work, Joseph Arleo's *The Grand Street Collector,*[32] which concerns itself very directly with the temptations of heroic language in Italian America. The novel's title refers to one Don Natale Sbagliato, a numbers collector in New York whom Fascist agents flatter into becoming the murderer of Guido Sempione (a thinly disguised Carlo Tresca). These are the words Don Natale finds filling his reverie just before he engages himself to commit the crime:

> *"The American right hand of Mussolini."* A sudden surge of joy flooded through him. "That of all those in this country he knows so well, I, *I* am the one he reaches for. That the brotherhood of suffering is undeniable. That the Eternal Father makes me worthy."[33]

Arleo leaves us no doubt that this is the rhetoric of delusion. Don Natale is thoroughly *Sbagliato* (Puzo has no monopoly of allegorical nomenclature) in his reading both of Mussolini and of his own role, and he comes to an elaborately terrible ending. A little too elaborate, it may be, and a little too terrible, but the ending is worth arriving at; and Arleo's book may be still finding readers when Puzo's will only have historians.

In Arleo's narrative, it is the loss of heroic illusions that acquires a tragic heroism. A more straightforward heroism than that, and a less doubtful one than Don Corleone's, belongs to the humble bricklayers who are the protagonists of DiDonato's *Christ in Concrete.* Here, the presence of Italian words and ways adds an entirely noble dimension to the narrative. But I shall reserve discussion of this until we have added the last of our tetrad of epithets to the analysis.

Diplomatic

Dante calls his vernacular *curial* "because curiality is nothing other than a balanced rule for things which must be done" and "we have come to call all of our actions which are well-balanced, curial"—and, as he says, his language has "been balanced in the very highest Italian court."[34] The notion of a language sifted by many judicious users with similar purposes in mind is a useful one to us here. I am employing a term which suggests something of balance as well, but *diplomatic* particularly suits the language of Italian American fiction because it points to mutual presence there of an Italian which is, as we have seen, liturgical and patriarchal and heroic, alongside and English which is—what? I shall propose here that in the gestures of the Italian component and in the language of Italian American fiction, we find a play of reciprocal Italian and American gestures; that this interplay formalizes each of the two components out of the need each has to reply to the other, so that the character of this language is diplomatic.

The reciprocity of diplomatic discourse is no mere matter of binary alternation but more closely resembles the gestural interchange of a dance, where distinct roles for the partners remain visible while every action of each somehow reflects or predicts the movement of the other. To call a literary language diplomatic, then, is perhaps to add an unwelcome complication to the act of reading: for the reader must not only follow the ordinary intricacies of language and structure, but he must also attend a drama that is purely linguistic, the encounter of two languages in the prose of the narrative. Unwelcome as this complication may be, the material forces it upon us. As a strategy of reading, the discovery of diplomatic play in language offers necessary light in the scrutiny of Italian American fiction and may well provide similar illumination elsewhere in multi-ethnic literature. I shall use as a specimen passage here a few paragraphs from the opening chapter of *Christ in Concrete;* the narrator here describes bricklayers at work:

> The Lean pushed his barrow on, his face cruelly furrowed with time and struggle. Sirupy sweat seeped from beneath his cap down his bony nose and turned icy at its end. He muttered to himself. "Saints up, down, sideways and inside out! How many more stones must I carry before I'm overstuffed with the light of day! I don't understand . . . blood of the Virgin, I don't understand!"
>
> Mike "the Barrel-mouth" pretended he was talking to himself and yelled out in his best English . . . he was always speaking English while the rest carried on in their native Italian. "I don't know myself, but somebodys whose gotta a bigga buncha keeds and he alla times talka from somebodys elsa!"
>
> Geremio knew it was meant for him and he laughed. "On the tomb of Saint Pimple-legs, this little boy my wife is giving me next week shall be the last! Eight hungry little Christians to feed is enough for any man."[35]

We might begin here without the aid of any of the analytic language we have been using. Reading simply as linguists, we can discriminate three clearly marked registers. First, there is careful idiomatic English, sometimes marked by a degree of artiness, that the narrator employs: "Sirupy sweat seeped from beneath his cap, down his bony nose and turned icy at its end." Second, there is the English equivalent of the Italian the characters are actually speaking, and DiDonato persistently emphasized this doubleness by using locutions which appear literally to translate Italian expression: "Blood of the Virgin is scarcely something Americans say, while *sangue della Vergine"* has a plausible ring. The third register is the broken English of "Mike 'the Barrel-mouth,'" which DiDonato places here on the second page of his novel, to indicate that the other characters are speaking not a pidgin or creole but rather an Italian that DiDonato is portraying in English. So much is clear.

But, having established these categories, we find that we must immediately begin to dismantle them. The narrator's English in particular evades easy classification because, though it generally has a highly self-conscious texture and shows a keen sensitivity to American idiom, it uses as well the Englished-Italian of the characters when the need arises. The narrator, for example, habitually and plausibly calls his characters by the agnomina that *contadini* devised for one another: Nick is "the Lean" and Mike is "the Barrel-mouth." But DiDonato can strategically refrain from using the sobriquet. Geremio, the Christ in the concrete, remains *Geremio* in the narrator's discourse, as indeed he does in the dialogue itself, where he even rises at times to the dignity of *Master Geremio*. Here, we might pause and see how this language is *diplomatic* in the sense we are using. Both the Italian and the English in the narrator's prose are transformed by one another's presence. The nicknames of the characters, sure signs in Italian that these men are peasants, acquire in English a thematic emphasis, so that these *braccianti* become masks for spiritual states (and subtler in their names are precisely *not* diplomatic). Thus, a familiar rustic habit of speech in Italian assumes in literal translation a fresh eloquence which, in turn, exerts a pressure upon the idiomatic English of the narrator, moving it upward in tone, so that it treats even minor details with poetic precision, in a language that has enough compression and visual attentiveness to suggest Dante as exemplar: again, "Sirupy sweat seeped from beneath his cap, down his bony nose and turned icy at its end."

Nor is the narrator's English the only language here that evades easy categories. When "the Lean" says, "Saints up, down, sideways, and inside out," the noun and the first two adverbs echo an Italian sequence, but *sideways, and inside out* is American music. The joining of the two pairs of adverbs gives the whole expression the resonance of an epic formula or comprehensive spell, a dignity of estate that neither of the conjoined elements, each drawn as it is from the demotic idiom of its native tongue, could ever alone possess. Some of the other "translated" locutions seem to be the very least *mis*translated: *sangue della Madonna* is a more likely exclamation that *sangue della Vergine;* "On the tomb of Saint Pimple-legs," though it begins recognizably, ends in such a way that we can only suppose that the Italian original is very local indeed or else that DiDonato has invented it for the occasion. The latter supposition seems to me the correct one. For DiDonato writes this novel in a language that he pieces together as he goes, an inspired *bricolage* that draws constantly upon the dance in his mind of the peasant eloquence of his childhood and the bookish discourse acquired in the youth he spent, as he boasts, as "probably the only apprentice-bricklayer in the United States who [came] to the job site with the *Divine Comedy,* the *Golden Bough* and Lampriere's classical dictionary under his arm."[21] We can, I think, without troubling to annotate its every gesture, see the elaborate dance of the Italian and English in such a passage as the following where Geremio's wife grieves for him after his death:

> O Jesu in Heaven, and husband near, whither . . . and how? Pieced from the living we are now both. Bread—bread of Job and Job of Bread had crushed your feet from the ground and taken your eyes from the sun, but nowhere are we separate—never-never in this breathing life shall I be away from you. Day and night will I kiss your wounds, with my flesh shall I keep the rain from you, these tears shall comfort you in heat, and with the cold shall I breathe upon you my warmth . . . husband great.[36]

Here is the language of neither Italy nor America. This tongue—liturgical, patriarchal, heroic, diplomatic—belongs to a people whose expression arises in two countries, employing the mythical dignity of a mythical Italy as a consolation for, as an incantation over, a real America.

Jerre Mangione writes that his mother enforced a rule that her children speak only Italian at home.

> Outside the house she expected us to speak English, and often took pride in the fact that we spoke English so well that none of our relatives could understand it. . . .

> We gradually acquired the notion that we were Italian at home and American (whatever that was) elsewhere. Instinctively, we sensed the necessity of adapting ourselves to two different worlds. We began to notice that there were several marked differences between those worlds, differences that made Americans and my relatives each think of the other as foreigners.[37]

The double consciousness, entirely identified with language, that Mangione describes here characterizes the situation of the Italian American novelist. If he writes, as he generally does, without DiDonato's poetic inventiveness, still he must confront the confusions of his situation. He must play the diplomat. He must translate, explain, mediate. Mangione often takes on the role of interpreter, carefully explaining the difficulties that arise from an Italian Americanism like baccauso.[24] D'Angelo offers catalogues of proverbs and nicknames as a necessary initiation for a reader who would understand the insides of an Italian American household. For, finally, it is the diplomatic imperative that conditions every aspect of the language of Italian American fiction. To mediate between two languages is to maintain the existence of both.

The accommodation, it may be, is a fragile one; it may be that coming generations will see the Italian American recede into a dim ancestry. Or it may be that the diplomatic counterplay will merely employ new terms to make the most of new relationships. The situation of the Italian American is changing. No longer an immigrant or the son of an immigrant, he fares forth now as a pilgrim. His grandfather has become a brown photograph of an old man where one can see *ravioli, vino, taralli*. The photograph curls in the dresser drawer, but the grandson is flying to Rome for the summer. Waiting for him somewhere south or east of there, his innumerable cousins have prepared him a vast ritual meal. He will sit among them, rosy with embarrassment of the anthropologist, not quite master of the dialect. Still, there will be blood between them and him, and one will touch his arm and claim him. One such touch will open a passage for him. At the other end of it, he will find the long, steep panorama of his grandfather's lost patrimony. Vittorini, Verga, Manzoni, Petrarca, Boccaccio, Dante will fill his ears. In that new music, he will hear a new complexity. Like many another returning American—like Irving in Westminster, or Eliot in Russell Square, or Henry James in Rye—he will find echoes in the ancient sounds that the natives never hear. He will discover then, it may be, as Eliot and James before him, another music of paradox, policy, and hesitation. For he will have passed between two worlds and, belonging to both, belong then to a third, a world whose initiates are those whose ears have been opened and can hear in every word, like the shadow of a doubt, the echoes it will have in a foreign place. Such writers as he will be must always recognize themselves as *diplomats*, in the oldest sense, for they are doubled, folded double, turning at every corner to hear the ghosts of voices from the place in which they no longer find themselves.

Notes

1. Nonetheless, it remains an option. Nicholas Delbano, who has allowed himself more freedom than most in this direction, manages generally to deflate his Latinity with irony, as in the following: "Mind unstrung with inventiveness, hands fashioning animals, an erector set in four dimensions, two-way windows that seemed to be one-way, one-way mirrors that seemed to be two, Alessandro moved through parlors of the farm, frame-house, upon a pogo-stick that rolled. Perpetually litigating over patents, preparing manifestoes, ordering millenia, his shirt-tail tied in Windsor knots to prod remembrance, tie soup-stained, he mechanized a rocking-chair and practiced archery." *Consider Sappho Burning* (New York: William Morrow, 1969), p. 80.

2. Lou D'Angelo, *What the Ancients Said* (Garden City: Doubleday, 1971), p. 9.

3. *What the Ancients Said*, p. 9.

4. *What the Ancients Said*, p. 11.

5. *What the Ancients Said*, pp. 16-24.

6. See his *A Circle of Friends* (Garden City: Doubleday, 1977) and his *How to Be an Italian* (Los Angeles: Price/Stern/Sloan, 1978); the latter of these, particularly, accomplishes its distancing of Italian by conceding to the inventors of stereotypes about Italians and Italian Americans so much as to make for painful reading.

7. Pietro Di Donato, *Christ in Concrete* (New York: Bobbs-Merrill, 1939), p. 142.

8. *Christ in Concrete*, p. 123.

9. *De Vulgari Eloquentia*, p. 29.

10. Lawrence Ferlinghetti, for example, changed his name back to the paternal form from Ferling, which his brothers used. See Neeli Cherkovski, *Ferlinghetti: A Biography* (Garden City: Doubleday, 1979), pp. 23, 82.

11. Garibaldi M. LaPolla, *The Grand Gennaro* (New York: Vanguard Press, 1935), p. 3.

12. Robert Canzoneri, *A Highly Ramified Tree* (New York: Viking Press, 1976), p. 41

13. *A Highly Ramified Tree*, p. 3.

14. *A Highly Ramified Tree*, p. 3.

15. *A Highly Ramified Tree*, p. 189.

16. Louis Forgione, *The River Between* (New York: E.P. Dutton, 1928).

17. Joseph Arleo, *The Grand Street Collector* (New York: Walker, 1970).

18. Rocco Fumento, *Tree of Dark Reflection* (New York: Knopf, 1962).

19. Mario Puzo, *The Fortunate Pilgrim* (New York: Athenuem, 1965).

20. Mario Puzo, *The Godfather* (New York: G. P. Putnam's Sons, 1969).

21. *De Vulgari Eloquentia*, p. 30.

22. *The Grand Gennaro*, pp. 3-4.

23. *The Godfather*, p. 31.

24. *The Godfather*, p. 32.

25. A good, idiomatic performance is "La luna mezzu o mari," transcribed by Franco Li Causi, performed by Antonio Vasquex, Maria Lupo, Franco Li Causi, A. Principato, and G. Vaccara, on Folklore Siciliano, Centra LPP 7.

26. *The Godfather*, p. 290.

27. *The Godfather*, p. 291.

28. Arleo's novel and Puzo's were compared even when they were published, notably by Barton Midwood, "Fiction," *Esquire*, Feb. 1971, p. 51: "Advertising copy for *The Grand Street Collector* compares it to *The Godfather*, but the two books have very little in common, except that they are both about Italian immigrants in New York in the Thirties. Moreover, the intentions of the two books are diametrically opposed. *The Godfather* is essentially exhibitionist and makes its appeal to ignorance and fear, while *The Grand Street Collector* is essentially introspective and makes its appeal to reason." In truth, the issues raised here are complex enough to merit separate attention. A good discussion of the difficulties with *The Godfather* is Giovanni Sinicropi, "The Saga of the Corleones: Puzo, Coppola and *The Godfather*," *Italian Americana*, 2 (1975), 79-90. The best defense of the novel is that of Rose Basile Green in her comprehensive and indispensable study, *The Italian American Novel: A Document of the Interaction of Two Cultures* (Rutherford, N.J.: Fairleigh Dickinson University Press, 1980), pp. 352-368.

29. *The Grand Street Collector*, pp. 29-30.

30. *De Vulgari Eloquentia*, p. 30.

31. *Christ in Concrete*, p. 12. On Di Donato's language, see also Giovanni Sinicropi, "Christ in Concrete," *Italian Americana*, 3 (1977), 175-183.

32. Pietro Di Donato, "Mister Nicky, The Floatin' Bricky," in *Naked, As an Author* (New York: Pinnacle Books, 1971), p. 109.

33. *Christ in Concrete*, p. 49.

34. Jerre Mangione, *Mount Allegro* (Boston: Houghton Mifflin, 1942), p. 52.

35. *Mount Allegro*, pp. 54-55.

Chapter 15

The Evolution of Italian American Literary Studies

Fred L. Gardaphe
State University of New York at Stony Brook

This paper orients three aspects of Italian American literary studies by first recounting the neglect of Italian American culture by mainstream America's cultural institutions, then by describing what happened when Italian Americans read, write and act, and finally by offering a sense of future directions for the field.

The Unused Past

A history of the Italian American intellectual is yet to be written, but when it is, one of the stories it will tell is the tension between what Antonio Gramsci has identified as the organic and the traditional intellectual. It will present a gallery of rogue scholars whose voices are vulgar and vital and whose place in American culture has never been stabilized by political lobbies, cultural foundations, or endowed chairs. It will tell the tale of the pre-Christian paganism of Italian culture that has resurfaced in popular culture through the antics of Madonna and the controversial cultural analyses of Camille Paglia. While both of these American women of Italian descent seem to be innovators in interpretation, they are in fact, popularizers of ideas that have long remained submerged in the shadows of Italian American culture. One need only look to Diane Di Prima's *Memoirs of a Beatnik* or the cultural criticism of Luigi Fraina and Robert Viscusi to find their modern antecedents. The major problem facing Italian American intellectuals is not a lack of preparation for or sophistication in their critical methods, but a lack of self-confidence that the culture they come from can be used to express themselves to the American mainstream audience. The lack of this self-confidence is one result of the immigrant experience.

What was referred to as "The Southern Problem" in Italy, a problem that even today is raised by Italians of northern Italy through the *Lega Lombarda*, became the "Italian Problem" in America. Antonio Gramsci analyzed this problem with his article entitled "The Southern Question." Written in 1927, this essay identified the activity of the southern intellectual as the tie between the southern peasant and the big property owners. In effect, the activity of such representative southern intellectuals as Benedetto Croce and Giustino Fortunato kept the southern bloc from becoming a revolutionary element. Without help from the intellectual many southerners decided that the uncertain future through emigration was a better option than the future they envisioned by staying. And so for many of those southerners, the answer to the southern question was to leave Italy. This fate is doomed to be repeated today; without a strong show of leadership by Italian American intellectuals, Italian Americans will opt to assimilate into mainstream American culture at the expense of losing contact with both the past and the present of Italian culture.

The vast majority of American writers of Italian descent can trace their ancestors back to those who left Italy during the late and early nineteenth century. The earliest voices of Italian Americans heard publicly were those of political and labor activists such as poet/organizer Arturo Giovannitti, Frances Winwar, journalist/organizer Carol Tresca and Luigi Fraina. In the early 1900s Luigi Fraina, who later changed his name to Lewis Corey, was one of the earliest to publish Marxist literary criticism in America. In David Madden's *Proletarian Writers of the Thirties* (1968) attention is given to Louis Fraina, also known as Lewis Corey. But Fraina, while producing some of the earliest Marxist cultural criticism in this country, concentrated his efforts on social, economic and political analysis and did not write fiction. During this period he was a union activist and a prolific Marxist critic and journalist. Early on Fraina investigated the clash between paganism and the Christian culture that attempted to annihilate it. While Fraina paid no attention to the cultural products produced by his fellow Italian Americans, his work represents the preoccupation of Italian American intellectuals with the obstacles they encountered in adapting to life in America. In one of his few directly anti-fascist articles, "Human Values in Literature and Revolution," Corey speaks out against fascism and argues that the only good literature is that which concerns "itself primarily with consciousness and values, with attitudes toward life" (8). Of the literature of his time that does this, Fraina notes three types: "The literature of capitalist disintegration," "The literature of fundamental human values and defense of those values," and "The literature of conscious revolutionary aspiration and struggle." Fraina saw fascism as "the final proof" that "in any period of fundamental social change, particularly as the old order decays, there is an increasing degradation of human values" (8).

Without scholarly societies or formal programs inside institutions dedicated to the study of Italian American Culture, American intellectuals of Italian descent who were intent on defining and developing Italian American culture had to do so independently, and more often than not their work was considered adjunct to their "real" work. While there were many Italian American newspapers in which appeared creative and critical work by Italian American writers it would not be until the children of Italian immigrants came of age in the 1930s that an articulate voice of *Italian Americana* would be heard in the mainstream media.

One of the earliest acts of indigenous Italian American criticism was Jerre Mangione's 1935 *New Republic* review of Garibaldi Lapolla's *The Grand Gennaro*. Mangione introduces the rarity of meeting Italian Americans in American literature and credits Lapolla for "creating Italo-Americans who are vivid and alive and probably a novelty to the average person who, not knowing them intimately, is likely to draw his conclusions about them from the gangster movies" (313). A few years later, Mangione reviewed Pietro Di Donato's *Christ in Concrete* in the *New Republic*, and while he praised the beginning writer's rendition of the Italian American life, he did not succumb to what I call Paesan Patting or blind boosterism; he did not hesitate to point out the novel's roughness and its "minor deficiencies" (111). During this early stage of his writing career Mangione took on the task of interpreting Italian culture and life under Mussolini. He reviewed translations of Pirandello's books: *Better Think Twice About It* and *The Outcast*, in the August 28, 1935 issue of the *New Republic*. During the same year, Mangione reviewed Mr. Aristotle, a translation of Ignazio Silone's collection of short stories. He wrote articles and short sketches for national publications such as *The Nation* and *The New Masses* and went on to be a spokesman for Italian and Italian American culture through his many books. His critical analysis of the dual identity in urban ethnic writing, his many reviews of books by Italian American writers and most recently his survey of literary history in *La Storia* have all served to both establish a serious presence of Italian American literature and criticism in American culture.

Giuseppe Prezzolini, a member of the executive council which directed the Institute of Italian Culture in the United States, founded in 1923, and director of the Casa Italiana of Columbia University in 1930, while denounced as a proponent of Fascism, often published commentaries on Italian American writers and encouraged Olga Peragallo to produce a survey of Italian American literary activities. Olga Peragallo's *Italian American Authors and Their Contribution to American Literature* was edited by her mother and published posthumously in 1949. Prezzolini wrote the preface to this first attempt to historicize American authors of Italian descent. This primal text paved the way for the next major step in the development of Italian American literary history by an indigenous intellectual.

A subsequent attempt to organize Italian American literature was Rose Basile Green's 1962 dissertation at the University of Pennsylvania: "The Evolution of Italian American Fiction as a Document of the Interaction of Two Cultures." Published in 1974 as *The Italian American Novel: A Document of the Interaction of Two Cultures*, Green's study was the first major attempt to identify and critically examine the contribution that American writers of Italian descent have made to American culture. Her work, typical of the ethnic revival period in which it was written, reflects an early stage of cultural examination, one that invites readers and critics to consider the fiction of Italian American writers through an essentially universal sociological paradigm related to understanding the process of Americanization through the experience of immigration. Green's scholarship enabled the formation of new dimensions of critical examination of the Italian American contribution to American literature.

The Unknown Present

While early intellectuals such as Green were well acquainted with what had happened in Italian American culture, few knew what was coming in the future. A number of contemporary critics of Italian American narrative have produced exciting and vital alternatives to Green's methodology by turning their gaze into the direction of the future. Such critics as Helen Barolini, Robert Viscusi, Frank Lentricchia, Mary Jo Bona, Anthony Tamburri, Louise Napolitano, Justin Vitiello, Franco Mulas, and Paolo Valesio (who has tapped into new ground in his work on the American writers of Italian descent who write in Italian) represent the major contemporary voices of Italian American narrative criticism. These critics represent the development of an indigenous criticism and are those whom Robert Viscusi refers to as interpreters "of the minority culture to which [they belong] by birth" ("A Literature Considering Itself," 278).

Helen Barolini, an essayist, novelist and translator, knew the importance that creating and reading literature plays in self-development. "Literature," she says, "gives us ourselves" ("Introduction," 51). Without experiencing models created by Italian American women, Barolini says, we cannot expect Italian American women to pursue literary careers. She believes that the Italian American women can contribute to a revitalization of American literature which might begin with writing about the self in the manner of keeping journals and writing memoirs and autobiographies. Achieving identity as an Italian American woman would not be achieved without difficulty. Barolini's search for self through her own writing, and the creation of her American identity through the creation of literature, enabled her to go in search of her sister authors. The results of that search are found in *The Dream Book: An Anthology of Writings by Italian American Women*. In the houses of Italian America were women writers, who, until Barolini gave them *The Dream Book*, often felt they wrote in a void, isolated from the Anglo/Saxon literary tradition as well as the beginnings of a male-dominated Italian American tradition. Faced with the restrictive barriers erected by family and tradition, the Italian American woman who would be a writer could only become one by directly challenging the forces that tied her down. Part of that challenge would require fighting the image that the larger society had created for her to emulate. She proved not only that and Italian American woman could write, but also that any consideration of Italian American culture would be incomplete if the literary works produced by women were ignored.

Early on, in what has proven to be an illustrious career as a literary critic and scholar, Frank Lentricchia began toying with the idea of Italian American literature. Until he took on the introduction to and interpretation of the fiction of Don DeLillo, Lentricchia had done little work on Italian American writers. While his earliest work does evidence signs of acknowledgment of his Italianita, it is during the mid-1970s, while he was working on his second book, a study of Robert Frost, that Lentricchia makes two brief appearances in the first two issues of *Italian Americana*. The first was a short review of John J. Soldo's *Delano* in *America and Other Early Poems*; the second was an intriguing essay which attempts to set the record straight on the origins of Italian American fiction. In the contributor notes he is said to be working on compiling an anthology of Italian American fiction, a work that if it had been produced would have been the first of its kind. What is most interesting in these two articles is his definition of Italian American writing as: "a report and meditation on first-generation experience, usually from the perspective of a second-generation representative; in such writing Italian American experiences and values are delineated as they appear in dramatic interaction with the mainstream culture. In other words, a book of poems or stories authored by a person of Italian background is not ethnic in character unless the writer engages his ethnic heritage. I make these preliminary remarks because it is believed in certain academic and publishing circles that ethnicity in imaginative literature is a value, when in fact ethnicity is only a descriptive concept that helps us to classify, not judge, literature." (124) This definition limits the impact, and thus the relevance of Italian American ethnicity, to the first two generations by keeping third generation members like Lentricchia outside the experience. No doubt this early definition is one that Lentricchia would probably have revised had he continued working on "ethnic" literature. However, Lentricchia's subsequent work, while not on Italian American subjects, is certainly done quite self-consciously as an Italian American. In fact, Lentricchia has only recently published his first autobiographical writings. In an interview with Imre Salusinszky, Lentricchia states: "I think it's easy to become sentimental about what I'm talking about [his Italian American background], and that's one of the reasons why I don't talk about it very much. I feel impelled to write an autobiographical essay once in a while about this stuff, and I've always held back, because I fear this goddam sentimentality about it" (*Criticism in Society*, 182-3). In "My Kinsman, T.S. Eliot," Lentricchia has finally let go and written an essay that is part fiction, part criticism and very autobiographical. This essay has since become part of a book-length memoir entitled *The Edge of Night*, published by Random House in 1994. In his most recent publications and appearances Lentricchia has employed his Italian Americaness in new and exciting ways.

One key stage in the *risorgimento* of Italian American studies occurred in 1967 through the founding of the American Italian Historical Association, which while not dedicated to literary studies (its founding members were primarily historians and sociologists) did welcome and encourage literary analysis and dedicated its second conference to the Italian American novel. It is through that association that some of Italian Americana's best literary criticism has come to be known. Robert Viscusi, whose work on Italian American literature has paved the way for subsequent critics, has contributed tremendously to the construction of a foundation upon which an Italian American discourse can be built. In many of his articles he offers a culture-specific approach that educates the reader about Italian culture and the context it creates for interpreting Italian American narrative. Viscusi was the first critic bold enough to challenge the nostalgia that permeated Italian American studies through his creation of complex essays that were the result of rigorous thought and an incredible sense of humor. Even when his brow is the highest, his tongue is hilariously pushed against his cheek. As a critic, he opened the door to a higher level of expectation for Italian American readers and writers; however, his greatest contribution to the field is his culturally critical novel *Astoria*. It is with Viscusi that we begin to see the beginning of a real revolution in Italian American literary studies, for his writing stopped speaking for Italian American writers and started speaking to them.

The critical work by Anthony Tamburri and Mary Jo Bona is characterized by their attempts to situate the ethnic difference evident in Italian American writing and relate it to its multicultural contexts. Their work treats Italian American literature as a colonized body of writing that gains its identity through its interaction between Italian and American culture. Tamburri has employed post-structuralist and semiotic approaches in creating cultural specific readings of Italian American literature and culture. His "manifesto," "To Hyphenate or Not to

Hyphenate," has played a key role in bringing Italian American literature into the field of multicultural studies. As one of the co-developers of the anthology, *From the Margin: Writings in Italian Americana*, and co-founder/editor of the bi-annual literary and cultural review *Voices in Italian Americana*, he has helped move Italian American literary criticism from the margins, where it has existed for too many years, and into the mainstream. Mary Jo Bona has contributed to the understanding of the literature produced by Italian American women. Besides a dissertation, "Claiming a Tradition: Italian American Women Writers," she has written a number of seminal articles. Her most recent contribution is *The Voices We Carry* (Guernica, 1993), an anthology of contemporary fiction by Italian American women writers. She is currently working on a critical study of Italian American women writers.

Justin Vitiello's *Oral History and Storytelling: Poetics and Literature of Sicilian Emigration*, a reading of Sicily through the people of the village of Trapetto, connects the contemporary to the classic, the scientific to the mythic and preserves what makes Sicily continue to be a major crossroads of world cultures. Throughout this study Vitiello weaves a narrative that renders the entire experience in the best tradition of travel writing. Sing fiction and poetry, he captures insights that seldom find their way into traditional scholarship. Thomas J. Ferraro's analysis of Mario Puzo's *The Godfather* in his important *Ethnic Passages: Literary Immigrants in Twentieth Century America* (University of Chicago Press, 1993), Frank Lentricchia's work on Don DeLillo, Louise Napolitano's *Christ in Concrete: An American Story* (1995) and Matthew Diomede's forthcoming study are both long overdue book-length studies of Pietro Di Donato's work. The sound scholarship of Edvige Giunta, whose work on such Italian American artists as Agnes Rossi, filmmaker Nancy Savoca and others is a further indication that the indigenous critic has arrived on the critical scene with valuable insights into the literature produced by Americans of Italian descent. In light of the exciting work being done today, more and more of the previously submerged American scholars, critics and writers of Italian descent are surfacing on the pages of *Differentia, Italian Americana, VIA*, and the few other ethnic specific publications dedicated to Italian Americana. The latest issue of *Differentia* is perhaps the most significant of the recent developments. By devoting an entire volume to the subject of Italian American culture, the journal, long a leading resource for disseminating Italian thought in America, sends a strong signal to Italian scholars and critics that there is much to be gained in giving serious consideration to the contributions of American writers of Italian descent. Now that we've established a solid tradition of criticism, it is time to move beyond our literary neighborhoods and into the larger world of American literature.

In the publishing arena, more and more writers are being accepted by mainstream presses such as Antonio D'Alfonso's Guernica Editions of Canada and the USA. Guernica is spearheading an attempt to enable the various branches of the Italian diaspora to speak to each other: *From Australia to Argentina, From Italy to Italian/North America*, this publishing effort has provided vital forums for Italian American literature.

The Uncertain Future

One thing about the work that I have just surveyed is that most of what has been developed thus far in the field of Italian American literary studies has been accomplished by individuals. And while the efforts have been valiant, there is little hope that this field will thrive unless individual intellectuals come together to identify tasks, share existing resources and co-develop new resources. The future of Italian American literary studies needs a new sense of cooperation among scholars of Italian and American cultures. Collaboration is the key word for the future, especially as public funding, which has never been generous to Italian American projects, is being threatened.

Interdisciplinary conferences, which foster a greater understanding of the intracultural situation, are but one of the tools we need to develop a greater sense of the importance of Italian American studies. Through these conferences we need to develop beyond identity politics and begin to use the ideas of aesthetics, religion and class to situate the contributions of Italian American writers so that what is said about them matters not only to Italian Americans but all Americans. We need to concentrate on the creation of such institutions as archival centers where the papers of our writers, our intellectuals, can be of use to a new generation of scholars. Right now, most of those papers are in basements gathering dust and mildew when they should be garnering attention. From these archives we need to create critical editions of works that have too long been out of print. We need to take advantage of new developments in technology to create electronic databases, to create multimedia programs which introduce and document the careers of our writers. And in order for all this to be developed and put to use, we need presence in academic programs which can provide encouragement and direction for graduate students. In terms of publications, the current situation is that we have a number of interesting islands, which is better than earlier when intellectuals were floating in the mainstream or in ponds; but the future needs to see a greater sense of interaction between and among publications. We need a good, ongoing bibliography project which would identify, locate, and annotate relevant primary and secondary publications. We need book-length studies on all of our major writers—the two new studies of Pietro Di Donato represent the greatest critical depth we've achieved, but we are standing deep in the shallow end; we need studies of all of our writers; we need to reprint deserving books that are out of print. While we have activists and politicians, too few have turned attention to their own culture. While we have a few journals, none is quarterly; we also lack a publishing center, and while a press would be nice, a more feasible alternative would be to create a publishing/editorial network that could be used as a clearinghouse to recommend books to publishers, and if possible, with a subvention. Yes, this all takes money, but before we can achieve the necessary financial support we need to connect the streets to the academe by uniting the efforts of such organizations as the National Italian American Foundation, the Sons of Italy and UNICO to the needs of the intellectual community. We, the intellectuals, must create products that they need, and they need to be able to see that we are creating products that can further their agenda. In conjunction with a greater development of intracultural studies, we need to establish a strong Italian American presence in the field of intercultural studies. This requires a greater awareness of the history and evolution of the cultural studies of other groups which make up America.

In this direction we need to develop new and attend existing conferences in which the cultural products of Italian American artists are compared to other Americans; we need to explore the possibilities of co-publications, co-criticism, and start publishing our articles in mainstream journals. We need to build intercultural coalitions. In order to achieve this goal, there are a number of obstacles that need to be confronted and surmounted; the mighty Modern Language Association has twice rejected a discussion group on Italian American literature, not to mention the rejection of frequent attempts by qualified scholars to introduce special sessions on Italian American literature to the annual conference; the National Endowment for the Humanities has rejected two successive grant proposals which were co-written by scholars and leaders—we need to create summer symposia through the NEH. Like our immigrant grandparents who were kept on economic leashes, we are on cultural leashes; we must stop looking outside and start working inside. We need to overcome our own pride, an often greedy sense of turf, and create national and international networks through which these objectives might more easily be achieved. These are ways in which Italian American culture can not only be preserved, but continue to evolve. We cannot rely solely on our past to create a sense of our future. This reliance tends to foster ideas such as the "twilight" of ethnicity, treating Italian Americaness as though it were a fixed entity with an expiration date. The future of Italian American literary studies depends on the commitment of all elements of Italian American culture. From the streets to the academies, there needs to be a united effort to support, promote, criticize and historicize the work that's being done.

Note

1. One moving account of how going to college affected an Italian American woman is Tina DeRosa's "An Italian American Woman Speaks Out," *Attenzione*, May 1980: 38-9.

References

Aaron, Daniel. "The Hyphenate American Writer." *Rivista di studi anglo-americani*, 4-5 (1984-85): 11-28.

Barolini, Helen. "Introduction." *The Dream Book*, ed. Helen Barolini. New York: Schocken, 1985, 3-56.

———. "Preface." *The Dream Book*. New York: Schocken Books, 1985.

Bona, Mary Jo. "Claiming a Tradition: Italian American Women Writers." Diss. University of Wisconsin, 1989.

———, ed. *The Voices We Carry*. Montreal: Guernica Editions, 1994.

Diomede, Matthew. *Pietro Di Donato, The Masterbuilder*. Cranbury, NJ: Associate University Presses, 1995.

Ferraro, Thomas J. *Ethnic Passages: Literary Immigrants in Twentieth Century American Literature*. Chicago: University of Chicago Press, 1993.

Fraina, Louis. "Socialism and the Catholic Church." *Daily People*, 12, 128 (November 5, 1911): 5.

Gambino, Richard. *Blood of My Blood*. New York: Anchor, 1975.

Goody, Jack and Ian Watt. "The Consequences of Literacy." *Comparative Studies in Society and History 5* (1963): 304-45.

Gramsci, Antonio. "The Southern Question." *The Modern Prince and Other Writings*. New York: International Publishers, 1957.

Green, Rose Basile. *The Italian American Novel*. Cranbury, NJ: Associated University Press, 1974

Kolb, Harold. "Defining the Canon." *Redefining American Literature History*. Ed. A. LaVonne Brown Ruoff and Jerry Ward. New York: MLA, 1991.

Lentricchia, Frank. "The American Writer as Bad Citizen." *Introducing Don DeLillo*. Ed. Frank Lentricchia. Durham: Duke University Press, 1991, 1-6.

———. *The Edge of Night*. New York: Random House, 1994.

———. "Introduction." *New Essays on White Noise*. Ed. Frank Lentricchia. New York: Cambridge University Press, 1991, 1-14.

———. "Libra as Postmodern Critique." *Introducing Don DeLillo*. Ed. Frank Lentricchia. Durham: Duke University Press, 1991, 193-215.

———. "Luigi Ventura and the Origins of Italian American Fiction." *Italian Americana*, 1, 2 (1974), 189-95.

———. "My Kinsman, T.S. Eliot." *Raritan*, 11, 4 (Spring 1992): 1-22.

———. Rev. of *Delano in American & Other Early Poems*. *Italian Americana*, 1, 1 (1974), 124-5.

———. "Tales of the Electronic Tribe. *New Essays on White Noise*. Ed. Frank Lentricchia. New York: Cambridge University Press, 1991, 87-113.

Madden, David. *Proletarian Writers of the Thirties*. Carbondale, IL: Southern Illinois University Press, 1968.

Mangione, Jerre. "Acrobat to Il Duce." Rev. of *Better Think Twice About It* and *The Outcast* by Luigi Pirandello. *New Republic*, 84, 1082 (August 28, 1935): 82-3.

———. *America is Also Italian*. New York: G.P. Putnam's Sons, 1969.

———. "Comments." *Contemporary Novelists*. 4th ed. Ed. D. L. Kirkpatrick. NewYork: St. Martin's Press, 1986, 570-2.

———. "A Double Life: The Fate of the Urban Ethnic." *Literature and the Urban Experience*. Ed. Michael C. Jaye and Ann Chalmers Watts. New Brunswick, NJ: Rutgers University Press, 1981, 169-83.

———. *The Dream and the Deal: The Federal Writers' Project 1935-1943*. Philadelphia: University of Pennsylvania Press, 1983.

———. *An Ethnic at Large: A Memoir of America in the Thirties and Forties*. Philadelphia: University of Pennsylvania Press, 1983.

———. (Pseud. Mario Michele). "Fontamara Revisited." *New Republic*, 91, 1173 (May 26, 1937): 69-71.

———. "Happy Days in Fascist Italy." Rev. *Fontamara* by Ignazio Silone. *New Masses*, 13, 1 (October 2, 1934): 37-8.

————. "Little Italy." Rev. *Christ in Concrete, The New Republic*, 100, 1291 (August 30, 1939): 111-12.

————. (Pseud. Jay Gerlando). "Pirandello Didn't Know Him." Rev. *Mr. Aristotle* by Ignazio Silone. *New Masses*, 17, 7 (November 12, 1935): 23-24.

————. Rev. *The Grand Gennaro*. *The New Republic*, 84, 1090 (October 23, 1935): 313.

————. and Ben Morreale. *La Storia*. New York: HarperCollins, 1992.

Mulas, Francesco. *Studies on Italian American Literature*. Staten Island, NY: Center for Migration Studies, 1995.

Napolitano, Louise. *Christ in Concrete: An American Story*. New York: Peter Lang, 1995.

Peragallo, Olga. *Italian American Authors and Their Contribution to American Literature*. New York: S.F. Vanni, 1949.

Ruoff, A. LaVonne Brown and Jerry W. Ward, eds. *Redefining American Literary History*. New York: MLA, 1990.

Tamburri, Anthony Julian. "In (Re)cognition of the Italian American Writer: Definitions and Categories." *Differentia*, 6-7 (Spring/Autumn 1994): 9-32.

————. *To Hyphenate or Not to Hyphenate*. Montreal: Guernica Editions, 1991.

Tamburri, Anthony Julian, Paolo A. Giordano and Fred L. Gardaphe, eds. *From the Margin: Writings in Italian Americana*. West Lafayette, IN: Purdue University Press, 1991.

Tamburri, Anthony Julian and Ron Scapp, eds. *Differentia*. Special Double Issue on Italian American Culture. 6-7 (Spring/Autumn 1994).

Viscusi, Robert. "Breaking the Silence: Strategic Imperatives for Italian American Culture." *VIA*, 1, 1 (1990): 1-14.

————. "A Literature Considering Itself: The Allegory of Italian America." *From the Margin: Writings in Italian Americana*. Ed. Anthony J. Tamburri, Paolo Giordano and Fred L. Gardaphe. West Lafayette, IN: Purdue University Press, 1991, 265-81.

Vitiello, Justin. *Poetics and Literature of the Sicilian Diaspora: Studies in Oral History and Story-Telling*. Lewiston, NY: The Edwin Mellen Press, 1993.

Chapter 16

From Italophilia to Italophobia: Representations of Italian Americans in the Early Gilded Age

John Paul Russo
University of Miami, Florida

"Never before or since has American writing been so absorbed with the Italian as it is during the Gilded Age," writes Richard Brodhead.[1] The larger part of this fascination expressed the desire for high culture and gentility, or what Brodhead calls the "aesthetic-touristic" attitude towards Italy. It resulted in a flood of travelogues, guidebooks, antiquarian studies, translations, drama, poems, and historical novels, peaking at the turn of the century and declining after World War I. The golden age of travel writing lasted from 1880 to 1914, and for many Americans the richest treasure of all was Italy.

This essay, however, focuses upon Brodhead's other category, the Italian immigrant as "alien-intruder." Travel writing's golden age corresponded exactly with the period of greatest Italian emigration to the United States. The causes of this negative attitude go back several generations before the arrival of the mass of Italian immigrants: "economic transformations that had been underway at least since the 1830s had produced, by the mid-1880s, a sense of widespread crisis in America . . . the new, more 'foreign' immigrant of the 1880s could easily be read as the cause of the painful changes of the present."[2] Shortly after the Civil War, Italian immigrants begin to appear on the margins of

American fiction. Their representation would change dramatically with each passing decade.[3]

Among American writers William Dean Howells was especially well suited to portray the fortunes of the Italian immigrant. He possessed broad social sympathies, a midwesterner's interest in the burgeoning cities on the Eastern seaboard, and a realist orientation in fiction. For having written a campaign biography on Lincoln, he was rewarded with a consulship in Venice (1861-64).[4] Subsequently he published *Venetian Life* (1866) and *Italian Journeys* (1867) which won the praise of James Russell Lowell and Charles Eliot Norton (the Venetian letters make "the most careful and picturesque *study* I have ever seen on any part of Italy," wrote Lowell, "they are the thing itself").[5] A strong admirer of the Risorgimento, Howells offered a written panegyric when he could not attend an event in honor of Italian unification in New York: "the liberation of Italy is a fact that all real Americans will celebrate with you . . . since the citizen of every free country loves Italy next to his own land, and feels her prosperous fortune to be to the advantage of civilization."[6] In 1870 Howells delivered the Lowell Lectures in Boston on "Modern Italian Poets" (published in 1887); he taught at Harvard on the same subject, and periodically reviewed Italian literature. His Italian was so good (better than that of most Cambridge italophiles) that one of his fictional immigrants, "as if too zealous for the honor of his beautiful language to endure a hurt to it," politely corrects the narrator's Italian: "Morde, non morsica, signore!"[7] While living in Venice he became engrossed in Goldoni's realist drama with its middle- and lower-class characters; Goldoni, he wrote, is "almost English, almost American, indeed, in his observance of the proprieties."[8] James L. Woodress only slightly exaggerates when he claims that Goldoni, "more than any other writer, turned him from Romantic poet into prose Realist."[9] Four of Howells's ten travel books concern Italy and five of his three dozen novels have an Italian setting; many characters in his other novels have visited it, discuss it, and extol it. Italian immigrants appear in his first book of fiction, *Suburban Sketches* (1871), and in five of his novels.[10] His knowledge of Italy and Italian gave him an ideal vantage from which to survey the immigrants and their confrontation with Americans and other ethnic groups.

Set a few miles from Boston in the fictional suburb of "Charlesbridge" (that is, Cambridge, where Howells lived from 1866 to 1877), *Suburban Sketches* consists of ten chapters on the urban sprawl and social dislocation following the Civil War. Charlesbridge is a place of mixing, between city and country, upper and lower classes, Yankee and immigrant, one ethnic type and another. The chapter "Flitting" is about moving a house, and the title captures the gist of so many of the sketches: that the "fundamental reality of modern American life was its impermanency."[11] Another sketch, "Doorstep Acquaintance," conveys the sense of transience, informality, and "pseudo-intimacies."[12] The building of the suburbs, their ethnic quarters, slums and street life, public transportation such as horse cars to Boston, their festivals, these provide the background and in some cases the main matter for the book. The narrator's study of horse-car passengers anticipates Basil March's unsettling meditations on the elevated train to the Lower East Side in *A Hazard of New Fortunes*.

Portraying immigrant groups for the American public of the *Nation* and the *Atlantic*, Howells gives the Italians space out of proportion to their numbers in the late 1860s. This reflects his own familiarity with and fondness for Italians, and his willingness to defend and excuse them. Besides, it was only a step from writing about Italians in their own country to writing about them in the United States.[13] James Russell Lowell, a fellow Cambridge italophile, reacted so favorably to one of the sketches that he wrote Howells, "I am not quite sure whether Cambridge is in Italy—though now I think of it, I know Italy is sometimes in Cambridge."[14]

The narrator of *Suburban Sketches* has "had the fortune to serve his country" in Venice (91) and has just returned to America. He is setting up house in a new section of a suburb, so that he shares the novelty with his fellow suburbanites—a convenient leveling device. His Italian enables him to speaks to immigrants with relative ease; dialects never present a problem.[15] In short, the narrator is closely modeled on Howells himself. At the same time, as with Washington Irving and his fictional "Geoffrey Crayon," Howells distances himself from his narrator and his materials, ethnic or otherwise, and this distance permits a (gently) satiric treatment of traits and foibles.

The sketch of Ferry Street in "Doorstep Acquaintance" is among the first portraits of an Italian neighborhood in American fiction.[16] "Ferry" means a passage over water, with the added implication of regularity: Italians have crossed over, yet one of Howells's recurrent themes is the Italian desire to return to Italy. Because they had left the home country mainly for economic reasons, not on account of religious or political persecution, repatriation was common among Italians and it distinguished them from all other immigrant groups. (As many as half of the Italians at the height of immigration repatriated.[17]) Ferry Street is situated in Boston's North End, by the wharves, "since the 1840s the first place of settlement for the poorest immigrants"; in the late 1860s a single street, with perhaps a few side streets, suffices to contain a future Little Italy.[18] The winter setting emphasizes the displacement of the Italians "born to a happier clime" (37) and balances any tendency to romance by a framing image with a realist bite.

"It was winter even there" (36). Even the collective and colorful Italian presence in Ferry Street cannot dispel the snows and chill of New England—but for the "figured" moment:

> It was winter even there in Ferry Street in which so many Italians live that one might think to find it under a softer sky and in a gentler air, and which I had always figured in a wide unlikeness to all other streets in Boston,—with houses stuccoed outside, and with gratings at their ground-floor windows; with mouldering archways between the buildings, and at the corners feeble lamps glimmering before pictures of the Madonna; with weather-beaten shutters flapping overhead, and many balconies from which hung the linen swathings of young infants, and love-making maidens furtively lured the velvet-jacketed, leisurely youth below: a place haunted by windy voices of blessing and cursing, with the perpetual clack of wooden-heeled shoes upon the stones, and what perfume from the blossom of vines and almond-trees, mingling with less delicate smells, the travelled reader pleases to imagine. I do not say that I found Ferry Street actually different from this vision in most respects; but as for the vines and almond-trees, they were not in bloom at the moment of my encounter with the little tambourine-boy. As we stood and talked, the snow fell as heavily and thickly around us as elsewhere in Boston. (37)

While the Italians make Ferry Street look like an ordinary street in an Italian town, the narrator has a "vision," in Howells's terms, an imaginative re-presentation of the concrete, in this case overturning Yankee Boston in the very site of its origins by the wharves. Ferry Street differs from "all other streets" in the city because it is "haunted" by Italy. The people have their own sacred imagery in this quintessential Puritan town (with its distaste for religious icons): the Madonna (queen of heaven as opposed to the Calvinistic Father-God). There are noise-making (instead of bourgeois quiet) and cursing (potential violence);

clutter (and by implication dirtiness); perfume (sensuousness) and "less delicate" odors (smells of urine, strong cooking, as of primitive encampments); "leisurely" conduct (laziness instead of the work ethic); and Romeo and Juliet figures (almost figurines) as symbols of art and breakaway sexuality. Though the negatives lurk just beneath the surface and give a disturbing tension to the "vision," the general impression is that Italians succeed in making themselves at home in an otherwise hostile environment. As it began with a winter image, the passage ends abruptly with a second winter image to enclose the "vision" within a realist frame: the implied contrast is between life and death. Grammatically, one sentence—a relative clause and its dependents—contains the street scene and gives it a sense of richness and plenitude; whereas two, much shorter sentences convey the narrator's swift mental return to the winter's day.

No immigrant emerges from *Surburban Sketches* as a fully formed, complex character and many are picturesque stereotypes in the Anglo-American cultural tradition.[19] Nonetheless, some are conceived with sufficient imaginative force to establish a point of human contact; many are given dialogue, which is facilitated by the Italian-speaking narrator, thereby upholding a canon of realist fiction.[1] The Italian immigrants are typically associated with peddling, vagabondage, street entertainments, child-like joy, and uncomplicated pleasures. Though Americans in Italy complained unceasingly of the *lazzaroni* and nasty beggars, Howells does not object to panhandling. As for idleness, the "children of the summer" (35) protest that the lack of English prevents their "practicing some mechanical trade"—"'What work could be harder,' they ask, 'than carrying this organ about all day?'" (35)—but he feels that they protest too much and really love their open-air life. Open air, but not countrified; Howells knows that Italians are a town-oriented people, even if their town had been a small southern village. The narrator calls them "friends," partly ironically; they are not even "acquaintances" because he does not expect to see them again. They are a displaced instance of the picturesque, a "vision" constantly undercut by their being out of place, and this opposition between romance and realism is intensified by the Italians and the narrator's capacity to find themselves at home and take pleasure wherever they are.

One "friend" is a coal-heaver in winter and an organ-grinding "troubadour" in summer: the opposition of paleotechnic drudge and carefree singer of love songs corresponds to the seasons with their alternation of death and life which had characterized the "vision" of Ferry Street. The friend's "lazy," "soft-eyed" boy, who collects coins with his tambourine, informs the narrator that the family has enough money to return to Italy. His mother is an "invalid" and "must be taken home" (37), as if to die. In fact most of the immigrants are "sick" for home. With one exception they say nothing of economic necessities that have driven them across the sea; they do not complain, nor does Howells question them on the matter. The exception is a journalist from Trieste, then under Austrian rule. He voices mild, unspecified criticism but he wants to return as much as the others.

Another "friend" is a chestnut-roaster from Tuscany who sells twice as many chestnuts for the same money as could be bought from an English-speaking merchant. In other words, Italians lack business sense, at least in America where the language is a problem. Many Italians failed to learn English because they lived in the hope of speedy repatriation. Yet they paid dearly for their failure as they could not find more remunerative jobs that would hasten their return. The disincentive for learning English had another untoward consequence: "the tendency of Southern Italian immigrants to return to Italy and their cultural and physical isolation from Boston's Yankee culture made them particularly unsuitable American citizens."[21] Howells depicts the immigrants as clinging tenaciously to their native language. The chestnut-roaster addresses the narrator in Tuscan, as if unaware that "Tuscan is not the dialect of Charlesbridge" (38). The Italians' tacit assumption that "there is no other tongue in the world but Italian . . . makes all the earth and air Italian for the time" (39)—another instance of the at-home-in-the-world theme which recurs frequently in Howells's treatment of Italians. The narrator enjoys speaking in Italian because it "flatters with an illusion" of being in Italy; if he stood and stared in astonishment, even a moment, at the chestnut-roaster's speaking to him in Italian, the pleasing illusion would vanish and their exchange would shrink to "vulgar reality" (39). The "swarthy fruiterer" in *The Rise of Silas Lapham* is "not surprised when he is addressed in his native tongue" by a Boston Brahmin italophile.[22]

With his wares before him on the ground, an "image-dealer" from Lucca reclines before a meeting house and answers questions, at his own speed, as he drops morsels of food into his mouth. He barely notices the busy life that goes on around him. Although the narrator is amused, his Yankee neighbors would probably have disdained the Italian's lack of ambition and industry. In quiet sympathy with him, however, the narrator becomes a dealer of illusion as he imagines the peddler "doing his best" to transform the meeting house into the "cathedral" of Lucca, the piazza of which "probably has a fountain and statuary" and is "not like our square, with a pump and horse-trough in the midst" (40). Again, romance balances realism. And to compensate for the lack of romance, the Cambridge square has a "towering" elm tree: if Italy has art, America has nature. The Italian peddles plaster statuettes of Apollo, classical deities, and "Canovan dancers": paganism and Dionysian life. As the narrator thinks, the Puritans beneath their "moss-grown headstones" in the cemetery would start if they saw such pagan and erotic images in their midst.

Among the other immigrants is an old Lombard scissors-grinder, "very red in his sympathies" (42), who had worked in Naples and Athens before coming to America. He too wants to return to Italy *"per goder un po' di clima prima di morire"* (41). He marvels at the new Boston Public Library from which he, a poor man, may borrow books. The narrator is embarrassed that the immigrant knows more than he himself about American history, mainly from having read Carlo Giuseppe Botta's famous *History of the War of the Independence of the United States of America* (1809).[23] The "cynical" journalist from Trieste is finally not so cynical when he sings a Venetian barcarole at the thought of going home. A "little old Genoese lady" has the most delicate manners and the face of a child expressing "kindliness" and "sympathy." She sells pins and needles, thread, tape, "and the like *roba*" (45) but does not even count the money paid her. Wondering how she manages to eke out a living from her small basket, the narrator recalls Italian simplicity and economy from his days abroad. The lady will not end the conversation before she presents two or three small gifts from her seemingly boundless basket, which takes on a magical quality. "The truth is, we Northern and New World folk cannot help but cast a little romance about whatever comes to us from Italy, whether we have actually known the beauty and charm of that land or not" (45).

Despite having been cheated of his wages and left destitute in *South America*, the "swarthiest" of Neapolitan organ-grinders possesses "that lightness of temper which seems proper to most northern Italians, whereas those from the south are usually dark-mooded, sad-faced men" (though they have "fine eyes," they are "not so handsome as the Italians of the north") (50). "South" may connote trouble in Howells's text:

South America, the U.S. South, southern Italy. As John F. Stack observes, "Brahmins distinguished between Northern and Southern Italians from the very beginning of the Southern Italian invasion of Boston in the 1880's." For the Brahmins, only Northern Italians were "part of Western civilization"; their "Germanic blood and artistic achievements sharply distinguished them from the ignorant peasants of Southern Italy."[24] *Suburban Sketches* shows this distinction already in place a decade earlier. The narrator's stereotyping of the Neapolitans as sad and sullen contradicts their reputation for cheerfulness and amiability. "Nothing surpasses for unstudied misanthropy of expression the visages of different Neapolitan harpers who have visited us; but they have some right to their dejected countenances as being of a yet half-civilized stock, and as real artists and men of genius" (50). Again, the narrator indulges in romantic primitivism, though he mocks gently in calling them "artists" and "men of genius," who are conventionally saturnine. Yet Howells is not deceived by appearances: however rough in look, the Neapolitans are "not so surly at heart as they look" (50). In the late 1860s and early 1870s, when perhaps a thousand Italians lived in Boston, there was not yet the preponderance of southern Italians, so they do not dominate Howells's panoramic sweep. The immigrants of *Suburban Sketches* are drawn rather evenly from the entire length of the peninsula.

As if to subvert the defensive pose implied by "doorstep acquaintance," the narrator remarks that he invited his first Italian acquaintance into his home. Glad "but not . . . surprised" (38) to be greeted in Italian, she is the widow of a "Vesuvian lunatic," Giovanni Cascamatto (crazy helmut), who kept setting fire to their houses until he perished in a blaze, another pejorative allusion to the fiery southern temperament. Yet the widow epitomizes "tranquil courtesy." Since her "object in coming to America was to get money to go back to Italy," she is raising a subscription to which the narrator makes a pledge. But when he invites her to dinner, she answers with an "insurpassably flattering" compliment that "she had just dined—in another palace." Quite likely she had not—she is being courteous—and just as likely the word *palazzo* was spoken. Saying it, she touches his house "with the exquisite politeness of her race." Her delicate action has a talismanic quality because the real house, a "little box of pine and paper," suddenly becomes in the narrator's mind "a lordly mansion, standing on the Chiaja, or the Via Nuovissima, or the Canalazzo" (38). By word and gesture she expresses the longing for a home, humbler than his imagining, but in the same city, her husband having burned down her own; such an act is more terrifying because of the sense of the sacral with which Italians invest the domus.[25] In his fiction Howells attaches enormous significance to the house as a symbol both of the individual and social status, Silas Lapham's new Back Bay house (which also burns down) being a prominent example. The narrator concludes, "we had made a little Italy together" (38), not meaning a "Little Italy" in the sense of an urban neighborhood—too early for that—but the enchantment of being in Italy. With its diminutive, affectionate wording and with the inner rhyme of "little" and "Italy," the phrase suggests the pleasing, the precious, the gracious, at once concrete and yet seen by the light of imagination.

Is this a false communion? a cozy sentimentalism? It could be that the woman's plight has given the bourgeois narrator a sense of aristocratic exclusivity with a palace on the Bay of Naples. Perhaps, too, the woman is faking it a bit; Italians are masters of playing up to foreign travellers in their land and participating in the fantasy in an ingratiating way—not one of their more attractive qualities. Questioning Howells's "self-satisfied exercises in multiculturalism," Brodhead comments that "speaking their language verbally may only conceal how little Howells 'speaks their language' in any other sense."[26] Still, the passage strikes the note of sincerity; the narrator has assisted the lady financially, not merely emotionally.

Charlesbridge, then, is a place of mixing. Yet where distinctions are threatened or lost, as René Girard has shown, scapegoating is sure to follow. In Boston of the 1860s and 1870s this role had been filled by the Irish, far more numerous than the Italians.[27] On Irish and Italian street life Howells's narrator cautions that the comparison "does not hold good in any way or at any time, except upon the surface." He reasons that "there is beneath all this resemblance the difference that must exist between a race immemorially civilized and one which has lately emerged from barbarism 'after six centuries of oppression'" (66). Southern Italians, who had just been described as only "half-civilized" (50) are now included in the general race which is "immemorially civilized." Despite the contradiction, Howells probably means that southern Italians are civilized in comparison to the Irish or other ethnic groups, an instance of his favoring the Italians.[28] In her study of race and class in Howells, Elsa Nettels comments that "the Italians are not stigmatized by the solecisms and the eye dialect that disfigure the speech of Irish and black figures."[29] Venting his prejudices, the narrator employs the Italian as a stick to beat the Irish by the carefully built-up theme of *cortesia*. "You are likely to find a polite pagan under the mask of the modern Italian; you feel pretty sure that any of his race would with a little washing and skillful manipulation, *restore*, like a neglected painting, into something genuinely graceful and pleasing; but if one of these Yankee-fied Celts were scraped, it is but too possible that you might find a kern, a Whiteboy, or a Pikeman" (66-67). The painting simile may imply the "neglected" Italian as unclean, but, at the same time, it is an aesthetic image.

The narrator's prejudice towards the Irish was hardly unusual after the Civil War among both Brahmins and the Yankee middle class of bureaucrats, shopkeepers, tradesmen. Oscar Handlin and Stack comment on the increasingly bitter edge given to anti-Irish prejudice. Though identified by common ancestry and religion with the Brahmins, unlike them the Yankees had never tolerated the Irish immigrants who were competitors in the labor market and whose Roman Catholicism was anathema. More idealistic and far more insulated economically and socially from the immigrants, the Brahmins had "deplored the excesses of anti-Catholic and anti-Irish hysteria during the 1840s and 1850s." "The Irish assault on Boston did not provoke xenophobia and nativism until after 1860," writes Stack, "the egalitarianism of the Adamses and of Hancock and Emerson persisted in spite of the unpleasant burdens that Irish immigration presented to the Brahmins."[30] But when the Irish population of Boston jumped from 3,936 in 1840 to over 50,000 in 1855, and when they began to form a political bloc opposed to the Brahmin program of reform, the Brahmins joined ranks with their Yankee brethren. "At that moment," notes Oscar Handlin, "the tradition of tolerance was breached and long repressed hostilities found highly inflammable expression."[31] The rising tide of Italian immigration takes place against this backdrop.

In another sketch some Neapolitan boys play violin and harp, while Yankee boys stand around with "impassive" faces, "warily guarding against the faintest expression of enjoyment" (51).[32] At a certain point the "minstrels played a brisk measure, and the music began to work in the blood of the boys"; one boy shuffles his "reluctant" feet and breaks into "a sudden and resistless dance," as if caught up by a life-force. However, the boy dances "only from the hips down": the music has only taken over half his body. The split between mind and body makes him dance "in an uncoordinated way" and with "no expression"; dancing neither comes naturally nor gives pleasure. The Yankee is ungainly, his gestures stiff and awkward. Is this in contrast to the common image of the musical Italian with fluid gestures and graceful comportment?[33] None of the other boys is "infected" and the narrator turns away: "The spectacle became too sad for contemplation" (51). The musical Italian also appears in "Jubilee Days," based on the National Peace Jubilee in Boston in June 1869. The diva "Parepa-Rosa" sings arias and "The Star Spangled Banner" in the make-shift "Coliseum" erected up in Back Bay (203). In a rendition of Verdi's Anvil Chorus a hundred "fairies in red shirts" marched like garibaldini and played on "invisible anvils," while a hundred fireman beat on anvils with sledgehammers, a thousand musicians played, and ten thousand people sang.[34] Later an immigrant tells the narrator "never in my life, neither at Torino, nor at Milano, nor even at Genoa, never did I see such a crowd or hear such a noise, as at that Colosseo" (212). New World gigantism and vulgarity combine to make a public spectacle and if the immigrant seems wowed by American demographic muscle, the narrator prefers the "chorus" of birds in the tree outside his suburban window.

Just as Italians were emigrating to Boston, African Americans arrived from the upper South and, between 1865 and 1880, doubled their number.[35] Howells's comparison of African Americans and Italians is more complex than the one with the Irish. Like the Italians' Ferry Street in Boston, the African American quarter of Charlesbridge has a "ragged gaety"; like the Italians who are "childred of the summer" (35), the African Americans have "summer in the blood" (20); both stand in contrast to the Yankees who take their pleasures either in the "pocket" or the "conscience" (20), that is anhedonically. Like the Italian quarter too, the African Americans' quarter is contrasted with the "aggressive and impudent squalor" of the Irish section and with the "surly wickedness of a "low American street" (20). Walking in the black neighborhood, the narrator has the pleasing illusion that an "orange-peel" in the street might have come from an orange tree "in the soft atmosphere of those back courts" (20), but the orange is also a totemic fruit of the Italians. The blacks have "supple cunning" and "abundant amiability" (28); the Italians are "wily and amiable" (39). The blacks possess an "inward music" (20); music is often linked to the Italians (though Richard Gambino points out differences between black and Italian music, the one emphasizing rhythm, the other melody[36]). Lynn observes that the narrator's part African American, part Native American servant Mrs. Johnson is a "turbaned, pipe-smoking, black equivalent of an Italian servant."[37] Howells refers to skin color, Mrs. Johnson's being "coffee soothed with the richest cream" (20, 26); Italians are often "swarthy," one of Howells's ethnic code words (here the representation and reality match, as Italians are in many cases swarthy[38]). Mrs. Johnson is so "full of guile" and "goodness," the same odd pairing of qualities found among the Italians, and she reminds him "pleasantly of lowly folk in elder lands" (30). What other "elder" land did Howells know better than Italy? Like the Italians, she has a "lawless" (21) side, a "child-like simplicity" (22), and manners marked by "tranquillity and grace" (20). Not having been bourgeoisified, again like the Italians, Mrs. Johnson only works when she wishes. And she has the culinary disposition of the Italians, and is particularly noted for having learned how to cook Italian dishes: "visions of the great white cathedral, the Coliseum, and the 'dome of Brunelleschi' floated before us in the exhalations of the Milanese *risotto*, Roman *stufadino*, and Florentine *stracotto* that smoked upon our board" (22). Finally, in unspoken sympathy, the ex-slave learns a Garibaldi liberation song, "Camicia rossa" (28), which she sings in Italian.

The type of the mysterious, uncanny Italian is explored in the sketch "By Horse-Car to Boston," in which Howells describes an Italian women on a trolley. Tall and dressed in black, she has arms which "showed through the black gauze of her dress with an exquisite roundness and *morbidezza*" (93) or the softness, realistic flesh tones, and chiaroscuro-like qualities of a painting. She wears "heavy bracelets of dead gold, fashioned after some Etruscan device," gold Etruscan earrings that touch her "white columnar neck" (the column as symbol of Italy), a "massive" Etruscan necklace, and "a multitude of rings." The Etruscan link enhances the uncanniness, the association with death, and the primitive history of Italy—about as far from Boston as one can get. Her "very expressive" hand "took a principal part in the talk which the lady held with her companion, and was as alert and quick as if trained in the gesticulation of Southern or Latin life somewhere." Her face is "strange," "death-white"; her eyes are "liquid." She was "altogether so startling an apparition, that all of us jaded, commonplace spectres turned and fastened our weary, lack-lustre eyes upon her looks, with an utter inability to remove them." This Medusa-like "mystery" (94) is in the vein of the Romantic Fatal Woman analyzed by Mario Praz: beautiful, exotic, pallid (the color of death), often innocent and therefore more enticing, having an uncanny, dreamlike gaze, and possessing a vampire wisdom.[39] When she departs, everyone "woke from a dream," or "as if freed from a potent fascination," and she never "reappeared" again (94).

While Howells's Italians receive the benefit of every doubt, he reserves harsh criticism for a Yankee vagrant. A veteran of the Civil War, "American, pure blood" (56), he has fallen so low on the social scale as to have been employed by an Irishman, a descent in social status that the narrator considers especially disconcerting. The vagrant refuses to work hard and prefers panhandling and an occasional day job to steady employment. Without friends or family he expresses the essential plea of the immigrant: "What I want is a home" (59). But the narrator, whose patience has been exhausted, responds, "Why don't you get married?" and dismisses him callously, "Do you know now, I shouldn't care if I *never* saw you again" (59). What for an Italian immigrant is acceptable or at least tolerable behavior in the new country is considered outrageous and humiliating in an "American."

By the mid-1880s it was evident that many Italian immigrants were not returning home. On the contrary, they arrived each year in greater numbers, and their presence was beginning to assume weight and density in Boston. The geographical triangle of *The Rise of Silas Lapham* (1885) consists of the lower-class North End (with a slowly growing Italian population), the South End (Yankees and Irish middle and lower-middle class; Lapham's old house), and patrician Beacon Hill with its recent adjunct Back Bay ("New Land") reclaimed from the Charles River (Lapham's new house). "Its first streets thrown open in 1872, the present Back Bay filled up in the next thirty years, and became equal to Beacon Hill in the status it conferred on inhabitants. Its air of Victorian prosperity and gentility made the North End appear even more squalid and the South End even more dreary."[40] Lapham builds his house on Beacon Street, Back Bay, facing the river, "the clean, fresh smell of the mortar in the walls mingling with the pungent fragrance of the pine shavings neutralized the Venetian odor that drew in over the water" (906). The morbid "odor" of the Venetian lagoon mixes with the "fragrance" of New England pine, like death and life. Back Bay also resembles Venice in being reclaimed from swampy waters and tidal lagoons; the image has a way of insinuating Lapham's future catastrophe. Three of Howells's five Italian novels have a Venetian setting and in every case the city has an aura of decadence and stands for the "demoralizing influences" of Italy.[41] Lapham's unfinished house goes up in flames, bringing him to near ruin.

The Italian immigrant as an "explosive" element is a topic of conversation at an elegant Beacon Hill dinner party at the home of Bromfield Corey. This italophilic Brahmin dabbled in art studies as a young man in Rome and, though he may have not have fought in the American Civil War, he boasts "a little amateur red-shirting" (1047) with Garibaldi in 1848. His tastes are described as "simple as an Italian's" (948), and his amiable nature, if shallow and ineffectual, is put down to "Italianized sympatheticism" (1186)—the phrase shows Howells in command of this subject. At the party Corey slyly proposes a scheme to help the Italian immigrants with their severe housing problem: "The occupation, by deserving poor of neat habits, of all the beautiful, airy, wholesome houses that stand empty the whole summer long, while their owners are away in their lowly cots beside the sea" (1040). The Beacon Hill ladies register immediate disapproval, but Corey, stung to the quick, teases his guests: "nothing but the surveillance of the local policeman prevents me from applying dynamite to those long rows of close-shuttered, handsome, brutally insensible houses. If I were a poor man, with a sick child pining in some garret or cellar at the North End, I should break into one of them, and camp out on the grand piano" (1041). The squatter image combines italophilic and italophobic elements, the grand piano denoting high culture and music preeeminent among the Italians (Lapham's daughters take dancing lessons "at Papanti's" [883][42]), "camping out" referring to the desperate plight of the immigrants, "dynamite" conveying their anarchic, potentially violent character. When one of the matrons asks about the fate of the furniture, Corey withdraws his proposal. A minister adds, "It's wonderful how patient they [the Italians] are," (1041)—southern Italian fatalism—and the subject is dropped. But Howells's British editor Richard Watson Gilder insisted that he remove the word "dynamite": "Not but a crank would misinterpret your allusion, but it is the crank who does the deed." His British publisher Roswell Smith wrote that the reference to dynamite "suggests nihilism, destructiveness—revenge."[43] Fearing a legal ban, Howells removed the passage, restored by later editors.

In the North End Corey buys an apple from a "swarthy fruiterer" (993) and enjoys exercising his Italian. Later Howells satirizes Corey's "sympatheticism" to the point where the proper Bostonian loses some of his dignity—significantly, over fruit. Corey eats his breakfast orange "in the Neapolitan fashion" (1184), a habit probably picked up as an art student in Rome. His morning orange reminds him both of his carefree days and the warm south. Eating an orange this way means to cut it in quarters, and to tear and suck out the pulp with one's teeth[44]: voracious, full of gusto, but in upper Boston a trifle *volgare*.

Howells's *The Vacation of the Kelwyns* was written around 1906-7 and published posthumously in 1920, but its setting in New England of 1876 places it in the pre-immigration period, and its view of the Italians is accordingly mild and suffused with nostalgia. Parthenope Brook, the main character, was born in Naples of American artists who named her after the siren protectress of the city. They themselves died of fever in Rome, leaving her to be raised in rural New England. In Parthenope's wistful remembrance of her Italian childhood, Nathalia Wright reads Howells's poignant memories of his own youth, as Howells writes, "in those simple days when living in Italy was almost a brevet of genius."[45] At one point an itinerant Italian family of organ-grinders pass by the New Hampshire vacation house:

> There were two men—an older man who sat silently apart in the shade and a young man who came forward and offered to play. He had the sardonic eyes of a goat, but the baby in the arms of a young mother had a Napoleonic face, classic and mature. She herself was beautiful, and she said they were all from the mountains near Genoa and were presently on their way to the next town. They were peasants, but they had a grace which made Parthenope sigh aloud in her thought of the contrast they offered to the mannerless uncouthness of the Yankee country-folks. (151)

From the "goat" (and scapegoat) to "Napoleon," "classic and mature," Italians in Howells have come full circle. To their credit, they appear courteous, sincere, individualistic, quick-witted, and artistic. On the debit side, they are anarchic, though nonviolent, slow to adapt to American commercial society, and weakened by their lack of English. Wright contends that Howells's Italian immigrants are "representative less of their own country than of the American melting pot."[46] But they have not yet "melted." They bear a family resemblance, if more nuanced and sympathetic, to the ideal of the Italian in northern European and American Romantic literature. These stereotypes have been investigated by Camillo von Klenze, Herbert Barrows, and Andrew M. Canepa, each of whom demonstrates the necessity of examining these representations and their changes at the micro-historical level.[47]

The representation of Italian Americans alters for the worse when, like the Irish, the Italians were perceived to be in America to stay. An occasional nuisance perhaps, but more often colorful and engaging, Howells's kindly Italians of the 1860s and '70s in *Suburban Sketches* plan to repatriate; yet their steadily growing number pose a nagging social problem in the '80s in *The Rise of Silas Lapham*. By the 1890s Howells wonders by what "malign chance" the Italians have metamorphosed from the "friendly folk" they are "at home" in Italy to the "surly race they mostly show themselves here: shrewd for their advancement in material things, which seem the only good things to the Americanized aliens of all races, and fierce for their full share of the political pottage" (*Impressions and Experiences* [1896]).[48] From "friendly" to "surly," from carefree to "shrewd" and materialistic, Italians are being "Americanized" into—what else?—Italian Americans and, as such, have begun to claim their social and political rights.

Let us remain in the '80s, the transitional decade, in examining the American representation of Italians. In 1884 Arlo Bates published *The Pagans*, the first of a series of novels once known for their brisk satire on Bostonian art circles. The italophilic theme emerges in the situation of two of the central characters who had studied art in Rome, and in the fateful circumstance of one of them becoming betrothed to an Italian. The novel also contains an italophobic scene in the North End, and what only a decade earlier seemed picturesque was now disturbing. But though Bates's Little Italy has none of the simple charm of Ferry Street, his immigrants are not just a huddled mass. Hitherto Italian immigrants appeared on the margins of American fiction. As their presence grew in Boston, the point was to find some way of bringing them forward into the central plot, of mixing the Americans and the Italian immigrants in a convincing manner. This too was the task of *The Pagans* and its sequel *The Philistines*,[49] which Bates accomplished by means of a stalwart character who moves between both worlds: a southern Italian peasant female art model. In this way ideological and social conflict between italophilia and italophobia comes narratively to life.

In the circle of George Whitefield Chadwick, who may figure in *The Pagans* as the "musician," Bates (1850-1918) was the son of a surgeon from East Machias, Maine and was graduated from Bowdoin College in 1876. Like Howells, he pursued a literary career as a journalist and novelist in Boston, becoming editor-in-chief of the Boston *Sunday Courier* in 1880 and professor of English at the Massachusetts Institute of Technology in 1893. But the rise of Arlo Bates was neither as fast nor as high as the rise of William Dean Howells. Howells came from genteel, well-connected Ohio stock, married into a prominent New England family, and on arriving in Boston was invited to attend Dante Club meetings with Longfellow, Norton, and Lowell. He subsequently became editor of the *Atlantic*, taught at Harvard, and was asked to succeed Lowell in the Smith Professorship of Modern Languages there. He was the friend of Presidents Hayes and Garfield, two fellow Ohioans. Bates was a Sunday magazine editor and taught in the English department of what was then a new technical school. Nonetheless he was a respected member of the Boston community and, like Howells, gave a set of Lowell Lectures, *Talks on the Study of Literature*, published in 1895.

An informal club of seven artists, the "Pagans" stand for "the protest of the artistic soul against shams," by which they meant custom and authority; profess an "unformulated although by no means unexpressed antagonism against Philistinism"; and believe truth is "that which one sincerely believes." For them, Puritanism is the "preliminary rottenness of New England" while Philistinism is the "substitution of convention for conviction."[50] They obviously like thinking in big abstractions. In surroundings that are not inimical to artists—rather, too hospitable, for Bostonians champion their artists into dull submission[51]—the Pagans endeavor to open a space between the Puritanism of their ancestors and the Philistinism of their contemporaries, as they hover between gentility and bohemia. Theirs is an altogether precarious situation, a Bostonian outpost of the Decadence: drifting beyond this space spells disaster for all but the hardiest souls, and the space ultimately proves too small for any of them to produce genuine art. To hear them talk, it is hard to say whether the Philistine or the Puritan is the bigger threat. Arthur Fenton, a Pagan with a penchant for making epigrams, sells out to become a society portrait-painter.[52] Another Pagan complains that Emerson did not go far enough—he "lacked the loftiness of vice; he was eternally narrow" and knew "only half of life" (80). In *The Philistines* Bates extends his critique: even where individuals have liberated themselves from Puritan dogma, its lasting imprint is upon conduct. The "essence" of Puritanism is "its strenuous earnestness, its exaltation of self-denial, and its distrust of the guidance of the senses."[53] Santayana and Van Wyck Brooks have been anticipated.

In *The Pagans* Bates connects the two Italies, of high culture and the impoverished immigrants, by means of the "peasant girl" Ninitta whom Grant Herman, a Boston sculptor, met on an excursion to Capri, "loved or believed he loved," and "induced" to come to Rome and be a model (37, 38). "Loved or believed he loved" and "induced" (or seduced?) are among the many vague words or phrases employed to excuse Herman, Bates's ideal artist, whenever his conduct is closely scutinized. "Black-haired" (159), Ninitta has a "dark, homely face, only redeemed from positive ugliness by her deep, expressive eyes" (34). Perhaps her face is not at issue because Herman is a sculptor and initially is attracted by her body: "rather slender, lithe and sinewy," long limbed "like Diana," "superb," "splendidly shaped" (34, 159). Yet in terms of the novel's thematic conflict, the division between beauty and ugliness, between body (sexuality) and head (conscience), expresses the split response to the Italian.

The diminutive "Ninitta" conveys slightness, a ninny, a nonentity; we never learn her family name, as if she had none, having cut her ties in running off to Rome. With an "Italian's passionate nature" (110), "passionate southern heart" and "crude, simple emotions," Ninitta is the archetypal "undisciplined Italian" (171).[54] Lacking a bourgeois manner and drive-control, she is "tender, loving, pathetically submissive" one day, jealous as a "fury" (116) on another. She is "superstitious" (114); jealous (109, 110, 114, 215); suspicious (120); impulsive (270) and theatrical (12, 139); but also "a good girl" (40, 119), "true and pure" (118) in her loyalty; unpredictable (the only unpredictable element in the novel) and dangerous: she holds her hair up with a "stilletto" (119) (which is silly and melodramatic—Bates is descending[55]). When one Pagan, who employed her as a model, tried kissing her against her will, she "offered to stab him with some sort of a devilish dagger arrangement she carries about like an opera heroine" (12). He hollers for help, other artists rush in like a "chorus," but she leaves "without a fuss" (13)—she can fight her own battles. Ninitta's mind is a mystery, a "strange" amalgam of "simplicity" and "worldly wisdom" (75). She thus combines purity, sincerity, strength, "character," and violence (when justifiably provoked): the noble savage. Finally, Ninitta comes from Capri: the island has associations of the "aesthetic-touristic" and is located in the South, the origin of an increasingly larger percent of the "alien-intruders." (Eventually almost 80 percent of Italian immigrants came from southern Italy.)

In Rome, Grant Herman had faint-heartedly proposed to Ninitta and was "too honorable to betray her" (38). Then, believing mistakenly that Ninitta is having an affair with his friend, he leaves Rome without consulting either. Perhaps he wants to believe anything that will soothe his conscience in leaving her. Though he learns after his friend's death that Ninitta had been faithful to him, he is not so honorable as to renew his pledge because he has fallen in love with a fellow sculptress, Helen Greyson, who is estranged from her husband. As the novel opens Ninitta has arrived in Boston after seeking Herman for seven years. Her presence on the scene throws the Pagans, the Puritans, and even some of the Philistines into consternation. Ninitta is the one and only Pagan.

Unlike Bates's Puritans, Ninitta is guided by her senses, or maybe "driven" is the better word. When she confronts Herman with his obligation, he is cool towards her, gives her a handshake, says he has a headache, and asks her to come back tomorrow (40). It is hard to think of a character who has ever recovered from such an initial poor showing in the eyes of the reader. Bates blames Ninitta for not understanding why, on having learned the truth of her honesty, Herman would still renege. But Ninitta cannot be blamed; it is Bates who appears never to have read *I Promessi Sposi* and who shows no comprehension of Italian *rispetto* involving "obligations and reciprocal arrangements" between the marital parties. Since Herman has given a ring and Ninitta has remained faithful, his personal feelings do not override the principle: "affection did not constitute an essential component of *rispetto*, even if its presence was desirable."[56] Yet Bates would have us believe that, coming from her background, she should accept Herman's change of heart and end the engagement. To understand the change, writes the patronizing Bates, "would have required not only a knowledge of facts of which she could have no cognizance, but far keener powers of reason than were centered in Ninitta's shapely head" (77). (Though this is badly written, "shapely" implies a sculptural quality—the *face*, symbolic of the personality, has a "positive ugliness.") The "facts" are seven years, cultural and class differences, a new country, and another woman. While the first three mean nothing to Ninitta, "instinct" (77) leads her to suspect another woman. Herman's unfounded suspicion of Ninitta in Rome is passed over lightly; Ninitta's well-grounded suspicion of Herman manifests a glaring defect in her character.

Embarrassed and seeking reconciliation, Herman visits Ninitta's threadbare attic room[57]and, for the first time, sees her as a person. "She was no longer simply the model, she was an Italian woman in her own home" (115). Against much of what one already knows about her, Bates allows Ninitta an extraordinary act of self-transcendence, as if he would make her do what is "right" from the point of view of the other characters' interests. Ninitta rejects Herman's renewed proposal because she refuses to force him into a loveless marriage. The psychological motivation is surprising, and just barely plausible, but the scene has unquestionable impact, and if Bates could have multiplied such scenes, he might have deepened understanding of the immigrants. Soon afterward, having agreed to pose for a statue by Helen, Ninitta discovers that Helen is sculpting a large work, *The Flight of the Seasons*, and that Herman is the model for the head of December (at thirty-five Herman is prematurely gray and complaining of his age). It is noteworthy that Helen is sculpting a face and head, with Herman as the model; with Ninitta, only the physical body (and head insofar as it is "shapely," but not the face) is seen as beautiful. Ninitta goes to Helen's studio and smashes the head of December to bits. "She didn't make any attempt to conceal it," reports Helen, "she came stalking melodramatically into his studio with the mallet and laid it down. 'There,' said she, 'now kill me. I have broken her work.' It was like a fashion magazine story" (139). Helen does not get angry; that would be bad *behavior*, the expression of the very histrionic emotion she mocks in Ninitta. But if her sculpture meant more to her, she might not compare its destruction to cheap sensationalism.

Ninitta's action has the immediate effect of freeing Herman from the obligation of being "Her Man," but will he now be Helen's man? In the novel's chief moral crisis Herman's conscience does not let him off so easily with regard to his pledge to Ninitta and he has second thoughts. Meanwhile, ill and bereft, Ninitta grows despondent and drifts aimlessly towards the North End, her surrogate home country. Ferry Street has grown into a large Italian neighborhood, which social workers at the time called "Boston's classic land of poverty"[58]:

> The poorer classes of foreigners in any city [writes Bates] are led by similarity of language and occupations to gather into neighborhoods according to their nationality, and the Italians are especially clannish. The fruit-venders and organ-grinders form separate colonies, each distinguished by the peculiarities incident to the calling of its inhabitants, the crooked courts in the fruit-sellers' neighborhood being chiefly marked to outward observance by the number of two-wheeled

hand-carts which, out of business hours, are crowded together there. (164)

An immigrant family, recognizing her speech, takes pity on Ninitta and brings her home to their tenement. She is eventually found by Mrs. Edith Fenton, wife of the "Pagan" Arthur and an upper-class volunteer in social work.[59] Already involved in social service, many Brahmins and Yankees would shortly embrace the settlement house movement (a noted settlement house would be the North End Union, founded in 1892 by the Benevolent Fraternity of Unitarian Churches).[60]

The interior of the tenement is presented through Mrs. Fenton's eyes: "The children have just been put into our schools, but they have not advanced very far as yet . . . they are wretchedly poor. I wish you could see the place, Mrs. Greyson. Eight people in a room not so large as this, and such poverty as you could hardly imagine. Yet these people had taken in another" (160). It was not uncommon for whole families to live in a single room, and the population density led frequently to health and sanitation problems.[61] Hoping to make conversions, Protestant churches set up "missions" in the slums, but with limited success. "They are Catholics, naturally," Mrs. Fenton says, "but they do not seem to have much religion of any kind, and keep clear of the priest for some reason" (161).[62] That they lack religion is plainly wrong, but their keeping clear of priests seems to have been the case with many arriving immigrants. According to Anna Maria Martellone, "even if [the immigrant] was a practicing, convinced Catholic, the conditions in which he found himself within the ambience of English-language parishes, governed by the Irish clerics, distanced him after a short time from the influence of the church."[63] But it was not long before the Italians had their own priests. Italians in the West End, for example, made a point of having their children baptized by Italian priests in Sacred Heart Church in the North End.

After communicating Ninitta's whereabouts, Mrs. Fenton returns to the North End with Helen whose knowledge of Italian will be helpful in persuading Ninitta to come back with them—yet another "crossing" for Ninitta, and not her last. In addition to charity, virtues mitigating the situation are (Yankee) thriftiness and cleanliness, seen as exceptional:

Ninitta was found in a room tolerably clean for that portion of the city, the old fruit woman who was its mistress having retained more of the tidiness of thrifty peasant ancestors than most of her class. One room

was made to accommodate the mother and seven children, and during
the absence of the former from home the premises were left in charge
of a girl just entering her teens [who] was engaged in preparing the
family dinner of maccaroni. (164-65)

Why is there no mention of the father? Here only women are helping
other women, from Helen and Mrs. Fenton to the young Italian girl doing
the cooking. If a woman is scapegoated as the cause of trouble, women
are the only ones who appear actively sympathetic. Yet Bates draws
upon another stereotype and feminizes the Italians, rendering them (in
his eyes) weak, abandoned, and vulnerable to exploitation—a mimesis of
their historical condition.

After Ninitta goes back to proper Boston, Helen persuades Herman
to honor his pledge and marry Ninitta. Since Helen's husband has just
committed suicide and she is free to marry, her self-sacrificing act is
explained by a strong Puritan conscience. Similarly, Herman's
temptation to marry Helen is great, and so his sacrifice in marrying
Ninitta is made to seem the greater. Bates leaves the impression that the
sacrifice is wrong, that the Puritan conscience is at fault; at the same time
Ninitta represents dangerous sexual desire that must somehow be
controlled or repressed. The novel ends with Helen's gloomy departure
for Rome, Herman's reluctant marriage, and the disbanding of the
Pagans. But this is not the real ending, only a suspension, because
everything points all too clearly to a marriage that is doomed and a love
between Helen and Herman that will not die.

More disposed towards Herman's indecisiveness and opportunism
than sympathetic with Ninitta's seven-year odyssey and social ostracism,
Bates scarcely conceals his prejudices where a Brahmin, at least in
public, would have been more detached and oblique. If with an air of
social superiority Helen says that Ninitta's behavior is like a magazine
story, Bates's own writing rarely rises above the level of the Sunday
papers. But whether he was shaping the moral perceptions of his
audience or merely expressing them, crudity of presentation is altogether
stronger in *The Philistines*, published in 1889 five years after *The
Pagans*. At the end of the first decade of large-scale Italian immigration
to Boston, the expansion of their community has intensified nativist
social prejudice.[64]

In *The Pagans*, virtually against the intentions of the novelist, Ninitta
is a forceful, if impractical, individual with a capacity for love and
endurance; in *The Philistines* she is blamed unjustly for a failed

marriage, commits a single indiscretion, and pays with her life. Six years have passed and Herman and Ninitta have grown emotionally apart. As he looks across the breakfast table, he "continually tried to discover what process of reasoning led Ninitta to given results" (60). Not fluent in English, she still speaks to him in Italian, which Bates implies is a failure to adapt. They have a "swarthy" (62) boy, named Nino after Ninitta who is also "swarthy" (388). To the inheritance of physical traits are added psychological ones. Herman accuses his wife of spoiling him and is angry that the *bambino*, as she insists on calling him, is not at the table: "He has all the Italian laziness in him," says Herman, who goes to rouse the boy and finds him lying "luxuriously" in his little bed (he is only five). One recalls the "lazy" boy with the tambourine in *Suburban Sketches*. Child-like themselves, Italians infantilize their children, which is no way to prepare them for life. "He will be a *bambino* to you when he is as big as I am" (62).

Isolated in Boston, Ninitta has made sacrifices to conform to her husband's society. "She used to have a few Italians come to see her; people she met that time she ran away, you remember, and we brought her home," Mrs. Fenton says, "but they don't come now." She raises her eyebrows, "A question of caste." Rejecting her compatriots for the sake of social climbing for her child, Ninitta told her Italian friends that "the *bambino* was born a gentleman" and "couldn't associate with them" (108). Yet when Ninitta is desperate, she goes to see "Italian friends of former days" (436), the only people to whom she can turn. Normally, Helen says with unbecoming prejudice, Ninitta is as out of place at an afternoon tea as "the pope at a dancing-party" (107), mocking both Ninitta and the papacy.

Herman's attempt to fathom his marital troubles and Ninitta's conduct involves him in rationalization and self-deception: "as the larger nature, it should be his place to make concessions, to master the situation, and to secure Ninitta's happiness." For her, he had made the "great sacrifice of his life" and he never lets himself forget it:

> But his patience, his delicacy, his steadfastness counted for little with Ninitta. She had been separated from him for long years of betrothal, during which he had developed and changed utterly. . . . Even Ninitta, little given to analysis, could not fail to recognize that her husband was a very different being from the lover she had known ten years before. One fervid blaze of the old lover would have appealed more strongly to

her peasant soul than all the patience and tender forbearance of years. (222)

He has all the patience; she, all the passion; and Bates would have us think that, were it not for her "peasant soul," she would know better. Indeed, if Herman had been more brutal with her, had he made a "slave" of her, she would have "accepted her lot as uncomplainingly as the women of her race had acquiesced in such a fate for stolid generations." Given her unfulfilled desire Ninitta is tempted to model again, her work supposedly being an outlet for her sexuality; an opportunity is provided by the Pagan-turned-Philistine Arthur Fenton. Vice attracts itself and then feeds on itself: "the time came when her ardent Italian nature was so kindled that she became involuntarily the tempter in her turn" (223-24). While Herman had posed for the married Helen Greyson in *The Pagans* without a trace of shame, Ninitta's modeling for Fenton is seen as scandalous. Bates traces Ninitta's fault to her background: "There was, too, who knows what trace of heredity in the readiness with which Ninitta tacitly adopted the idea that infidelity to a husband was rather a matter of discretion and secrecy; whereas faithfulness to her lover had been a point of the most rigorous honor" (223). Again, Bates misreads Ninitta because he does not comprehend *rispetto*.

Fenton's *Fatima* ("Shining One") portrays Ninitta as an oriental beauty "lying with long sleek limbs amid bright-hued cushions" (379), linking the Italian woman to oriental luxury and wantonness (a familiar stereotype: the Venetian courtesan, the *dama* of the cicisbeo). Fenton has tried to conceal Ninitta's identity by only taking her body for the model—her face was not beautiful in any case—and by transposing the head from another model, but the ruse will not work: her "true" identity is the body and will be recognized as such. The dichotomy between italophilia and italophobia, already present in Ninitta's person (beautiful body, ugly face), is now expressed by decapitation (a castration). The theme appears in both novels. Helen's head of December modeled on Herman might also be read as a castration image, December being the month of death. Helen's last name "Greyson" also contains a deathly color, her first name being the mythical beauty; in her own way she, too, evokes a split response, of love and death. Helen and Herman are entering middle age, typified by Helen's *The Flight of the Seasons*. The various doublings express fears of dwindling potency and a consequent arousal of sexuality. Bates himself was in his later thirties at the time of writing the novel and his wife had recently died, leaving him with a young son about Nino's age. The biographical relations cannot be coincidental, but more attention must first be given to Bates's life, and there is no biography.

At the gallery exhibition Herman recognizes his wife's body (with its "sensuous enticement") and it "choked" him (382-83). Scandal has broken out over Ninitta, and it fills Herman with shame and anger. He confronts Ninitta whose "swarthy passionate face was an image of terror" (388). The rhetoric is virulently racist and sexist:

> She was not far enough away from her peasant ancestors not to be moved by the size and strength of her husband's large and vigorous frame. Many generations and much subtlety of refinement must lie between herself and savagery before a woman can learn instinctively to fear the soul of a man rather than his muscles in a crisis like this. (388-89)

This is a rather circumlocutionary way of saying that Italians are wife-beaters, an Anglo-American trope.[65] Herman asks how she could have betrayed him, though whether she has ever sexually betrayed him is only insinuated and highly doubtful. Besides, an artist like Herman might have understood, at least vaguely, her desire to pursue her line of work in the studio instead of staying home. So he punishes her where it hurts most: what will Nino think of her when he grows up? The question, a veiled threat, plunges her into deeper grief. "Could he have known what was passing in her heart; it would have moved him to a deeper respect and a keener pity than he had ever felt for her. No more than a dumb animal had she any language in which she could have made him understand her feelings had she tried" (391). Not Ninitta, Bates himself lacks the language of her feelings, for it is the gift of language that a novelist should bestow upon such a character, either directly through speech and action, or indirectly through description and symbol.

Ninitta decides to flee Boston, leaving Nino with his father, and go back to Italy; it will be her final crossing. Yet a second exile is not a sufficiently severe penalty for her transgression; she might return; and she is blocking the marriage of Herman and Helen. There is no other solution to the scandal but for the scapegoat to die. And the partner of the deed, Arthur Fenton, must die for "seducing" Ninitta and (it is another part of the plot) for trafficking in bad business ventures. Moreover, he is a Pagan turncoat. On a steamer bound for New York she meets Fenton on his way to placate his creditors. In dense fog the steamer crashes into another ship and Ninitta and Fenton are drowned. As Bates explains, Fenton would have survived the disaster, were it not for his heroic attempt at trying to *save* her. If this is to grant Fenton a measure of redemption, Ninitta must again appear responsible for bringing trouble to men. Further, since both Ninitta and Fenton believe that Boston will think they had run off together, and never learn the truth, their deaths are spiritually as well as physically tormenting.

Herman and Helen marry and raise Nino in proper Boston. The Italian Americans would have to wait a generation before becoming the central focus of interest in serious works of art.[66]

Epilogue

To jump forward seventy-five years, italophilia and italophobia inform two books that examine urban redevelopment in the 1950s, Fred Langone's *The North End: Where It All Began* and Walter Muir Whitehill's *Boston: A Topographical History.*

Langone, a lawyer and Boston City Councillor, comes from a distinguished Italian American family long settled in the North End. In 1927 his grandfather Joseph A. Langone, Sr., state representative and owner of a funeral home in the North End, organized and led the massive funeral procession of Sacco and Vanzetti. Langone's father was election commissioner and state senator; his mother was a powerful figure in state and national immigration politics.[67] *The North End* is both a personal memoir and an historical portrait of a neighborhood over two centuries of changing ethnic groups and economic fortunes, with the Italians lodged in it for roughly the past hundred years.

Langone's strongest theme is protecting one's own backyard from the rapacity of politicians, city planners, "greedy developers," special interest groups, and Washington. He had fought a losing battle against the expansion of Logan Airport, which meant increased noise pollution and the destruction of neighborhoods and marshlands in the predominantly Italian East Boston. He also lost out when in the 1950s the Southern Artery, an elevated superhighway, tore through one side of the North End and left it haemorrhaging for years and choking with congestion. (Recently, planners decided that the Southern Artery was a big mistake and now want everything underground; the current ten-to-fifteen year project again threatens serious dislocation.) But Langone had his successes; when politicians wanted to end the open market in the old

Haymarket Square, he not only helped save it, but was able to give it an extra day. He won the fight to preserve the famous North End waterfront and got the city to build senior citizen housing and provide for a park.

His book's most painful chapter does not concern the precariously preserved North End, but the West End, contiguous and fluid with it, and as Langone says, vibrant, safe, even more cosmopolitan in its ethnic mix of Italian, Irish, Jewish, African, Polish, Ukrainian. In the late 1950s and early 60s the West End was "redeveloped" in what some sociologists consider among the worst examples of its kind in American urban history. The West End is the North End's dark shadow.

Showing no understanding of the heritage they were enjoined to protect, lacking in any real culture to guide them in their momentous decisions, planners and politicians seized and condemned the West End's forty-eight acres and 3,200 households and cut the heart out of the city. Along with the demolition of Haymarket, Bowdoin, and Scollay Squares to make room for the architectural catastrophe of Government Center (by I. M. Pei) and the no less hideous City Hall, the razing of the West End sundered the North End from Beacon Hill and Back Bay, forever destroying the architectural integrity of Old Boston. If the reclamation of the marshlands to make Back Bay was the finest urbanistic achievement for the nineteenth-century city, the West End demolition ranks as its most significant twentieth-century event. Back Bay enhanced Boston, the West End Urban Renewal Project was an unmitigated disaster.

Where were the city elders and the venerable sages when the West End was on the chopping block? One can find no better example of WASP decadence after World War II than the way their leaders turned a blind eye. In *Boston: A Topographical History*, published in 1958, a year after the unveiling of the West End redevelopment plan, Walter Muir Whitehill, director of the Boston Athenaeum (and former Allston Burr Senior Tutor at Lowell House, Harvard), reviewed the decision and blandly expressed his opinion. "This [plan] is less to be regretted in that the area, having been open country in the eighteenth century, had fewer points of historic interest than the other parts of the town." How easily the sentence slips from the mandarin's pen! Elevation of an "historic" eighteenth century of Brahmin-Yankee pride; "open country," the pastoral myth; suppression of the immigrant-laden nineteenth century which had its own storied myths; "fewer points" revealing that he is merely counting, not seeing the West End in its aesthetic and urbanistic relations to other quarters; no hint of the human cost, "less to be regretted."[68]

Ten years later, in a second edition, Whitehill sang a different tune, harsh and grating. Now that the character of the central city had been transmogrified, he woke to a nightmare. Conducted by the Boston Redevelopment Authority, the West End project "brutally displaced people, disrupted neighborhoods and destroyed pleasing buildings, only to create a vast approximation of a battlefield in the center of the city. . . . [the new apartment towers of Charles River Park are] as complete a break with the traditional architecture and habits of Boston as the adjacent shopping center-motel-movie house in Cambridge Street which has the air of having wandered in from the suburbs of another city." But there is no admission of his earlier error in judgment, and the new chapter in which he reviews the West End fiasco is called, without a trace of self-irony, "A Decade of Renewal." As if he had just come upon the scene, he writes: "total demolition of large areas, without regard for the feelings of people, and their eventual reconstruction—after long periods as a desolate dump—in unfamiliar form for new uses was neither good sense nor good politics." In a footnote Whitehill, however, betrays the feelings that had guided him in the first place: "there were streets and courts that were quite as suitable for economical living in the center of the city as the streets of the north slope of Beacon Hill or of Bay Village"; the West End had "many of the virtues that Jane Jacobs found" in Greenwich Village. So the West End wasn't a slum after all. "In Poplar Court, for example, a number of young physicians and their families lived pleasantly in nineteenth-century red brick houses converted into apartments." These future members of the WASP elite are the only specific group that Whitehill mentions as displaced among the 3,200 households. "They were near the Massachusetts General Hospital, and their wives made full use of the nearby foreign groceries and bakeries." Those happen to have been Italian American and Jewish American groceries and bakeries, not "foreign" ones.[69]

A tribune of the people, Langone made certain that the lessons of the West End would not be lost on the North End or, for that matter, elsewhere in the city. Developers did not tear down a single house in the North End, which, having retained its distinctive character, is one of the major tourist attractions on the East Coast. Yet Langone's *pietas* includes not only his Italian heritage; he embraces all the ethnic populations who have nourished the spirit of the place, from the early British immigrants to the Italians. Then, he welcomes future inhabitants of whatever origin, as if to say that the "twilight" of one ethnicity (in Richard Alba's phrase) only just precedes the dawn of another. The book's subtitle *Where it All Began* calls attention to the birth of the American Republic and to its rebirth in the consciousness of each successive ethnic group. Balancing many expressions of passing, nostalgia, and death in Langone's memoir are metaphors of birth and living process: "The North End will never die out as a good, viable community because it is here that our great country was born. No matter what ethnic strain of immigrants came here, it never changed its character." Its people have always pulled together as a community, a fact powerfully expressed in their participation in numerous civic and religious events. One of the most culturally interesting and uplifting—and one which Langone had no small hand in saving after World War II—is the annual Veterans Parade.

In the spirit of renewal, this large parade starts from Paul Revere's grave in the King's Chapel Burial Ground and proceeds to the original Paul Revere House in North Square, North End. Here the mayor of Boston hands a scroll to a "Paul Revere," who rides on horseback down Prince Street, nearby the Old North Church where the warning lanterns were hung, across Charlestown Bridge, and into Middlesex County with the cry "The British are coming!" If Old Boston has preserved its heritage for the next century, it has to thank Langone and those like him, for their historical imagination, civicness, and courage.

Notes

1. Richard H. Brodhead, "The Double Dream of Italy in the American Gilded Age," a paper read at a conference entitled "America's Italy," sponsored by the Fondazione Giovanni Agnelli, Washington, D.C., 17-19 Sept. 1992, p. 11, forthcoming in the acts of the conference (by permission). Brodhead's title would have better referred to one dream and one nightmare.

2. Brodhead, "The Double Dream of Italy in the American Gilded Age," p. 9.

3. There were Italian Americans in American literature before Italian Unification. This essay is concerned with their appearance in the post-bellum period. The 1850 census reported 3,645 Italians living in the United States; in 1910, there were 1,343,125 (Emiliana P. Noether, "As Others Saw Us," *Transactions of the Connecticut Academy of Arts and Sciences*, 50 [Sept. 1990]: 125).

4. He had to turn down the consulship in Rome because it came without a salary; the Venice post provided $1500 a year.

---

5. Quoted in James L. Woodress, Jr., *Howells and Italy* (Durham: Duke University Press, 1952), p. 40. *Italian Journeys* has been reprinted by the Marlboro Press, VT and is reviewed by Giuseppe Gadda Conti in *Italian Americana*, 11, no. 2 (1993): 285-86.

6. Quoted in Woodress, Jr., *Howells and Italy*, p. 199.

7. *Suburban Sketches* (1871; Boston: Osgood, 1872), p. 45. "Bites, not nibbles, signore!": the reference is to the growling house-dog. Hereafter page numbers are cited in parentheses in the text and notes.

8. Quoted in Nathalia Wright, *American Novelists in Italy: The Discoverers: Allston to James* (Philadelphia: University of Pennsylvania Press, 1965), p. 176. William L. Vance remarks on *Venetian Life* that Howells focuses on the middle and lower classes, on everyday work habits, foods, local customs, etc.: "his way of seeing Venice was transformed from one of exclusively visual externality to one of dramatic involvement, vision enlarged by language" (in "Seeing Italy: The Realistic Rediscovery by Twain, Howells, and James," *The Lure of Italy: American Artists and the Italian Experience, 1760-1914*, ed. Theodore E. Stebbins, Jr. [Boston and New York: Museum of Fine Arts and Harry N. Abrams, 1992], p. 99).

9. Woodress, Jr., *Howells and Italy*, pp. 131-32.

10. Wright, *American Novelists in Italy*, pp. 195-96. Brodhead remarks that Howells's italophilia had a measure of shrewd self-interest given the fascination with Italy in Boston literary circles, then deeply immersed in Dante and Italian culture ("Double Dream of Italy in the American Gilded Age," p. 12). Such ambition does not preclude a genuine interest in Italy (cf. Woodress, Jr., *Howells and Italy*, pp. 102, 113, 186, 198, 200-201).

11. Kenneth S. Lynn, *William Dean Howells: An American Life* (New York: Harcourt Brace Jovanovich, 1970), p. 206. See also *Suburban Sketches* (21); and James Russell Lowell, "Leaves from My Journal in Italy and Elsewhere: III. Italy," in *Fireside Travels* (Boston: Houghton Mifflin, 1904), p. 149: "Coming from a country where everything seems shifting like a quicksand, where men shed their homes as snakes their skins, where you may met a three-story house, or even a church, on the highway, bitten by the universal gadfly of bettering its position, where we have known a tree to be cut down merely because 'it had got to be so old,' the sense of permanence, unchangeableness, and repose which Italy gives us is delightful."

12. Brodhead, "Double Dream of Italy in the American Gilded Age," pp. 13-14.

13. Lynn (*William Dean Howells*, p. 199) says that it was "comparatively easy" for Howells to make the transition, but the sketches show him grappling with American prejudices; his narrator is in some sense his foil. This was not the case in his travelogues where he writes in his own voice.

14. Lowell to Howells, 2 May 1869, quoted in Lynn, *William Dean Howells*, p. 199. For the italophilic milieu in which Howells moved in

From Italophilia to Italophobia 367

Cambridge, see my "The Harvard Italophiles: Longfellow, Lowell, and Norton," *L'Esilio romantico*, ed. Joseph Cheyne and Lilla Maria Crisafulli Jones (Bari: Adriatica Editrice, 1990), pp. 303-24.

15. Perhaps somewhat implausibly in view of the diversity of dialects. Yet Howells had spent four years in Italy and knew his way around the language.

16. "Doorstep Acquaintance" was published in the *Atlantic* in 1869 and reprinted in *Suburban Sketches* in 1871.

17. Italians ranked first among ethnic groups in repatriation between 1908 and 1931 (Betty Boyd Caroli, *Italian Repatriation from the United States, 1900-1914* [New York: Center for Migration Studies, 1973], p. 9; see tables on pp. 11 and 38 and the discussion of statistical problems, chaps. 1 and 2 passim). Of the so-called "birds of passage" syndrome R. F. Foerster explained: "Between 1860 and 1880, as the fresh arrivals increased, the immigration assumed a much more definite character. Where before there had been individuals there were now types and classes. From small beginnings the contingent from South Italy had swelled to substantial proportions. After 1870, for the first time, it became evident that, following a somewhat indeterminate state, many repacked their chattels and went home again. No previous immigrants into this land of promise had done that" (*The Italian Emigration of Our Times* [Cambridge: Harvard University Press, 1919], p. 324). Pino Arlacchi, who cites this passage, locates the reasons for return-migration in "balanced reciprocity," a social system in crisis after the Unification (*Mafia, Peasants and Great Estates: Society in Traditional Calabria* [Cambridge: Cambridge University Press, 1983], chap. 1). For return-migration see also Thomas Kessner, *The Golden Door: Italian and Jewish Immigrant Mobility in New York City, 1880-1915* (New York: Oxford University Press, 1977), pp. 27-28.

18. Arthur Mann, *Yankee Reformers in the Urban Age* (Cambridge: Harvard University Press, 1954), p. 4. This may be Ferry Way, off Prince St., and now absorbed into Commercial Street. In the seventeenth and eighteenth centuries the ferry took people to and from Charlestown (Walter M. Whitehill, *Boston: A Topographical History* [Cambridge: Harvard University Press, 1959)], pp. 28-29). For the ethnic composition of the North End, see Anna Maria Martellone, *Una Little Italy nell'Atene d'America: La communità italiana di Boston dal 1880 al 1920* (Naples: Guida Editori, 1973), pp. 235-36. In 1900 there were twenty-five nationalities domiciled in the North End.

19. Lynn refers to "picturesque vignettes of Italian characters" (*William Dean Howells*, p. 199).

20. James criticized Howells for not writing about Italians "as from equal to equal" in *Italian Journeys* (quoted in Lynn, *William Dean Howells*, p. 198). Thirty-five years later James would have a similar problem with the immigrants in *The American Scene*.

21. John F. Stack, Jr., commenting on Frederick A. Bushee's "The Invading Host" (1902), in *International Conflict in an American City: Boston's Irish, Italians, and Jews, 1935-1944* (Westport: Greenwood, 1979), p. 24.

22. William Dean Howells, *The Rise of Silas Lapham*, in *Novels 1875-1886*, The Library of America (New York: Viking Press, 1982), p. 993.

23. Botta's was probably the most respected history until George Bancroft's multi-volume *History of the United States* began appearing in the 1830s. Harvard University adopted Botta for its course on the American revolution in 1839 (Noether, "As Others Saw Us": 133).

24. Stack, Jr., *International Conflict in an American City*, p. 24. This was the heyday of the Teutonic myth in Anglo-Saxon culture. In *Mont Saint Michel and Chartres* (1904) Henry Adams goes so far as to transform St. Thomas Aquinas into a Swabian-Norman, uniting "the two most energetic strains in Europe" (chap. 16), as if Italy could not produce a philosopher of such standing. See Edward N. Saveth, *American Historians and European Immigrants, 1875-1925* (New York: Columbia University Press, 1948), chaps. 1, 2.

25. Robert Anthony Orsi, *The Madonna of 115th Street: Faith and Community in Italian Harlem, 1880-1950* (New Haven: Yale University Press, 1985), pp. 75 ff.

26. Brodhead, "Double Dream of Italy in the American Gilded Age," p. 14.

27. There were 35,287 Irish-born residents in Boston in 1850 compared to 134 Italians; by 1880 the number of Irish stood at 64,793 (an additional 8,366 in Cambridge) and Italians at 1277 (36 in Cambridge) (Oscar Handlin, *Boston's Immigrants: A Study in Acculturation*, rev. ed. [Cambridge: Harvard University Press, 1959], pp. 243, 261). These figures may be compared with the 1875 Massachusetts Census which lists 2,389 Italian residents in Boston (Stack, Jr., *International Conflict in an American City*, p. 23).

28. The norm was otherwise, the Italians' usually being compared unfavorably. "The lowest Irish," said John Fiske, "are far above the level of these creatures" (John Higham, *Strangers in the Land: Patterns of American Nativism, 1860-1925* [New York: Atheneum, 1963], p. 65).

29. Elsa Nettels, *Language, Race, and Social Class in Howells's America* (Lexington: University of Kentucky Press, 1988), p. 92.

30. Stack, *International Conflict in an American City*, p. 21.

31. Handlin, *Boston's Immigrants*, p. 191.

32. See John E. Zucchi, *The Little Slaves of the Harp: Italian Child Street Musicians in Nineteenth-Century Paris, London, and New York* (Montreal and Kingston: McGill-Queen's University Press, 1992).

33. Oddly, Richard Gambino does not see the Italian as particularly graceful. Commenting on black and Italian stereotypes, he remarks that black body language is "fluid, agile, graceful, easy, and seemingly relaxed and uninhibited," whereas the Italian American "stands and moves in a controlled, guarded way"; "his shoulders and hips remain locked even during the fastest

dancing, in contrast to the focus on pelvic movement of black dance. It is a code of a self-contained rocklike body punctuated by deliberate staccato movements" (*Blood of My Blood: The Dilemma of the Italian Americans* [New York: Doubleday, 1974], p. 303). One can only disagree. The words "controlled" and "guarded" do not spring to mind when one thinks of the *passeggiata*. Italians are known to be excellent dancers: the Italian dancing master is a common type from the eighteenth century (see n. 43 for an example). In Palermo in the early ninetenth century George Russell noted that "the deportment of these lovely women, their dancing, and their attitudes, are attractively elegant" (*A Tour through Sicily in the Year 1815* [London, 1819], p. 48).

34. Martin Burgess Green, *The Problem of Boston: Some Readings in Cultural History* (New York: Norton, 1966), p. 103: "John S. Dwight, Boston's Yankee music critic, left town for the occasion."

35. Handlin, *Boston's Immigrants*, p. 212.

36. Gambino, *Blood of My Blood*, pp. 302-303.

37. Lynn, *William Dean Howells*, p. 197.

38. "'You don't call . . . an Italian a white man?' a West Coast construction boss was asked. 'No, sir,' he answered, 'an Italian is a Dago.'" Ralph Waldo Emerson was "thankful that immigration brought 'the light complexion, the blue eyes of Europe'"; "'the black eyes, the black drop, the Europe of Europe is left'" (Higham, *Strangers in the Land*, pp. 65, 66). As James Fenimore Cooper saw the *lazzaroni* in Naples, "Naked men, resemble Indians with breech cloths. Colour not very different" (*Letters and Journals*, ed. James Franklin Beard [Cambridge: Harvard University Press, 1960], 1: 380).

39. Mario Praz, *The Romantic Agony*, trans. Angus Davidson, 2nd ed. (London: Oxford University Press, 1970), p. 207.

40. Mann, *Yankee Reformers in the Urban Age*, p. 5.

41. Wright, *American Novelists in Italy*, p. 187. These influences are countered by positive ones that enable Howells to criticize what he found "bad" in modernity.

42. "Lorenzo Papanti, an exiled Italian count, established the one 'proper Boston' dancing school of the century" (1214, note by Edwin H. Cady). Lapham's daughters take lessons in the public classes; the Brahmins presumably send their daughters to the private ones.

43. Quoted in William Dean Howells, *The Rise of Silas Lapham*, ed. Walter J. Meserve (Bloomington: Indiana University Press, 1971), pp. 385-6. The entire scene is an expression of the turmoil in Howells: "In the spring [of 1885, shortly before the novel was published] a sudden overwhelming sense of guilt—a Swedenborgian 'vastation'—turns Howells to Tolstoy and deeper, more radical social inquiries" (1205, note by Edwin H. Cady, Library of America edition).

44. This information is owed to a private communication with Giuseppe Gadda Conti, author of *William Dean Howells* (Rome: Edizioni di Storia e Letteratura, 1971). Gaddi Conti claims an "intimate sympathy" between

Howells and Bromfield Corey and notes that on occasion Howells chooses him as his mouthpiece (p. 182). Corey is partially a Howells surrogate, like the narrator in *Suburban Sketches*.

45. William Dean Howells, *The Vacation of the Kelwyns* (New York: Houghton Mifflin, 1920), p. 51.

46. Wright, *American Novelists in Italy*, p. 195. In her chapter on Howells and Italy, Wright devotes only one paragraph to the Italians in America; Woodress in his book-length study even less (*Howells and Italy*, pp. 63-64, 153).

47. Camillo von Klenze, *The Interpretation of Italy during the Last Two Centuries: A Contribution to the Study of Goethe's "Italienische Reise"* (Chicago: University of Chicago Press, 1907); Herbert Barrows, "Convention and Novelty in the Romantic Generation's Experience of Italy," in *Literature as a Mode of Travel*, intro. by Warner G. Rice (New York: New York Public Library, 1963), pp. 69-84; and Andrew M. Canepa, "From Degenerate Scoundrel to Noble Savage: The Italian Stereotype in 18th-Century British Travel Literature," *English Miscellany*, 22 (1971): 107-46.

48. *Impressions and Experiences* quoted in Wright, *American Novelists in Italy*, p. 196. The Italians were not particularly "fierce"; it took longer for them to receive their share of the "pottage."

49. I limit myself to these novels, though Bates's *The Puritans* (1898) has some of the same characters.

50. Arlo Bates, *The Pagans* (New York: Henry Holt, 1884; fac. rpt. Upper Saddle River, N.J.: Literature House, 1970), pp. 56, 211, 234-35.

51. Green, *The Problem of Boston*. p. 136.

52. According to Van Wyck Brooks, Boston's general suspicion of the plastic arts excepted portrait-painting on account of its association with "family pride," "wealth," and "public spirit" (*The Flowering of New England* [New York: Dutton, 1936], p. 3).

53. Arlo Bates, *The Philistines* (Boston: Ticknor, 1889), p. 324.

54. Helen Greyson's Roman art teacher is "Flammenti," another image of the fiery, passionate Italian (*Philistines*, p. 107).

55. A common attribute of the southern Italian stereotype (Higham, *Strangers in the Land*, p. 90).

56. Arlacchi, *Mafia, Peasants and Great Estates*, p. 28.

57. Which Ninitta's flair has rescued "from the common-place. A bit of flimsy drapery, begged from some studio, hung over one of the windows; a rude print of the Madonna was pinned to the wall, and under it, on the wooden table, was a bunch of withered flowers" (114). As in *Suburban Sketches*, the Madonna symbolizes the Italian view of religion.

58. Quoted in Mann, *Yankee Reformers in the Urban Age*, p. 4.

59. "While Italian women will receive an American parish visitor with a sweet smile, the next day they will tell the Italian pastor that they thought her

somewhat crazy or at least very peculiar. There is such a chasm between the mentality of simple Italian women and that of the American lady visitor and there is such a strong tendency in the Anglo-Saxon race to enforce its views without much consideration for the views and traditions of the other race, that the results are not lasting" (Enrico C. Sartorio, *Social and Religious Life of Italians in America* [Boston: Christopher Publishing, 1918], republished [Clifton, N.J.: A.M. Kelley, 1974], p. 123).

60. Martellone, *Una Little Italy nell'Atene d'America*, pp. 203n, 487-88. As Allen F. Davis notes, 40 percent (33) of the total number of settlement houses in the United States in 1911 were in Boston (*Spearheads for Reform: The Social Settlements and the Progressive Movement, 1890-1914* [New Brunswick: Rutgers University Press, 1984], p. 268). According to T. J. Jackson Lears, "Among the educated bourgeoisie [at the turn of the century], this quest for 'real life' was the characteristic psychic project of the age. It energized the settlement house movement, as legions of sheltered young people searched in the slums for the intense experience they felt they had been denied at home" ("From Salvation to Self-Realization: Advertising and the Therapeutic Roots of the Consumer Culture, 1880-1930," in Richard Wightman Fox and T. J. Jackson Lears, eds., *The Culture of Consumption* [New York: Pantheon, 1983], p. 10).

61. Martellone, *Una Little Italy nell'Atene d'America*, pp. 237-38.

62. Much of the social work was organized by the Protestant churches of Boston. See Francis D. De Bilio, "Protestant Mission Work among Italians in Boston," dissertation, School of Theology, Boston University, 1949; Antonio Mangano, *Religious Work among Italians in America: A Survey for the Home Missions Council* (New York: Missionary Education Movement of the United States and Canada, 1917). De Bilio writes that "Our view of the American Christian world outside our slum was an extension of our experience with the solicitous American women who made up the *Ladies Auxiliary*, who were in turn the vital connection between the mission and the denomination. Christmas parties were a week or more after Christmas, so that the left-over or discarded Christmas gifts of parties in American churches could be collected and brought to the 'poor mission children'" (p. 165) (cited in Martellone, *Una Little Italy nell'Atene d'America*, p. 452). Not to be outdone, the Italians usually went along to get the presents for their children at Christmas and Easter, but did not change their religion. Since Italians traditionally gave out gifts at the Epiphany (Jan. 6), the fact that they had to wait a week or two after Christmas would have made little difference to them.

63. Martellone, *Una Little Italy nell'Atene d'America*, p. 443.

64. The population of the North End rose from 16,904 in 1880 (perhaps less than 1000 of them Italians) to 18,447 in 1890 and 30,546 in 1900 (when 13,738 are Italian).

65. There is an example of this trope in De Sica's film *Indiscretion of An American Wife* (*Stazione Termini*) (1954) where a married women from

Philadelphia (Jennifer Jones) is tempted into an affair with an Italian
(Montgomery Clift). She asks him whether, if she becomes his wife, he will beat
her, and it appears that at some level the idea arouses her.

66. In two works of art just before World War I, Italian immigrants are the
central interest, and it seems appropriate that those works should be in opera, a
genre in which the Italians were closely associated: *The Padrone* (1912) by
Bates's friend George Whitfield Chadwick, and *The Immigrants* (1914) by
Frederick Shepherd Converse. Regrettably, neither opera has been performed or
even published. Victor Fell Yellin's *Chadwick: Yankee Composer* (Washington
and London: Smithsonian Institution Press, 1990) raises hopes for an
improvement in Chadwick's fortunes, particularly regarding his stage works.
Yellin informs me that a portion of *The Padrone* was performed in a concert
version in the 1960s.

Dean of American composers, Chadwick (1854-1931) wrote one of the first
large-scale musical works portraying Italian immigrants in the United States,
almost prophetically entitled *The Padrone*. Set in Boston's North End in the
"Summer of the Present Day," the opera capitalizes on the verismo style of
Puccini and Mascagni to paints a dark picture of social conditions, exploitation,
immigration politics, and violence. Chadwick submitted *The Padrone* to the
Metropolitan Opera whose managing director Giulio Gatti-Casazza had recently
instituted a policy of staging one new opera by an American composer each
season. Gatti-Casazza turned Chadwick down without explanation, the more
unusual given the composer's eminence. Chadwick made his own inquiries and
later told a friend that Gatti-Casazza "disliked the book because it was a drama
of life among the humble Italians,—and probably too true to life" (Yellin,
Chadwick, p. 211).

What was Gatti-Casazza's motivation? It was not on account of the music
because the prize went (in part, according to Yellin, for political reasons) to
Victor Herbert's *Madeleine*, "theatrical fluff" set in the eighteenth-century salon
of a French actress. Was Gatti-Casazza, a bourgeois "northerner" from Udine,
embarrassed or scandalized by the revelations of sordid life among fellow
Italians, mainly from the south? Or was he trying to protect them and prevent
their image from being further maligned? In the event, Chadwick locked away
his stage masterpiece. Yellin speculates that, at fifty-nine and in failing health,
Chadwick may have wanted to devote his remaining years to his educational
duties and to the promotion of his orchestral works. He never wrote again for the
stage.

The son of a New Hampshire carpenter turned insurance salesman,
Chadwick grew up in the mill town of Lowell, Massachusetts amid crowded
immigrant conditions. His stepmother may have been a mill worker. After study
abroad he returned to Boston, established a career in teaching and composition,
and became director of the New England Conservatory of Music. Yellin writes
that *The Padrone* is a "sympathetic outsider's understanding, far in advance of

its time, of the way cultural forces act on the everyday lives of ordinary people of a specific ethnicity" (p. 212). But when Chadwick wrote *The Padrone*, in some sense he was returning to the scenes of his youth and may have had an "insider's" understanding too. The "completed orchestral score bears all the hallmarks of a noble, viable work," notes Yellin, who praises its "sensitivity to the intimate relationship between the prosody of the words and his musical invention" (p. 73).

The plot of *The Padrone* would do justice to *The Godfather*. Divided into two acts with an orchestral interlude, it tells the story of Marietta, a tambourine girl in the pay of a local *padrone* named Catani. She lives in hope of saving enough money to pay the passage of Marco with whom she is in love. The opening scene is laid in a North End restaurant where Marietta rejects Catani's advances. Vowing revenge, Catani convinces Francesca, Marietta's elder sister who has been spurned by Marco, to denounce Marco to the immigration authorities on a trumped-up charge of abandonment. Marietta's savings would then go for nought and she would be forced to stay in Boston and marry Catani, while Francesca would be free to return to Italy with Marco. After an orchestral interlude, act two takes place at the Boston docks where Marco is about to land. Three choruses interact: wealthy Americans returning from a tour of Italy, the new Italian arrivals getting off the boat, and the dockside Italian Americans to welcome them and to celebrate the wedding festivities (Broadhead's categories hold good). Marietta and Marco meet, but Francesca's denunciation succeeds, and he is led back to the ship. In a rage Marietta stabs Catani to death.

"As a dramatic composer," concludes Yellin, "Chadwick advances into the big leagues of continuous lyric drama, the most flexible and theatrical medium before the invention of cinema" (p. 213). Oddly enough, the work that could have been the bridge between the classical American composers and the new generation of young immigrant composers or first-generation Americans was denied a hearing: "The very process of immigration, which *The Padrone* sympathetically examined, was to be the cause of a gap in the continuity of American musical history between older composers of Yankee stock and young modernists, many of whom were first- or second-generation immigrants. As the Yankee 'fathers' tended not to recognize the ethnic (i.e. American) legitimacy of the upstart 'sons,' the sons, in turn, denied their musical 'parents' the usual filial affection and respect and even, at times, their existence." Unpublished, *The Padrone* could not influence the next generation(s) of American opera composers: George Gershwin, Virgil Thomson, Marc Blitzstein, and Gian-Carlo Menotti. "When the American style was demanded during the New Deal days, it had to be reinvented" (p. 218). In his review of Yellin's book (*TLS* 26 Oct.-1 Nov. 1990: 1154), Wilfrid Mellers writes that "On the strength of [*The Padrone*]—dealing with low, modern American life—it would seem that Chadwick had the aptitude and technique to have anticipated Menotti": it is "a major opera of genius like Gershwin's *Porgy and Bess*."

Frederick Shepherd Converse (1871-1940) was another "Yankee" composer engrossed by the saga of the immigrants. According to Robert Joseph Garafolo ("The Life and Works of Frederick Shepherd Converse, 1871-1940 [diss., Catholic University of America, Washington, D. C., 1969], pp. 66-68), Converse visited Naples in 1909 and was "moved by the plight of the Italians emigrating to America." Three years later he began composing *The Immigrants*, with a libretto by Percy MacKaye. Its original title appears to have been "The Emigrants"; the change indicates that Converse had decided to establish the viewpoint in the United States rather than the land of departure. He finished the work in 1914 and submitted it unsuccessfully to the Los Angeles Prize Contest. Meanwhile, Henry Russell wrote Converse that he would arrange to have the work reviewed by Gatti-Casazza and Cleofonte Campanini at the Metropolitan. Gatti-Casazza had produced his *The Pipe of Desire* in 1910 (the first opera by an American at the Metropolitan), but "it appears as though the Metropolitan Opera Company was unwilling or unable to produce these works [*Beauty and the Beast* and *The Immigrants*]." The Boston Opera Company, with which Converse was associated, went into bankruptcy in 1914 after five seasons, thereby dashing any hopes that the opera would find an audience.

67. William Foote Whyte was often a guest at Langone's home when he was conducting research for *Street Corner Society* (Langone's father appears as the political figure "George Ravello"). Yet Langone rankles defensively: "What his book did to the North End was to make it look like everybody was in some kind of racket." But Whyte was treating only one segment of North End life and did not examine the role of women, the family, health, education, or religion. Besides, far from being wholly negative, Whyte recognized in his corner boys the virtues of friendship, solidarity, fair-mindedness, patriotism and community. Still, he inaccurately referred to the North End as a "slum" (Fred Langone, *The North End: Where It All Began* [Boston: *Post-Gazette*, American Independence Edition, 1994], p. 20). See also Whyte's memoir "My Friend, Angelo Ralph Orlandella," *Italian Americana*, 13, no. 2 (1995): 166-176, and Orlandella's contribution in the same issue.

68. Whitehill, *Boston: A Topographical History*, pp. 195-96.

69. Whitehill, *Boston: A Topographical History*, pp. 201-202, 274.

Chapter 17

Mater Dolorosa No More? Mothers and Writers in Italian American Literary Tradition

Mary Jo Bona
Gonzaga University

> She muttered and sobbed as she plodded
> blindly on. . . . This one was even saying
> the same crazy stuff, about "my son, my son."
> It must be catching.
>
> Dorothy Bryant,
> *A Day in San Francisco* (1982)

> I have seen them wrap their souls
> around their children
> and serve their own hearts
> in a meal they never share.
>
> Gianna Patriarca, "Italian Women,"
> from *Italian Women and Other
> Tragedies* (1994)

The epigraphs that begin this essay examine the position of mothers of Italian ancestry, women who traditionally define themselves according to the needs of their families. Writers such as Dorothy Bryant and Gianna Patriarca enliven one of the most persistent images of Italian cultural history and Western iconography: the figure of the *mater dolorosa*, the eternally suffering and beseeching mother.[1] In their works, these writers neither reduce Italian women to a stereotypical image of a suffering servant nor exclude that image as a vital and complex aspect of their identity. Exploring the relationship between Italian women's role and definition within *la famiglia* and the figure of Mary, one of whose manifestations is in the role of the *mater dolorosa*, reveals an insistent social reality for women from Southern Italian culture. Italian Americans of second and third generation also continue to be fascinated by this image, incorporating, negotiating, and interrogating the figure of the pining mother in poetry and in fictional narratives.

Pietro Di Donato's *Christ in Concrete* (1939) remains one of the most provocative novels from a second-generation Italian American. His depiction of the mother in this novel seems traditional enough until Di Donato reaches the conclusion of the narrative, where he reverses the role of the grieving suppliant in a surprisingly unconventional way. Although not known nearly as well as Di Donato, Mari Tomasi, also a second-generation Italian American, wrote compellingly about an Italian immigrant mother in her 1949 novel, *Like Lesser Gods*. Tomasi expanded the traditional role of the *mater dolorosa* by attributing to the mother characteristics traditionally reserved to men: aggressiveness, stoicism, and strength. An analysis of Di Donato's *Christ in Concrete* alongside Tomasi's *Like Lesser Gods* reveals each author's attempt to integrate the cultural image of the *mater dolorosa* with the actual conditions of living in a strange and harsh American environment. In doing so, both Di Donato and Tomasi give dimension to their fictional Italian immigrant women, whose role in America is often determined by their cultural identities as sorrowful mothers.

Second-generation writers such as Di Donato and Tomasi introduced the Italian family to American readers in portrayals that emphasized the centrality of the immigrant mother's role. Recent writers continue to represent mothers in the family, but in doing so, they often oppose or challenge features that are fundamental to the image of the *mater dolorosa*. Two third-generation Italian American writers, Tony Ardizzone and Rita Ciresi, create narratives that self-consciously incorporate mother figures who belie basic features of the *mater dolorosa*. Like Di Donato, Tony Ardizzone at first seems more conventional than his female contemporary, Rita Ciresi. Yet a close reading of his story "Nonna" (1986) reveals the ways in which the author himself grieves over the often damaging expectations placed on women in Italian families. Rita Ciresi's "Mother Rocket" (1993) creates a fictional *mater dolorosa* who shocks as much as she delights. While Di Donato and Ardizzone represent seemingly conventionalized versions of the suffering mother, Tomasi and Ciresi more directly oppose the concept at the beginning of their narratives, recreating an image of the mother that suits the highly particularized personalities of their female characters. To examine the relationship between the role of Italian women in the family and the image of the suffering mother, I offer below a brief overview of the cultural definitions of the *mater dolorosa* which sheds light on the ways in which these writers manipulate such meanings in their prose.

Images and Definitions of the *Mater Dolorosa*

In *Protocols of Reading*, Robert Scholes analyzes a 1972 photograph, taken by W. Eugene Smith, of a Japanese mother gazing at the misshapen face and deformed body of her daughter as she bathes her in a square bath tub. Disturbing and painful to view, the picture is "firmly and terribly grounded in history," as Smith was photographing victims of mercury poisoning in Japan. Scholes warns that it would be an error to read the photograph *only* as a document of the ravages of industrial pollution, as effective as a "work of agitation and propaganda" it was (25). Instead, Scholes believes that the photographer knew what he was looking for "because he knew one of the most persistent and elaborate linkages of image and concept in our cultural history: the iconographic code of the *pieta*: the image of the *mater dolorosa*, holding in her arms the mutilated body of her crucified child" (26).[2]

Crossing cultures, continents, and historical periods, the image of the wounded child draped over her grieving mother's knees has a five-thousand-year-old history. Analyzing the polyvalent figure of Mary in *Alone of All Her Sex: The Myth and the Cult of the Virgin Mary,* Marina Warner explains that throughout the centuries Mary has assumed various roles: Virgin, Queen, Bride, Mother, and Intercessor. Her manifestation as *mater dolorosa* has its roots in one of the world's oldest surviving literatures—"the liturgies of Sumer, written around 3000 B.C." (208). As Warner explains, five thousand years ago, in southern Mesopotamia during the scorching month of August, the priests invoked the annual liturgies of Dumuzi, the shepherd, and Inanna, the queen of heaven, his mother and bride. Sacrificed and tortured by underworld demons, Dumuzi suffers just as Christ suffers the tortures of his passion. Inanna, the goddess, weeps for him: "O the agony she bears,/shuddering in the wilderness,/she is the mother suffering so much." The words of the goddess, Warner argues, "could be a poem on a Christian icon of the Pieta: the dead Christ laid out on his grieving mother's knees" (206). Warner traces the beginnings of the suffering mother from ancient times to modernity, suggesting a shared interest in a more passionate and immediate form of worship, which the *mater dolorosa* embodies.

The cult of the *mater dolorosa* in fact begins "to rise in Italy, France, England, the Netherlands, and Spain from the end of the eleventh century to reach full flowering in the fourteenth" (Warner, 210).[3] Warner attributes the "spontaneous vernacular character that the cult of the mourning mother acquired" to the creation of the Franciscans, who preached the gospel to the illiterate and impoverished through the language of drama and image (210). In doing so, they dramatized the Stations of the Cross, a cycle of meditations that recreated Mary's participation in her son's Passion. While the Synoptic gospels do not present Mary in any stage of Christ's journey to Calvary, the friars in Europe reanimated Mary's participation in the *Via Dolorosa*, producing a series of stories contained in the Stations of the Cross, and in paintings and sculptures. What remains essential to Mary's role in the Passion is "the intense belief in the mother and son's communion . . . which always seeks out a parallel to Christ's life in hers, [and which] made her Calvary the nodal point of his Passion" (Warner, 211).

What continues to undergird the Virgin's importance to practicing Catholics in modern Christendom is her ubiquitous "participation in mankind's [sic] ordinary, painful lot; . . . the Virgin retained the common touch" (Warner, 216). Even though the Church carries the rider that Christ himself is the only savior, the only redeemer, the only mediator, Warner relates the popular sentiment, "expressed independently of theology," which recognizes that Jesus could not have been born a man without his mother, thus according "Mary a crucial place in the economy of salvation."[4]

No expression more precisely captures the role of Southern Italian women than the "economy of salvation," for both in practical and in moral terms, Italian mothers were essential to their family's survival in an impoverished land. Recognizing the inviolate nature of the role of Italian women within the family simultaneously requires an awareness of their often profoundly intimate connection to the Madonna.[5] As Barolini states, "the woman's role and definition in the family was gained through the strong cult of the Madonna—the Holy Mother who prefigured all other mothers and symbolized them" (1985, 9). Understanding the difficult life of Southern Italian women provides a way of reading the narratives of Italian American writers contextually, that is, as part of a larger cultural and social fabric.

The Role of Southern Italian Mothers

In her role of succoring the bereaved, the *mater dolorosa* also shares their sorrow, a role that the Southern Italian woman was expected to perform for her family, the one abiding and stable social reality in a life of constant impoverishment, few resources, and political oppression in the *Mezzogiorno*. While nominally Roman Catholic, the peasants of Southern Italy and Sicily regularly expressed a faith that embraced popular belief rather than church doctrine. As religious as they were, the sentiments of the contadini were enclosed "within the spirit of *campanilismo* [village-mindedness]," as Rudolph Vecoli explains: "Each village had its own array of madonnas, saints, and assorted spirits to be venerated, propitiated, or exorcised. . . . God, like the King, was a distant, unapproachable figure, but the local saints and madonnas, like the landlords, were the real personages whose favor was of vital importance" (228).[6] For peasant women, whose responsibility to the family was central, the Marian cult became interwoven within their roles as the "all-forgiving, all-protecting" Madonna. As Ann Cornelisen puts it, "Women can identify immediately with the all-suffering Mother. . . . Much as the Vatican may deplore it, in the South Christ is on the altar, but the people pray to and worship the Virgin Mary" (27).[7]

If it was believed in the *Mezzogiorno* that the Virgin Mary stood "as the highest ideal of Christian womanhood," then peasant women were required to approximate that ideal within the context of marriage and motherhood (Williams, 82). As Cornelisen points out, however, peasant mothers were seldom able "to carry the weight of total responsibility," in representing the ideal Madonna (27). Nonetheless, girl children were early apprenticed by their Italian mothers and instructed in lessons on their future roles as the economic and cultural sustainers of the family.

Because the family was the only institution that could be trusted in a land where natural conditions were as fierce as political oppression, women's function as mothers and keepers of the household was all the more valued. In *Blood of My Blood*, Richard Gambino describes the role of Southern Italian women as one requiring *serieta*, seriousness, "life-supporting qualities" in a land ravished by *miseria* (miserable poverty) (148-149).

When they came to America, Italian women saw their role modified and transformed by the economic and social values of the new country. Nonetheless, immigrant mothers often remained on the margins of the assimilative process and as a result created "a cultural universe in their homes and neighborhoods that was made out of the values and principles of their own world" (Ewen, 203). In describing the reaction of first-generation mothers to their new environment of tenement houses, Elizabeth Ewen deliberately employs elegiac language to express their "feelings of alienation and unfamiliarity": "The loss of sunshine was . . . an image of mourning for a world left behind, a plaintive moan of entry into the unknown" (62).[8] Such language reinforces the role of immigrant women as sorrowful mothers, in this case, grieving the loss of their homeland, which they cradle in their memories.

Although the maternal authority of the immigrant generation was not necessarily diminished in America, the position of Italian mothers as women of *serieta* was not unilaterally maintained in the new world.[9] As much as they were idealized in their motherly role, Italian women were also constrained if not trapped by the image of the always beneficent, always suffering mother. As Andrew Rolle explains, the image of the Italian mother was "overwhelmed by a masculine mystique. The Madonna had been a mother but scarcely a wife. Accordingly, the Italian woman has historically reduced the power and importance of sexuality by accepting a *mater dolorosa* role" (111). In addition, other sources such as interviews and fictional representations of Italian mothers have strongly asserted that such roles were often reductive and damaging, especially when the Italian women tried to transmit those ideals to their Americanized daughters.[10] Implicit in the definition of the *mater dolorosa* is self-nullification, a sacrificing of any potential unrelated to the succoring and sorrowful role. At the same time, the image of the mother of sorrows has been both provocative and challenging for Italian American writers, many of whom invoke that role in order to incorporate its meanings into a twentieth-century context.

Italian American Writers: Reimagining *Mater Dolorosa*

Pietro Di Donato's *Christ in Concrete* and Mari Tomasi's *Like Lesser Gods* articulate the second generation's response to the Italian family's adjustment to American society. Although they obviously differed in their opinions about American values, both authors fictionalized with compassion and depth the immigrant mother's difficult, if not tragic, relationship to American culture. In doing so, Di Donato and Tomasi offer images of the mater dolorosa that both expand and reconsider traditional meanings.

Pietro Di Donato's autobiographical first novel, *Christ in Concrete*, became a best-seller that was chosen over Steinbeck's *Grapes of Wrath* as a main selection of the 1939 book-of-the-month club.[11] The quintessential *mater dolorosa* figure, Annunziata, the mother of Paul and seven other children, is presented as the suffering widow. Her husband, Geremio, was literally buried alive under concrete at a construction site where he worked. Paul, the eldest child, whose voice is central to Di Donato's novel, takes up trowel and climbs dangerous scaffolds, replacing his father as *paterfamilias*. After he enters the workaday world, Paul begins seriously to challenge his mother's piety, which he ultimately believes oppresses immigrants by encouraging them to accept poverty as their fate. After witnessing the gruesome and avoidable death of his godfather at the end of the novel, Paul loses his faith. Refusing to live any longer in ignorance of his oppression, Paul crushes the cross that Annunziata later places in his hands, a violent gesture which thereafter ushers in his mother's death.

Although she is shocked and dismayed to observe her beloved son destroying the cross, Annunziata's first reaction is, in fact, just the opposite of the traditionally swooning supplicant: she attacks her son, catches him by the throat, and "with a heart-ripping cry [she] thrust him to the wall beating his face hysterically and screaming, 'Out! Out! The Lord's Paul is no more! . . . My sainted son is dead!'" (231). Repeatedly punching her stomach, Annunziata thinks to herself "Fruit of this belly have I devoured" (231). Such behavior does not overtly recall the Christian mother, but it certainly recalls the pre-christian mother described by Warner as the "all-devouring savage goddess of myth" (221). At the same time, Di Donato invokes the Christian mother who avidly gazes upon the features of her son because she mourns her loss (Warner, 221). Unlike the devouring goddess of pre-christianity, however, who sacrifices a substitute to the powers of darkness to save herself, Annunziata sacrifices herself in order to save her son.

What follows is a depiction of Annunziata's Passion, which becomes a determining force in Paul's life. The final scene is conventional insofar as it depicts mother and son as mutual sufferers. As Adrienne Rich writes in *Of Woman Born* "whether in theological doctrine or art or sociology or psychoanalytic theory, it is the mother and son who appear as the eternal, determinative dyad" (226).[12] However, Di Donato also reverses the positions of mother and son, thereby transforming the traditional conception of the *mater dolorosa*: it is Annunziata who dies and her son who holds her as she sings her death lament, crooning a final lullaby for Paul and her soon-to-be orphaned children: "'Little Paul my own/Whose Jesu self/Glorified our home/. . . . Children wonderful . . . love ever our Paul. Follow him'" (236). As Fred Gardaphe explains in the introduction to *Christ in Concrete*, the image that readers are left with is an "inversion of the *Pieta* in which son is holding a mother . . . [who hails] her son as a new Christ, one that her children should follow. But this haunting image also suggests that it is the mother who has become the new Christ, who in witnessing what America has done to her son, dies and through her death frees her son from the burden of his Catholic past" (xv).[13] Annunziata's position as the new Christ in fact liberates her from the passivity inherent in the traditional role of the grieving mother who watches helplessly the crucifixion of her son. In her new role, Annunziata allows her son to live by a new dispensation, in which salvation is individual and not determined by organized religion. Despite the fact that Annunziata is often depicted throughout Di Donato's novel as frail and ultimately capitulating to the other world, the final scene reverses the positions of mother and son in the Passion: Annunziata is the blood-offering; her son, Paul, the principle of the abiding earth (Warner, 221). At the same time, Di Donato's final scene reinforces one of the preeminent images of the Passion: the tragedy and dissolution of a loving family (Warner, 217).

Gardaphe rightly contends that Di Donato's portrayal of Annunziata is much more subversive than has been previously recognized (1996, 69). However, Annunziata's status as an immigrant mother and a widow problematizes her radically reenvisioned status. Di Donato portrays Annunziata as decidedly powerless because of her status as an immigrant woman in capitalistic American society, despite the solidarity among the Italians in the community. Helen Barolini's description of the Italian mother in America focuses on this kind of attenuated status: "Not able to Americanize on the spot, the immigrant woman suffered instant obsolescence (an American invention), and became an anachronism, a displaced person, a relic of a remote rural village culture" (13). That Annunziata dies young (at thirty-five) reinforces her inability to effect change for herself or her family *and* still live in the world. That she is a "widow," a term that Adrienne Rich reminds us means "without," places her in a category of "pure negation" (249). Although it seems inconceivable to suspect a newly widowed mother of eight to be a bearer of evil (in Italian culture, a bestower of *il mal'occhio*), Annunziata's status as a widow makes her a candidate for such a role.[14] To maintain her sacred status as the all-good mother, Annunziata functions both as a *mater dolorosa* figure and the savior of her son. Uniting both images in *Christ in Concrete*, Di Donato at the same time must sacrifice the actual woman, Annunziata.

Mari Tomasi's second novel, *Like Lesser Gods*, tells a different story.[15] The author introduces a model of *serieta* in the character of Maria, the pragmatic and assertive mother of the Dalli family. Maria's husband, Pietro, a carver in the Vermont granite industry, works in closed sheds, which contributes to the tuberculo-silicosis from which he eventually dies. Unlike Annunziata, who prays to a merciful God to protect her husband at dangerous work sites, Maria expects of herself the command and foresight to effect change for the better. Maria's abiding concern for her husband's health stems from what Michael Gold has called "female realism": she is concerned for her children's welfare.[16] Receiving a regular pay envelope from her husband is necessary to maintain the family's economy. As deeply as she loves her husband, Maria defies his artistic predilections in order to save her family from economic and personal ruin.

To ensure that Pietro quits his job at the stone quarries, Maria takes matters literally into her own hands by sneaking into the stonecutters' shed at night and destroying Pietro's nearly finished carving of a cross. She genuinely desires to save her beloved husband from a crucifixion, but her violence against the stone is so savage and passionate that Pietro's employer cannot mistake it for an accident. Rather than vent her anger on those whom she loves (and risk losing the only role she possesses—her position as mother and protector), Maria takes arms against the unreasoning stone. In contrast to her husband, who regards stonecutting as sacred artistry—stonecutters memorialize life like lesser gods—Maria does not have the luxury of perceiving carving from an artist's perspective. Stripped from aesthetic value, Maria's attitude toward stone remains pragmatic. Maria's rash action fails her: Pietro never quits the stonesheds. Nor does he discover whose hand savagely vandalized his greatest work to date.

Maria's role as *mater dolorosa* is envisioned by Tomasi in ways uniquely different from Di Donato's portrayal of Annunziata. Like Mary of the gospels, Maria Dalli silently ponders her troubles in her heart. Never once does she function as the pining and inconsolable mother. Maria's sexuality is never reduced in favor of accepting the role of *mater dolorosa*. In fact, Tomasi clearly intends for her reader to know that the Dalli couple enjoys each other sexually, and despite disagreements about Pietro's vocation, both husband and wife love each other passionately (15, 27-28). Tomasi endows Maria's character with sacred and aesthetic resonance as the narrative advances, connecting her less to an image of the *Pieta* and more to an image of Mary firmly rooted in the world.

Like Mary of spontaneous vernacular character created by the Franciscans, Maria Dalli participates in her husband's suffering and death. On the way to the sanatorium, where Pietro lives his final days, Maria and her eldest daughter, Petra, walk on either side of Pietro, holding his arms. Tomasi, like Di Donato before her, employs the language of the Passion to suggest a connection between Jesus Christ and the immigrants, who suffered and died excruciating deaths. Tomasi describes the *Via Dolorosa* in the walk to the sanatorium as Pietro's final "plodding to his Calvary" (220). Like the Mary depicted in the Stations of the Cross, Maria Dalli is not only beside the suffering Pietro on his way to Calvary, but she staunches his wounds and watches his body take flight over the "hills of northern Italy" (257).

Before dying, Pietro's final thoughts focus on his wife's strength and determination, and he compares her to the permanence of stone: "he was proud of her. As strong and as unflinching as granite she was" (256). It is no coincidence that Tomasi refers to Da Vinci's role at the Carrara quarries, mentioning specifically the artist's painting of the *Madonna of the Rocks*, connecting Maria with the mother of mothers. Although she grieves for the death of her husband, Maria leads the family, like Paul in *Christ in Concrete*, into a healthy future. Maria's role as *mater dolorosa* is ultimately transformed by the marvelous symbol of granite that unifies the novel and its characters. As Alfred Rosa astutely points out, like the ice of Walden Pond that is cut from the top and sent all over the world, the granite not only "celebrates a region," but is artistically "tooled into sculptures that are unique in the mixture of boldness and mysticism they reflect" (Afterword, 297). Maria Dalli may very well be the silently suffering mother, but she is also the strongly capable immigrant woman, who continues to act effectively for her family. Tomasi's dedication to writing a novel out of the tradition of realism may very well have allowed her to portray the mother as an active participant in matters of daily living. As a result, Tomasi expands the definition of the *mater dolorosa* by portraying a suffering mother, who continues to love and work in order to maintain the coherence of family life in America after the tragedy of her husband's death.

The second-generation writers, represented here by Di Donato and Tomasi, depicted immigrant families struggling to survive their early years in a new world. *Christ in Concrete* and *Like Lesser Gods* are family narratives that emphasize the development of the children of immigrants, who are influenced as much by their suffering mothers as they are by American cultural values. Writers from the third generation continue to concern themselves with the fate of the Italian family in America, though their narratives at times depict an attenuated family status and communities in dispersal. In particular, Tony Ardizzone and Rita Ciresi incorporate the image of the *mater dolorosa* in order to explore its dire implications on the women characters that they fictionalize.[17] Both authors examine how this image influences the internal perceptions of women who are haunted by specific occurrences in their past. Both writers critique and ultimately enlarge the meaning of the suffering mother, offering an inventive recreation of this figure in Italian American literature.

"Nonna," the concluding story in Tony Ardizzone's collection, *The Evening News* (1986), features the internal ruminations of an elderly Italian American woman as she walks around a neighborhood that has undergone wholesale dismantling: the Little Italy of Chicago's West side.[18] Throughout her reflective journey down the streets of her changing neighborhood, Nonna reveals the primary reason that underlies her ongoing torment: the fact that she was unable throughout her married life to conceive children. Despite the explanation of the doctors who told her that not she, but her husband was infertile, Nonna ceaselessly punishes herself for her "barrenness," blaming it on her sexual indiscretion with Vincenzo before they were married. As Harriet Perry explains in her essay on female honor, the main task of a good Italian immigrant wife is to become pregnant: "the female is not fully a woman until she is a wife, and not fully a wife until she is a mother" (229). Throughout her long life, Nonna has internalized cultural definitions of womanhood, which regard the childless woman as "a failed woman, unable to speak for the rest of her sex, and omitted from the hypocritical and palliative reverence accorded the mother" (Rich, 251). A widow for many years, Nonna roams the streets, creating stories about the neighborhood people, revealing her unabated grief about being unable to bear children. After deciding that the long-haired girl behind the counter of a local bookstore is actually praying to the Madonna for children, Nonna remembers all the novenas she made and prayers she said to the saints, but to no avail. In frustration, Nonna thinks, "And even God knows that each woman deserves her own baby. Didn't he even give the Virgin a son?" (151). The fact that Nonna recalls the Virgin reaffirms her own connection to the role of a *mater dolorosa*. Moreover, Nonna's reference to Mary's status as a virgin reinforces her belief in the miraculous nature of creation itself.

Ardizzone's portrayal of Nonna ultimately reconfirms her own role as a creator, in her case as a storyteller, a voice of a community that has been obliterated. She is able not only to speak for her sex, but for her community at large. Nonna remains in the neighborhood that has been drastically reduced in size, the Italian community scattering to other places. Thinking that "her punishment was nearly over," Nonna's afternoon walk through the streets recalls a *Via Dolorosa* as she weeps for her motherless state and for the state of the Italian community that has been buried and reduced to rubble in the name of urban renewal. Her final gesture of purchasing Mexican flat breads in the Mexican grocery store reveals her symbolic recognition that she no longer needs the yeast of the Speranza Bakery to know that "perhaps bread is just as good this way" (161). That she is called Nonna (grandmother) throughout the story connects her ineluctably to motherhood; as Warner contends, "a woman who weeps always becomes, in the very act, a mother" (223). Ardizzone simultaneously critiques and alters the image of the *mater dolorosa*, endowing Nonna with the authority to reconsider her status.

Rita Ciresi is similarly concerned with the ability of one of her female characters to reconsider her past. Her book of stories, *Mother Rocket* (1993), includes both an absurd and a grotesque rendering of the sorrowful mother figure in her title story "Mother Rocket." Her protagonist, Jude Silverman, is a Jewish American whose cultural identity unceasingly torments and defines her. After her parents accidently electrocute themselves in the bathtub, her Aunt Mina and Uncle Chaim adopt her, and eventually take her to Israel where they intend to move. After arguing with her pious, "so Old World" aunt and uncle about moving to the sacred homeland, Jude flees the Jerusalem cafe where they are having breakfast. Later on, her Aunt and Uncle nearly catch up with Jude, but they are killed by an explosion that blows glass and furniture out into the street. This memory stifles, defines, and determines much of Jude Silverman's behavior when she returns to New York to a career as a dancer in the modern troupe called Future/Dance/Theater, a name that ironically contrasts with Jude's obsessive devotion to the past.

That she suffers from the horrifying memory of watching her Aunt Mina and Uncle Chaim get blown to pieces in an explosion in Jerusalem in 1967 is reflected regularly in Jude's perverse humor and maudlin emphasis on her tragic self. Jude's cultural identity and her ties to the Holy Land threaten to extinguish any possibility for future change. What freezes Jude's sense of herself, interestingly, leads to a Pulitzer Prize winning photograph that features Jude kneeling on the cobblestones, "surrounded by blood. . . . In her arms Jude cradled the man's amputated arm, which . . . bore the tiny blue tattoo of numbers that branded inmates of concentration camps" (61). Years later, Jude's husband, also a photographer (who envies the award-winning photo), describes the famous picture as "bogus," full of "symbolic pathos" (61). But like Smith's deliberate decision to photograph Tomoko in the bath with her mother, the photographer in the Jerusalem street highlighted an image that crosses cultural and religious boundaries. In other words, both photographers—historical and fictional—knew what they were looking for: the iconographic code of the *Pieta*. Ciresi, like Di Donato, reverses the position of parent and child, as the niece cradles the mutilated remains of her crucified uncle, doubly reinforced by his status as a Jew and a concentration-camp survivor.

As a result of this experience, Jude Silverman risks becoming the *mater dolorosa in extremis*, since she faithfully believes that "she wasn't anything, she wasn't anybody, without all that behind her" (69). However, instead of sacrificing herself in order to erase the burden of her cultural past, Jude Silverman reinvents herself by the end of the narrative, freeing herself from her earlier conviction that she "was born to die." Instead, Jude has a baby. The conclusion of the story does not recapitulate to sacrificially laden motherhood, but rather offers a realization that motherhood is liberating and frees Jude from self-loathing and her obsession with the past. In fact, Jude reinvests the evils of nuclear warfare encapsulated by the term *Die mutterrakete* (the mother rocket) by applying the term to herself, aware of the life-enhancing beauty inherent in giving birth. Becoming a mother saves Jude from a cloying and histrionic performance she plays as the hyperbolic *mater dolorosa*.

Ciresi, like Ardizzone, reconsiders the meaning of the sorrowful mother in terms other than that of the traditional Italian American mother within the confines of *la famiglia*. As a result, these writers are invoking the role in order to move beyond the traditional narrative of sorrowful mother and crucified son, though all the writers discussed in this essay are decidedly indebted to this image. Ardizzone, like Di Donato, seems to portray a traditional Italian American woman, but ultimately complicates her character by endowing her with characteristics that verge on the mystical. In contrast, Ciresi's narrative, like Tomasi's, begins with a female character who directly confronts the image of the sorrowful mother, and ultimately chooses not to wear the mantle of suffering suppliant. Motherhood for Tomasi's Maria and Ciresi's Jude means living actively and responsively in a world that has taken away so much from them.

Other writers in the Italian American literary tradition likewise incorporate and reimagine the mother's role in modern American culture, reinforcing her significance as a shaper and creator of family and community structures. Such works include Emanuel Carnevali's *The Autobiography of Emanuel Carnevali*, John Fante's *The Wine of Youth*, Carole Maso's *Ghost Dance*, Denise Giardina's *Storming Heaven*, and Renee Manfredi's *Where Love Leaves Us*. In each of these narratives, the writers include images of the sorrowful mother, whose laments resonate within the larger narrative of the story. For example, a fascinating re-interpretation of this image can be found in Carole Maso's *Ghost Dance* and Renee Manfredi's *Where Love Leaves Us* in which Italian American fathers assume the role of the grieving suppliant. A fuller analysis of the father's role in the Italian American family as represented in these texts compels a reconsideration of the complicated nature of the ethnic family in America.

Fathers, too, are portrayed as plodding blindly on, grieving for the death of what they perceive to be the culture of *italianita*: customs and rituals specific to the local villages from which they or their parents emigrated. The recurring image of the *mater dolorosa* may very well symbolize the Italian American writer's allegiance to an insistent social reality not only for the women in the family, but for the Italian-descended family at large. By recalling the image of the suffering mother (father, grandparents, children), Italian American writers simultaneously examine the fate of the Italian American family. What they find there is undoubtedly as various and complicated as analyzing any contemporary American family, but the recurring image of the *mater dolorosa* is grounded in a religious and cultural history rich in meaning. Writers probing the intersection between the *mater dolorosa* and the Italian family in America have produced works of literature that create as much as they reveal ideas about the relationship between nurturing and suffering. In doing so, these writers construct themselves and their relationship to Italian American identity, creating texts of nuance and beauty that assume resonance and depth when read alongside other texts and contexts.

Notes

1. Dorothy Bryant, an Italian American, primarily writes novels; Gianna Patriarca, an Italian Canadian, published her first book of poetry in 1994. Other poets from the Italian American literary tradition examine and interrogate the image of the suppliant mother in their poetry: see Rose Romano's "Praises of the Madonna," in *The Wop Factor* (malafemmina press, 1994); several poems in Romano's edition *la bella figura: a choice (malafemmina press, 1993)*; and Jean Feraca's "Nursing My Child through His First Illness," in *Crossing the Great Divide* (Madison: Wisconsin Academy of Sciences, 1992). References to other fiction writers will be made in the text.

2. In *Protocols of Reading* (New Haven, Conn.: Yale University Press, 1989), Scholes reproduces W. Eugene Smith's photograph of *Tomoko in the Bath.*

3. It is not surprising to learn that one of the most popular poems of fourteenth-century Italy was the "Passion of Our Lord Jesus Christ," which, Warner explains, "paints the Passion as the private tragedy of a loving family" (217). In fact, *cantastorie* (storytellers, history singers) were employed to recount the tale of the Passion, and such popular invocations slowly seeped into the rule-laden established church.

4. In *Black Madonnas: Feminism, Religion, & Politics in Italy*, Lucia Chiavola Birnbaum explains that in Italian vernacular belief Easter is celebrated "not as the resurrection of the son, but the son rejoining his mother on Sunday afternoon *outside* the Church" (italics, mine). Modeled on the ritual of the giunta (reunion), Easter was a day for "peacemaking" (141, 142).

5. For a good overview of the mother's centrality within the family and her connection to the Madonna see Colleen L. Johnson's "The Maternal Role in the Contemporary Italian American Family," in *The Italian Immigrant Woman in North America* (Toronto: The Multicultural History Society of Ontario, 1978): 234-244.

6. See also Phyllis Williams's chapter "Religion and Superstition," in *South Italian Folkways in Europe and America* (New York: Russell & Russell, 1938): 135-159.

7. As Leonard Covello notes, "if the personality of Jesus was, in the Roman Catholic Church, subordinate to that of the Madonna, it was in southern Italy, almost entirely eclipsed by the worship of the Madonna and the innumerable saints. . . . Just as, pictorially, Jesus (as child) is overshadowed by his mother the Madonna, so in the sentiments of the peasants, the chief deity of the Christian Trinity is the Madonna." In *The Social Background of the Italo-American School Child* (Leiden: E. J. Brill, 1967): 120-121.

8. For another essay that describes in detail the unrelieved lives of drudgery for Italian immigrant women see Valentine Rossilli Winsey's "The Italian Immigrant Women Who Arrived in the United States Before World War I," in *Studies in Italian American Social History: Essays in Honor of Leonard Covello*, ed. Francesco Cordasco (Totowa, N.J.: Rowman and Littlefield, 1975): 199-210.

9. As Barolini writes in her introduction to *The Dream Book*, "the Old World Family style and mother role developed in response to la miseria are no longer relevant in a democratic society nor tolerated in affluence" (13). For an anthropological interpretation of the changing material conditions and personal values of Italian American families, see Micaela di Leonardo's *The Varieties of Ethnic Experience: Kinship, Class, and Gender among California Italian Americans* (Ithaca, N.Y.: Cornell University Press, 1984).

10. Besides the already cited article by Valentine Rossilli Winsey and Elizabeth Ewen's book (which is replete with interviews from Jewish and Italian mothers and daughters), see also Robert Orsi's chapter

"Conflicts in the Domus" in *The Madonna of 115th Street: Faith and Community in Italian Harlem, 1880-1950* (New Haven: Yale University Press, 1985): 107-149; and Connie A. Maglione's and Carmen Anthony Fiore's interviews in *Voices of the Daughters* (Princeton, N.J.: Townhouse Publishing, 1989). References to fictional representations will be made in the essay.

11. *Christ in Concrete* was reprinted in 1993 (New York: Penguin) with a preface by Studs Terkel and an introduction by Fred L. Gardaphe. All citations in the essay refer to this text.

12. Two chapters in Rich's *Of Woman Born* are useful to an analysis of the mother-son relationship portrayed in Di Donato's novel: Chapter VIII, "Mother and Son, Woman and Man" and Chapter IX, "Motherhood and Daughterhood."

13. See also Gardaphe's analysis of Di Donato's novels in *Italian Signs, American Streets: The Evolution of Italian American Narrative* (Durham: Duke University Press, 1996): 66-75.

14. As Lawrence Di Stasi notes in his superb study of the evil eye, those most likely to bestow *il mal'occhio* are the ones outside the regenerative process—widows, childless women, spinsters, priests and monks. See *Mal Occhio: The Underside of Vision* (San Francisco: North Point Press, 1981): 37.

15. Tomasi's first novel, *Deep Grow the Roots* (1940), is set in Northern Italy (the Piedmont) and centers around the tragic love story of two peasants during the Fascist regime. *Like Lesser Gods* is set in a fictionalized Barre, Vermont. It has recently been reprinted by The New England Press (Shelburne, Vermont, 1988). Alfred Rosa writes the Afterword. All citations in the essay refer to this text.

16. As quoted in Elizabeth Ewen's *Immigrant Woman in the Land of Dollars* (New York: Monthly Review Press, 1985), 191.

17. Both Tony Ardizzone and Rita Ciresi write short stories and are winners of the Flannery O'Connor Award for Short Fiction. Ardizzone won the award for *The Evening News* in 1986 and Ciresi won the same award in 1993 for *Mother Rocket*. That they are writing in the same genre and share an interest in the image of the *mater dolorosa* makes for an interesting comparison.

18. Ardizzone's story "Nonna" is included in *From the Margin: Writings in Italian Americana* and in his recently published *Taking It Home: Stories from the Neighborhood* (Urbana: University of Illinois Press, 1996). For a novel-length portrayal of Chicago's Little Italy see

Tina De Rosa's *Paper Fish*, which has been reprinted by The Feminist Press (1996). All citations from "Nonna" are taken from *The Evening News*.

Chapter 18

In Recognition of the Italian American Writer: Definitions and Categories

Anthony Julian Tamburri
Purdue University

For Maria, again

Most men do not think things in the way they encounter them, nor do they recognize what they experience, but believe their own opinions.

Heraclitus

And I thought, "Does this son of a bitch think he is more American than I am?" Where does he think I was brought up? Because my name is Ciardi, he decided to hyphenate the poem. Had it been a Yankee name, he would have thought, "Ah, a scholar who knows about Italy." Sure he made assumptions, but I can't grant for a minute that Lowell is any more American than I am. . . .

John Ciardi, in *Growing Up Italian*

"If every picture I made was about Italian Americans, they'd say, 'That's all he can do.' I'm trying to stretch."

Martin Scorsese, in *Premiere (1991)*

393

Part One—A Premise of Sorts

Ethnic studies in any form or manner—for instance, the use of ethnicity as a primary yardstick—do not necessarily constitute the major answer to filling in knowledge gaps with regard to what some may consider ethnic myopia in the United States. Nevertheless—by now a cliche—we all know that the United States of America was born and developed—at times with tragic results[2]—along lines of diversity. What is important in this regard is that we understand, or at least try to understand, the origins of the diversity and difference which characterize the many ethnic and racial groups which constitute the kaleidoscopic nature of this country's population.[1] Accepting literature as, among many things, the mirror of the society in which it is conceived, created, and perceived, we come to understand that one of the many questions ethnic literature addresses is the negative stereotypes of members of ethnic/racial groups which are not part and parcel of the dominant culture. By ethnic literature, I mean that type of writing which deals, contextually, with customs and behavioral patterns that the North American mind-set may consider different from what it perceives as mainstream. The difference, I might add, may also manifest itself formalistically (i.e., the writer may not follow what have become accepted norms and conventions of literary creation, or s/he may not produce what the dominant culture considers good literature). This last point notwithstanding, one of the goals of ethnic literature is, to be sure, the dislodging and debunking of negative stereotypes. In turn, through the natural dynamics of intertextual recall and inference, the reader engages in a process of analytical inquiry and comparison of the ethnic group(s) in question with other ethnic groups as well as with the dominant culture. In fact, it is precisely through a comparative process that one comes to understand how difference and diversity from one group to another may not be as great as it initially seems; indeed, that such difference and diversity can not only co-exist but may even overlap with that which is considered characteristic of the dominant group. This, I believe, is another of the goals/functions of ethnic literature: to impart knowledge of the customs, characteristics, language, etc. of the various racial and ethnic groups in this country. Finally, partial responsibility for the validity or lack thereof of other[3] literatures also lies with the critic or theorist. In fact, the theorist's end goal for other literatures, perhaps, should not limit itself only to the invention of another mode of reading. Instead, it should become, in itself, a strategy of reading which extends beyond the limits of textual analysis; it should concomitantly, and ultimately, aim for the validation of the text(s) in question vis-à-vis those already validated by the dominant culture.

The fortune of Italian American literature is somewhat reflective of the United States mind-set vis-à-vis ethnic studies. Namely, until recently, ever since the arrival of the immigrants of the 1880s, the major wave of western European emigration, the United States has considered ethnic/racial difference in terms of the melting-pot attitude. The past two decades, however, have constituted a period of transition, if not change, in this attitude. Be it the end of modernism, as some have claimed, be it the onslaught of the postmodern, as others may claim, in academic and/or intellectual circles today, one no longer thinks in terms of the melting pot.[4] Instead, as is well known by most, one now talks in terms of the individual ethnic/racial culture and its relationship—and not necessarily in negative terms only—with the long-standing, mainstream cultural paradigm. It is, therefore, with the backdrop of this new attitude of rejecting the melting pot and supplanting it with the notion of America as a "kaleidoscopic, socio/cultural mosaic," as I have rehearsed it elsewhere,[5] that I shall consider an attempt to (re)define Italian American literature and recategorize the notion of the hyphenate writer. By using the phrase "kaleidoscopic, socio/cultural mosaic," I mean to underscore how the socio/cultural dynamics of the United States reveal a constant flux of changes originating in the very existence of the various differentiated ethnic/racial groups that constitute the overall population of the United States. As an addendum, I would suggest that, as people, we must still come to understand that the population of the United States is indeed similar to that of a mosaic in that this country consists of various bits and pieces (i.e., the various peoples, ethnic and/or racial, of the United States), each one unique unto itself. The kaleidoscopic nature of this aggregate of different and unique peoples is surely descriptive of this constant flux of changes that manifests itself as the various peoples change positions, physical and ideological, which ultimately change the ideological colors of the United States mind-set.

Bouncing off notions immediate to post-colonial literature, of ethnic—or for that matter any other—literature we may indeed state that, first of all, such a notion cannot be constructed as an internally coherent object of theoretical knowledge; that such a categorization "cannot be resolved . . . without an altogether positivist reductionism."[6] Secondly, other "literary traditions [e.g., third world, ethnic, etc.] remain, beyond a few texts here and there, [often] unknown to the American literary theorist" (5). While it may be true that Ahmad's use of the adjective "American" refers to the geopolitical notion of the United States of America, I would contend that the situation of ethnic literatures within the United States is analogous to what Ahmad so adroitly describes in his article on, for lack of a better term, "third-world literature." Thus, I would suggest that we reconsider Ahmad's American within the confines of the geopolitical borders of the United States and thereby reread it as synonymous to dominant culture. Thirdly, "Literary texts are produced in highly differentiated, usually over-determined contexts of competing ideological and cultural clusters, so that any particular text of any complexity shall always have to be placed within the cluster that gives it its energy and form, before it is totalised into a universal category" (23). Thus, it is also within this ideological framework of cluster specificity that I shall consider further the notion of Italian American literature as a validifiable category of United States literature and (re)think the significance of the Italian American writer within the recategorization of the notion of the hyphenate writer.

Finally, I should specify, at the outset, that which I have in mind for the Italian American writer throughout this essay. Because of language plurality—standard Italian, Italian dialect, and United States English[7]—I believe that there are different types of writers that may fall under the general category of Italian American writer. They range from the immigrant writer of Italian language to the United States-born writer of Italian descent who writes in English; and in between, of course, one may surely find the many variations of these two extremes.[8] Here, in the pages that follow, therefore, I shall use the phrase Italian American writer in reference to that person who—be s/he born in the United States or in Italy—is significantly involved in creative literary activity in the English language.[9]

Part Two—Definitions and Categories

The notion for an enterprise of this type is grounded in a slightly unorthodox mode of thought. In this poststructuralist, postmodern society in which we live, my essay therefore casts by the wayside any notion of universality or absoluteness with regard to the (re)definition of any literary category vis-à-vis national origin, ethnicity, race, or gender.

Undoubtedly, one can, and should, readily equate the above-mentioned notion to some general notions associated with the postmodern. Any rejection of validity of the notion of "hierarchy," or better, universality or absoluteness, is characteristic of those who are, to paraphrase Lyotard, "incredul[ous] toward [grand or] metanarratives."[10] Indeed, one of the legitimized and legitimizing grands recits—metanarrative—is the discourse built around the notion of canon valorization. By implicitly constructing an otherwise nonexistent category, or subset, of American letters (i.e., Italian American literature) the notion of a centered canon of the dominant Anglo American culture is rattled once more. Rattled once more precisely because there already exist, fortunately, legitimized—that is, considering the Academy as the legitimizing institution—similar categories such as African American or Jewish American fiction; one need only peruse the list of graduate courses in American and English literature in the various catalogues of most American universities."[11]

In the past, Italian American art forms—more precisely, literature and film—have been defined as those constructed mainly by second-generation writers about the experiences of the first and second generations. In a recent essay on Italian American cinema, for example, Robert Casillo defined it as "works by Italian American directors who treat Italian American subjects."[12] In like fashion, Frank Lentricchia had previously defined Italian American literature as "a report and meditation on first-generation experience, usually from the perspective of a second-generation representative."[13] Indeed, both constitute a valid attempt at constructing neat and clean definitions for works of two art forms—and in a certain sense we can extend this meaning to other art media—that deal explicitly with an Italian American ethnic quality and/or subject matter.[14] Such definitions, however, essentially halt, though willy-nilly by those who offer them, the progress and limit the impact of those writers who come from later generations, and thus may result in a monolithic notion of what was/is and was/is not Italian American literature. Following a similar mode of thinking, Dana Gioia has more recently proposed yet another limiting definition in his brief essay, "What Is Italian American Poetry?"[15] There, Gioia describes "Italian American poetry . . . only as a transitional category" for which the "concept of Italian American poet is therefore most useful to describe first- and second-generation writers raised in the immigrant subculture" (3). Together with his restrictive definition of Italian American poetry, Gioia also demonstrates a seemingly furtive sociological thought pattern in not distinguishing the difference between ethnicity passed from one generation to the next vis-à-vis a member's decision of the subsequent generation to rid him/herself of and/or deny his/her ethnicity, when he states that "[s]ome kinds of ethnic or cultural consciousness seem more or less permanent" (3).[16]

One question that arises is: What do we do about those works of art, written and/or visual, that do not explicitly treat Italian American subject matter and yet seem to exude a certain ethnic Italian American quality, even if we cannot readily define it? That is, can we speak to the Italian American qualities of a Frank Capra film? According to Casillo's definition, we would initially have to say no. However, it is Casillo himself who tells us that Capra, indeed, "found his ethnicity troublesome throughout his long career" (374) and obviously dropped it. My question, then, is: Can we not see this absence, especially in light of documented secondary matter, as an Italian American signifier in potentia?[17] I would say yes. And in this regard, I would suggest an alternative perspective on reading and/or categorizing any Italian American art form.[18] That is, I believe we should take our cue from Scorsese himself and therefore "stretch" our own reading strategy of Italian American art forms, whether they be due to content and/or form—explicitly Italian American or not, in order to accommodate other possible, successful reading strategies. Indeed, recent (re)writings of Italian American literary history and criticism have transcended a limited concept of Italian American literature. New publications (literary and critical) have created a need for new definitions and new critical readings, not only of contemporary work, but of the works of the past. In addition, these new publications have originated, for the most part, from within an intellectual community of Italian Americans.[19] Therefore, I would propose that we consider Italian American literature to be a series of ongoing written enterprises which establish a repertoire of signs, at times, sui generis, and therefore create verbal variations (visual, in the case of film, painting, sculpture, drama, etc.) that represent different versions—dependent, of course, on one's generation, gender, socioeconomic conditioner what can be perceived as the Italian American signified.[20] That is, the Italian American experience may indeed be manifested in any art form in a number of ways and at varying degrees, for which one may readily speak of the variegated representations of the Italian American ethos in literature, for example, in the same fashion in which Daniel Aaron spoke of the "hyphenate writer."[21]

Within the general discourse of American literature, Daniel Aaron seems to be one of the first to have dealt with the notion of hyphenation.[22] For him, the hyphen initially represented older North Americans' hesitation to accept the newcomer; it was their way, in Aaron's words, to "hold him at 'hyphen's length,' so to speak, from the established community" (213). It further "signifies a tentative but unmistakable withdrawal" on the user's part, so that "mere geographical proximity" denies the newly arrived "full and unqualified national membership despite . . . legal qualifications and official disclaimers to the contrary" (213).

Speaking in terms of a passage from "hyphenation" to "dehyphenation" (214), Aaron sets up three stages through which a non Anglo American writer might pass.[23] The first-stage writer is the "pioneer spokesman for the . . . unspoken-for" ethnic, racial, or cultural group (i.e., the marginalized). This person writes about his/her co-others with the goal of dislodging and debunking negative stereotypes ensconced in the dominant culture's mind-set. In so doing, this writer may actually create characters possessing some of the very same stereotypes, with the specific goals, however, of 1) winning over the sympathies of the suspicious members of the dominant group, and 2) humanizing the stereotyped figure and thus "dissipating prejudice." Successful or not, this writer engages in placating his/her reader by employing recognizable features the dominant culture associates with specific ethnic, racial, or cultural groups.

Aaron considers this first-stage writer abjectly conciliatory toward the dominant group. He states: "It was as if he were saying to his suspicious and opinionated audience: 'Look, we have customs and manners that may seem bizarre and uncouth, but we are respectable people nevertheless and our presence adds flavor and variety to American life. Let me convince you that our oddities—no matter how quaint and amusing you find them—do not disqualify us from membership in the national family'" (214). What this writer seems to do, however, is engage in a type of game, a bartering system of sorts which ignores the injustices set forth by the dominant group, asking, or hoping, instead, that the very same dominant group might attempt to change its ideas while accepting the writer's offerings as its final chance to enjoy the stereotype.[24]

Less willing to please, the second-stage writer, instead, abandons the use of preconceived ideas in an attempt to demystify negative stereotypes. Whereas the first-stage writer might have adopted some preconceived notions popular among members of the dominant culture, this writer, instead, presents characters who have already sunk "roots into the native soil." By no means, therefore, as conciliatory as the first-stage writer, this person readily indicates the disparity and, in some cases, may even engage in militant criticism of the perceived restrictions and oppression set forth by the dominant group. In so doing, according to Aaron, this writer runs the risk of a "double criticism": from the dominant culture offended by the "unflattering or even 'un-American' image of American life," as also from other members of his/her own marginalized group, who might feel misrepresented, having preferred a more "genteel and uncantankerous spokesman."

The third-stage writer, in turn, travels from the margin to the mainstream "viewing it no less critically, perhaps, but more knowingly." Having appropriated the dominant group's culture and the tools necessary to succeed in that culture—the greater skill of manipulating, for instance, a language acceptable to the dominant group—and more strongly than his/her predecessors, this writer feels entitled to the intellectual and cultural heritage of the dominant group. As such, s/he can also, from a personal viewpoint, "speak out uninhibitedly as an American."[25] This writer, however, as Aaron reminds us, does not renounce or abandon the cultural heritage of his/her marginalized group. Instead, s/he transcends "a mere parochial allegiance" in order to transport "into the province of the [general] imagination," personal experiences which for the first-stage ("local colorist") and second-stage ("militant protester") writer "comprised the very stuff of their literary material" (215).[26]

An excellent analog to Aaron's three stages of the "hyphenate writer" can be found in Fred L. Gardaphe's threefold Vichian division of the history of Italian American literature.

Gardaphe proposes a culturally "specific methodology" for the greater disambiguation of Italian American contributions to the United States literary scene. In his essay, he reminds us of Vico's "three ages and their corresponding cultural products: the Age of Gods in which primitive society records expression in 'poetry' [vero narratio], the Age of Heros, in which society records expression in myth, and the Age of Man, in which through self-reflection, expression is recorded in philosophic prose." These three ages, Gardaphe goes on to tell us, have their parallels in modern and "contemporary [socio-]cultural constructions of realism, modernism, and postmodernism" (24). And, ultimately, the evolution of the various literatures of United States ethnic and racial groups can be charted as they "move from the poetic, through the mythic and into the philosophic" (25).

In making such an analogy, it is important to remember, as Aaron had already underscored, that personal experiences "comprised the very stuff of . . . literary material" for both the first-stage ("local colorist") and second-stage ("militant protester") writers; whereas the third-stage writer, on the other hand, travels from the margin to the mainstream without either renouncing or abandoning his/her cultural heritage. For Gardaphe, Vico's three ages (read, Aaron's three stages) constitute the premodernist (the "poetic" = "realism"), the modernist (the "mythic" = "modernism"), and the postmodernist (the "philosophic" = "postmodernism").

For the first-stage writer, then, a type of self-deprecating barterer with the dominant culture, the vero narratio constitutes the base of what s/he writes. S/he no more writes about what s/he thinks than what s/he experiences, his/her surroundings. His/her art, in a sense, then, records more her/his experiential feelings than her/his analytical thoughts. This writer is not concerned with an adherence to or the creation of some form of objective, rhetorical literary paradigm. S/he is an expressive writer, not a paradigmatic one—his/her ethnic experiences of the more visceral kind serve more as the foundation of his/her literary signification.

The second-stage writer, the "militant protester" who is by no means conciliatory as was the first-stage writer, belongs to the generation that rediscovers and/or reinvents his/her ethnicity. While s/he may present characters who have already "sunk roots in the native soil," s/he readily underscores the characters' uniqueness vis-à-vis the expectations of the dominant culture. As Gardaphe reminds us, before this writer can "merge with the present," s/he must recreate—and here I would add, in a sui generis manner—his/her past: s/he must engage in a "materialization and an articulation of the past" (27).

The use of ethnicity at this second stage shifts from the expressive to the descriptive. As a rhetorico-ideological tool, ethnicity becomes much more functional and quasi-descriptive. It is no longer the predominantly expressive element it is in the premodernist, poetic writer (i.e., the bartering, first-stage expressive writer). Whereas in the premodernist, poetic writer, ethnicity, as theme, is the conduit, hence expressive, through which s/he communicates his/her immediate, sensorial feelings, for the modernist, mythic writer, ethnicity becomes more the tool with which s/he communicates his/her ideology. In this second case, the ethnic signs constitute the individual pieces to the ethnic paradigm this second-stage writer so consciously and willingly seeks to construct.

While this modernist, mythic second-stage writer may engage in militant criticism of the perceived restrictions and oppression set forth by the dominant group, expressive residue of the evolution from the pre-modernist to the modernist stage, the third-stage writer (i.e., Gardaphe's postmodernist, philosophic writer) may seem at first glance to rid him/herself of his/her ethnicity.[27] This writer, as Aaron reminds us, will often view the dominant culture "less critically" than the previous writers but indeed "more knowingly." This should not come as any surprise, however, since, as Gardaphe later tells us, this writer finds him/herself in a decisively self-reflexive stage for which s/he can decide to transcend the experiential expressivity of the first two stages by either engaging in a parodic tour de force through his/her art or by relegating any vestige of his/her ethnicity to the background of his/her artistic inventions.[28] In both cases, the writer has come to terms with his/her personal (read, ethnic) history, without totally and/or explicitly renouncing or abandoning cultural heritage. This writer, that is, transcends "mere parochial allegiance" and therefore passes completely out of the expressive and descriptive stages into a third and final (?) reflexive stage in which everything becomes fair game. All this is due to the "postmodern prerogative" of all artists, be they the parodic, the localizers, or others simply in search of rules for what will have been done.

What then can we finally make of these writers who seem to evolve into different animals from one generation to the next? Indeed, both Aaron and Gardaphe look at these writers from the perspective of time; their analyses are generationally based—and rightfully so. However, we would not err to look at these three stages from another perspective, a cognitive Peircean perspective of firstness, secondness, and thirdness as rehearsed in his Principles of Philosophy.[29] All three stages, for Peirce, represent different modes of being dependent on different levels of consciousness. They progress, that is, from a state of nonrationality ("feeling")[30] to practicality ("experience")[31] and on to pure rationality ("thought")[32] or "potentiality," "actuality," and "futuribility."

If firstness is the isolated, sui generis mode of possibly being Peirce tells us it is, we may see an analog in the first-stage writer's vero narratio. For it is here, Gardaphe tells us, that primitive society records expression in poetry, in unmitigated realism, by which I mean that which the writer experiences only.[33] In this sense, the writer's sensorial experiences, his/her "feelings," as Peirce calls them, constitute the "very stuff of [his/her] literary material." Namely, those recordings of what s/he simply experiences, without the benefit of any "analysis, comparison or any [other] process whatsoever, by which one stretch of consciousness is distinguished from another."

As the second-stage writer shifts from the expressive—"that kind of consciousness which involves no analysis," Peirce would tell us—to the descriptive, s/he now engages in some form of analysis and comparison, two processes fundamental to Peirce's secondness. This writer, that is, becomes aware of the dominant culture—"how a second object is"—and does not repeat the conciliatory acts of the first-stage writer; s/he undergoes a "forcible modification of . . . thinking [which is] the influence of the world of fact or experience."

The third-stage writer transcends the first two stages of experiential expressivity either through parody or diminution of significance of his/her expressivity because s/he has seen "both sides of the shield" and can therefore "contemplate them from the outside only." For that "element of cognition [thirdness, according to Peirce] which is neither feeling [firstness] nor the polar sense [secondness], is the consciousness of a process, and this in the form of the sense of learning, of acquiring, mental growth is eminently characteristic of cognition" (1.381). Peirce goes on to tell us that this third mode of being is timely, not immediate; it is the consciousness of a process, the "consciousness of synthesis" (1.381), which is precisely what this third-stage, postmodern writer does. S/he can transcend the intellectual experiences of the first two stages because of all that has preceded him/her both temporally (Aaron, Gardaphe) and cognitively (Peirce).[34]

What we now witness after at least three generations of writers is a progression from a stage of visceral realism to that of incredulous postmodernism, with passage through a secondary stage of mythic modernism in which this monolithic, modernist writer believes to have found all the solutions to what s/he has perceived as the previous generation's problems. In light of what was stated above, we may now speak in terms of a two-fold evolution—both a temporal and intellectual process—that bears three distinct writers to whom we may now attach more precise labels. The expressive writer embodies the poetic realist who writes more from "feelings." Through the process of analysis, on the other hand, the second is a comparative writer who sets up a distinct polarity between his/her cultural heritage and the dominant culture in that s/he attempts to construct a sui generis ethnic paradigm. The third writer, instead, through "mental growth," as Peirce states, can embrace a consciousness of process (i.e., self-reflexivity) and consequently engage in a process of synthesis and "bind . . . life together" (1.381)—this I would consider to be the synthetic writer. The following graph charts my use of the above-mentioned terminology in what I have proposed as three possible categories of the Italian American writer—or, for that matter, any ethnic/racial writer:

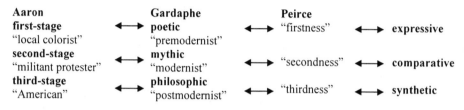

Aaron		Gardaphe		Peirce		
first-stage "local colorist"	←→	poetic "premodernist"	←→	"firstness"	←→	expressive
second-stage "militant protester"	←→	mythic "modernist"	←→	"secondness"	←→	comparative
third-stage "American"	←→	philosophic "postmodernist"	←→	"thirdness"	←→	synthetic

Having proposed such a reclassification, I believe it is important to reiterate some of what was stated before and underscore its significance to the above-mentioned categories. First and foremost, it is important to emphasize that the three general, different categories, while generationally based for Aaron and Gardaphe and cognitively based for Peirce, should not, by any means, represent a hierarchy—they are, simply, different. For in a manner similar to Peirce's three stages, these three general categories also represent different modes of being dependent on different levels of consciousness. The key word here, of course, is different. These categories are different precisely because, just as literary texts in general, as Ahmad reminded us, "are produced in highly differentiated, usually over-determined contexts of competing ideological and cultural clusters," so too do each of the three categories constitute specific cognitive and ideological clusters that ultimately provide the energy and form to the texts of those writers of the three different stages.

Second, these stages do not necessarily possess any form of monolithic valence. What I am suggesting is that writers should not be considered with respect to one stage only. It is possible, I would contend, that a writer's opus may, in fact, reflect more than one, if not all three, of these stages.[35] In this respect, we should remind ourselves that pertinent to any discourse on ethnic art forms is the notion that ethnicity is not a fixed essence passed down from one generation to the next. Rather, "ethnicity is something reinvented and reinterpreted in each generation by each individual,"[36] which, in the end, is a way of "finding a voice or style that does not violate one's *several components of identity*" (my emphasis), these components constituting the specificities of each individual. Thus, ethnicity—and more specifically in this case, italianita[37]—is redefined and reinterpreted on the basis of each individual's time and place, and is therefore always new and different with respect to his/her own historical specificities vis-à-vis the dominant culture.

This said, then, we should also keep in mind that we may now think in terms of a twofold evolutionary process—both temporal and cognitive—which may and/or may not be mutually inclusive. The temporal may not parallel the cognitive and vice versa. Hence, we may have, sociologically speaking, a second- or third-generation writer—according to Aaron's distinction, s/he would have to be a "second-" or "third-stage" writer—who finds a voice or style in his/her recent rediscovery and reinvention of his/her ethnicity. This writer, though a member of the second or third generation, may actually produce what we may now expect from the expressive or comparative writer—namely, the first- or second- generation writer. Conversely, we may actually find a member of the immigrant generation—undoubtedly, a "first-stage" writer from a temporal point of view—whose work exudes everything but that which we would expect from the work of a first- or even a second-generation writer (that is, Aaron's "first-" or "second-stage" writer). This immigrant writer may indeed fall more easily into the category of the synthetic writer rather than that of the *comparative* or *expressive* writer. For my first hypothesis, then, I have in mind a writer like Tony Ardizzone, a third-generation Italian American whose work fits much better the category of the expressive and/or comparative writer. My second hypothesis is borne out by the example of Giose Rimanelli, an Italian born, raised, and educated in Italy, who has spent the past four decades in the United States. His first work in English, *Benedetta in Guysterland*, is anything but the typical novel one would expect from a writer of his migratory background.

Part Three—Some General Considerations

An analogous discourse of one's own cultural and historical specificities may indeed be constructed around the notion of the reader. For the manner in which texts are interpreted today—the theoretical underpinnings of a reader's act of disambiguation, that is—is much more broad and, for the most part, tolerant of what may once have seemed to be *incorrect* or *inadequate* interpretations. Today the reader has as many rights as the author in the semiotic process. In some cases, in fact, the reader may even seem to have more rights than the writer. Lest we forget what Italo Calvino had to say about literature and the interpretation thereof: the reader, for Calvino, relies on a form of semiosis which places him/her in an interpretive position of superiority vis-à-vis the author.[38] In "Cybernetics and Ghosts" Calvino considers "the decisive moment of literary life [to be] reading" (15), by which "literature will continue to be a 'place' of privilege within the human consciousness, a way of exercising the potentialities within the system of signs belonging to all societies at all times. The work will continue to be born, to be judged, to be distorted or constantly renewed on contact with the eye of the reader" (6). In like manner, he states in "Whom Do We Write For" that the writer should not merely satisfy the reader; rather, he should be ready "to assume a reader who does not yet exist, or a change in the reader" (82), a reader who would be *"more cultured than the writer himself"* (85; Calvino's emphasis).[39]

In making such an analogy between reader and viewer I do not ignore the validity of the writer. For while it is true that the act of semiosis relies on the individual's time and place and is therefore always new and different with respect to its own historical specificities vis-à-vis the dominant culture (i.e., the canon) it is also true that the writer may willy-nilly create for the reader greater difficulties in interpretation. Namely, if we accept the premise that language—verbal and/or visual—is an ideological medium that can become restrictive and oppressive when its sign system is arbitrarily invested with meanings by those who are empowered to do so (i.e., the dominant culture/the canon-makers) so too can it become empowering for the purpose of privileging one coding correlation over another (in this case the canon), by rejecting the canonical sign system and, ultimately, denying validity to this sign system vis-à-vis the interpretive act of a noncanonical text.[40] Then, certain ideological constructs are de-privileged and subsequently awarded an unfixed status; they no longer take on a patina of natural facts. Rather, they figure as the arbitrary categories they truly are.

All this results in a pluralistic notion of artistic invention and interpretation which, by its very nature, cannot exclude the individual— artist and reader/viewer—who has found "a voice or style that does not violate (his/her) several components of identity" (Fischer), and who has thus (re)created, ideologically speaking, a different repertoire of signs. In this sense, then, the emergence and subsequent acceptance of certain other literatures, due in great part to the postmodern influence of the breakdown of boundaries and the mistrust in absolutes, have contributed to the construction of a more recent heteroglossic culture in which the "correct language" is deunified and decentralized. In this instance, then, all "languages" are shown to be *"masks [and no language can consequently]* claim to be an authentic and incontestable face." The result is a "heteroglossia consciously opposed to [the dominant] literary language," for which marginalization—and thus the silencing—of the other writer becomes more difficult to impose and thus less likely to occur.[41]

Turning now to a few writers, we see that their work represents to one degree or another the general notions and ideas outlined above. John Fante, Pietro Di Donato, and Joseph Tusiani—two fiction writers (Fante and Di Donato) and a poet (Tusiani)—have produced a corpus of writing heavily informed by their Italian heritage. Their works celebrate their ethnicity and cultural origin, as each weaves tales and creates verses which tell of the trials and tribulations of the Italian immigrants and their children. Fante and Di Donato confronted both the ethnic dilemma and the writer's task of communicating this dilemma in narrative form. Tusiani, on the other hand, invites his reader, through the medium of poetry, to understand better, as Giordano points out, the "cynical and somber awareness of what it means to be an immigrant," and to experience the "alienation and realization that the new world is not the 'land of hospitality' he/she believed it was."[42] So that, be it the novelist Di Donato, or the short-story writer Fante, Tusiani's "riddle of [his] day" figures indeed as the riddle of many of his generation, as it may also continue to sound a familiar chord for those of subsequent generations: "Two languages, two lands, perhaps two souls . . . / Am I a man or two strange halves of one?"[43]

In a cultural/literary sense, it becomes clear that these and other writers of their generation belong to what Aaron considers stage one of the hyphenate writer. They are, from the perspective of what is stated above, the expressive writers. For this type of writer is indeed bent on disproving the suspicions and prejudices his/her stereotyped figure seems to arouse and, at the same time, win over the sympathies of the suspicious members of the dominant culture. Fante, Di Donato, and Tusiani, as also their co/ethnics, indeed both examined in a sui generis way their status in the new world and, insofar as possible, presented a positive image of the Italian in America.

In turn, writers who have securely passed from the first through the second and onto the third stage of hyphenation may include the likes of Mario Puzo, Helen Barolini, and Gilbert Sorrentino. While it is true that each writer has dealt with his/her cultural heritage, each has done so both differently from each other as also from those who preceded them. No longer feeling the urge to please the dominant culture, these writers adopted the thematics of their Italian heritage insofar as it coincided with their personal development as writers. In his second novel, *A Fortunate Pilgrim* (1964), that recounts the trials and tribulations of a first-generation immigrant family, Mario Puzo figures as a fine example of the comparative writer. Ethnically centered around Lucia, the matriarch of the Corbo family, the novel examines the myth of the American dream and the real possibility of the outsider to succeed in realizing it. To be sure, Puzo, as he does later in *The Godfather*, does not always paint a positive picture of the Italian American in this novel. Yet, considered from the perspective of a greater social criticism, Puzo may indeed engage in a form of "militant criticism." His use of a sometimes sleazy, Italian American character—especially those involved in the stereotypical organized crime associations—may readily figure as an indictment of the social dynamism of the dominant culture which refuses access to the outsider.[44] The novel's expansive theme of survival and the desire to better one's situation lie at the base of the variegated, kaleidoscopic view of a series of seemingly overwhelming tragedies which the family, as a whole, seems to overcome.

In considering another example, we see that Helen Barolini's *Umbertina* (1979) could not be more Italian American. The author of a novel which spans four generations of an Italian American family, she is, undoubtedly, acutely aware of her ethnicity and hyphenation. Her main characters are all women, and each represents a different generation. In a general sense, they reflect the development of the Italian American mind-set as it evolved and changed from one generation to the next. Yet, with this novel, it becomes increasingly clear that Barolini has gone one step further than those who preceded her, both the men and women. She is now able to reconcile her ethnic/cultural heritage with her own personal specificities of gender and generational differences in order to transport these personal experiences into the province, as Aaron stated, of the general imagination. In Umbertina, Barolini, as synthetic writer, combines her historical awareness of the Italian and Italian American's plight with her own strong sense of feminism, and, ultimately, the reader becomes aware of what it meant to be not just an Italian American but indeed an Italian American woman.[45]

In a different vein, yet also "bind[ing] life together," as Peirce would state, Gilbert Sorrentino attempts to fuse his inherited immigrant culture—represented by terms of nature in his poetry—with his artistic concern, as John Paul Russo has demonstrated.[46] Yet, references to Italian American culture are most infrequent throughout his opus. In his own words, Sorrentino surely "knew the reality of [his] generation that had to be written,"[47] as he too contributed to this cultural and literary chronicle. However, he took one step further than his co/ethnics (Italian Americans) and, so to speak, dropped the hyphen. Yet the dropping of the hyphen, according to Aaron, does not necessarily eliminate a writer's marginality. He states that the writer "has detached himself, to be sure, from one cultural environment without becoming a completely naturalized member of the official environment. It is not so much that he retains a divided allegiance but that as a writer, if not necessarily as a private citizen, he has transcended a mere parochial allegiance and can now operate freely in the republic of the spirit." In Sorrentino's case, while he was keenly aware of the American literary tradition that preceded him, in dropping the ethnic hyphen he appropriated yet another form of marginality; with the likes of Kerouac and Ferlinghetti as immediate predecessors, Sorrentino chose the poetics of late modernism over that of mainstream literary America.[48]

In dealing with his/her Italian American inheritance, each writer picks up something different as s/he may perceive and interpret his/her cultural heritage filtered through personal experiences. Yet, there resounds a familiar ring, an echo that connects them all. Undoubtedly, Italian American writers have slowly, but surely, built their niche in the body of American literature. Collectively, their work can be viewed as a written expression par excellence of Italian American culture; individually, each writer has enabled American literature to sound a slightly different tone, thus bringing to the fore another voice of the great kaleidoscopic, socio/cultural mosaic we may call Americana—kaleidoscopic mosaic precisely because the socio/cultural dynamics of the United States reveal a constant flux of changes originating in the very existence of the various differentiated ethnic/racial groups that constitute the overall population of the United States. What emerges, as Fischer has stated, "is not simply that parallel processes operate across American ethnic identities, but a sense that these ethnic identities *constitute only a family of resemblances*, that ethnicity cannot be reduced to identical sociological functions, that ethnicity is a process of *inter-reference between two or more cultural traditions* (my emphasis)" and, I would add, between two or more generations of the same ethnic/racial group.

Thus, perhaps, an appropriate way to close would be to borrow from Marshall Grossman and, again, from Lyotard. For if the "power of the hyphen [as Grossman states] lies in its openness to history [or, better still] in the way it records and then reifies contingent events," since the "ideology of a particular hyphen may be read only by supplying a plausible history to its use,"[49] the person who opts to eliminate it, to use something else in its place, or, as I have suggested elsewhere,[50] turn it on its side, does so in the search "for new presentations," to quote now from Lyotard. In this manner, then, the text the writer creates, the work, s/he "produces are not in principle governed by pre-established rules [i.e., canon formation], and they cannot be judged according to a determining judgment, by applying familiar categories to the text or to the work. Those rules and categories are what the work of art is looking for. The artist and the writer, then, are working without rules in order to formulate the rules of what *will have been done*" (81; emphasis textual).

In an analogous manner, so does the reader of these same texts work without rules, establishing as s/he proceeds similar interpretive rules of what will have been read. Such is the case with the reader of ethnic texts, who proceeds to recodify and reinterpret the seemingly arbitrary—non-canonical (read also ethnic)—signs in order to reconstruct a mutual correlation of the expressive and content functives, which, in the end, do not violate his/her intertextual knowledge. Moreover, such an act of semiosis relies on the individual's time and place, and is therefore always new and different with respect to its own historical specificities vis-à-vis the dominant culture—the canon.

It is, in final analysis, a dynamics of the conglomeration and agglutination of different voices and reading strategies which, contrary to the hegemony of the dominant culture, cannot be fully integrated into any strict semblance of a monocultural voice or process of interpretation. The utterance will always be polyvalent, its combination will always be rooted in heteroglossia and dialogism,[51] and the interpretive strategies for decoding it will always depend on the specificities of the reader's intertextual reservoir. For the modernist reader, therefore, one rooted in the search for existing absolutes, an Italian American sign system may appear inadequate, perhaps even contemptuous. For the postmodernist reader, instead, one who is open to, if not in search of, new coding correlations, an Italian American sign system may appear significantly intriguing, if not, on occasion, rejuvenating, as these texts may indeed present a sign system consisting of manipulated sign functions which ultimately (re)define the sign. To be sure, then, in defense of a sustained but fluctuating Italian American category of creative works, one may recall Lyotard's "incredulity toward metanarratives" (xiv), late twentieth century's increasing suspicion in narrative's universal validity, for which artistic invention is no longer considered a depiction of life—or, stated in more ideological terms, artistic creation is no longer executed/performed according to established rules and regulations. Rather, it is a depiction of life as it is represented by ideology,[52] since ideology presents as inherent in what is represented that which, in actuality, is constructed meaning.[53]

Notes

1. For more on the use of the slash in place of the hyphen, see my *To Hyphenate or Not To Hyphenate? The Italian American Writer: An Other American* (Montreal: Guernica, 1991). With regard to the Italian American writer, see especially 20-27, 33-42.

This essay is a slightly modified version of the opening essay to the special issue on Italian American culture of *Differentia* 6/7 (1974): 9-32; it also appeared subsequently as the first chapter of my *A Semiotic of Ethnicity: In (Re)cognition of the Italian American Writer* (Albany: SUNY, 1998).

2. Of numerous historical cases, I have in mind the egregious examples of Native Americans and African Americans.

3. I use the adjective "other," here, in this essay, as an umbrella term to indicate that which either has not yet been canonized (i.e., considered a valid category) by the dominant culture (here, read, for instance, MLA) or, if already accepted, has been so in a seemingly conditional and a

somewhat sporadic manner. Namely, when it is a matter of convenience on the part of the dominant culture.

4. This is also true for the more popular press. In a *Gannett News Service Daily, Journal and Courier* (Lafayette, IN), DeWayne Wickham, a national columnist for the Gannett News Service, wrote in favor of using the metaphor of "stew" rather than "melting pot" in describing the racial/ethnic composition of the United States. See his "U.S. is stew, not a melting pot" (11 March 1992).

5. See my *To Hyphenate or Not To Hyphenate?* 48.

6. See Aijaz Ahmad's response: "Jameson's Rhetoric of Otherness and the 'National Allegory,'" *Social Text* 17 (1987): 4.

7. Because of nuances, subtleties, and semantic and grammatical differences among the various English languages spoken throughout the world, I believe it is necessary to recognize these different languages. And since "American," as adjective, can refer to any one of the many geographical and cultural zones of the Americas, for the sake of convenience and economy, I shall refer to United States English in the following pages as, simply, English.

8. While there does not yet exist an exhaustive study on the various categories of the Italian American writer, Flaminio Di Biagi has offered us a valiant first step in that direction. See his "A Reconsideration: Italian American Writers: Notes for a Wider Consideration," *MELUS* 14.3/4 (1987): 141-151.

Also, with regard to the Italian writer in the United States, I would remind the reader of Paolo Valesio's substantive essay, "The Writer Between Two Worlds: The Italian Writer in the United States," *Differentia* 3/4 (Spring/Autumn 1989): 259-276. Gustavo Perez Firmat, in an analogous manner, takes the matter one step further and offers an equally cogent exegesis of the bilingual writer—in his case the Cuban American—who, in adopting both languages (at times separately, at other times together in the same text), occupies what he considers the "space between" (21); see his "Spic Chic: Spanglish as Equipment for Living," *The Caribbean Review* 15.3 (Winter 1987): 20ff.

9. In stating such, I do not intend to ignore the bilingual Italian American writer: s/he who operates in both linguistic milieus. Hence, the presence of Joseph Tusiani in this essay and possible topics of discussion in any further versions of this type of study may indeed include the works in English by someone like Giose Rimanelli, Peter Carravetta, and/or Lucia Capria Hammond.

10. Jean-Francois Lyotard, *The Postmodern Condition: A Report on Knowledge*, trans. Geoff Bennington and Brian Massumi with a foreword by Fredric Jameson (Minneapolis: University of Minnesota Press, 1984): xiv.

A most recent rehearsal of a "postmodern," critical analysis specifically focused on Italian American literature can be found in Fred L. Gardaphe's excellent essay, "Visibility or Invisibility: The Postmodern Prerogative in the Italian American Narrative," *Almanacco*, Vol. II, No. 1 (1992): 24-33.

11. With regard to a discussion on the general notion of canon, I leave that for a larger setting, one which allows more space for such an encompassing argument. For more on the notion of canons, see *Canons*, ed. Robert von Hallberg (Chicago: University of Chicago Press, 1984), especially Charles Altieri, "An Idea and Ideal of a Literary Canon" and Richard Ohmann, "The Shaping of a Canon: U.S. Fiction, 1960-1975": 41-64, 377-402.

12. See his "Moments in Italian American Cinema: From Little Caesar to Coppola and Scorsese," *From the Margins: Writings in Italian Americana*, ed. Anthony Julian Tamburri, Paolo A. Giordano, and Fred L. Gardaphe (West Lafayette: Purdue University Press, 1991): 374.

13. He then continues to say that "in such writing Italian American experiences and values are delineated in dramatic interaction with the mainstream culture." See his review of Delano in *America & Other Early Poems*, by John J. Soldo, *Italian Americana* 1. 1 (1974): 124-125.

14. One problem with definitions of this sort is that they exclude any discourse on the analogous notion of, for example, the "hyphenate" filmmaker. I refer to Daniel Aaron's "The Hyphenate Writer and American Letters," *Smith Alumnae Quarterly* (July 1964): 213-217; later revised in *Rivista & Studi Anglo-Americani* 3.4-5 (1984-85): 11-28.

15. Dana Gioia, "What Is Italian American Poetry?" in *Poetry Pilot* (December 1991): 3-10.

16. One may also take issue with Gioia's revisionist history of Italian American poetry dating back to Lorenzo Da Ponte; or his statements on Italian language that "Toscano [is] the standard literary dialect of written Italian." Da Ponte was an Italian who, as an adult socialized in Italy, came to the United States under questionable circumstances and, as [one of ?] the first Italian professor[s] in North America, became a member of a privileged class. This, I would contend, is quite different from that Italian American literature one finds rearing its head at the beginning of

the twentieth century. With regard to the questions delta lingua, I would only point out that Italian is a national language which has evolved over the centuries, influenced heavily by its many dialects, fiorentino included. But there is not really any one dialect, today, that is considered the nucleus of standard Italian.

17. At this point I would wonder if Casillo's definition of Italian American cinema with regard to his opening remarks on Capra may not possibly create a type of have your cake and eat it too?

18. What is important to keep in mind is that one can perceive different degrees of ethnicity in literature, film, or any other art form, as Aaron already did with his "hyphenate writer."

19. Origins of recent Italian American self-inventory can be dated back to Rose Basile Green's 1974 book-length study, *The Italian American Novel: A Document of the Interaction of Two Cultures* (Fairleigh Dickinson LJP). Since then, the field of Italian American criticism has emerged sporadically in conference proceedings and, more specifically, in an acutely original contribution by Robert Viscusi ("De vulgari eloquentia: An Approach to the Language of Italian American Fiction," *Yale Italian Studies*, Vol. I, No. 3 [1981]: 21-38) and in Helen Barolini's best-selling anthology, *The Dream Book: An Anthology of Writing by Italian American Women* (Schocken, 1985). The recent publication of the above-mentioned *From the Margin: Writings in Italian Americana*, the establishment of journals such as *la bella figura* and *VIA: Voices in Italian Americana*, and the resumption of the journal *Italian Americana* further represent the rise of an indigenous interest in the critical study of Italian American culture. Still to appear is a special issue of *Differentia* due out in fall 1992.

In addition, the fall 1987 issue of *MELUS* was devoted to Italian American literature and film, and the *South Atlantic Quarterly* dedicated an entire issue to the work of Don DeLillo. These are but two examples of interest in Italian American cultural studies by non-Italian American scholarly organizations.

20. The basic tenets of this definition came out of a collaborative brain-racking session, in the office of City Stoop Press, with Fred Gardaphe, with the specific intent of defining Italian American literature. Therefore, the I may better be read as We.

21. See his "The Hyphenate Writer and American Letters." Here, I quote from the original version.

22. Aaron is not alone in discerning this multistage phenomenon in the ethnic writer. Ten years after Aaron's original version, Rose Basile Green spoke to an analogous phenomenon within the history of Italian American narrative; then, she discussed her four stages of "the need for assimilation," "revulsion," "counterrevulsion," and "rooting" (See her *The Italian American Novel: A Document of the Interaction of Two Cultures*, especially chapters 4-7).

As I have already said elsewhere (*To Hyphenate or Not To Hyphenate? The Italian American Writer: An Other American*), I would contend that there are cases where a grammar rule/usage may connote an inherent prejudice, no matter how slight. Besides the hyphen, another example that comes to mind is the usage of the male pronoun for the impersonal, whereas all of its alternatives (e.g., s/he, she/he, or he/she) are shunned.

23. In order to avoid repetitive textual citations, I should point out that Aaron's description of these three stages are found on page 214.

I would also point out that Daniel Aaron's three stages of the hyphenate writer have their analogues in the different generations that Joseph Lopreato (*Italian Americans* [New York: Random House, 1979]) and Paul Campisi ("Ethnic Family Patterns: The Italian Family in the United States" [*The American Journal of Sociology* 53.6 (May 1948)]) each describe and analyze: i.e., "peasant," "first-," "second-," and "third-generation." With regard to this fourth generation—Lopreato's and Campisi's "third generation"—I would state here, briefly, that I see the writer of this generation subsequent to Aaron's "third-stage writer," who eventually returns to his/her ethnicity through the process of rediscovery.

24. The danger, of course, is, metaphorically speaking, of adding fuel to the fire, since there is no guarantee that such a strategy may convince the dominant culture to abandon its negative preconceptions

25. There are undoubtedly other considerations regarding Aaron's three categories. He goes on to discuss them further, providing examples from the Jewish and Black contingents of American writers.

26. One caveat with regard to this neat, linear classification of writers should not go unnoticed. There undoubtedly exists a clear distinction between the first-stage writer and the third-stage writer. The distinction, however, between the first- and second-stage writer, and especially that between the second- and third-stage writer, may at times seem blurred. In his rewrite, in fact, Aaron himself has recognized this blurring of boundaries, as these "stages cannot be clearly demarcated'

(13). This becomes apparent when one discusses works such as Mario Puzo's *The Godfather* or Helen Barolini's *Umbertina*. More significant is the fact that these various stages of hyphenation may actually manifest themselves along the trajectory of one author's literary career. I believe, for instance, that a writer like Helen Barolini manifests, to date, such a phenomenon. Her second novel, *Love in the Middle Ages*, revolves around a love story involving a middle-aged couple, whereas ethnicity and cultural origin serve chiefly as a backdrop. Considering what Aaron states in his rewrite, and what seems to be of common opinion—that the respective experiences of Jews and Italians in the United States were similar in some ways (23-24 especially)—it should appear as no strange coincidence, then, that the ethnic backgrounds of the two main characters of Barolini's second novel are, for the woman, Italian, and, for the man, Jewish.

27. For a cogent example of ethnic signs relegated to the margin— what at first glance may seem to be an absence—see Gardaphe's discussion of DeLillo (30-31), where he also rehearses his notions of the "visible" and "invisible" Italian American writers.

28. Again, I refer to Gardaphe's analyses of Rimanelli and DeLillo (28-31), the first the parodist (the "visible"), the second the assimilated (the "invisible").

29. *Principles of Philosophy in Collected Papers*, ed., Charles Hartshorne and Paul Weiss, Vol. 1 (Cambridge, MA: Harvard University Press, 1960). Peirce offers numerous versions of his definitions of these three modes of being and examples throughout his writings, especially in this volume.

30. "By a feeling, I mean an instance of that kind of consciousness which involves no analysis, comparison or any process whatsoever, nor consists in whole or in part of any act by which one stretch of consciousness is distinguished from another" (1.306).

31. Secondness, as "the mode of being of one thing which consists in how a second object is" (1.24), provokes a "forcible modification of our ways of thinking [which is] the influence of the world of fact or *experience*" (1.321; emphasis textual).

32. "The third category of elements of phenomena consists of what we call laws when we contemplate them form the outside only, but which when we see both sides of the shield we call thoughts" (1.420).

33. I make this distinction in order not to contradict myself vis-à-vis Peirce's use of the term "real" when he discusses secondness. There, he

states: "[T]he real is that which insists upon forcing its way to recognition as something other than the mind's creation" (1.325).

34. As an aside, I would merely point out that Gadamer's notion of one's anterior relationship to the subject may also come into play. I shall reserve this, however, for another time and place.

35. Indeed, I would also contend that, in a similar vein, any number of these stages may even be inferred in a single work of a writer.

36. Michael M. J. Fischer, "Ethnicity and the Post-Modern Arts of Memory," in *Writing Culture: The Poetics and Politics of Ethnography*, ed. James Clifford and George E. Marcus (Berkeley: University of California Press, 1986): 195.

37. For more on italianita, see Tamburri, Giordano, Gardaphe, "Introduction," *From the Margin: Writings in Italian Americana*

38. See his "Cybernetics and Ghosts" and "Whom Do We Write For," in *The Uses of Literature*, tr. Patrick Creagh (New York: Harcourt Brace Jovanovich, 1986). These essays were originally published, respectively, in 1967 and 1967-68, and are now available, in Italian, in Italo Calvino's volume of collected essays, *Una pietra sopra* (Turin: Einaudi, 1980).

39. That is, Calvino foresaw a reader with "epistemological, semantic, practical, and methodological requirements he [would] want to compare [as] examples of symbolic procedures and the construction of logical patterns" ("Whom Do We Write For," 84-85).

Caveat lector: What I have in mind here is that any reader's response in this semiotic process is, to some degree or another, content/context-sensitive.

40. See, for example, V. N. Volosinov, *Marxism and the Philosophy of Language*, trans. Ladislav Matejka and I. R. Titunik (Cambridge, MA: Harvard University Press, 1986): "A sign does not simply exist as a part of reality—it reflects and refracts another reality. Therefore, it may distort that reality or be true to it, or may perceive it from a special point of view, and so forth. Every sign is subject to the criteria of ideological evaluation (i.e., whether it is true, false, correct, fair, good, etc.). The domain of ideology coincides with the domain of signs. They equate with one another. Wherever a sign is present ideology is present also. Everything ideological possesses semiotic value" (10).

41. This, for Bakhtin, is dialogized heteroglossia. A work, language, or culture undergoes dialogization "when it becomes relativized, depriviliged, aware of competing definitions for the same things." Only

by "breaking through to its own meaning and own expression across an environment full of alien words and variously evaluating accents, harmonizing with some of the elements in this environment and striking a dissonance with others, is [a word or for that matter, language, or culture] able, in this dialogized process, to shape its own stylistic profile and tone" (Mikhail M. Bakhtin, *The Dialogic Imagination*, ed. Michael Holquist, trans. Caryl Emerson and Michael Holquist [Austin: University of Texas Press, 1981]: 258ff).

42. See Paolo A. Giordano, "From Southern Italian Immigrant to Reluctant American: Joseph Tusiani's *Gente Mia and Other Poems*" in *From the Margin*: 317.

43. See his "Song of the Bicentennial (V)," in *Gente Mia and Other Poems* (Stone Park, IL: Italian Cultural Center, 1978).

44. Basile Green expresses an analogous notion in her section on Puzo in *The Italian American Novel*.

45. For more on the gender/ethnic dilemma in Umbertina, see my "Helen Barolini's *Umbertina*: The Ethnic/Gender Dilemma," in *Italian Americans Celebrate Life: The Arts and Popular Culture*, ed. Paola A. Sensi-Isolani and Anthony Julian Tamburri (Staten Island, NY: The American Italian Historical Association, 1990): 29-44; for a larger version of this essay dealing also with the intertwining themes of ethnic and gender dilemma in *Umbertina*, see my "*Umbertina*: The Italian American Woman's Experience," in *From the Margin*: 357-373.

As already mentioned, in her later novel, *Love in the Middle Ages*, the subject matter is much more universal insofar as ethnicity and cultural origin are backdrops to a love story involving a middle-aged couple.

46. See Russo's essay, "The Poetics of Gilbert Sorrentino," *Rivista di Studi Anglo-Americani* 3 (1984-85): 281-303.

47. *Vort* 2 (1974): 19. I owe this quote to John Paul Russo, "The Poetics of Gilbert Sorrentino."

48. Again, I refer the reader to John Paul Russo's "The Poetics of Gilbert Sorrentino."

49. Marshall Grossman, "The Violence of the Hyphen in Judeo-Christian," *Social Text* 22 (1989): 115-122.

50. See my *To Hyphenate or Not To Hyphenate?* 43-47.

51. For more on the notions of heteroglossia and dialogism, see Bakhtin, *The Dialogic Imagination*: 426, 428 passim.

52. Lenard J. Davis, *Resisting Novels: Ideology and Fiction* (London: Methuen, 1987): 24.

Index

421

About the Editors

Frank M. Sorrentino received his B.A. in political science from St. John's University and his M.A. and Ph.D. in politics from New York University. Dr. Sorrentino has been a Professor of Political Science at St. Francis College for the last twenty-two years and is presently Chairman of the Department of History, Political Science, and Social Studies. Dr. Sorrentino has taught at New York University, Long Island University, and Kean College. In addition, he has lectured extensively at various universities in the United States and Europe.

Dr. Sorrentino has written several books, including *American Government: Power and Politics in America, Ideological Warfare: The FBI's Path Toward Power*, and *Soviet Politics and Education*. He is presently completing a new book entitled *"The Presidency and The Bureaucratic State."*

In addition, Dr. Sorrentino has authored numerous articles and has delivered papers at various professional conferences. He has written many newspaper columns that have been circulated throughout the United States on subjects ranging from American politics, law, and international relations to Italian American issues.

Dr. Sorrentino has received many awards for his lecturing at New York University and St. Francis College. He received The Distinguished Faculty Member Award of St. Francis College in 1998 and an Award for Outstanding Teaching in Political Science by The American Political Science Association and Pi Sigma Alpha, the National Political Science Honor Society.

Dr. Sorrentino has led study tours of Italy, Greece, France, Spain, Russia, Ukraine, China, and Japan. He is Associate Director and Program Director of the Italian Historical Society and Vice President of the JL Better World Institute.

Dr. Sorrentino lectures frequently on Italian culture and politics, Italian American politics and issues, as well as topics relating to American politics, U.S. foreign policy, constitutional law, the presidency, public administration, and organizational problems and theory.

Jerome Krase is Murray Koppelman Professor and Chairperson of Sociology at Brooklyn College of The City University of New York where he also teaches courses on urban sociology and interethnic group relations. He received his Ph.D. from New York University in 1973, completing a dissertation "The Presentation of Community in Urban Society," which dealt with the problems and prospects of maintaining the viability of minority and racially integrated urban neighborhoods. Subsequently he worked as an activist-scholar in the field of community organizations, publishing articles and presenting papers while deeply involved in the neighborhood organization movements in New York City. His recent articles in the *Journal of the Michael Harrington Center for Democratic Values and Social Change* and *Publico e Privato* were based on his experience in the community organization movement.

During the last two decades his interests have expanded into Italian American and Polish American studies, as well as visual sociological studies of ethnic communities.

He has coauthored and/or coedited *Self and Community in the City, Ethnicity and Machine Politics, The Melting Pot and Beyond: Italian Americans in the Year 2000, Italian Americans in a Multicultural Society, Industry, Technology,* and *Labor and the Italian American Communities,* as well as many other articles on urban life and culture. He has forthcoming with Philip Cannistraro the *Proceedings of the 1998 Annual Meeting of the American Italian Historical Association, Italian American Politics: Local, Global/Cultural, Personal.*

He has lectured and conducted research on "Spatial Semiotics" at the Jagiellonian University in Krakow, Poland, and at the universities of Pisa, Perugia, Trento, and Trieste, and in 1998 he was Visiting Professor of Sociology at the University of Rome, "La Sapienza." Among other things Italian American, he has served as President of the American Italian Historical Association, Vice President of the American Italian Coalition of Organizations, Director of the Center for Italian American Studies at Brooklyn College, and a member of the National Council's African American and Italian American dialogue. Most recently he was on the Exhibition Planning Committee of "The Italians of New York: Five Centuries of Struggle and Achievement" at the New York Historical Society. As a student of "ordinary" urban neighborhood life, he lectures, gives photographic exhibitions, and writes a regular column for *The Free Press*, an alternative newspaper in New York City.

About the Contributors

Richard D. Alba is Professor in the Department of Sociology at The State University of New York, Albany.

Mary Jo Bona is Professor in the Department of English at Gonzaga University in Spokane, Washington.

Philip V. Cannistraro is Professor in the Department of History at The City University of New York.

Frank Cavioli is Professor Emeritus at The State University of New York, Farmingdale.

Angela D. Danzi is Professor in the Department of Sociology at The State University of New York, Farmingdale.

Judith N. DeSena is Professor in the Department of Sociology at St. John's University.

Donna R. Gabaccia is Professor in the Department of History at The University of North Carolina.

Richard Gambino is Professor Emeritus at The State University of New York, Stony Brook.

Fred L. Gardaphe is Professor in the Department of European Languages, Literatures and Cultures at The State University of New York, Stony Brook.

Jerome Krase is Murray Koppleman Professor in the Department of Sociology at Brooklyn College.

Salvatore J. LaGumina is Professor Emeritus at Nassau Community College, N.Y.

Daniel J. Monti, Jr. is Professor in the Department of Sociology at Boston University.

Gary R. Mormino is Professor in the Department of History at The University of South Florida.

George E. Pozzetta was Professor of History (deceased) at The University of Florida, Gainsville.

Salvatore Primeggia is Professor in the Department of Sociology at Adelphi University.

John Paul Russo is Professor in the Department of English at The University of Miami, Florida.

Frank M. Sorrentino is Professor in the Department of History, Political Science, and Social Studies at St. Francis College, N.Y.

Anthony Julian Tamburri is Professor in the Department of Foreign Language and Literatures at Purdue University, Indiana.

Joseph A. Varacalli is Professor in the Department of Sociology at Nassau Community College, N.Y.

Rudolph J. Vecoli is Director, Immigration History Center and Professor in the History Department at the University of Minnesota.

Robert Viscusi is Professor in the Department of English at Brooklyn College.